Memoirs of a Nobody

Henry Boernstein in the 1870s. Carte de viste photograph by Jean Baptiste Feilner, Vienna and Bremen. Courtesy of the Missouri Historical Society.

Memoirs *of a* Nobody
The Missouri Years *of an* Austrian Radical, 1849-1866

Translated and edited by Steven Rowan

Missouri Historical Society Press
St. Louis

©1997 by the Missouri Historical Society Press
Published in the United States of America by the Missouri Historical Society Press,
P.O. Box 11940, St. Louis, Missouri 63112-0040
5 4 3 2 1 01 00 99 98 97

Library of Congress Cataloging-in-Publication Data

Börnstein, Heinrich, 1805-1892.
    [Fünfundsiebzig Jahre in der Alten und Neuen Welt. English]
    Memoirs of a nobody : the Missouri years of an Austrian radical, 1849-1866 / [by
Henry Boernstein] ; translated and edited by Steven Rowan.
        p. cm.
    "…a translation and edition of roughly half of the two-volume autobiography of
Heinrich Börnstein, known in America as Henry Boernstein…" –Pref.
    Includes bibliographical references and index.
    ISBN 1-883982-20-0 (cloth) — ISBN 1-883982-21-9 (pbk.)
    I. Börnstein, Heinrich, 1805-1892–Biography. 2. Authors, Austrian–19th century-
–Biography. 3. Austrians–Missouri–Saint Louis–Biography. 4. Saint Louis
(Mo.)–History–Sources.
I. Title.
PT1823.B2F813 1997
909'.0431081—dc21   97-20637
                                                                          CIP

Distributed by the Wayne State University Press

Designed by Robyn Morgan, Production by Arista Graphics, Inc.
Printed by: Comfort/Fiedler Printing

∞ This paper meets the requirements of the American National Standard for Permanence of Paper for Printed
Library Materials, Z39.48, 1984.

Cover illustration:
View of St. Louis, Missouri. Steel engraving by E. B. Krausse after G. Hofmann, 1854.
Missouri Historical Society Photograph and Print Collection.

This edition is dedicated to the memory of Aloysius J. Schuster (1900-1994)

Contents

Illustrations

Foreword

Memoirs of a Nobody? A sly, knowing title for a book if ever there was one. I suspect that Henry Boernstein, having outlived many of his enemies and writing out his story for future generations, had a sense that to be a "nobody" in a time of great upheaval was to be "somebody" indeed.

True, Boernstein was often one or two persons removed from a Lincoln or Goethe or Bismarck, though he had seen them with his own eyes and had worked with their associates. He had been a colleague of Karl Marx and was intimate with the Bentons and Blairs, two great American political families of the era. Compared to these famous names, though, Henry Boernstein is surely a "nobody."

This is not the proper comparison to make, however, and I believe Henry Boernstein understood this. The "nobodies," whether European peasants, American slaves, or middle-class citizens on both continents, were becoming "somebodies" with a force that the avatars of reaction could not suppress forever. This does not imply a self-satisfied sense of historical inevitability, however. Boernstein had witnessed the era of Napoleon, participated in the intellectual ferment that led to the revolutions of 1848, and had taken up arms in what he conceived to be a war for liberty in America. Such were the times, and Henry Boernstein, looking back on decades of risk on two continents, knew that because of such personal commitments from "nobodies," the world would never be the same. As he writes in his preface, the people "actually make cultural history"; for this reason, memoirs such as his provide "rich material for the comparison of the past with the present."

So Henry Boernstein's memoirs remind us of the past's persistence, of the continuing relevance of previous choices and chances. We are still trying to understand the debilitating nature of racial and ethnic division; in Boernstein's St. Louis of the 1850s, such tension was evident in perhaps more vivid terms than those we have become comfortable with. Slavery still existed, Irish and German Americans competed for political and ecomonic influence, and "nativists" worked to maintain hegemony over any group considered to be outside the mainstream. For all his patriotism and belief in fundamental American political values, Boernstein himself does little in his narrative to erase ethnic and cultural boundaries. His characterizations of African Americans are not free of stereotype, and he speculates that German-speaking Americans will come to dominate America in the coming decades. St. Louis, like America itself, was still becoming, still testing whether diverse groups with strong cultural affiliations could coexist. It didn't always work then, as the New Year's slave auctions, occasional election riots, and eventual civil war made plain, and it doesn't always work today.

Despite this democratic turbulence, Americans have always believed in the notion of almost limitless opportunity. As Boernstein describes his migration to America and embraces the notion that by working hard one can get ahead, surely his words have continuing resonance for our later generations. Boernstein is torn between immersing himself in a market-driven culture (which he does with remarkable success) and maintaining a sense of higher aesthetic and cultural purpose. He also recognizes, as we must, that there are limits to American possibility. "America is the proper soil for young people," he decides as he contemplates returning from his consular post in Bremen. "Everyone works as long as he can, and he only lives as long as he works." He notes that he rarely saw gray or white hair in St. Louis. Surely America has gone a long way toward providing for all citizens, but the problems of how to equitably manage opportunity and provide lives of dignity for those not able to take full advantage of those opportunities continue to dominate our public discourse, not only in the St. Louis region, but in the nation at large.

Perhaps the best reason to read Henry Boernstein's words is that in his struggles we recognize something of ourselves. Surely his strong personality and high idealism guaranteed him nearly as many enemies as friends, but in his memoirs we find life's highwire balancing act lived out to the fullest. Not only does Boernstein continually take on more work and activity than he can handle, but even at his noblest hour, the point where he volunteers for the great conflict of his adopted home, his fundamental humanity breaks through and he is self-deprecating enough to write it down for us.

Boernstein and the volunteer company under his command is stationed at the Marine Hospital in St. Louis when he receives orders in the night to march to the river, embark on a steamer, and deliver needed military supplies to Alton, Illinois. As he and his company report to Captain Lyon, Boernstein plays something of a real-life comic after years of specializing in such roles on the stage. "We had marched in such haste," he writes, "that I had not even found time to put on my boots, so that I performed my first military expedition in my slippers." As we contemplate our hero marching about the banks of the Mississippi in his house slippers, he joins in the fun. "I only lacked my dressing gown to make it complete," he laughs, thankful that he had quit wearing one "in those troubled times." He somewhat optimistically concludes that "I was fortunate that it was a dark night and no one saw my slippers."

My guess is that Captain Lyon did see Henry Boernstein's slippers, and perhaps had a chuckle of his own when he stranded Boernstein without orders for three days in Alton after the successful completion of the mission. In any case, we can see the slippers, and as we grin at the sight of them, we see our own ways of improvising under duress. At the same time, we can be grateful that in those dark days so many new Americans, many who were not accepted by the "native-born," were willing to undertake deadly serious missions in the dark. That Henry Boernstein and his fellow German American "nobodies" put their lives on the line at the beginning of the Civil War not merely for the preservation of the Union, but for the liberation of African Americans, reminds us that high ideals do matter, even if we must improvise a little in our commitment to them.

ROBERT R. ARCHIBALD, PRESIDENT
MISSOURI HISTORICAL SOCIETY

Preface

What follows is a translation and edition of roughly half of the two-volume autobiography of Heinrich Börnstein, known in America as Henry Boernstein, published serially in German-language American newspapers and in book form in Leipzig in 1881. *Fünfundsiebzig Jahre in der alten und der neuen Welt. Memoiren eines Unbedeutenden [Seventy-Five Years in the Old and the New World: Memoirs of a Nobody]* is an argumentative, partisan, and very personal vision of a colorful, controversial man who made a major mark on the American Midwest in the middle years of the nineteenth century. Henry Boernstein was, among other things, a writer, playwright, theater director, actor, journalist, soldier, physician, photographer, revolutionary, diplomat, and entrepreneur. In the end he came to be disliked by many of those who had the occasion to deal with him, but he personally brought together the many regions and spheres of life that made up mid-nineteenth-century culture, connecting Bohemian Paris with St. Louis, frontier Galizia with frontier Missouri, and Karl Marx and Heinrich Heine with Abraham Lincoln.

The ultimate purpose of this edition is to restore to our perception of American life in that period some of the verve and color lost in the process of making history all too orderly and proper. Henry Boernstein was a troublemaker, an irritant and a rabble-rouser who had the courage of his convictions and who participated as a major player in the first phase of the American Civil War in Missouri.

As a historian I am aware that it is certainly an act of mutilation to present only an excerpt of an autobiography to the public. However, this has been partly remedied by providing a précis of the first volume in the introduction and a small précis of the remaining portion between the end of the "American" section of the memoirs and the author's conclusion. Everything between those two points has been translated without any excisions. Within those limits some material was included, such as Boernstein's description of Bremen and his consular service there, that might seem irrelevant to the purpose of the edition but that gives the reader an idea of the author's descriptive powers. I felt that the rest of Boernstein's autobiography, enjoyable as it is, would not interest American readers so much as the narrative of his strange career in the United States, which contains in it a vision of America that is fresh and thoughtful, and that stands on its own.

The introduction cannot take the place of a thorough history of St. Louis or of Missouri. Instead, it is intended to prepare the reader for the text he or she will encounter, as well as to provide information hitherto unavailable in English.

Time to translate and annotate this text was generously provided by the exchange program between the College of Arts and Sciences of the University of Missouri–St. Louis and the Missouri Historical Society, and I made use of the considerable collections at the Society's Research Center. Additional work was done at the New York Public Library, the Bavarian National Library in Munich, the municipal archives of Vienna, the Austrian National Library in Vienna, the International Institute of Social History in Amsterdam, and the Baker Library of the Harvard University Graduate School of Business Administration. Over the years I have been assisted in various capacities by Professor Dr. Wilhelm Brauneder of the University of Vienna Law School (and now of the Austrian National Assembly), by Dr. Walter Schmidt, formerly director of the Zentralinstitut für Geschichte bei der Akademie der Wissenschaften der DDR, and by both Dr. Harald Steindl and his wife Mag. Ulrike Steindl of Vienna.

I received special permission to cite passages from the credit reports of R. G. Dun & Company from the R. G. Dun & Company Collection, Baker Library, Harvard University Graduate School of Business Administration.

Editorial assistance was provided by Elizabeth Sims Bowling, who earlier worked with me on editing the Friedrich Münch translation of Boernstein's novel, *The Mysteries of St. Louis*, in 1990. Indispensable assistance in completing this project was granted to me by Tammy Sumpter.

STEVEN ROWAN

Translating and Editing Boernstein's *Memoirs*

Although these memoirs were received by those who had known Henry Boernstein with the sort of bemused charity which one always extends to a long-defeated enemy, over the years it has been regarded as an important source for the history of St. Louis German journalism. In this century, it was a major reference source for such German-speaking American scholars as Carl Wittke, A. E. Zucker, Karl J. R. Arndt, and Mary Olson, though their reliance on Boernstein has often been a result of desperation. The original files of German-language newspapers have become hard to find, and some issues, even whole titles, are now forever lost.

With the decline of bilingualism in the Midwest following the turn of the century, it became necessary for important texts about the German immigration to be translated if they were to be used by historians interested in regional development. William Godfrey Bek of Grand Forks, North Dakota,[1] translated a long series of writings by Missouri Germans, particularly his "Followers of Duden," published in the *Missouri Historical Review* from 1919 to 1924. This series included letters, diaries, and published prose of such Missouri pioneers as Friedrich Münch. In 1942, the State Historical Society of Missouri in Columbia received the typescript of a translation Bek had made of Boernstein's memoirs. The Society had the typescript bound in two volumes, and it is presently Collection 1054 in the Western Historical Manuscripts Collection at the University of Missouri–Columbia. This translation, entitled Heinrich Börnstein, *Seventy-Five Years in the Old and the New World: Memoirs of an Unimportant Person*, was based on the second edition of the memoirs published in 1884.[2] The two volumes, corresponding to Boernstein's division of his German original, consist of a first volume of 252 typed pages, with 215 pages in the second.

As is to be expected from any work by William G. Bek, the translation was careful and precise, rendering Boernstein's words into a prose that appears rather

---

1. See the obituary of Bek (1873-1948) in *MHR* 43 (1948-49): 186. Bek studied at the University of Missouri through 1905, received his Ph.D. from the University of Pennsylvania in 1907, and taught at the University of Missouri from 1907 to 1911. He then moved to the University of North Dakota, where he became dean of arts and sciences in 1930.

2. *MHR* 36 (1941-42): 496, referring to what is now WHM Columbia 1054. The second edition differed from the first (which was the edition reprinted by Peter Lang in 1986) only through an additional preface and an aphorism at the beginning. Mrs. William G. Bek later donated what was supposedly a Boernstein manuscript entitled *Germans in Missouri, MHR* 43 (1948-49): 177, but this is an error. The text in question, WHM Columbia 1047, is actually the manuscript of a book by Bek on Missouri Germans, composed c. 1905.

archaic and overly elegant to a more recent eye. But the translation never attempts to be complete, for translated portions are repeatedly interspersed with bridging summaries of those parts not directly translated. Usually this was a result of an editorial decision that readers would not be interested in a particular passage, but frequently the motivation was that Boernstein's subject matter was offensive to contemporary morality or taste. In volume I, p. 58, for example, "... there follows five pages in which Mr. Boernstein tells about a morbid curiosity about the origin of man and particularly the birth of human beings. When a cousin of his died in childbirth, his vivid but unrealistic imagination actually caused him to be seriously ill . . ." Bek goes on to omit lists of names, sometimes whole chapters even in the Missouri portions of the translation, such as Boernstein's description of Highland, Illinois, or his attempts to outline the early history of St. Louis. Scandalous portions, such as the career of Ned Buntline, vanish as well. The very important political chapter, "Through the Desert of Nativism"; descriptions of theatrical performances; and anything even remotely related to sexuality, let alone criticism of the Lincoln administration, are cut out. Some excisions are not noted in the manuscript, making it worthless even as a "pony" for those with halting German.

On the whole, then, Bek's translation is at best only partial, necessarily reflecting the tastes and anxieties of an earlier era. Those who could not easily read German, or who understood German but had difficulty reading the old German *Fraktur* typeface, were out of luck. Further, because Boernstein's book is a tendentious document which often has a shaky relation to the facts, annotation is a useful tool. Bek provided none. A completely new translation was needed, and with a scholarly apparatus that would make the text understandable to those who are new to the era and culture of mid-nineteenth-century immigrant America.

The principle of the present translation has been to remain true to the sense of the original so far as possible, and to translate Boernstein's prose into an English that best reflects for a modern reader what he wrote. No effort has been made to create fake nineteenth-century English; if a translation had been made in the nineteenth century it would have been quite different, and my own approach differs considerably from the previous translations of William G. Bek or Elizabeth Gempp. Portions of the Boernstein memoirs have already been translated piecemeal, and I took care to examine those translations only after my own work was finished, citing them for further reference. Interestingly enough, it turns out that my method of exposition was foreshadowed by that of William G. Bek, though I decided at the outset to exclude nothing within the limits of the Missouri period of Boernstein's memoirs. The period outside those limits has been summarized, but not so as to cover any of the author's blemishes.

Annotation has been provided where there appears to be a clear need to identify the participants in Boernstein's story, and where identification has proved possible. There has been no effort to annotate everything, since Boernstein wrote in a dense style typical of the nineteenth century, in which every line contains echoes of literary models and period references. Instead, explanation has been made in order to make the text lying before the reader comprehensible, and to open the way for further exploration. Since the main purpose of this volume is to open a window on the mind of German-speaking expatriate life in mid-nineteenth-century America, it has not been my purpose to correct all of Boernstein's misperceptions or downright errors. In the end his memoirs should not be judged simply as a source but enjoyed as an artifact which can tell us a great deal about a forgotten dimension of our own past.

STEVEN ROWAN

Memoirs of a Nobody

Introducing Henry Boernstein, a.k.a. Heinrich Börnstein

Steven Rowan

About Boernstein and his *Memoirs*

The memoirs composed by Henry Boernstein (Heinrich Börnstein) in Baden (Niederösterreich) and Vienna beginning at the end of the 1870s looked back over a long life lived, as his original title had it, in both the "Old World" and the "New World." What he wrote was as partisan and tendentious as the man who lived those events.[1] Particularly when Boernstein looked back on his American years, he was reaching into controversial territory, to a time when he was regarded as a dangerous radical and a subversive. He was also reliving an experience that had ended with failure and his own defeat. Not only did the political radicalism for which he fought much of the twelve years he lived in America suffer eventual defeat with the end of Reconstruction, but even within the radical movement he had long been isolated, rejected, and forgotten. This later fate colored his memories as well as his memoirs. Last, certain elements of his own personality failed to register clearly in his memoirs because he never faced them himself, leaving them to others to report. Certain parts of that difficult personality emerge only after a great deal of dredging, and at this long distance we can only catch a glimpse of the devils that drove him in his personal as well as his public life.

---

1. For a summary of scholarship on Henry Boernstein, see my introduction to Boernstein, *Mysteries*, vii-xv, though here it would be proper to mention Alfred Vagts, "Heinrich Börnstein, Ex- and Repatriate," *BMHS* 12 (1955-56): 105-27; and Vagts, *Deutsch-Amerikanische Rückwanderung*, Beiheft zum Jahrbuch für Amerikastudien, no. 6 (Heidelberg, 1960), esp. 114-116; also Ludwig Eisenberg, *Das geistige Wien. Künstler- und Schriftsteller-Lexikon*, vol. 1 (Vienna, 1893), 48. Generally, see Rowan/Primm and Steven Rowan, "The Cultural Program of Heinrich Börnstein in St. Louis, 1850-1861," *In Their Own Words*, vol. 3, no. 2 (1986), 187-206; Rowan, "Anticlericalism, Atheism and Socialism in German St. Louis, 1850-1853: Heinrich Börnstein and Franz Schmidt," in Henry Geitz, ed., *The German-American Press* (Madison, Wis.: Max Kade Institute for German-American Studies, 1992), 43-56. Manuscript materials on Boernstein are in the Archiv der Stadt Wien, the Theatersammlung and the Handschriftensammlung of the österreichische Nationalbibliothek. Portrait materials are to be found in the Bildsammlung of the österreichische Nationalbibliothek.

The external facts of his life are easy enough to extract. Henry Boernstein was born in Hamburg in 1805 to a Protestant mother and a Catholic father. His father abandoned a promising career as an actor for more mundane pursuits in order to be allowed to marry. Franz Sigmund Boernstein was not from Hamburg like his wife, but from distant Lemberg (now L'viv in Ukraine) in the Austrian-ruled Polish Kingdom of Galizia and Lodomeria. When Hamburg was ravaged by the last phase of the Napoleonic Wars, the elder Börnstein gathered his family and returned to his native land, where he found a living managing a liquor and perfume factory. Henry Boernstein was permanently marked by this early move from Hamburg's civility to the primitive frontier existence of Galizia. He would spend much of his own active life in regions where his culture and language were in the minority, addressing an often isolated German community beset by other peoples whose attitudes toward his were less than benign.

Despite a good deal of self-censorship, his memoirs provide rather penetrating information about his own adolescence. His earliest efforts to discover something on his own about unmentioned subjects led him to sneak from a locked cabinet a book labeled as dealing with suicide; he found instead a book filled with horrifying pictures of obstetrics. This episode was intermingled in his memory with glimpses of a beloved cousin dying in childbirth and then being laid out with her dead child in the parlor downstairs. His early affair with a Viennese ballerina, as well as his headstrong efforts to elope with his fifteen-year-old future wife Marie Steltzer, demonstrated strong emotional drives over which he had only marginal control.

As a father and husband, Boernstein was patriarchal, gathering around himself a vast brood of real and adopted offspring that generated a portable refuge from the tumultuous world he helped create for himself. Even here the reality was much more complex than the mid-Victorian appearances. For one thing, his Hungarian-born wife Marie Steltzer was no passive *Hausfrau;* she was a cheerful, talented dancer and comic actress with a much greater following than her husband. Boernstein himself, noted on the stage chiefly as a comic dialect actor, would find his forté on other side of the scenery as a manager and writer for stage productions.

Boernstein's professional life exhibited a repeating pattern of self-sabotage, with episodes of almost Faustian creativity punctuated by depression, doubt, and turbulence arising from his own impertinence toward those in authority. Despite his own pretentions to higher culture, he was more *Schlockmeister* than *auteur*, pitching sensationalism and scandal with a thin admixture of tony material. He also had a deep and abiding hostility to the institutions of Christianity. Far from being an incidental detail in his life, this inveterate anticlericalism was essential to this approach, since he would never relent from campaigning against religion even when such a course would have been wise.[2]

The first volume of the memoirs (summarized following this introduction) follows the experiences of Henry Boernstein as he lurches through a youth entranced with acting and writing. Hopes of going to Italy with an Austrian regiment lead him to blunder into military service before accidentally becoming a journalist in the 1830s while studying medicine at the University of Vienna. He later moves to acting, then to directing and managing theaters, and his perennial fascination with life in a culturally marginal situation draws him to the Bohemian Paris of the 1840s. His activities there amounted to a dress rehearsal of his later experiences in St. Louis, combining journalism, entrepreneurial innovation, politics, and theater. Although he participated in the events of the Paris revolution of 1848, he was regarded as too old and too personally slippery to be a true "Forty-Eighter" by the self-conscious emigrant community those failed uprisings created abroad.

After Boernstein emigrated to America in 1849, he passed a year in Highland, Illinois, where he developed a practice as a homeopathic physician. But his true American career began in 1850, when he became editor of the *Anzeiger des Westens* in St. Louis. His experiences in St. Louis formed the heart of his memoirs, and they also dominate the portion translated here. The St. Louis Boernstein entered in 1849 was a raw, expanding boomtown, burgeoning on the trade of the American river system and from the overland trade to the opening West and Southwest. Boernstein was enthralled by the amoral energy of a growing community, and his memoirs are a striking record of the entrepreneurial spirit. The account translated takes him from these beginnings through the end of his career as United States consul in Bremen in 1866. As editor and owner of the most important German-language newspaper in Missouri, Boernstein was directly involved in the increasingly stormy political life of the state, culminating in the secession crisis of 1860-1861. To him, the battle at the outset of the Civil War was a confrontation between Missouri's future (railroads, industry, and trade based on free labor) and its own past, represented by slavery and all which went with it. The result in Missouri was a war not so much between the North and the South as between St. Louis and the rest of Missouri. In 1861 Boernstein worked with Republican political leaders and pro-Union military to overthrow the Missouri state government, and for a time he controlled what was left of that government as military commander in Jefferson City, the state capital. Boernstein then took the post in Bremen, a patronage plum from the Lincoln Administration. Boernstein's absence

---

2. See Boernstein, *Mysteries*, xii.

from St. Louis undermined his shaky power base in that city, and his split with anti-Lincoln radicals eventually resulted in his newspaper, the *Anzeiger des Westens*, ceasing publication in its original form in early 1863.

Following the end of his United States governmental service in 1866, Boernstein decided to remain in Europe, eventually gravitating to Vienna. At the time he completed his memoirs (1881), as he indicates in his forewords and prefaces, he was still working as a columnist for German-language American papers. He died in September 1892, followed within weeks by his wife Marie. In their joint will, Henry and Marie Boernstein declared they died citizens of the United States, and they directed that their tombstone indicate they were citizens of Missouri.[3] They were buried in Matzleinsdorfer Protestant Cemetery in Vienna; their grave was obliterated by official action in December, 1941.[4] A *Heinrich-Börnstein-Strasse* was named after him in the Strebersdorf district of Vienna, but there is no memorial of any kind in St. Louis, save for his misspelled name (as "Henry Bernstein") on the Camp Jackson memorial now in Lyon Park, opposite the Anheuser-Busch Brewery.

Because of the stormy St. Louis years and the way they ended, Boernstein left a memory behind in St. Louis that was both unclear and negative. Those who had always hated him continued to loathe him as a radical and an anti-religious bigot, and many of those who had supported him in the 1850s now denigrated him as a traitor to his original ideals for supporting the gradualist policies of Francis Preston Blair, Jr. and President Lincoln against the radical antislavery cause. Lincoln's sudden death at the end of the Civil War made the president a political martyr to the very radicals who had excoriated his policies while he lived, but Boernstein's reputation remained under a cloud.

Henry Boernstein Meets Karl Marx, or, How Radical Was Boernstein?

One of the perennial accusations against Boernstein in his Missouri years was that he was a dangerous radical, an irresponsible demagogue intent on overthrowing American social and political institutions. As the unidentified reporter for the R. G. Dun & Company credit agency termed it, his newspaper was "adverse to good morals & American institutions," and

---

3. Archiv der Stadt Wien, Nachlassenschaft von Marie Boernstein, 1892, joint will signed 13 August 1891.

4. Thus the manuscript register of Matzleinsdorfer Friedhof, seen by me during my visit to Vienna in April 1988. It is still unclear to me whether the obliteration was due to superannuation or because of a Nazi-inspired destruction of graves with "Jewish" names.

"devoted to the diffusion of Infidel principles."[5] Yet Boernstein eventually lost his footing in Missouri not because he was radical, but because he was not radical enough to keep up with the revolutionary changes taking place in America in the depths of the Civil War. Where he was truly subversive in American terms was in his uniform hostility to organized religion in its many forms, a position more revolutionary in the United States than in Europe, and in his dedication to ending slavery, which he conceived to be a barrier to the flourishing of free labor. This position earned him the intense hatred of the vested social and economic interests of St. Louis and interior Missouri. On arriving in America, he tended to separate himself from the political causes of the "Forty-Eighters," partly because he was older than most of them, but partly also because he was probably already better apprised than they of American political and social conditions. Throughout his period in Missouri, he remained an advocate of gradualist policies on the national scene, and it was as a supporter of middle-of-the-road policies that he would lose his power and property in St. Louis.

It thus comes as a bit of a surprise that Boernstein had once been closely involved with Karl Marx and other adherents of what would become known as the Communist Party. Although this association was brief, lasting mere months, Boernstein played a considerable role in providing an environment for the development of communist ideology at a crucial stage of its formulation.[6] Boernstein's political evolution would later make him a pariah among members of the Marxist movement, but his crossing of Karl Marx's path did win him the major collaborator of his middle years, Karl Ludwig Bernays.

Boernstein's original intention in late 1843 had been to publish a German-language Parisian cultural biweekly entitled *Vorwärts!* ["Advance!"] to supplement his other projects, which then included a cultural information bureau, a "translation factory" reworking French dramas for the German stage, and columns for German-language newspapers in America. Using money invested by such backers as the composer Giacomo Meyerbeer, who was just leaving Paris to serve the royal court in Berlin, Boernstein intended to produce a reformist journal that could be distributed without trouble to subscribers all over Germany, as well as to the sizable German-speaking communities in France, England, and America. His first coworker in this

---

5. R. G. Dun & Co. Collection, Baker Library, Harvard University Graduate School of Business Administration, Missouri vol. 36, p. 286, report of 21 November 1851, and Missouri vol. 37, p. 340, report of 20 May 1853.

6. Walter Schmidt, "Zur Geschichte des Pariser Vorwärts von 1844," *Vorwärts! . . . Unveränderter Neudruck* (Leipzig: Zentralantiquariat der Deutschen Demokratischen Republik, 1975), v.

enterprise was Adalbert von Bornstedt, a writer who was then also working for the Prussian government as a secret agent.[7] Bornstedt sought to keep the journal innocuous and to steer any discussion of foreign policy in a Prussian (anti-Russian) direction. Because the French press law required any political daily or weekly to post a large bond against libel judgments, Boernstein declared the paper to be nonpolitical, although it was openly liberal in demanding freedom of the press and an end to secret proceedings of courts and other governmental bodies. Despite the paper's blandness, it was still universally banned from the German mails, with the result that the number of subscribers remained small.

The result of being banned from the mails in Germany was that the paper grew more radical in the course of the spring and summer of 1844, ending in the fall as the principal mouthpiece of international communism under the direct control of Karl Marx and his associates. What happened, in effect, was that *Vorwärts!* was absorbed by the group that had published the radical *Deutsch-Französische Jahrbücher*, which Boernstein and Bornstedt had sharply criticized when it appeared. In early May, a major contributor to the *Jahrbücher*, Ferdinand Cölestin Bernays (later known as Karl Ludwig Bernays) was made the editor of *Vorwärts!*; and by the start of July the journal's defining subtitle was changed from "Paris Signals from Art, Science, Theater, Music and Social Life" to the less cultural rubric of "Paris German Newspaper."[8]

Where was Boernstein in all this? In his memoirs he confesses to having been made a radical democrat as a result of unpleasant experiences butting heads with the aristocrats of Linz as a theater director, an engagement which ended in 1839.[9] Although he had become acquainted with the writings of the Young Germany movement, he had come to political convictions by his own route and as a result of his own experiences. Boernstein describes the next stages of his conversion:

> Through Bernays I came to get to know Dr. Arnold Ruge, a man as amiable as he was highly educated, and later I came to know the other collaborators on the *Deutsch-Französische Jahrbücher*. A new world of ideas, ever expanding, opened itself to me, so that from being Saul I became Paul, and I was soon won for the principles and doctrines of humanism. In

7. Adalbert von Bornstedt (1808-1851), former Prussian officer, writer, and major collaborator in the German Democratic Society in Paris as well as in the German Legion, was a secret agent for the Prussians in the late 1830s and the early 1840s. *MEW*, 27: 712; Schmidt, "Zur Geschichte des Pariser Vorwärts," xl, n. 16, for citation of one of his reports.

8. Schmidt, "Zur Geschichte des Pariser Vorwärts," xi.

9. Boernstein, *Memoiren*, I: 261.

those days they termed humanism what today would be called socialism, except that in those days humanism was simply a matter of writing and talking, of scholarly research and speculation, while today socialism has grown to practical life and even dominates the politics of the day. The program of "humanism" consisted of the proposition: "Mankind on this earth should not be divided from one another or used against one another on the grounds of any natural or artificial borders, diversity of languages or religious prejudice. There should be no nationality, no states, no more divisions, but instead only an association of united mankind, founded on the great eternally valid principles of Liberty, Equality and Fraternity, and the purpose of this unity would be to dissolve all Europe's historic and cultural development, all distinctions between rulers and ruled, between capital and labor, between owners and non-owners, between rich and poor, between superstitious and freethinkers, into a harmony satisfying all. This would finally establish the grand, free, general political system of unified mankind and the realm of eternal peace." As young and lively as I was at the time, I quickly became enthused for this program for the future, making my *Vorwärts* available to these humanists, who had no mouthpiece of their own.[10]

By June the journal had taken on the entire range of leftists grouped around Karl Marx and Arnold Ruge, and the editorial offices became the setting for intense discussions over the direction of socialism. Boernstein increasingly became a passive spectator in the operations of his own paper:

During editorial meetings twelve to fourteen persons gathered together [in Michael Bakunin's room], some sitting on beds or chests, some standing or pacing about, all of them smoking like mad, debating with the greatest agitation and passion. We could not open the windows, since a crowd would then form in the street to discover what all the yelling was about. As a result, the room soon became so filled with clouds of smoke that someone just entering would be unable to recognize those present, and we could not even see one another.[11]

The end result of these debates was a split between Karl Marx and his entourage and the more "humanistic" Arnold Ruge, leading to Ruge's departure by the end of summer. It was in the columns of the Paris *Vorwärts!* that the outlines of scientific socialism, which is the Marxist term for Marxism, were first clearly laid down. These were, of course, the last days of

---

10. Boernstein, *Memoiren*, I: 350.
11. Boernstein, *Memoiren*, I: 351.

what has been called the "humanist Marx" of the *Economic and Philosophical Manuscripts* of 1844, a brief and passing phase popular out of all proportion with Western leftists in the 1950s and 1960s. This was also the period in which Friedrich Engels permanently entered Marx's orbit, and his submissions included part of what would become his classic, *The Condition of the English Working Class in 1844.* Other contributors to the journal included the Russian Michael Bakunin, Georg Weber, Hermann Ewerbeck, and the great German satiric poet Heinrich Heine. The period of most intense radicalization coincided with the aftermath of shocking weavers' revolts in Silesia, as well as the bizarre spectacle of the display of Christ's Holy Tunic in Trier, both providing fodder for the journal's social criticism and anticlericalism.

Boernstein well described the lurch the *Vorwärts!* took to the left, but he was less than candid in saying that the closure of the paper came before the split between Ruge's humanists and Marxists had been completed.[12] In fact, for the last few months of its publication, Ruge had departed and *Vorwärts!* had become a genuinely radical paper, the like of which was not to be seen in Europe again until the revolutions of 1848.

At the end of 1844 the French government finally gave in to the demands of the Prussian government to suppress the journal, using as its pretext the change in format, which had resulted in a political paper's operating without posting the bond required by law. The police acted with special speed to close the paper after Bernays authored an article that appeared to endorse the political assassination of monarchs. The result was that most of the participants scattered or made bargains, with Marx going into exile in Brussels and Boernstein cutting a deal with the police to remain in Paris but to abstain from politics. Karl Ludwig Bernays "took the fall" and went to prison for two months. This brief imprisonment would prove to be a turning point for Boernstein as well as Bernays.

During the revolution of 1848, which began with a street riot in Paris in February and quickly led to the flight of King Louis-Philippe and the establishment of the Second Republic, Boernstein played a significant supporting role. He helped organize a German Legion to assist an uprising in Germany, and his younger brother Arnold actually saw combat with that force, whose disastrous march into Baden coincided with the collapse of Friedrich Hecker's revolt on behalf of a German republic.[13] He withdrew

---

12. Boernstein, *Memoiren,* I: 352.

13. On Arnold Bernhard Karl Börnstein (1806-1849), who would die of cholera in St. Louis shortly after arrival in America, see *MEW,* 27: 712. Henry Boernstein's participation in the German Democratic Association drew the special scorn of Karl Marx's wife. See Jenny Marx to Joseph Weydemeyer in Hamm, Paris, 16 March 1848,

from the leadership, however, as soon as proletarian revolutionaries won the upper hand in Paris, and he became a passive observer of the later phases of the revolution, working with Bernays to report events in the French National Assembly. Bernays was eventually called upon to assist a legation the Republic sent to Vienna, so that he became an official of the new régime. Out of curiosity, Boernstein took to collecting newspapers, fliers, and ephemera day by day during the revolution, donating them as a collection to the Mercantile Library after arriving in St. Louis. Boernstein had a ringside seat in downtown Paris for the violent suppression of the leftists by General Cavaignac in June 1848, and he blamed the subversion of the Second Republic on the efforts of socialists to take the French Republic further to the left than the rest of France was willing to go. He was scathing in his criticism of the leftists' demand for a "right to labor." Whatever his socialism had ever consisted of, he no longer held a revolutionary leftist position by June 1848. Despite this, however, Boernstein continued to regard Marx with an awe he bestowed on few persons he had actually met. To him, Marx remained the "powerful thinker, the much-tested author of that epoch-making work, *Das Kapital*, . . . who remains the terror of all European governments."[14]

So far as Marxists were concerned, Boernstein had become a mere petty-bourgeois democrat and anticlerical agitator, and beyond that, in their eyes, both a traitor to the proletarian cause and a probable spy for the French secret police.[15] The last charge has never been proved, but it stuck to such an extent that leftists often conspired to keep Boernstein from knowing what they were doing. Unknown to Boernstein, various associates of his continued to keep in touch with Marx and the Central Committee of the Communist Party. Karl Ludwig Bernays filled Marx and Engels in on the lurid details of Boernstein's personal life in Sarcelles, outside of Paris. In St. Louis as well, Boernstein's comrade in anticlerical crusades, Franz Schmidt, provided reports to the Central Committee secretary Wilhelm Wolff in Brussels, using

---

MEW, 27: 604. Friedrich Hecker (1811-1881) of Mannheim was a leader of radicals in Baden beginning in the early 1840s, and in 1848 he rejected compromises with the ruling princes and led a rebellion on behalf of a German Republic. After his defeat in battle, Hecker fled to America, eventually settling as a farmer in Summerfield, Illinois. He would play a prominent role in Republican Party politics in Illinois before the Civil War, and during the Civil War he commanded two successive regiments, receiving serious wounds at Chancellorsville. His papers are at WHM, University of Missouri—St. Louis. He remained throughout his life the symbol of the uncompromising German radical, set apart by his dashing soft broad hat with a feather.

14. Boernstein, *Memoiren*, I: 354.

15. Friedrich Engels to Karl Marx in Brussels, Paris, 19 August 1846, *MEW*, 27: 35; Friedrich Engels to Joseph Weydemeyer, 27 February 1852, *MEW*, 28: 500.

the code name Theseus.[16] Far from being a tool of socialist movements, Boernstein was regarded by the real revolutionaries as a hopeless liberal, in their hierarchy one of the lowest forms of life.

First Great Friendship: The Strange Tale of Boernstein and Bernays

The relationship between Henry Boernstein and the man known as Karl Ludwig Bernays was central to Boernstein's life from 1845 to at least 1862, and is the counterpart to the association with Carl Bukovics von Kis-Alacska that would dominate his last three decades after 1862. Born in 1815 in Mainz to a Jewish family which converted to Christianity when he was still a child, Bernays was baptized Ferdinand Cölestin Bernays and received a law degree from Heidelberg in 1838. After working as a journalist, he ran afoul of censorship authorities in Mannheim and fled to Paris in 1843.[17] As previously mentioned, he was a major contributor to the *Deutsch-Französische Jahrbücher*,[18] and he served as the vanguard of the Jahrbücher group in their infiltration and takeover of the Paris *Vorwärts!*, besides at least temporarily converting Boernstein to socialism. Up until his condemnation to two months of imprisonment in St. Pélagie, Bernays's course of life appeared intimately intertwined with the Marxists, and the expectation would have been for him to continue as a wheelhorse of communist journalism in Marx's entourage. Particularly noted for his humorous satiric style, he held much the position with Marx later to be occupied by Friedrich Engels.

Yet the two months he spent at St. Pélagie prison left the diminutive Bernays (whom Engels jokingly called "*der Kleine*," "the little man") broken,

---

16. Walter Schmidt, *Wilhelm Wolff. Kampfgefährte und Freund von Marx und Engels, 1846-1864* (Berlin/East: Dietz, 1979), 263; Franz Schmidt ("Theseus") to Wilhelm Wolff, St. Louis, 28 December 1850, in Rolf Weber, ed., *Das Land ohne Nachtigall. Deutsche Emigranten in Amerika, 1777-1886* (Berlin/East: Der Morgen, 1981), 159-168, 436-7.

17. MHS, Bernays Papers, box 1, folder on genealogy, includes a summary sheet on "The Life of Charles Louis Bernays" as well as two sketches of a Bernays family tree. Karl Ludwig Bernays was a distant cousin through his great-grandfather to Martha Bernays, the wife of Dr. Sigmund Freud of Vienna, as well as to Ely Bernays, husband of Dr. Freud's daughter Anna.

18. Joachim Höppner, ed., *Deutsch-Französische Jahrbücher, herausgegeben von Arnold Ruge und Karl Marx* (Frankfurt a. M.: Röderberg-Verlag, 1982) for a paperback edition. Bernays wrote "Schlussprotokoll der Wiener Ministerialkonferenz vom 12. Juni 1834 mit dem Einleitungs- und Schlussvorträge des Fürsten Metternich, nebst einer rühmlichen Nachrede" ["The final Protocol of the Vienna Ministerial Conference of 12 June 1834 with the Introductory and Concluding Addresses of Prince Metternich, Along with a Positive Appreciation"], 208-232; and he also edited the "Deutsche Zeitungsschau" ["Review of the German Press"], 300-324.

humiliated, and disoriented. He worked off his prison experience by writing a book on penology so savage and bitter that not even leftists would publish it. In this vulnerable moment, he fell into Boernstein's orbit and would not manage to extricate himself for almost two decades. He fell in love with Boernstein's foster daughter, "Pepi," who was also sexually involved with Boernstein, and when Bernays declared his intention to escape the Boernstein farmhouse located in the village of Sarcelles outside of Paris (rented with Bernays' money) to join Marx in Brussels, both Pepi and Marie Boernstein declared their love for him. Bernays thereupon became the perpetually self-subordinating aide to all of Boernstein's enterprises, starting with operating a news service in Paris. Marx and Engels chuckled and sneered at great length over Bernays' foolishness, and in the end they wrote him off as a prisoner of love being kept by a cabal consisting of the wily Boernstein and a pair of calculating women.[19]

The ultimate resolution of this quandary was found in the respectable estate of marriage. Karl Ludwig Bernays married Pepi, now formally referred to as Josephine Wolf and whom Boernstein briefly described in his memoirs as "our foster daughter . . . a young Austrian from a respectable family, daughter of a brave officer. . . . "[20] A suitably bourgeois appearance was given to everything, including Pepi's two children of uncertain parentage. Of all of this, of course, there is not a breath in Boernstein's memoirs, although it clearly marked a turning point of Bernays's life. Shortly after the beginning of Boernstein's editing of the *Anzeiger des Westens* in St. Louis, Bernays authored a detailed refutation of communism, declaring at the outset, "I was once a communist myself; better still, I was not the least of its founders. And I was a battler against the most miserable class of human beings in Europe, which I still loath, the bourgeoisie!" [21]

Bernays and his wife would remain in Boernstein's wake until the American Civil War provided an occasion to separate for good. What the personal relations of these two couples consisted of over this period is an open question, since Bernays's confessional correspondence with Marx soon ceased.

Bernays joined Boernstein in Highland, Illinois, remaining there as a merchant for several years after Boernstein's departure, until Boernstein

---

19. For this soap opera, see Karl Ludwig Bernays to Karl Marx in Brussels, Sarcelles, 15-20 July 1846, MEGA 2, 3rd division, 2: 259, 261, 295-6; Friedrich Engels to Karl Marx in Brussels, Paris, 19 August 1846, ibid., 2: 28; Karl Ludwig Bernays to Karl Marx in Brussels, Sarcelles, 15-20 July 1846, ibid., 2: 256-262; Friedrich Engels to Karl Marx in Brussels, Paris, 15 January 1847, *MEW,* 27: 73-4; Friedrich Engels to Karl Marx in Brussels, Paris, 9 March 1847, ibid., 27: 78-9; Friedrich Engels to Karl Marx in Brussels, Paris, 25-6 October 1847, ibid., 27: 95.

20. Boernstein, *Memoiren,* 1: 364.

21. "Der Communismus und Amerika," *AW,* vol. 15, no. 145, 9 April 1850, p. 2.

finally managed to draw him to St. Louis to assist him at the *Anzeiger*. In St. Louis Bernays distinguished himself as secretary of the Missouri Republican Party during the 1860 presidential elections. After returning from his brief, unpleasant tour as a United States consul in Europe in 1862 (there had been protests over his Jewish origins in both America and Switzerland), Bernays served as a paymaster of troops, breveted a lieutenant colonel. After the Civil War, Bernays returned to German-American journalism in St. Louis, and after Boernstein lost his own consulship Bernays urged a renewal of their old partnership in America. Instead, Boernstein decided to remain in Europe. Karl Ludwig Bernays was buried in Bellefontaine Cemetery in St. Louis in 1879, the very destiny Boernstein had foreseen for himself had he stayed in the Midwest. On his deathbed, Bernays wrote a final letter to Henry Boernstein in distant Vienna, commemorating their lasting friendship.[22]

The Religious Question and the Civil War Crisis in Missouri

Boernstein's career as a red menace was short lived and long behind him by the time he reached America, and his reputation as a radical in Missouri rested on different criteria. The most fundamental aspect of his entire political life was his anticlericalism, expressed primarily in his hostility to the Catholic Church in general and the Jesuit Order in particular. This hostility arose in part from his personal experience as a Protestant growing up in Galizia, though one part of his personality had been drawn to the theatricality and beauty of the Catholic ritual. His anti-Jesuit ideology was reinforced by exposure to the doctrinaire anticlericalism of la vie de Bohème in Paris in the 1840s, preserved for us today chiefly in the popular leftist novels of Eugène Sue, *The Mysteries of Paris* and *The Wandering Jew*. Hatred of religious hierarchies was an essential characteristic of nineteenth-century liberalism, for established churches were the bane of political reform.

Transferred to an American setting, however, this hothouse anticlericalism lost much of its specious justification, for America had neither established churches nor princely courts to serve as foci of black-robed intrigue. In America the only way such polemic could be applied was by arguing that organized religion subverted democracy through corruption or conspiracy. It thus had to link itself with the "paranoid style" of American politics which went back at least to the critique of Freemasonry leveled in the 1820s, or even to the anti-Jacobin agitation of Jedediah Morse at the end of the eighteenth century. In his crusade against the Jesuits,

---

22. Boernstein, *Memoiren*, 2: 442.

Boernstein was promoting patterns of religious paranoia which would take on a life of their own in the twentieth century, turning against enemies not even imagined. It is a dreadful irony that Boernstein's anti-Jesuit fantasies in his novel *The Mysteries of St. Louis* probably provided one ultimate model for the infamous anti-Semitic screed, *The Protocols of the Elders of Zion*.[23] Ultimately, one variety of paranoid bigotry is pretty much like another.

Since Boernstein himself conformed to the general stereotype of a fire-breathing persecutor of religion, it was only a small jump to see him as the archenemy of Christianity itself, the Jew. Boernstein was assumed by informers to R. G. Dun & Company to be an "Israelite" or a "converted Israelite," with characteristics typical of his race.[24] The fact that many of his collaborators, particularly Bernays, were from Jewish families left the way open to more anti-Semitic speculation. The fact that Boernstein could be as hard on rabbis as priests in his publications did not change the popular judgment on the issue.[25]

The positive half of Boernstein's anticlerical message was that the American republic was secular in origin and had only been subverted over time by forces relying on the corruption and stupidity of the people. German radicals thus came to treasure Benjamin Franklin and Thomas Paine as true republicans, because those Americans had rejected doctrinaire Christianity in favor of a secularized deism or atheism. German-American radicals saw themselves as defenders of a "true Americanism" of which native American citizens in their religious blindness had lost sight.[26]

---

23. Boernstein, *Mysteries*, 158-62. Norman Cohn, *Warrant for Genocide: The Myth of the Jewish World Conspiracy and the Protocols of the Elders of Zion* (London: Eyre and Spottiswoode, 1967), outlines how the model for the Protocols was Maurice Joly's *Dialogues aux enfers*, which was in turn inspired by the chapter "In the Jewish Cemetery of Prague," from the novel *Biarritz* (Berlin, 1868) by Hermann Gödsche under the pen name of Sir John Retcliffe. Gödsche probably knew Boernstein's novel and used it as his own inspiration for a paranoid vision of world conquest by a conspiracy, though the conspirators are changed to suit the audience. More recently on this seamy milieu, see George F. Kennan, "The Curious Monsieur Cyon," *The American Scholar* 55 (1985-6): 449-75, esp. 468-73.

24. R. G. Dun & Co. Collection, Baker Library, Harvard University Graduate School of Business Administration, Missouri vol. 37, p. 589, report of 19 October 1857, "a German Israelite . . . The opinion as to his honesty is divided here, he is an Israelite, and every inch one. . . ." Ibid., Missouri vol. 36, p. 286, report of 10 July 1857 on Henry and August S. Boernstein, "'Father & Son' converted Israelites."

25. Rowan, "The Cultural Program of Heinrich Börnstein in St. Louis, 1850-1861," *In Their Own Words*, vol. 3, no. 2 (1986), 199: in 1856, as part of his supplementary volumes of literature, the *Haus-Bibliothek des Anzeigers des Westens*, he published an anti-religious comic novel entitled *Schief-Levinche mit seiner Kalle oder Judenthum und Katholizismus* by Dr. Schiff, protecting himself from the charge of publishing an anti-Jewish novel with citations from his old friend Heinrich Heine and a letter from the author, see *Haus-Bibliothek*, vol. 3, 33-35.

26. Rowan/Primm, 156-8; *AW*, 19 January 1861.

In concrete terms, the anticlerical movement expressed itself by arguing against the immunity of church property from taxation, as well as against the ability of churches to accumulate property without restriction. They favored legislation restricting ecclesiastical property such as prevailed in Europe at the time, if not outright confiscation. They intervened in the internal affairs of denominations by opposing the ability of hierarchies to ignore or abuse the interests of individual congregations. When the opportunity presented itself, German-American anticlericals advocated the removal of religious instruction from public schools and the establishment of schools that either avoided religious subjects or were openly rationalist.

Boernstein and other German-American radicals were particularly offended by the religiously sanctioned moralism of much of American public life, which tended to view political questions in terms of moral right and wrong predetermined by God. The point where this came to open conflict was over Sabbath legislation, which offended the social mores of religious Germans as well as freethinkers. Anglo-American efforts to restrict the sale and consumption of alcohol also brought Germans up against Yankee moralism. Although Boernstein himself did not consume alcohol as a result of personal convictions about health, he rejected the notion that religious groups had any valid argument for placing a religious sanction on drink or other social enjoyment, or that authorities had any business turning those prejudices into public law binding on others. The informants of the R. G. Dun agency pointedly noted that Boernstein's undertakings included a brewery and businesses such as the theater which profited from Sabbath performances.[27]

It was in the context of his anticlericalism that Boernstein moved from mere attack to constructive organization in St. Louis, creating a "Society of Free Men" as a framework for education and anti-Christian agitation. As a true mid-Victorian, however, he argued that there was a rational basis for a public and private morality which differed little from that supported by Christian reason. This led to his establishment of schools and rationalist associations to explore and expound science and philosophy, which was thought inevitably to promote the moral life as then understood. The fact that this tradition seems naïve and hollow to us today is a reminder that it was as much a product of its times as the flamboyant Catholic piety then being promoted by Pope Pius IX.

---

27. R. G. Dun & Co. Collection, Baker Library, Harvard University Graduate School of Business Administration, Missouri vol. 36, p. 286, report of 1 January 1856, and report of 10 August 1857; Missouri vol. 37, p. 588, report of 23 April 1860, "He is also lessee of the German Hotel . . . depending largely on Sabbath day exhibitions for support." Ibid., report of 5 July 1860, "H. B. is engaged in a variety of outside operations, some of them of a doubtful character."

At the same time, however, American moralism was having a field day *later ?* with another fundamental question at which we are less likely to scoff today, the issue of whether human beings could own others of their kind as slaves. In St. Louis, mainstream public opinion, supported by the principal churches, held that property in slaves was sanctified by both the holy scriptures and the United States Constitution. Abolitionist sentiment, in contrast, held that slavery could never be justified in Christian terms, and that Christian morality, in fact, demanded the obliteration of slavery from the earth. There is increasing doubt about the doctrinal integrity of abolitionism as a Christian movement, since its moralism is as dubious as the currently discredited arguments of the temperance movement (though the same arguments are currently still seen as somehow viable when applied to illegal drugs or even tobacco smoking). The civil rights movement of the twentieth century could equally be seen as just another American moralist movement, abusing Christianity for temporal ends. Boernstein would have agreed that Christian moralism was fallacious, but he still opposed slavery as economically and morally destructive to the community depending on it. Despite his convictions, Boernstein could still deal with defenders of slavery on a personal level, and he counted one of the most extreme among them, the cultured archreactionary Thomas C. Reynolds, as a friend until the crisis of secession. *(1861)*

Ultimately slavery was seen by Boernstein and his colleagues to be harmful because it provided inordinate power to a small elite and undermined the value of free labor. The maintenance of the slave regime mandated serious abridgements of freedoms of speech and press, and it turned all the residents of a slave state into accomplices in supporting a slavery that benefited very few. It also necessitated a brutal system of discipline that lowered the tone of public life. The existence of slavery discouraged immigration, degraded labor and craftsmanship, and subsidized a few agrarian industries (hemp, tobacco) that were of little intrinsic profit to Missouri. Slavery, always marginal to the economy of Missouri, functioned chiefly as a token of the attachment older Anglo-American elites felt for their lands of origin (usually Virginia, Tennessee, or Kentucky), as well as a reminder of the state's traditional role as supplier of food to the cotton plantations of the Deep South.

Boernstein not only locked horns on a regular basis with "mainstream" newspapers such as the *Missouri Republican* or the *Deutsche Tribüne*, but also with journals representing specific sectarian points of view. The Old Lutheran community centered on South Jefferson in St. Louis as well as in Perry County, which would eventually be known as the Lutheran Church, Missouri Synod, had its voice in C. F. W. Walther. Walther had become the principal figure in confessional Lutheranism in America following the expulsion of the wayward Bishop Martin Stephan shortly after the group's arrival from Saxony in 1838. Walther's voice had been heard in the fortnightly *Der Lutheraner*, read by Lutheran laity throughout the Midwest since 1844.[28] A more specialized doctrinal journal which began in 1855, *Lehre und Wehre*, was aimed primarily at pastors and theologians and rarely glanced at day-to-day events.[29] Boernstein had conflicts with Walther almost from the first day of his residence in St. Louis, and he attacked Walther through both the *Anzeiger des Westens* and the anticlerical weekly *Freie Blätter* edited by his friend Franz Schmidt. Schmidt took to describing the Old Lutherans as "mere Stephanites," whose works stank as badly as the St. Louis levee on a hot summer's day.[30] In April and May, 1861, Walther would note with horror the fact that Boernstein commanded a military force within sight of Concordia Seminary on Jefferson Avenue, and he expected to be stormed by the forces of evil united against him in the service of abolition and godlessness.[31]

Still, the Old Lutherans were a small and relatively isolated sect in comparison with the Catholic Church, and there the conflict was direct, prolonged, and merciless. Catholic Germans found themselves beset on several sides, against American Nativists as hostile to their religion as they were to the land of their birth, against German rationalist anticlericals who hated any replication of Old World religion in the New, and lastly against a Catholic Church which was increasingly an instrument of Irish-American political power and indifferent to the survival of "minority" Catholic cultures. Like the Lutherans, the Catholics in St. Louis tended to tolerate and even advocate nullification and slavery. This was partly a price of survival in the face of Nativist pressures, but it was partly also a response to the political polarization which grew out of the agitation of anticlerical radicals, an apostolic succession of which Boernstein was neither the first nor the last.

Throughout the 1850s, Boernstein's principal sparring partner was the Catholic daily, *Tages-Chronik*, launched under the editorship of August Böckling on 23 August 1851.[32] Boernstein immediately took umbrage at the launching editorial of the *Chronik*, which proclaimed its undying hostility to "Jews and

---

28. Arndt/Olson, I: 262-3, published 7 September 1844-1974.

29. Arndt/Olson, I: 262, published January 1844-1974.

30. *Freie Blätter*, vol. I, no. 20, 26 July 1851; see Steven Rowan, "Franz Schmidt and the Freie Blätter of St. Louis, 1851-53," in Elliott Shore, Ken Fones-Wolf, James P. Danky, eds., *The German-American Radical Press: The Shaping of a Left Political Culture, 1850-1940* (Urbana: University of Illinois Press, 1992), 31-48.

31. See letters of Pastor C. F. W. Walther to Pastor J. C. W. Lindemann, St. Louis, 27 April 1861; to Theodor E. Buenger, St. Louis, 7 May 1861, and to Jacob Matthias Buehler, St. Louis, 21 May 1861, all in the Concordia Historical Society.

32. The citation in Arndt/Olson, I: 271 is misleading and internally contradictory, but it correctly sees the paper as ending in 1861.

heathens," people Boernstein felt were entitled to full citizenship rights by the constitutions of the United States and Missouri.[33] When the *Tages-Chronik* declared its allegiance to "positive Christianity," Boernstein's response was to ask what might constitute "negative Christianity" in those terms.[34]

In the end, Boernstein split the difference with the Nativists by agreeing with them in treating the Catholic Church as the source of all evil in American society. It was this tactical sharing of enemies with the Nativists which made possible the cynical political coalition eventually institutionalized as the Missouri Republican Party, within which German leftists constituted the chief immigrant group. A symptom of this sharing of goals was the tactic Boernstein used in the presidential election of 1856, when the Republican candidate John C. Frémont was not on the ballot in Missouri. Boernstein perversely urged his followers to vote for the Know-Nothing candidate, former President Millard Fillmore, using a ticket headed "Under Protest!"

In crucial matters, then, Boernstein was a secular radical, advocating the elimination of privileges accorded to religious institutions and promoting a system of free labor that entailed depriving a powerful class of its property and power. He was a "small-r" republican through and through, and he became a member of the Republican Party as well when the time came. Although anticlericalism was regarded by most English-speaking Republicans with puzzled embarrassment, the secularist antislavery ideology coincided at crucial points with American religious abolitionism, even if the principles beneath the two traditions were profoundly different. What the anticlericalism of German radicals provided was the basis for what proslavery Democrats in Missouri regarded as a diabolical pact struck between Boernstein and his allies, in which secularists (often openly denigrated as "infidels" by sensitive Anglo-Americans) allied with Nativists by agreeing to pursue a mutual policy of anti-Catholicism. This tactic allowed the German radicals to join the new Republican Party *en masse*, leaving Catholic immigrants, including many Germans, behind in the Democratic Party. "The Germans" (as they presumptuously spoke of themselves) long remained the sole major immigrant group in the Republican Party, finding themselves in the strange company of temperance advocates, Nativists, and old Whigs. Boernstein would talk endlessly of the unity of German opinion under his leadership, so that eventually even those who should have known better came to believe it.

---

33. *AW,* weekly, vol. 16, no. 46, 30 August 1851, p. 4, for 24 August. Boernstein took the term "heathen" to be aimed against Native American polytheist cults, not against secularists such as himself.

34. *AW,* weekly, vol. 16, no. 46, 30 August 1851, p. 2, for 27 August.

The Critics Rave: The Persisting Memory of Henry Boernstein

Those who had extensive dealings with Boernstein in St. Louis in the 1850s were almost unanimous in their estimation of the man's energy and talent, though they frequently regarded him either as misguided or as a mere sensationalist and opportunist. The chilly Gustav Körner, a close friend and soul mate of Lincoln, was in a position to vouch for what he perceived in Boernstein:

> He was a man of undoubted talents and executive ability, but politics was more a matter of business with him than of principle. He wielded a ready pen, wrote novels in what we now call the "dime novel" style, far more realistic than the "Mysteries" of Eugene Sue, or the "Human Documents" of Zola. Having in some way obtained control of the *Anzeiger des Westens,* he became the first sensational writer of the German press. Of course, he was a reformer, and, like Eugene Sue, at once ran amuck against the Jesuits and Catholicism in general. He published sensationalist reports about cruelties inflicted in convents, kidnapping and other terrible misdeeds. Disturbances and even riots were engendered by his drastic representations. He used the press in order to make for himself a party, and he succeeded to a great extent. Those who would not follow his dictation, he relentlessly pursued. He was a master at advertising himself and his paper, and made the latter a business success. In some respects his stirring up of the people was not without its good effects, but no doubt he created strife and bad feeling, and above all roused the American population against the Germans and the newcomers in particular. A good deal of the very strong revival of the Native American feeling, just at this time and for some years to come, was owing to the arrogance, imperious and domineering conduct of the refugees.[35]

Körner himself wrote editorials in the *Belleviller Zeitung* in those years, and he believed that Boernstein's boasting of a superior intellect was mere vanity:

> It is true, the utterly hollow and vain pretenses to superior knowledge of Mr. Boernstein, and his palpable charlatanism, I occasionally castigated. As he had very soon managed, by his overbearing vanity,—his bull-dozing as it would now be called,—to make himself a good many enemies, the "Belleviller Zeitung" was readily taken and greedily read in St. Louis.

---

35. Gustav Körner, *The Memoirs of Gustave Körner,* vol. I, Thomas J. McCormack, ed. (Cedar Rapids, Iowa, 1909), 548-9.

It is no wonder that he assailed me bitterly, represented me as the great champion of the "Grays," gave me the epiphet of the "Gray Gustav," and called me a relic of olden times, though he, himself, was older than I. I gave him a Roland for his Oliver: he grew angry and I kept cool. At any rate he did not disturb my circles, whilst I did his to a considerable extent.[36]

An opinion from the other extreme of the political spectrum, that of the anti-Lincoln Radical Republicans who followed John Frémont in 1861 and 1864, can be gathered from Daniel Hertle in his evaluation written at the very end of hostilities in 1865. When Hertle thought back on the origins of what would become the Republican Party, he was inevitably drawn to the story of the Benton Democrats and their rivals, as well as to the phenomenon of Henry Boernstein:

The greatest portion of the older immigration along with a portion of the newer stood on the side of the anti-Benton party, which was represented by the *Demokratische Presse* under the leadership of Christian Kribben and F. A. H. Schneider. The newer part of the immigration, which in most cases did not yet have the right to vote, inclined to the Benton party, which was defended by the *Anzeiger des Westens* under Henry Boernstein. It must be remarked here that this extremely violent conflict between the two German newspapers combined so many personal motives that the principles were quite erased in the process and the matter deteriorated into a battle of Germans among themselves, a *querelle allemande* ["German quarrel"]. The *Anzeiger* . . . made great contributions to Germans and their social life in St. Louis under Herr Boernstein's leadership. Himself a passionate actor, he soon created a decent theater and united in himself the functions of an editor, director and reviewer; tirelessly active, he orchestrated the festivities and public entertainments for every German occasion. By this means he won great influence with the population, and the *Anzeiger* was an oracle for a long time and for many. But soon he fell into the error of every leader; he believed he, the sole tribune of the people, could command what the Germans had offered him freely. His vanity often misled him to unwise statements that he, the *Anzeiger*, could command the inclinations, the views and the votes of Germans. Persons and whole associations not subject to his will were attacked without mercy, and it was not unusual that he was successful. For a while it appeared as if he were the keeper of the seal of the Germans' favor, but that in itself

---

36. Körner, *Memoirs*, vol. I, 550. While Körner speaks of the *Belleviller Zeitung* obtaining readers in the St. Louis area, the *Anzeiger des Westens* always had considerable circulation in Southern Illinois, rivaling its competitor's circulation in outstate Missouri.

irritated them and awakened the pride of German self-esteem, particularly that of the educated. These educated persons opposed him first of all in the *Tribüne* and later in the *Demokratische Presse.* Irritated by this opposition, he committed even worse errors through the worst sort of demagoguery, denigrating the educated and making them an object of suspicion in the eyes of the uneducated. Instead of using his influence over the great masses to raise them, he flattered their coarseness by trying to make the educated and education itself laughable in the eyes of the masses, who never could separate the person from the principle. Using nicknames created by the older immigration, he called them "Latins, Bloats, Spartans" and other silly-sounding names. . . . The conflict, as unedifying as it was, at least contributed to getting the Germans to read newspapers.[37]

Throughout his professional life, Boernstein's almost demonic drive made enemies everywhere, but his most intense foes were those who had worked with him most closely. Repeatedly throughout his wild ride in St. Louis from 1850 to 1862, it was his closest collaborators who broke away and attacked him, whether it was Carl Dänzer and his creation, the *Westliche Post,* or Georg Hillgärtner and his *Neue Zeit.* The informants of R. G. Dun registered his unpopularity among "the intelligent portion of the Germans" in 1852, and in 1857 they tersely noted, "Becoming unpopular with the Germans here. . . . Has lost about 2000 subscribers to his paper during the last four months."[38] Through it all, only Bernays would remain solidly loyal, for his own reasons.

It is an open question whether Boernstein even helped the Union cause in the opening phase of the Civil War. Like Nathaniel Lyon, whom he described as a hot-headed Nativist and a poor general, Boernstein helped polarize the muddled political situation in Missouri in the late 1850s, but often to the disadvantage of his own party. His intense, unprincipled anticlericalism had the Catholic Church as its chief target, but he also harbored nothing but scorn for the Old Lutherans under C. F. W. Walther, or for rabbinical Judaism, which was strong in St. Louis. His opponents portrayed his efforts as simple bigotry, giving themselves the chance to picture support of slavery as an urbane and reasonable position, in harmony with toleration of religious diversity. The result was that the conflict which arose in Missouri could be seen as a battle between religion and irreligion,

---

37. Daniel Hertle, *Die Deutschen in Nordamerika* (Chicago, 1865), 52-53.

38. R. G. Dun & Co. Collection, Baker Library, Harvard University Graduate School of Business Administration, Missouri vol. 36, p. 286, report of 31 July 1852; and Missouri vol. 37, p. 589, report of 21 December 1857.

and in 1861 the first round went to irreligion.[39] The *Missouri Republican* repeatedly portrayed the Germans as antireligious in its "The Spirit of the German Press" series. As a result of Boernstein's efforts, the Irish in St. Louis were particularly alienated from the Union cause in its earliest phases, and Irish papers became mouthpieces for proslavery positions. Consequently, the force raised in the U.S. Arsenal in St. Louis in April 1861 was truly the worst nightmare of the Missouri establishment, a force of Germans and Czechs, many of them with revolutionary predilections, lead by colonels including an Anglo politician on the make (Blair), an unstable abolitionist Yankee (Lyon), their sworn enemy (Boernstein), an academic militarist (Sigel) and a thuggish street-gang leader (Nikolaus Schüttner). They had every reason to believe their world was coming to an end, and for fifteen years it did.

Ironically, despite his radical reputation with Anglos, Boernstein never wholly aligned himself with all radical goals, and in the end this ambiguity would lead to his downfall in Missouri. His hatred of organized religion would probably prove to be his only firmly held belief, along with his hostility to an entrenched privileged class. In an American setting, however, other questions were primary, and in those matters Boernstein tended to take a more gradualist approach. The man he most consistently supported through the Civil War in Missouri was Francis Preston Blair, Jr. who favored compensation for slaveowners, gradual emancipation of blacks, and their colonization overseas. By the time Boernstein reached America, whatever socialism he had supported as a member of Karl Marx's entourage in 1844 had been thoroughly washed out of him by his horror at the "right to labor" debacle of the early Second French Republic. As he confessed himself, he was a Green by personal experience, but a Gray in practical politics. In the end, Boernstein's support of Blair, and through him of Lincoln, would spell disaster for his own cause in Missouri.

"Books have their own fates": The *Memoirs*.

The memoirs, which were written after Boernstein's Missouri experience had been overlaid by more than a decade in Europe, are uneven as a historical source and must be treated with caution. His memoirs have long been regarded as a major source for the history of the German emigration as well as for the history of the German-language press in the United States, but it has suffered the fate of being a window looked through too often from only one side. To Austrian and German observers of the American

---

39. The best demonstration of this "pious proslavery" position, besides the columns of the *Missouri Republican,* is the post-war tract by W. M. Leftwich, *Martyrdom in Missouri,* 2 vols. (St. Louis: S. W. Book and Publishing Co., 1870).

scene, Boernstein is regarded as a primary source on German-American politics in the 1850s. In contrast, many who would be able to read Boernstein with critical care because they understand the complex history of the American Midwest have been barred access to him because they do not read German, the language of a high percentage of the regional population in the last century.

Boernstein's strong personality and wide background, together with his ready pen, means that his memoirs stand in the first rank of German emigrant autobiographies of the nineteenth century. The two with which it bears direct comparison were, significantly enough, both written in English, a sign of the fading of the German language even among German-Americans in the 1890s. The oral reminiscences of Gustav Körner and the memoirs of Carl Schurz were both produced by Germans who had made themselves thoroughly at home in America, and who could look back on successful careers in which they had earned status and respect in their new homeland.[40] Their origins in distant Germany cast an exotic light on their lives, but their success was a result of reaching beyond a single ethnic community. In contrast, Boernstein wrote as a man who had never received respect in exchange for his efforts, and his American career had been both colorful and ultimately disastrous. Above all, the exotic part of his story was not Central Europe but America, viewed in retirement from the distant vantage point of Vienna. Although he remained proud of being an American—and a Missourian—Boernstein persisted through his entire life in being an Austrian actor and journalist.

The more one knows about the German scene in mid-nineteenth-century St. Louis, the more problematic Boernstein's account becomes. He never takes nonradical Germans seriously, particularly those with religious commitments. He never even mentions his continuous battles with the Catholic *Tages-Chronik*, one of the few openly proslavery German papers in St. Louis, nor does he breathe a word about his perennial battles waged with C. F. W. Walther of the Lutheran Synod headquartered in St. Louis, through Walther's *Der Lutheraner*. He denies the existence of more than a smattering of German Whigs, and he never mentions any opposing German-language papers after the *Deutsche Tribüne*, such as Christian Kribben's *Demokratische Presse*, let alone the all-powerful *Westliche Post*, which buried the *Anzeiger des Westens*.

Still, above all else, the memoirs constitute a precise document of a personality. Factual details or names are occasionally incorrect, and the exact sequence of events is sometimes blurred. But the person who drove the Missouri establishment mad is clearly visible throughout. This is a presence

---

40. Körner; Carl Schurz, *The Reminiscences of Carl Schurz*, 3 vols. (New York: McClure, 1907-8).

which changed things in the American Midwest in complex and at times indiscernible ways. He was a wild card which made new combinations possible and even necessary. Intelligent he certainly was, but also perverse and mercurial, and his motivations were often hard to divine. Yet, in the last analysis, he was a good soldier when times grew grim and there was serious revolutionary work to be done. He was continuously bluffing, but that bluffing was ultimately guaranteed by personal courage. In his brief command in Jefferson City, when he held a strategic position with a handful of troops by keeping his enemy guessing, he was a showman and an actor in a situation where those rare qualities were desperately needed. Although he would wear many costumes in the course of an actor's life, his best role would be in a U.S. Army colonel's uniform, a brief part he played for more than mere applause. Although he spoke of himself in the end as a "nobody," an "insignificant man," he indeed made a difference, turning historical developments in directions that would never have been possible without his having been there.

The sea is made up of droplets, while mankind is made up of individuals—yet these droplets will eventually hollow out the hardest stone, just as in the course of time the individual will make and form the cultural history of the human race.[1]

The Author
Dedicates this book
to his dear and true friend

Carl von Bukovics

Director of the Vienna *Stadttheater*[2]

both respected and loved as an artist and as a human being.
Dedicated as a gift of friendship
and as a remembrance of beautiful times lived together.

---

1. This epigraph appears only in the second edition of Boernstein's memoirs, published in 1884.
2. Carl Bukovics von Kis-Alacska (died 1888), a close friend of Boernstein treated at the end of these memoirs, resigned military service in 1858 and made his debut as a singer in Graz in 1859. In 1865 he began a career as a comic actor at the *Theater in der Josefsstadt* in Vienna, and he served that theater as director through 1870, then taking directorships in Teplitz and Wiener Neustadt. In 1875 he became director of the Vienna *Stadttheater*, and he achieved the high honor of being director of the *Burgtheater* in Vienna from 1884 until his death. See Eva Obermeyer-Marnach, ed., *Österreichisches Biographisches Lexikon, 1815-1950*, I (Graz; Cologne, 1957), p. 126.

In Place *of a* Prologue

I began writing down my memories in my seventieth year, giving in to the desires of tried and true friends. Then after the completion of the first half, the work which I had begun was left lying for two years. It was only renewed urging of friends which moved me to continue it. As a result, these sketches were completed in 1879 and 1880, appearing in fragments in the widely read *Westen*, the Sunday edition of the *Illinois Staatszeitung* in Chicago.[3] The friendly reception they found moved me to have them appear as a whole in book form. I leave it to the benign judgment of the public to decide whether I have been right to do that. The grounds that moved me to this publication, which is perhaps too presumptuous, are contained in the following:

Open Letter to
Mr. Hermann Raster

Editor of the *Illinois Staatszeitung* in Chicago (United States of America)[4]

Dear Friend and Editor:

You were recently so friendly as to encourage me to send you reminiscences from my life from time to time for publication, and I have given this invitation a great deal of thought. There is much to be said both for and against such reports, and I have closely weighed both sides of the question. To be sure, I have written down some reminiscences from my very active life in leisurely hours, but because I regard myself as much too unimportant a personality in the great course of humanity, I have not regarded it as proper to burden the reading public with a couple more volumes of memoirs that would only contain banalities. The result is that these sketches have peacefully slumbered for a few years in a drawer of my writing desk. Perhaps I was wrong to hold them back, and your invitation gave me a chance to consider the question once more in detail.

Such private sketches by an individual are basically more or less valuable as contributions to cultural history. In his "Images from the German Past," Gustav Freytag has shown surprisingly well what individual descriptions

---

3. *Der Westen* appeared from 1854 to c. 1920, and it had a circulation of 10,000 in 1880. See Arndt/Olson, I: 88.

4. Hermann Raster (1827-1891), a participant in the 1848 revolution, arrived in New York in 1851, becoming the editor of the Buffalo *Demokrat*, the New York *Abendzeitung*, and in 1867 of the *Illinois Staats-Zeitung* of Chicago. See Zucker, 329.

from past times, family chronicles of simple citizens or reports of events by contemporaries can offer to historical research as well as to following generations as a whole. History only works in great strokes, giving us portraits of emperors and kings, of great statesmen and generals, portraying great acts and actions of states. It pays little attention to civil life, the ways and actions of individuals who compose that great mass which is called "the people." These people, however, actually make cultural history, insofar as they support the efforts of their rulers and leaders or resist them to some degree. In every epoch of history, such phenomena have been propagated by the masses, though little has been preserved for posterity from the period before the invention of printing.

To be sure, such reports are of little interest to living contemporaries, who already know the spirit and dynamics of their own time. But for following generations they offer more interest, providing rich material for comparison of the past with the present. Perhaps this motivation was the chief one that moved me to allow these memoirs to lie in peace, for their publication can offer contemporaries little that is new, and even less of interest. Their small value can be realized only after long aging, as they say with wine, and will merit some attention from cultural historians.

Naturally you and your readers have every right to ask why I wrote these memoirs, if they were never intended for publication. I will answer that straightaway. I wrote them as a legacy to my children and grandchildren, and partly for my own entertainment, for by writing I lived once more in spirit in past times, both happy and sad. Now it is certainly possible that someone else might enjoy these accounts, and even discover some pleasure because his own experiences are similar. This is why memoirs and autobiographies excite so much interest in Germany, and especially in England and France.

When I began considering writing these sketches, I asked Friedrich Kapp,[5] experienced in these matters. He wrote me in reply, "It is certainly your right to write your memoirs; . . . whoever has lived a life of thought and action has not only the right but the obligation to make this contribution to cultural history." These sketches are intended to do no more than that, providing a handful of sand to the mortar with which the great structure of the history of humankind is raised over centuries, that structure whose first foundations from the age of rocks and pilings is only beginning to be

---

5. Friedrich Kapp (1824-1884), born in Hamm, Westphalia, participated in the uprising in Frankfurt am Main. He arrived in America in 1850, becoming a lawyer in New York, and later commissioner of immigration for New York, from 1867 to 1870. He wrote extensively. He returned to Germany in 1870, becoming a member of the *Reichstag* as a National Liberal. His son was the instigator of the "Kapp Putsch" against the Weimar Republic in 1921. Zucker, 307-8.

uncovered. World history as we know it concerns itself with great events, and the events of a single life are nothing so far as it is concerned; but it is the total of these episodes that is handled by cultural history. Cultural history tells us what our predecessors have done and left undone, and from this we learn what we are to do or leave undone. In this respect the memoirs of a single nobody could be of some use, and this was certainly one of the reasons that moved me to write down these memoirs.

The reader must be assured that he will not find truth and poetry; what I am writing is what I myself experienced and saw. I might remain silent about many things that did not happen to me but to others, but I have invented nothing. If I mention historical events in which I was actively or passively engaged, I have neither the faith nor the intention to bring up new or unknown things. I mention events only for the sake of completeness.

So I have come to the decision to send you some fragments from these sketches for publication, and it will soon be seen whether they are of interest to your readers. If this is the case, I can continue them from time to time. If the contrary is the case, all you need to do is whisper a soft, "Stop!" These sketches will then sink back into the dark drawer of my writing desk. Now to business!

With a hearty greeting
Your old friend
Henry Boernstein
Vienna, 15 March 1879

Foreword *to the* Second Edition
(1884)

My publisher has been so good as to ask me to write a short foreword to the second edition of my book. As flattering and pleasant as such an invitation might be to me, it still puts me in some disarray. This book is nothing more, after all, than an unpretentious narrative of my experiences, and I am now in that age when one has, so to speak, "experienced nothing further." I have added three more years to the seventy-five years of the first edition, as I am now celebrating my seventy-eighth birthday. That is about all I can add to my autobiography.

Despite my age, I still enjoy untroubled physical and psychological health, as well as an undiminished capacity for work. Under the direction of my dear friend Carl von Bukovics, I still oversee the duties of a booking agent at the Vienna *Stadttheater*, and in the last four-and-a-half years I have read fourteen hundred newly submitted pieces. I continue to serve as European correspondent for American newspapers and, as my editors tell me, my *"Europäische Plaudereien"* ["European Chit-Chat"] still enjoys applause from a steadily growing circle of readers. In great, lively Vienna I lead a rather quiet, withdrawn life entirely devoted to the conscientious practice of my profession and my journalistic labors, but I pay lively interest to all new phenomena in the area of science, culture and literature. That is all I have to add to my autobiography. I have no desires except to be the same until the end, but I also have no complaints, either about the past or about the present. I belong to that minority of humanity which is satisfied with its lot.

If I do not have much of a right to speak of myself, I still cannot let the occasion slip to fulfill an obligation, which is the obligation of gratitude. I therefore express my deepest thanks to the esteemed public who has received my book with such friendliness. Above all else, I thank the entire daily press of Germany and Austria, which has been so supportive and sympathetic to an old colleague and which leveled this book's way to the public through their positive reviews. This good reception pleased me. It was a warm, bright glimpse of sunlight in the winter of my adventurous life.

May these lines also receive as friendly a reception.

Written in Vienna on 4 November 1883, my seventy-eighth birthday.
Henry Boernstein

Summary of the First Volume of Boernstein's Memoirs

From My Childhood (1805-1813)

Boernstein was born in Hamburg on 4 November 1805, a time when Hamburg had been little altered by the changes begun by the French Revolution. Even with the beginning of French occupation, the traditional forms of bourgeois life changed slowly. He was the eldest surviving son of Franz Sigmund Börnstein and his wife Ilse Sophie, née Hesse. Franz Börnstein had been a Catholic actor who left the stage in order to marry Ilse, the Protestant daughter of a Hanoverian ship's captain. The children were raised Protestant, and Boernstein was baptized Georg Christian Heinrich. The French occupation of Hamburg in 1810 led to the quartering of forces on bourgeois houses, and the Wars of Liberation beginning in 1813 later brought Russians and Swedes. The French retook the city, leading to heavy fines and the loss of personal fortunes, specifically the Börnstein family's valuable silver.

Time of Terror and Emigration (1813)

The French occupation of 1813 and 1814 led to systematic ruination of bourgeois Hamburg at the hands of a savage soldiery.

Departure and Journey (1813)

Franz Börnstein and his family left Hamburg in July 1813 to go to his native Lemberg, partly by boat and partly by carriage. They crossed a Germany aroused against Napoléon I in the War of Liberation. Near the Bohemian border Henry Boernstein saw Napoléon with his own eyes, and in Karlsbad he saw the poet Goethe. They reached Lemberg after a hard journey in September.

Polish Economy (1815-1817)

Boernstein describes the basic form and history of Polish Galizia, occupied by Poles, Ruthenians, along with some Jews and Germans. The crude conditions there horrified Ilse Börnstein, particularly the Polish peasant practice of kissing the boots or skirt-hems of persons of higher status.

Life Begins in Earnest (1815-1817)

Lemberg had some of the character of a civilized town, with paved streets and large buildings. Although Jews dominated much of the industry, delivery, and retail business, the tone of the town was German.

The Religious Question (1815-1817)

As Protestants, Ilse Börnstein and her children were part of a tolerated but second-class minority in a society dominated by the privileges historically accorded the Catholic Church. Because Boernstein's father was a Catholic, however, the Austrian state required that he attend Catholic catechism. His mother provided Protestant instruction at home, but he was forced to attend mass. Boernstein, looking back, sees religion as a man-made effort to rationalize morality.

The First Prayer (1815-1817)

As a boy, Boernstein would compose prayers in which he thanked God for not making him a woman. Once, due to his curiosity, he managed to obtain a book normally locked in a cabinet in his home. He was stunned to discover it was a particularly horrifying illustrated manual on obstetrics. This led to very confused questions about sexuality. At this time, the death of a cousin in childbirth increased his distress. He became increasingly drawn to the esthetics of the Catholic mass, and his father declared his son would become either a preacher or an actor.

In Gymnasium (1815-1820)

On a visit of the Austrian Emperor Francis I to Boernstein's Gymnasium (high school) in Lemberg, Boernstein spoke the school's greeting and received a pat from the ruler. He began to be convinced by theological arguments, and he was interested in going to seminary, although his mother stridently opposed it.

Years of Apprenticeship (1821)

After leaving high school, Boernstein became involved with friends who composed poems and plays, performing them for acquaintances and relatives.

At *the* University (1821)

Due to official repression after the murder of the poet Kotzebue, there was little of traditional fraternity life at Lemberg University. Boernstein was an avid attender of theatrical productions.

To Italy (1821)

In early 1821 the Carbonari rebellion broke out in Italy, and Austrian troops were sent there both to repress rebellion and to reinforce occupation. Boernstein assumed that if he joined a particular infantry regiment as a cadet, he would be sent to Italy. Against his parents' desires he joined, but he was erroneously registered as a native Lemberger, binding him to fourteen years' service. Contrary to expectations, the unit stayed put in Olmütz, Bohemia.

Soldier's Life (1821-1826)

Boernstein regarded his five years as a soldier as a complete waste of time, although the experience did help him forty years later as a colonel in the United States. The tactics of the Austrian army were archaic and discipline brutal in a unit with French or British officers and illiterate Polish privates. Boernstein was promoted to corporal and transferred to Lemberg.

A Duel *and its* Results

While Boernstein was on duty elsewhere, his mother died. At the funeral, he experienced a laughing fit that continued for days until ended by narcotics. During a march in Galizia, a dueling frenzy ran through the officer corps, then the cadets. Boernstein became involved in a duel with another cadet, leading to a badly wounded arm. He rejected amputation and recovered, but he was released from military service.

Merry Youth (1826)

After much effort, Boernstein received an honorable discharge, and his arm was made to work by a daring therapy. He returned to the university, but he led a rather silly life with his friends. Finally, his father determined to send him to Vienna to study medicine.

Disappointments (1826)

After two weeks of continuous travel, Boernstein reached Vienna. He soon wasted most of his father's money on theater and fell into poverty, unable to find any employment.

Twenty-One *and* Starving (1826)

Utterly down on his luck, Boernstein was rescued in the Prater by a publisher who needed an editor for his Vienna cultural journal. Boernstein began his career as a journalist. He had great success at publicizing a balloon ascension, which made him more in a day than he had brought with him from Lemberg. He registered as a student in medicine, and he never took money from his father again.

In Journalism (1826-1827)

In the service of his publisher, Boernstein wrote several plays and undertook extensive publishing projects. He did theatrical reviews at the Theater an der Wien *and the* Leopoldstädter Theater *for journals. He also learned how to manipulate censorship authorities.*

From Scylla *into* Charybdis (1826-1827)

As a journalist, Boernstein covered the death and burial of Beethoven. From being a theatrical reviewer, he was offered the post of manager of a theater. He also became involved with a notorious ballet dancer.

Across *the* Rubicon (1827)

Boernstein covered a famous murder trial that arose from the liaison between a young man and an actress he knew, all ending in a dramatic execution. Boernstein began working as a comic actor, despite his father's misgivings. He returned to Lemberg with a troupe.

Theatrical Life (1828-1829)

Boernstein established himself as a character actor in dialect and accent roles. In Lemberg he first met the Hungarian actress Marie Steltzer, then fourteen. He returned to Vienna with Marie's family to perform variety productions, including comedy, dance and singing. Marie's mother rejected Boernstein's request to marry Marie because the mother foresaw a profitable acting career for her daughter. Boernstein decided to abduct Marie and take her to Hungary, where they could legally marry.

The Abduction (1829)

Boernstein was arrested while trying to flee with Marie, and he was charged with abducting a minor. Marie insisted to the police that it had been she who had abducted Boernstein, an action which was not covered by the law. On his release from detention, Boernstein learned that his father had died in Ofen, Hungary. Marie's mother permitted the marriage only after receiving a payoff.

Marriage *and* Honeymoon Trip (1829-1830)

After a successful engagement in Ofen, Boernstein and Marie were married on 12 November 1829. They went to Transylvania in the dead of winter to perform at a playhouse in Temésvar (Timisoara). Marie taught dancing. Back in Ofen, Boernstein wrote a play with a Hungarian theme that had great success when translated into Magyar.

First Directorship (1830-1831)

Boernstein and Marie arrived in Vienna from Pest on the first steamboat to travel the Danube, then went on to perform in Laibach. They briefly visited Trieste and Venice. On his return to Austria, Boernstein obtained the directorship of the theater in St. Pölten, though the season was restricted by an outbreak of cholera.

An Artistic Journey

August Sigmund Boernstein was born on 13 February 1832. After finishing the season in St. Pölten, Boernstein, Marie, her sister, and brother-in-law, all went to present a variety show in Italy. The first performance in Venice was a total catastrophe.

Stable *at* Last (1832-1839)

In Trieste and Gorizia the troupe found a better reception than Venice, and further performances in Laibach made money. Boernstein obtained the directorship in Linz, where he worked for six years.

Alone *and* Independent (1835)

In Linz, Boernstein had repeated skirmishes with the nobility of the city, partly because the theater building belonged to the Upper Austrian estates. Boernstein also warred with the censorship authorities.

The End *of the* Linz Directorship (1837)

Boernstein mortally offended the nobility of Linz when he bought a coach and livery for his wife, which was regarded as pretentious for a bourgeois. He was convicted of allowing an offensive song performed in his theater, and he spent three days in jail. When his lease was finally up, he took over the theater in Agram (Zagreb, Croatia).

An Episode (1837)

By order of the Imperial court, Boernstein took the Linz troupe to Bad Ischl to perform for the Emperor as he took the waters. Boernstein describes charming incidents involving members of the Imperial family during this idyll.

Going South (1839-1840)

Six years of struggling with the censorship bureaucracy and nobility in Linz had turned Boernstein into a radical democrat. From Agram he tested the idea of opening a permanent theater in Trieste.

The Crisis *in* Trieste (1840)

In Agram, Boernstein helped create a Croatian national theater, greatly offending Hungarian nationalists. Boernstein's efforts to establish a theater in Trieste were undermined by the financial crisis created by the war between Turkey and Egypt. He decided to make a tour of Italy with his troupe.

Through Italy *to* Germany (1840-1841)

Good success was had in Padua, where there were many German students, then in Merano and Bolzano in the Tyrol. In Munich, Boernstein had a chance encounter with Prince Clemens von Metternich, the Austrian Chancellor.

Through Germany *to* Paris (1841-1842)

Because there was no work to be had in Munich, Boernstein went on to Augsburg, where he turned down a permanent position with the Augsburger Allgemeine Zeitung, *then the leading German paper. In Mannheim, however, he found himself forced to work as the editor of a journal, and he wrote for other papers as well. He organized a small troupe and set out for Paris to join an attempt to establish a German opera in Paris.*

The German Opera *in* Paris (1842)

The effort to establish a German opera was a disaster from start to finish. The result was that a large company of eighty members was stranded in Paris without any means of getting home.

The Rescue (1842)

A collection was taken up among Parisian Germans to save the actors stranded in Paris. Boernstein visited Heinrich Heine, among others, to raise funds. King Louis-Philippe asked for the chorus to perform at his court in Versailles. Although Boernstein was concerned that some radicals in his group might take the occasion to attempt an assassination, the royal concert was a great success, and Boernstein gained a very positive impression of Louis-Philippe as a person.

The Solution *to the* Problem (1842)

As a result of royal support, Boernstein was invited to many gatherings of nobility, where his chorus provided entertainment or simply background. Franz Liszt also helped by giving a concert with the chorus. As a result the actors raised the money to go home. Boernstein and his family remained in Paris.

A New Homeland (1842-1847)

Boernstein became involved once more in journalism, this time political rather than cultural. He began writing political columns for the Augsburger Allgemeine Zeitung *and the New York* Deutsche Schnellpost. *He also managed an Italian opera company.*

The Great Translation Factory (1843-1844)

Boernstein had close associations with the composer Giacomo Meyerbeer, the poet Heinrich Heine, and the pianist Franz Liszt. Boernstein translated about fifty French stage plays into German for the German market. Some nationalists protested that this flooded the German stage with cosmopolitan, un-German plays with suspect politics, and Boernstein was accused of subverting traditional German values.

A German Newspaper *in* Paris (1844)

Attacks on Boernstein alarmed the Augsburger Allgemeine Zeitung, and although he continued to work for the paper, he felt he should establish a paper of his own in Paris. The Italian opera had closed due to several mishaps, so Boernstein was left with journalism as his sole recourse. He founded a Central Bureau for Commission and Publicity for Germany to promote fashions, innovations, and news, and he met with great success. Mayerbeer invested money, and the first issue of the new journal Vorwärts! appeared on 1 January 1844. It was a moderate opposition paper at the start, favoring gradual progress and reform, but it was immediately banned in all of Central Europe.

The Founding *of the* German Support Association (1844)

The poverty of many Germans stranded in Paris led Boernstein to support the creation of an association for the needy regardless of political, religious, or social distinctions. A German reading room was also established, but there was more success with a lending library. A pretender to the Duchy of Mantua granted Boernstein a patent of nobility and a coat of arms, which he resolutely refused to use.

The Flourishing *and* End *of the Vorwärts!* (1844)

The publication of the Deutsch-Französische Jahrbücher by Arnold Ruge and Karl Marx in Paris excited a great deal of attention. Boernstein's review of that publication brought him together with one of its editors, Karl Ludwig Bernays, who became his closest friend. Through Bernays, Boernstein converted to humanism, which was the term then used for what would later be called socialism. The result was that the collaborators on the Deutsch-Französische Jahrbücher entered the Vorwärts!, and Boernstein came to know the magnetic Karl Marx, as well as the Russian revolutionary Bakunin. French authorities finally intervened and closed the journal. Bernays was sent to jail for two months, Marx was exiled to Brussels, and Boernstein made a deal with the police. Other participants scattered.

Experiences *and* Acquaintances (1842-1847)

After the closure of the Vorwärts!, Boernstein ran a press service for papers that could not afford a correspondent in Paris. Boernstein worked together with Bernays, who acted as a reporter. As a translator, Boernstein came to know Alexandre Dumas père, who treated him to some of his famous dinners. He also came to know nearly all of the writers for the French stage in this period. In April 1844 he was initiated into Freemasonry, although he dropped it even before leaving France. Marie Boernstein's sister at this time married a member of the Italian aristocracy, so that Boernstein could move in rather rarefied noble circles when he cared to, which was rare, although it was not to his taste.

The Vienna Children's Ballet (1845)

An old acquaintance appeared on Boernstein's doorstep in Paris with a large traveling troupe of children, and Boernstein had a comic time acting as an agent for the company. The troupe had great success in Paris before going on to London and America.

Idyllic Country Life (1846-1847)

Boernstein, Bernays, and their dependents settled in the peasant village of Sarcelles near Paris, leading a rather idyllic country life while commuting to Paris to do their reporting and journalism work. The family took on a Walloon wanderer named Léon, a young man without a past who worked for them as a servant.

Henrich Heine (1842-1848)

Resentment mounted against the régime of King Louis-Philippe, and the poet Heinrich Heine saw this most clearly. Heine had been impoverished by a market crash, and he was very ill in 1848 when Boernstein last saw him. In the course of the idyll in Sarcelles, Boernstein began considering emigrating to America. He was writing a great deal for German papers in America, and his dispatches were being translated into elegant English by Charles A. Dana and Bayard Taylor for Horace Greeley's New York Tribune.

The February Revolution (1848)

As a result of government ineptitude, a street incident escalated into a full-scale revolt in Paris. Boernstein was able to observe the revolt, as well as the proclamation of a French Republic.

The Paris German Legion (1848)

The Republic was proclaimed, but it had little support outside of Paris itself. The provisional government was benign but confused, and it proclaimed the "right to labor," which proved a disastrous error. Radicals gathered in Paris to organize a German Democratic Legion to aid revolution in Germany, and Boernstein headed the German Democratic Association, which helped raise the unit and arm it. Georg Herwegh proved utterly inept as leader of the Legion, a troop of about eight hundred men.

Under *the* Republic (1848)

With the collapse of the Baden Revolution, the German Legion was isolated and finally badly beaten at the Swiss frontier by Württemberg troops. Customers of Boernstein's Central Bureau dried up, causing him to look about for another source of support. In the course of the revolution, Boernstein made a systematic collection of the pamphlets and short-lived papers available on the Paris streets, which he later gave to the Mercantile Library Association of St. Louis. The elections of 4 May produced a conservative majority in the National Assembly, which doomed the Republic.

The May Days (1848)

Boernstein observed the development of events as a reporter at the National Assembly. Although the Assembly confirmed the Republic, leftists sought to overawe and terrorize it from the start. Disorder and confusion reigned, and newspapers were increasingly unable to pay for services. Boernstein desired increasingly to emigrate to America.

The June Battles (1848)

Demands that German workers join an armed confrontation with the government to achieve their "right to labor" led Boernstein to resign his presidency of the German Democratic Association. He watched the uprising and its repression by General Cavaignac over a period of four days, which put to rest the theory that barricades were an invincible weapon in the hands of the people. Charles A. Dana was in Paris at the time, bringing Boernstein a payment in gold from Horace Greeley for his many articles.

Under Cavaignac's Rule (1848)

General Cavaignac extended the state of siege indefinitely, becoming a dictator at the behest of the National Assembly. The first appearance of Louis Napoléon to take his oath as a member of the Assembly excited great interest, although he appeared clumsy and spoke "haltingly, with a strong Teutonic accent." After taking his seat, Napoléon kept his silence while others debated. The popular election of the president was set for 10 December. Bastide, the foreign minister, named Bernays the French consul to Jacmel, in Haiti. Members of Cavaignac's government expected Louis Napoléon to be elected president, and even before the election Boernstein reserved passage on the Sea Lion for Bernays and the women of the entourage to travel to New Orleans. On 11 December they left for Le Havre, leaving Boernstein and his brother Arnold in Paris to put affairs in order.

HENRY BOERNSTEIN, ESQ.,

Publisher of the "Auzeiger des Westens."

Henry Boernstein in 1860. Wood engraving based on a contemporary photograph from Edwards's Great West. Courtesy of the Mercantile Library Association, St. Louis.

Left Behind Alone

(1848-1849)

The *Sea Lion* had already put to sea on 16 December, and from that moment forward I did not hear a thing from or about my family until I arrived in New Orleans to find their first letters deposited with the French consulate.

I had plenty to occupy me in Paris. I had to collect fees due me from a mass of journals and theaters, the correspondence bureau just sold to Captain Demmler had to be run by me for a while with his assistance in order to initiate him in the business, and a myriad other preparations had to be made. As a result, I had little time for boredom or somber reflection. In August Bernays and I had received decrees from Minister of Justice Cremieux, granting us French citizenship, for we appeared on a list prepared by the Provisional Government granting French citizenship to a number of foreigners "for their services to the Republic *en recompense nationale.*"[1] This greatly speeded our getting passports and assured us a good reception from the French consul in New Orleans.

In the meantime, our traveling company had grown. First of all, I had gained an adoptive son, a schoolmate and friend of my eldest son. Both of them made such heartfelt requests not to be parted and to take Gustav along that I agreed. I was heartened by the thought that in America children were not a burden but a blessing. The more hands a family has, the less it has to rely on paying wages to strangers, and it is better guaranteed to survive and flourish.

The parents of my new adopted son, Gustav Prand, delivered their son to me. They were fine, honorable people. The father had once been a very prosperous grain dealer, and as such he had supplied the stables of Napoléon I. In 1814, with the fall of the Empire, his bills were not paid, and there followed years of failed harvests and inflation during 1816-17. Prand suffered great losses, and he had to sell his business and become a driver in a coach line. This hard duty was enough to get him a stroke, and he had to give the position up. The result was that he sank still further, and by this time he was concierge of a nearby house. Gustav was the youngest of the four sons and one daughter whom the old couple had. Their eldest was a soldier in Algeria, and now I took their youngest son.

---

1. French, "In national repayment."

From the very first time I saw him, I had a special affection for the boy. He reminded me of a friend of my youth, since died—there are such sympathetic physiognomies—and I took him into my heart. He also replaced my first-born, who had died after a few months of life. I have never regretted taking him on, and Gustav has always been a loving and grateful son to me, a true brother to his siblings. He is a thoroughly honorable and worthy character, and now, as a postal official in St. Louis, he is loved and respected by his superiors as well as his colleagues.[2]

On 20 December I attended the installation of the new president, Louis Napoléon. General Cavaignac laid down his powers at a solemn session of the National Assembly, and the newly elected president Louis Napoléon was led in. On this occasion he conducted himself with restraint and ease, but his Teutonic accent still prevailed.[3] The president of the National Assembly, Armand Marrast, gave a brief address on the Napoleonic House in which, certainly against his own heart, he congratulated Louis Napoléon, while exhorting him on the obligations of his government. Louis Napoléon barely paid attention to Marrast as he gazed about the hall. When the speech reached its end, the prince stared at the speaker with an extraordinary gaze that Parisians translated as, *"As-tu fini?"*[4] As Marrast finished, the new president gave him a threatening look that could be interpreted as, *"Je te ferai sauter, mon ami."*[5]

Marrast then read out the oath, with Louis Napoléon repeating after him: "In the presence of God and the French people, I swear to remain faithful to the democratic republic, one and indivisible, and to fulfill all the duties which the constitution imposes upon me." He would break this solemn oath in the coarsest possible manner not three years later.[6] This was certainly a low crime, but those who had done the same with their own oaths to Louis Philippe have no right to accuse him of it, particularly such as the two Dupins,[7] who had already sworn and broken a dozen oaths of fidelity.

---

2. Gustavus Boernstein was listed as a Post Office clerk in *Directory* 1871, 114. He died in 1893 and the MHS Photographs and Prints Collection has a photograph of him.

3. Louis Napoléon (Emperor Napoléon III), son of Queen Hortense of Naples, had been raised in Switzerland and retained the villa of Aranenburg on the southern shore of Lake Constance, to which his Empress Eugénie retired following Napoléon's abdication and death.

4. French, (very rude) "Are you finished?"

5. French, "I'll make you jump, my friend."

6. Louis Napoléon overthrew the Second Republic in December 1851, and a year later he was named Emperor Napoléon III, abdicating in 1870 after the defeat of France at the hands of the Prussians.

7. André-Marie-Jean-Jacques Dupin (1783-1865) was president of the French Chamber of Deputies and a leading Orléanist, then president of the National Assembly (1849-51)

The end of the unfortunate year of 1848 was the darkest and saddest New Year's Eve I ever experienced. I sat lonely and alone, having sent the youngsters to the theater, and wrote to New Orleans and my dears, who were probably at that moment struggling with the winter storms then to be expected in the Atlantic Ocean. It was a sad, depressing New Year's Eve, one which I shall never forget.

A young painter named Alexandre Boulet, whose wife had gone ahead of him to work as a *marchande de modes*[8] in New Orleans, joined us for the voyage, and I was able to oblige him in many ways. My brother, whose wife had also left with Bernays on the voyage, also hired an old Swiss named Gunziker as a "help"—a great hunter, farmer, cattle-breeder and, alas, loudmouth.

The arrears came in extremely slowly, and it proved even harder to introduce Captain Demmler to the mysteries of the correspondence bureau, but an aide with an open mind was discovered for him in person of the former Legionnaire Löwenfels,[9] who had a better grasp of what had to be done. Thus passed week upon week in impatience, and we still were not free. On 25 January I wrote my last letter to my dears in New Orleans—my wife has preserved it. It should also find its place here, since it best represents the feelings which moved me in this decisive time. The letter reads:

Paris, 25 January 1849
My dear, good Marie and all of you, my loves and my dears!

This is the last letter you will receive from me. Unless extraordinary events intervene, we shall embark on the 30th on the American ship *Espindola*, under Captain Barstow, in Le Havre for New Orleans. How our passage shall be, whether better or worse than yours, whether you are all still alive, or whether we shall ever see one another again—who knows all of this? I am profoundly sad and depressed. I am very concerned about this cursed cholera in New Orleans, but what can be done? It seems as if our undertaking is fated to struggle against all possible obstacles and

---

and a leading Bonapartist. See *MEW,* vol. 8, 692. His younger brother Baron Pierre-Charles-François Dupin (1784-1873) was a deputy from 1827 to 1837, a Peer of France, a representative in 1848-49, and a senator of the Second Empire; see on both Dupins, Adolphe Robert, Edgar Bouloton, Gaston Cougny, eds., *Dictionnaire des parlementaires français,* vol. Cay-Fes (Paris, 1891), 490-3. I owe this reference to my colleague Steven Hause.

8. French, "(female) seller of fashions."

9. The German Legion was a military organization formed in 1848 in Paris with the intention of aiding revolution in Germany. Boernstein played a role in its organization, described in vol. I of his memoirs.

difficulties, so that what has been won with such effort will seem all the more valuable.

Our liquidation goes slowly and not so well as we had hoped at first. Several journals have disappeared, and others will not pay. In short, I can barely bring together 5,000 francs, but we do have many strong arms, courage and good will on all sides. Once we are all together and can work as one, things will go forward quickly.

On 18 January, at eight in the morning, I had a semi-dream while waking, a sort of vision. Marie called out my name quite close to my ear. I felt that you had reached New Orleans at this moment, or was it an evil foreboding? Dreadful uncertainty.[10]

Brother Carl is bringing along old Gunziker, he who shall lead our ministry for hunting and be successor to Leatherstocking, with whom he shares many characteristics.[11] But shall we get that far? If we have a misfortune, if we have lost the women, then good evening to world and settlement, for we will be off to California or to Oregon Territory, and we will become Leatherstocking ourselves—we've already decided that. Boulet is also quite concerned about his wife, who is sickly in any case. We speak of you the whole day and calculate our chances of ever seeing you again. Oh, two more months of uncertainty!!!

We are all well and healthy, and we are now entirely ready for travel. We cannot wait for the moment of departure, however long the voyage shall be. Here everything seems dark and sad; any day we expect street battles worse than the June Days. There is a dearth of trade, misery, dissatisfaction everywhere. We can thank heaven if we get out of Europe with one blue eye.

Yesterday I dined with Pulszky and Tausenau, who were fortunate enough to escape. Haug, Mahler and other Vienna refugees are here as well.[12] To be brutally frank, I don't care much for Pulszky; at least, he does not live up to Bernays' enthusiasm for him. He appears to have a vast opinion of himself, and a very low one of everyone else.

---

10. The *Sea Lion*, stalled by contrary winds, only arrived in New Orleans on 30 January [Boernstein's note].

11. Natty Bumppo was "Leatherstocking," the hero of James Fenimore Cooper's novels of eighteenth-century New York, most notably *The Last of the Mohicans* (1826).

12. Karl Tausenau (1808-1873), a moderate leftist and chief of the Central Committee of

Our sale of the furniture has of course suffered from the poor times, hardly 700 francs from everything. My purchases amount to 1,800 francs. I am bringing three guns, three men's saddles and one woman's saddle, a complete carpentry shop with all tools, saddler's tools, a complete portable pharmacy with surgical instruments, clothing and shoes for five years, knitting needles, work shoes, socks and a myriad of other useful, even indispensable things—no luxury, nothing in excess!

Our baggage amounts to twenty-four chests and trunks, and you had twenty-two on the ships *Sea Lion* and *Lorena*, forty-six trunks in all—a small town. I am just curious where we are to keep all of that. Still, everything will come in useful, for sure, and in the course of settling it will save us a great deal of money.

Oh, I still do not believe in our settling down. I continue to fear that we will not all be together again. I am almost fixated on that! What would all these things do for me then? I encourage myself in vain. Each of us tries in vain to build up the other's confidence through serious or joking encouragement, but each fears for his beloved and has given up hope. If only Madame Boulet could come directly on board with the letters! If only the French consul could be moved by a letter from Bernays to intervene for us with Customs, so that they do not rip our bags apart, that would be a great fortune. Much of that could not be replaced.

Take care for your health—and give some attention to the others. Ignore nothing! Just as long as there is no sickness when starting out—Oh, what a horde of cares and fears lay upon me. It almost drives me mad.

And now all of you, fare well. Hope that we shall see one another soon. If it does not turn out that way, and the *Espindola* does not reach port, fare well and be blessed.

In life as in death, your
H. Boernstein

May all of you fare well. Until we meet again!

Democratic Societies in Vienna in 1848, emigrating to London after the revolution. See *MEW*, 8: 715. Ernst Haug was an Austrian officer, then a participant in the 1848-49 revolt in Austria, emigrating to England. See ibid., 8: 697. Ferenc (Franz) Pulszky (1814-1897), a Polish-born figure in the Hungarian revolution of 1848-49, emigrated to England and America, writing for Horace Greeley's *New York Tribune*, but returned to Hungary after achievement of national autonomy in 1867 and served in the Hungarian National Assembly. See *MEW*, 27: 735.

At last came our hour of salvation, and we were able to leave Paris after resolving all our affairs on 1 February. On 4 February the American three-master *Espindola* raised anchor and we sailed with her, brave and committed, toward our new homeland, America.

Thus ended my years of apprenticeship, and now began my years of wandering. Whether these wanderings would ever bring me to mastery remained an open question. I went to America with European ideas and plans, as appears from the letter just shown, loaded down with a mass of unnecessary things and my head full of plans difficult or impossible to carry out. As a result it was natural that I continued my apprenticeship even in the midst of my years of wandering. I had to forget a great deal and learn even more. Yet I was in the best years of manhood, full of energy and good will, and I was eager to learn. I always hoped for a joyous success in my new home, as well as for sure progress, albeit with difficulties. I will try my best in subsequent dispatches to tell how these expectations and hopes turned out. After a trying, difficult beginning, I found things better than I had ever expected. With good luck and against all expectations, my boldest hopes were fulfilled in a relatively brief time, even if the route there—my very profession—was not what I had planned or foreseen.

The Sea Crossing
(1849)

W e had been ready for the journey for a week, and with all our furniture, beds and utensils long since sold, we bivouacked miserably in the room of a little *hôtel garni*, every day expecting to be summoned to board our ship. We took our modest meals in the new Viennese restaurant in the Rue Montorgueil, where refugees of all lands, particularly Germans and Austrians, horded together, and where the most interesting acquaintances could be made. In the last week of January a letter arrived there from the shipping company in Le Havre with which we had reserved our passage. The letter exhorted us to come at once to Le Havre, for the *Espindola*, which we had booked, would go to sea on the twenty-ninth at noon, at the latest on the thirtieth in the morning. Of course we did not have to be summoned twice and, being impatient to get underway, we left with the night train for Le Havre on the twenty-eighth, arriving on the twenty-ninth at dawn.

We went to our shipping company to announce our arrival, wanting to go on board at once in order to spare ourselves our expensive life in hotels. But as usually happens, the ship was not yet ready to leave, for freight was still being loaded. Until it was correctly stowed, no passengers could be allowed on board. Beyond that, the wind was still unfavorable for leaving the harbor and putting to sea, and the captain was awaiting the first fresh breezes from landward. As soon as everything was ready we would receive notice at once; in the meantime, a little emigrants' hotel was recommended to us as being good and cheap. Because the ship would not be leaving on the twenty-ninth or the thirtieth for that matter, we had no alternative but to take up quarters in the hotel, where our modest needs found fulfillment and the prices were not out of reason. We had nothing whatsoever to do, however; our many trunks and chests lay ready for transfer in the train station, so we could only take a walk for the entire day, getting to know our future companions, investigating the beauties of Le Havre in all directions, and learning the many ingenious ways for exploiting emigrants and relieving them of their superfluous money before they set off across the ocean.

All of the other passengers sailing with the *Espindola* had also been called too soon to Le Havre, some of them as much as two weeks early, and they consumed in idleness and boredom the money they had brought with them. Our ship had, in fact, long since been made ready for passage and awaited no more freight, the export of articles from Paris having fallen to nil since the February Revolution and due to the uncertainty of circumstances. Even the

winds were favorable, as sailors assured me. The reason we were waiting was
that the captain and the company still expected a troupe of emigrants who
would only be underway on 1 February, something we, of course, only
learned later when we were at sea. As a result we did not leave on 31 January
or on 1 February, and it was only on the evening of the second when the
delayed emigrants arrived, that we were informed that the freight had been
loaded and stowed, and that we could go aboard the next morning. This
took place with mutual pleasure.

In truth no freight at all had been loaded, for the ship carried ballast, and
the only freight consisted of emigrants and their baggage. For it is a policy of
such harbors to retain emigrants in their hands as long as possible, so that
they leave a portion of their money behind in the harbor town. Thus it was
that almost every building along the harbor and in the neighboring street
displayed a sign announcing in large German letters, "German Money
Accepted Here!" They should more properly have read, "Germans Robbed of
their Money Here." There was one hellhole after another in which buxom
barmaids from Alsace served up *bière de Strasbourg* and enticed the emigrants in
their beloved German language, for they could not understand a word of
French. In the largest establishments of this type, in the evenings an old piano
from the days of Louis XV would accompany a violin perpetually out of
tune, and they would commit a dreadful dance music to which the emigrants
would twirl around like mad in *"Hoppswalzer"* or *"Gestampfen"* by the sweat of
their brows. In the back room enterprising gambling impresarios would
establish a table for Macao or Half-Twelve, where only the dealer or his
friends—but nary an emigrant—won. There also was no lack of temptations
in sex or drink, and hawkers and saleswomen of all sorts continually milled
among the emigrants offering them books or brochures ranging from German
prayerbooks to French illustrated obscenities, pressing on them all possible or
impossible items. They were assured with the greatest persuasion that these
items would be useful—even vital necessities—not only on the passage, but
also over there in America, the best that anyone could obtain. In short, there
was a systematic, refined exploitation of the poor emigrants that cost many
inexperienced fellows the larger part of their travel money.

As early as the second I received permission to go on board to inspect the
ship and the conditions between decks, for we were traveling in the 'tween
deck to save money. At the same time I oversaw the loading of my twenty-four
trunks and chests, which appears to have impressed both the captain and the
shipping company.

The *Espindola* was a large, splendid American three-master, one of the
handsome, respectable ships of the American merchant marine that was then
still in a leading position, competing even with English ships and controlling
much of the emigrant trade from French, Dutch, Belgian, and even English

harbors. The *Espindola* had its name from a famous or infamous pirate of the Antilles who was still making the Gulf of Mexico insecure in the opening years of this century through his clever coups. The bow of the ship was decorated with his bust in romantic pirate costume, but neither the captain nor the officers of the ship could tell me more about his adventurous life, and the shipping company could only reply to my inquiries, *"Ah, c'était un fameux coquin, mais je n'en sais plus."*[1] This *fameux coquin Espindola* has remained an unsolved mystery to me, and I cannot even find him in Professor Schem's *Deutsch-amerikanisches Konversations-Lexicon,*[2] which incidentally consoles me for the fact that I have no entry there either. My name and actions are mentioned on several dozen pages, but always without the crucial remark, "See the article."

Once aboard, I learned from the first officer that Captain Barstow was still in Paris settling his affairs, that the ship had come from New Orleans with a cargo of cotton, and that it would be taking back three cabin passengers and 280 emigrants. The cabins for the captain and the officers were on the rear deck, and the officers had cleared their cabins for the cabin passengers in exchange for a payment, having established temporary quarters in the provisions hold for the few hours they were not on deck duty. I took a look at the 'tween deck and was horrified by the narrowness and closeness of the bunks, which were ranged side by side and on top of one another so that there was barely a narrow passage between them. In order to protect the captain and the cabin passengers from the noise and smell and other inconveniences of 'tween decks, the deck was blocked behind the last mast by a wall of planks, so that the entire rear of 'tween deck was empty, used only to store sails. I saw at once that this was the best, airiest part of the entire 'tween decks, for there was a window aft by the rudder, and it had its own staircase. When I asked the officer, he conceded at once that this was indeed the best place, and that he was ready to rent it to me as a sort of second-class cabin. My decision was quickly made, I rushed to land and to the shipping company, and we had an agreement after brief negotiation. With the payment of a small additional fee, the rear 'tween decks was cleared to be our cabin. A small area was set aside as a sail locker, and bunks and enclosures were erected in the remaining large, airy space for my brother, Boulet, my two sons, Gunziker and me. We all made ourselves at home. Now we had room and air, and we could have our baggage and provisions with us. We even had our own stairway, and we were isolated from the misery of life between decks. This was the luckiest of decisions, and we were often to have occasion to be thankful for it during the passage.

---

1. French, "Ah, he was an infamous rascal, but I don't know any more than that."
2. Alexander Schem, *Deutsch-amerikanisches Konversations-Lexicon,* 11 vols. (New York, 1869-1874).

The next morning, 3 February, the emigrants came on board. In those days it was not yet the practice on American ships (as it was on a German ship) for 'tween-decks passengers to be fed by the ship. Each family had to arrange its own provisions, cooking for themselves on crude stoves set up on the foredeck. Single passengers ordinarily joined with a family for meals, contributing their own provisions for the common meals and lending a helping hand as they could. These kitchens were extremely precarious affairs in which a wave could often put out the fire and pollute the pots, and a blow of wind often overturned the stove. As a result, the passengers often had to go three, four, or once even eight days with cold food, such as hardtack, ham and bacon. Despite this I still marvel that the ship did not go up in flames a thousand times, for the pots had to be held on the stove when the ship rolled, and the coals that spilled on the deck had to be dowsed and carefully picked up. It was, of course, impossible for all 280 passengers to cook at once, so that they had to wait turns, coming to the stove in shifts. There was no set order, and for this there was the old proverb, "First come, first served." On these terms, old Gunziker did us many a good service, for since he was always first at the stove with our pots as soon as the deck was swept and the cooking about to begin. My brother and I did the preparation of the food to be cooked, and this was not only the most pleasant pastime during the long sea journey, but also gave us tuition in the art of cooking, which served us well when we were starting out at the bottom in America.

As a consequence of the arrangement that prevailed in those days on American ships, passengers often had provisions that were slim, even running out during long journeys. To be sure, every passenger received a printed notice listing how much hardtack, flour, salt pork, ham, bacon and the like would be needed per head, and when the people came aboard the steersman checked their provisions and referred those with inadequate food to the stipulations of the contract. Still, there were always families who could not be caught by such measures in a group of 280 passengers. Either due to thrift or from sheer lack of money, they came aboard with bags of old clothes topped with a few hardtack or a side of bacon, as if loaded with provisions. On our own ship, which had a planned crossing of thirty-six days, it was to be expected that after forty days some of the poorer families found they had consumed all their provisions. For the last fourteen days genuine hunger reigned, and most fed themselves on hardtack, soaked in a little hot water with some salt. In the last thirty years things have much improved, and steerage passengers are provided up to the last day with simple but plentiful food. In those days, however, besides the inadequate provisioning of individuals, most spent the first weeks cooking and eating all day, due to idleness and boredom. The result was that the supplies ran low or even ran out early. We had supplied ourselves well, having not only the prescribed food in abundance, but also coffee, tea, condensed milk, sugar, wine, cognac and other pleasures in abundance. We even had a barrel of splendid apples, that had just been landed in Le Havre from America and that now made the trip back, providing us the finest services along the way.

The third of February passed with yet more fruitless hope and expectation. It was only early in the morning of the fourth that Captain Barstow arrived from Paris; the anchor was raised at once, and the *Espindola* left the harbor for the sea about noon. Once land had vanished from our sight, we took our separate quarters and lay down in our bunks, resting with good hopes of a swift journey as the ship sailed through the English Channel.

It was only the next morning, as we took up the routine of cooking, eating and sleeping already described, that we began to get to know the captain and our fellow passengers. Captain Barstow was a short, solidly built man, a genuine Yankee from New England—Providence if I'm not mistaken—friendly and cheerful in manner, a capable and experienced sailor. He was no friend to the talking and curious questioning of passengers, but when he said something, it was with a precision and exactness that awoke everyone's sense of security and trust. At the same time, as a true Yankee, for all his friendliness and good nature he was always calculating, and he knew how to keep his freight of emigrants in order, even to exploit it profitably when needed.

The three cabin passengers were Dr. Churchill, an English physician from London, Dr. Kratochwill, an Austrian physician from Prague, and a young Boyar from the princely house of the Cantacuzeno in Romania, then still called Moldavia and Wallachia. All three were educated, upstanding men who soon recognized in us kindred spirits, and it was thanks to our acquaintance with them that we were allowed to stay on the aft deck, rather than restricted to the foredeck with the other emigrants. In the course of the long journey our acquaintance became an intimate one, so that we parted in New Orleans with genuine regret.

All three were on their way to California, which had just then opened her golden gates. In those days there were no steamers from New Orleans, so they had to go by sailing ship from New Orleans in order to reach the Gulf of Darien, then across the isthmus and Panama, to continue their journey to California. We passed many pleasant hours with these men, who held off the awful boredom of a long sea voyage with stimulating conversation.

A generally hilarious situation led them often to invite themselves to dinner even after they had eaten, particularly on days when dinner in the cabin had been a catastrophe. It appears that Captain Barstow had brought a Negro from New Orleans to serve as a cook; the man, however, was merely a shoe-shiner who had once worked for a short time cleaning up a Negro cook-shop. On the voyage from New Orleans to Le Havre his cooking had sufficed for the captain and his two officers, who were satisfied with their American cuisine of pork and beans, ham and eggs, cornbread and the like. On the return voyage, however, he was supposed to produce decent meals for three cabin passengers used to European cuisine and he did not succeed, although Captain Barstow had supplied him with plenty of canned goods, vegetables and all manner of delicacies in Le Havre. Once he smothered a sweet pudding with a pepper sauce, all of his pastries failed utterly, and every attempt to refine his experiences from the Negro cook-shop produced disaster. The result was that the three cabin passengers often appeared before us in 'tween decks, laughing heartily but still hungry, and we invited them to our own frugal meals, which they loved. As their contribution they brought their own conserves, including splendid Chester cheeses, Verona salami and other worthy delicacies.

I never saw the two physicians again, but in St. Louis I heard from persons returning from California that they were doing well, and that they had achieved respectable eminence in San Francisco. I saw the young Boyar Cantacuzeno twenty-two years later, while I was managing the *Theater in der Josephstadt* in Vienna in 1871. One day I received a note from him asking me to visit him in the *Hotel zum goldenen Lamm*, as he could only pause for two days in Vienna while returning from the baths at Aachen, and he would dearly like to see me. Naturally I rushed to him, but instead of the young, blooming man I had known I encountered a prematurely aged patient plagued by gout, which often happens to those in the Orient. Now I had not grown any younger myself, but I was still more robust than he, who was a good twenty years younger. He was extremely happy to see me again, and we passed a couple pleasant hours in intense conversation, rousing faded memories of our voyage, both happy and sad. Then we parted, probably forever, for I never heard from him again.

The 280 steerage passengers, mostly Badeners and Palatines, were good-spirited, peaceful, friendly people free of excesses, and they had no brawls. We got along very well with them, we helped them when we could, and I was happy to encounter many of them later in America. I learned that most of them worked their way up to a secure position in life after hard struggles.

After a long cruise in the Channel due to contrary winds, during which we approached the English and then the French coast, and we could clearly see the landscape and towns, we at last entered the Atlantic Ocean. Now the land was completely lost to sight, and the first half of our voyage passed smoothly and pleasantly, helped by favorable winds. Our captain steered sharply south, and we were below the thirty-eighth parallel, south of the Azores, by the end of February. Yet the captain kept the bow pointed south, drawing close to the African coast until we had passed the Canaries. Here the tropical climate prevailing at the Tropic of Cancer made itself felt. We had left Europe in the hard winter of early February, and the farther down the Atlantic we went, the milder the air had become. Here below the thirty-sixth degree, however, the heat was unbearable. Everyone still wore the thick, warm winter clothes we had used on departure; summer clothes lay packed in trunks and chests stored away in the hold, and a change of clothing was out of the question. The cabin passengers and we were the only ones who had our baggage with us, so that we could at least put on some light clothing. In the steerage the solution was for the men to walk about in a shirt and underpants, the women in a blouse and half-slip. If they had not feared the captain, there probably would have been adventurous spirits who would have preferred the costume of Adam, with collar and maple leaf. At least we were able to run about on the sun-heated deck barefoot, saving considerable leather from shoes and boots.

One morning, as we all did our homage to *dolce far niente*[3] lying bathed in sweat about the deck in the most marvelous costumes and in the most astounding positions, we observed some agitation among the crew. The officers brought out their telescopes, and soon the news spread that a ship was approaching under full sail. Since we had left the English Channel, we had not had a single ship in sight, so this was an event that brought everyone upright, causing all of us to gape into the distance. From hour to hour the ship became ever sharper, and soon it came clearly into sight, steering toward us. It was a schooner with two masts, bearing the Spanish flag. Soon they were within hailing distance. We could clearly see the crew, all wild, wayward fellows with olive-yellow sunburned faces, red caps and brown ponchos. They signaled for a conference, and Captain Barstow ordered us to come about. The Spaniard drew near, and through the megaphone her captain asked to compare our readings of latitude and longitude and course with his. Our captain approved this, so they displayed a school blackboard with their own readings in large chalk numbers. At a glance, Captain Barstow and his officers broke into open laughter, for the estimates on the Spanish ship, which probably had no sextant, were so splendid that the good fellows appeared to believe they were on the Newfoundland Banks, though they were actually twenty degrees south of there, near the Canary Islands. On our ship, the large map was brought up on deck from the captain's office. The correct readings were signaled them with large figures, which led them to express great astonishment, pounding their heads with their fists. Then we were thanked through the megaphone, and they turned and took a course northeastwards, perhaps hoping to reach a Spanish port by chance.

This episode was a pleasant distraction, but the crew did not look on it positively, and an old sailor moaned something about "bad luck" and

---

3. Italian, "the sweet doing of nothing."

"damned scoundrels" into his gray beard. In fact from this very moment our luck appeared to have departed us. The poet says, "One does not dawdle beneath palms without punishment." In the same way, our cruise in the tropics had bad results. About an hour after we lost sight of the Spanish schooner, the fresh breeze that had sustained us until then ceased, and the sail hung flaccid and shrunken on the masts. The captain looked in every direction, contemplated the mirror-smooth sea and voiced the opinion that we were finished for a few weeks. His prophecy was literally true. The cessation of wind, unbroken by even a breath, continued. The ship lay as if nailed to the spot, rolling slowly from one side to another. It was a monotonous motion we landlubbers were not used to, continually shifting all the trunks back and forth. Everything movable had to be tied down, and we could not even sleep at night because we had to fear falling off the flat bed. This dreadfully useless situation, combined with the unbroken tossing of the ship back and forth lasted a full fourteen days. Everyone on board was completely demoralized. We lost all ability to act, all energy, all desire to read or write. Instead we abandoned ourselves to a twilight state, tormented by boredom and wakeful dreams. Only someone who has ever himself experienced a complete cessation of wind could adequately evaluate this situation and its evil results. Our captain knew all of this from years of experience, and with American determination he took the necessary measures.

On *the* Way *to* New Orleans
(1849)

On the evening of the fateful day our hitherto-pleasant voyage was suddenly interrupted by the cessation of wind and the ship began its fatal heaving to and fro, we went down to our berths without any inkling what dead calm in the tropics could mean. We all hoped that the next morning, when we awoke, we would again see our ship striking through the foaming waves with sails billowing in a favorable wind; we had not a care. When we arose the next morning, after a night rendered sleepless by the continual tossing of the ship, everything was as it had been the evening before. The sails still hung loose and empty from the spars, the crew not even regarding it as worth the energy to haul them in. The sea lay slick as a mirror as far as the eye could see, an unending glittering surface. There was not the slightest breath of wind. In contrast to the evening before, a glowing heat had descended even in the earliest morning hour that made staying below deck intolerable. All of us sat or lay about the deck, resigned to our fate and waiting for the wind we all desired. The ship continued its heaving to and fro, urging even those who had already had seasickness to new nausea.

The more apathetic and depressed we grew in the course of this and the following day of deadly boredom and inactivity, all the more active and energetic of a sudden became our captain. In the time when the wind had been favorable, he had seemed to take his ease, and now I discovered in him the first practical example of the proverbial shrewdness of the Yankee, which is partly learned, but partly inborn. Captain Barstow, who had already made this southern passage innumerable times and collected a treasure of maritime experience, was perhaps the only one on the ship who firmly foresaw the long duration of our becalming, and hence hit on the proper measures. He knew well that nothing could be so demoralizing for his crew as well as his passengers, as such a long, complete cessation of activity. He knew the saying, "The Devil makes work for idle hands." So he decided to keep both crew and emigrants at peace by some activity, and (as a true Yankee) he sought to exploit this activity to his advantage. If I report now what he did, and how he did it, I confess openly that at the time we had no idea of his intentions or of his total plan. Like all the others we listened to orders, and it was only gradually that we came to realize the actual reasons for the captain's actions after talking with the cabin passengers when the whole affair was virtually over.

So far as Captain Barstow was concerned, his major consideration was to keep the crew and the emigrants involved in any sort of activity. From the

very first day he was on deck at sunrise, against his usual practice, bringing
life and movement to the entire ship. Some of the sails were taken down
from the yardarms and stowed in the sail locker, to be patched and repaired
by a detail of sailors. At the same time the captain ordered two boats made
ready and manned by another detail of the crew. These boats were linked to
our ship with cables and were rowed to turn the bow of the ship in a
direction the captain ordered. There was a chance, the captain avowed, that
the calm reigned only in a small area, and that we could row our way into a
region where the wind was blowing. To be sure, the advance proved very slow,
but it seemed better to us than nothing at all. Soon, however, this effort
proved impractical, for the heat was so intense under the direct rays of the
sun that the rowing sailors had to be replaced after two hours at their oars.
They were bathed in sweat, and when one had sunstroke, the captain gave up
the effort; he himself knew it to be pointless and he had ordered the rowing
only to occupy his crew. The boats were called back in. A large sail was
spread over the aft deck as a tent, and another one over the foredeck, so
people could at least enjoy the blessing of shade. In order not to allow his
men to be idle, however, during the following days the captain had the ship
cleaned and washed inside and out and freshly painted. Paints were hauled
out, ground and prepared. Scaffolding was secured outside the ship, where
the sailors sat and painted. The tackle was carefully checked, and anything
lacking was replaced. In short, in the course of the fourteen days we were
becalmed, the captain completely occupied his men in a useful way.

The real problem was with the emigrants, and here the Yankee's
smartness came to the surface in the most original way. On the very first
day, while the unfortunate sailors were still rowing away, the captain invited
the three cabin passengers, my brother, Boulet and me along with three of
the most respectable heads of family among the emigrants to a discussion
in his cabin. The captain addressed this council of war with the greatest
seriousness for a long time in English, which we interpreted in German to
the others as best we could. The gist of the address was that the captain
thought the sudden appearance of the Spanish ship the previous day
seemed highly suspicious, and that he harbored concerns. He believed that
the request for bearings was only a pretext to approach the ship to
determine the strength of the crew and see whether an attack by night
would net good booty. He asserted with all seriousness that there were still
desperate adventurers in these southern climes on small islands who
pursued all sorts of illegal trades, even piracy, when the opportunity
presented itself. He told how such clever fellows discovered the vulnerable
side of a ship in such a way, then approached it in rowboats by night,
clambered aboard, killed or jettisoned crew and passengers. They would
plunder the cargo and leave the ship to its fate after setting it afire. In this

cursed calm, when it was impossible to use sail to avoid such an attack, there had to be special vigilance and preparations for defense. It was likely that scout boats would spy on the ship during one of the coming nights to see whether those on board were on guard, and it was important to display a guard, even to prepare to repel such an attack. He figured on the enthusiastic support of the passengers, affirmed that his officers and men would also do their duty. He moved that the emigrants be organized as a military company, saying he would arm them and permit them to participate in the defense of the ship. He then asked us, should we approve of this, to take over the organization of the male passengers, perhaps using former soldiers as squad commanders to train the people in the use of weapons and military order.

After some discussion, the captain's recommendation was unanimously accepted and immediately put into effect. There were about 120 male emigrants capable of bearing arms, including about twenty former soldiers who became noncommissioned officers in the company. Once we all had determined the basis and purpose for this organization and received general consent, the training began, filling most of the hours of the day. At first it was done without weapons, but later the captain had guns brought out of the hold, which the steersman distributed to the company. They were old flintlocks, shooting irons even older and more dangerous than those Floçon had given the German Legion. But in the general excitement no one was concerned, and so we trained from morning until night.

With the continual pitching of the ship, it was not unusual for the first rank to be thrown back into the rear rank, and as they disentangled themselves, laughing, they would be pitched on their noses, creating new jollity. Captain Barstow, who was always present at these practices, encouraged them. He declared his satisfaction and revealed his plan, which consisted of showing the pirates that the ship had a large, armed crew ready for a vigorous defense, and that the greatest vigilance reigned on board. Once the pirates received such an impression, they would of course renounce any intention of attacking the ship.

On board there was a small cannon, a real miniature gun. An artillerist would have called it a half-pounder. It was intended for firing a salute on entering a harbor, or for sounding a distress signal in an emergency. It was agreed that the company, together with the crew, would keep watch through the day; at night they would go to rest as usual until the cannon fired an alarm shot, when everyone would rush on deck and take his assigned post. This was tested, and a busy military life predominated on board, all the more so, because now and then the captain sighted a sail on the horizon that he described as suspicious. The first week of calm passed in earnest drill, changing of guards, and occasional alarms. Eventually, however, the

first enthusiasm cooled and everything remained quiet; no suspicious boat
appeared nearby, and an attack grew steadily less likely. The smarter ones
began to doubt that the matter was serious. They began to suspect that the
captain had only wanted to keep the people busy, but because they grasped
the usefulness of this, they avoided expressing their doubts out loud.
Gradually, however, greater casualness began to enter the drills, until they
were entirely suspended in the last few days of calm. The people did have
guns, but Captain Barstow never gave them any ammunition, saying it could
easily lead to an accident in the crowded 'tween decks; the ammunition was
in his cabin and the steersman would distribute it as soon as an alarm was
sounded. When there dawned a more-or-less conscious awareness of the
mystification of the previous days, the excitement subsided, and people
passed their time reviewing the plans and hopes they were to pursue on
arriving in America.

This was one of our own favorite occupations in these idle, boring
hours. As often as we sat together—my brother, Boulet and Gunziker and I,
we built castles in the air. We had learned our Bromme and our Duden[1] by
heart: seized by their brilliant, eloquent portrayals, we were totally
enthusiastic about the southern part of Missouri, particularly the area
around Cape Girardeau. There the climate was so mild that the Mississippi
never froze. The level, fertile country was enclosed by the primeval forest,
where we were sure to be impressed by the "sycamores, catalpas, platans,
ailantus, tulip trees, cedars and cypress, sumac and paw-paw, where wild
grape climbed, unfolding the full richness of their vines beneath the shadows
of flowering bushes." This sort of thing was printed in emigrant books, and
we believed in it as a gospel of the future. Bernays and our families were
supposed to be awaiting us there in Cape Girardeau; so it was settled, and as
soon as we were all back together, we each wanted to buy farms with
120–30 acres and work them communally, leading a quiet, peaceful country
existence. We were heartily tired of Europe and its politically heightened

---

1. Traugott Bromme (1802-1866) was the author of a series of maps, descriptions, and
    guides for emigrants from the early 1830s to the 1850s, published both in Germany and
    in Baltimore. His *Wohlfeile Hand-Bibliothek für Auswanderer nach den Vereinigten Staaten von
    Nordamerika und Freunde der Kunde fremder Welttheile* (Leipzig; Baltimore, 1838) was
    excerpted as *Illinois und Missouri, Taschenbuch für Einwanderer und Freunde der Länder- und
    Völkerkunde* (Baltimore, 1838); see Joseph Sabin, *Bibliotheca Americana*, vol. 2 (New York,
    1869), 516-18. Gottfried Duden (1785-1855) was the author of *Bericht über eine Reise
    nach den westlichen Staaten Nordamerikas* (Elberfeld, 1829), translated as *Report on a Journey
    to the Western States of North America and a Stay of Several Years Along the Missouri (During
    the Years 1824, '25, '26, 1827)*, James W. Goodrich, ed. (Columbia: University of
    Missouri Press, 1980); this very glowing, popular description of Missouri drew many
    immigrants to that region, despite scathing critiques of Duden's portrayal by such
    German-Americans as Gustav Körner.

goings-on. This was why we had taken care to equip ourselves, hauling over a good forty chests—including carpentry and saddler's tools, although we knew nothing about these trades, along with a mass of other things that seemed extraordinarily important to us—though in reality they were useless.

We drew plans for the house we wanted to build, drafted the garden on paper, figured the size of barns and stalls. In short we acted like all other emigrants, who based their plans on European attitudes in complete ignorance of American conditions. In those days we wallowed in these plans, dreams and hopes, and a year later we were completely disillusioned, laughing at our clever castles in the clouds. By then, we understood that we had brought along a mass of useless things, and we had learned that there is only one thing worth packing—*a great deal of money!* As much money as possible and as few things as possible, excepting perhaps clothing and linen, for everything needed in the way of tools, home furnishing, etc., can be bought in America better, more cheaply and more efficiently than in Europe. But then we were happily lodged in our illusions, and they at least had the positive quality of helping us pass the idle time of our voyage.

Most emigrants did just as we did. Near Highland I came to know a man who was wealthy but tired of Europe, who came to America to settle quietly in the countryside. He brought with him not only the plans for the villa he intended to build, but also all door locks, window frames and several chests of plate glass for his windows, besides other luxurious objects for the edifice. When I came to know him on his farm in the prairie, he had already built an American frame house and lived as did others, but he claimed to be intending to reside there only provisionally; he still intended to build his villa with the plate-glass windows. A year later he had been thoroughly cured of this madness and had sent the door locks, window frames and plate glass together with all the other European junk to St. Louis to be auctioned off, where they were dumped for a song.

At long last, as with everything else, the doldrums had an end. One evening the captain had all the sails set, and in the distance could be seen a somewhat ruffled patch of sea. A burst of wind was coming, the captain believed, which must be used as best one could. In fact it did arrive. The agitation and frothing of the waves approached ever nearer, and suddenly there was a solid blast of wind whose first burst knocked down the top spar of the middle mast and threw it to the deck, fortunately injuring no one. It was as if the touch of a magic wand had changed the entire situation on board. Everything was animated by new courage and high hopes. The sails unfolded, and the ship flew once more across the waves as swift as an arrow. The comedy was at an end, the guns were collected and taken below decks, and the pirates were committed to deserved oblivion. None of us suspected, however, that Captain Barstow had even more plans for playing soldier.

It was high time indeed that we got underway, because the provisions of most passengers had been considerably reduced, and there was a complete lack of other items. With every day the shortage of provisions showed itself more and more until it rose to disturbing heights, and in the last days there was literally nothing left to eat on the entire ship. One day, as we were sailing ahead with a favorable wind, Captain Barstow called his trusted representatives together and presented his newest plans in a long address. He well knew that most passengers were at the end of their provisions and that, if he held his present course passing Cuba to reach New Orleans, he would lose so much time that there was fear that some of the passengers might starve. He wanted to review his own stocks of provisions, and what could be spared would be sold to needy passengers at cost. But he had a further plan to shorten the voyage if the passengers would be willing to help. He said he knew of a passage through the Bermuda Islands, making the voyage four or five days shorter than going around the Bermudas and along the north coast of Cuba into the Gulf of Mexico. No fully loaded ship could pass this straight, however, only one with a shallow draft. He now had a great deal of ballast in the holds, consisting of stones and rubble, and if the passengers would help him dump this ballast, he would be in the situation to sail through the straight and significantly shorten the voyage. We now took the captain's proposal to the assembled passengers, and general agreement was reached, partly due to the shortage of provisions, partly due to the longing to have solid earth underfoot again. Everyone declared himself ready to throw the ballast overboard. The captain designated a couple of sacks of cornmeal and a barrel of salt pork to be excess provisions, and it was in fact sold by the pound to the emigrants as they needed it at the same low price at which it had been obtained in Le Havre. Despite this, there remained families who were low on provisions who were unable to afford even the cheapest supplies without leaving them bereft of money when they landed; these had to make it through the last few days on hardtack softened in hot water, as described.

Captain Barstow's plan worked. In Le Havre, he had made up for the lack of freight by loading a great deal of stone ballast, and he would have had to unload that in New Orleans before taking on the cargo of cotton that awaited him, thus losing several days before he could receive the new load. Further, the ship's crew would neither load nor unload ballast, so there were special harbor workers who did that who were well paid for their work and who took their time about the job. Captain Barstow hence made two good tosses with one die. It cost him absolutely nothing to have his passengers unload his ballast, and he could take on his new cargo in New Orleans on the first day in port, permitting him to take to the sea all that much sooner. This was a double profit for the clever Yankee. Even the military organization was of use. Everything went forward in an orderly fashion and on command. The squads relieved one another in order, the squad leaders oversaw the work, and everyone was given his post and duties according to military discipline.

The large hatches on the deck and between decks were opened, and a ramp was constructed to the hold. Baskets were distributed to the people. One squad was placed in the hold and another between decks, while the women helped out on the deck itself. Those below filled the baskets with stones and rubble, others passed them to the 'tween decks, and then they were passed to the upper deck, where the women dumped them into the sea. When the people were tired, another squad would come to work. And so it went on for *four whole days*, in a light mood with singing and jesting, from sunrise to sunset, until the greater part of the ballast lay in the sea. During this period we had already entered the Gulf of Mexico and approached the mouth of the Mississippi. To this day, I still do not know whether the captain really knew a quicker way and took it or not. He probably sailed his usual course, and it was done only in order to be rid of the ballast for free and without loss of time.

Finally, when we came out on deck one morning, we were shown a black point on the distance, interpreted to be our pilot and the steam tug that would take us up the river to New Orleans. There was a joyous "Hooray!" to this announcement; our redemption was near, and it really was high time it came. We were already on the sixty-second day of our voyage, and we had been so sorely tried by shortages of every sort that I have no doubt that the extension of the voyage by even a few more days would have led to illnesses due to shortages and hunger. The black point gradually became a distinct cloud of smoke, and finally we could clearly see the steamer. We exchanged signals, and the captain confirmed that we had reached our goal and would be towed to New Orleans without delay. There was general jubilation and unlimited joy. We washed and combed, and the Sunday clothes were unpacked. In keeping with tradition, the straw sacks and bolsters that had been bought in Le Havre for the voyage were thrown into the sea, where they were borne away by the current. In any case, they had already been worn thin and flat and were no longer usable, but they were tossed away a good twenty-four hours too soon, for we had to pass another night on board as the tug hauled us up the river, and during this night the improvident had to sleep on bare boards. I have no idea who told them to throw away their straw sacks, but I suspect the captain again had his hand in the game, for once in New Orleans he would have had to dispose of over two hundred bags of straw. So he saved the money for disposing of them and, what was more, he had the ship "clean and clear" all the earlier.

At last the steamer tug was alongside us. The pilot brought American newspapers aboard, in which I searched in vain for news of the ship *Sea Lion* and my people but where I found the bad news that cholera was raging in New Orleans and that there had been several cases of yellow fever.[2] We were filled with the darkest premonitions about the fate of our people, but that was of no use. We had taken the great step, and it could not be reversed. We had to go forward, whatever happened. Our ship was lashed to one side of the steam tug, and at the Southwest Passage a French ship was joined to its other side. The three ships passed in this manner up the Mississippi. The mood of all was raised by the banks of the mighty stream, blooming in the full majesty of summer; the charming landscape; the lush tropical vegetation; the refreshing land breeze and the consciousness that we were at our goal.

All of the emigrants had put on their holiday best. The women were decorated in their finest, the children were washed and combed, and the men had put on their new Sunday hats. They also bore their large painted porcelain pipes with silk tassels, puffing large clouds of the tobacco they had done without for so long, but which the dealer on the steamer tug had sold them. The joy of being finally at our goal shone on every face. Everyone was in the best of moods, and lovely German folk songs were sung, sounding harmoniously through the silent night. There was little sleeping, for no one could wait to get there at last. Now the first houses appeared, at first only a few, then in small clumps, then larger ones. The banks became steadily more alive with people and vehicles. Before us lay a forest of masts of ships at anchor, with the flags of all nations. Regular streets with splendid buildings ran up from the shore. One more great turn, then a shake, and the tug had freed us. We lay at the levee of New Orleans, separated from the shore only by a German ship across which we rushed without delay to the land, deeply desiring to have solid earth under our feet again. *We were in America.*

---

2. Cholera is an infectious intestinal disease transmitted by contaminated food and water. The victim suffers severe diarrhea and vomiting, leading to dehydration and eventual death after about five days. Cholera, which was endemic to India, became a major disease of heavily populated areas in Europe and America in the 1830s. Yellow fever is a virus disease carried by the bite of mosquitoes. Within three to six days of being bitten, the human victim has fever, headache, muscle pain, and dizziness. The skin is likely to turn yellow, and the victim bleeds from the gums and in the stomach. After an apparent recovery, some victims will experience a sudden return of fever, followed by coma and death. The specific vector of the disease was established by Walter Reed, and the viral nature of the disease was established in 1927. Until the development of a vaccine in 1937, the only means of control was to suppress mosquito breeding. Treatment includes complete bed rest and replacement of lost fluids. See *The Merck Manual of Diagnosis and Therapy*, 15th ed. (Rahway, N.J.: Merck Sharpe & Dohme Research Laboratories, 1987), 189-93.

First Impressions of New Orleans
(1849)

We had departed Le Havre on 4 February, and on 8 April we once again set foot on solid ground in America. Our journey had thus lasted a full sixty-two days. Only one who has experienced it himself knows how enervating and demoralizing a long sea voyage can be to people, how in the end there is only one ruling thought and desire, which is to reach the distant shore. Such a person can grasp the joyous feelings of release and reawakened hope and energy we felt on setting foot on American soil. Our ship had been announced to New Orleans by telegraph from the mouth of the Mississippi, so that Madame Boulet awaited us on the riverbank to give her husband a heartfelt greeting. Of course I wanted to go at once to the French consulate to get news about my own people, but Madame Boulet informed me that this would be pointless. It was already evening, and the consular bureau closed at four. She knew for a fact that the consul kept all the personal correspondence in his own valise, and he had long since gone to his family's villa, which was two hours out of town. I would be better advised go there the next morning.

It was more pressing for us to find our boarding house and assure ourselves lodging, and she offered to lead us to the house where Bernays and our families had lived and been quite satisfied. On inquiring with the captain on board, we learned that we had nothing better to do, for it was too late in the day to get clearance from customs. The baggage had meanwhile been brought from the hold to the deck, where it would remain under the watch of two customs agents who had come aboard when the ship entered the river. We were able to take hand baggage and trifles with us after inspection by the agents, but we were to report promptly the next morning, for the inspectors would come early. The emigrants scattered in every direction to find lodging, and we went to the house recommended to us.

The goal of our journey proved to be a mid-sized brick house with a sign in front reading "Boarding and Lodging. Mint Exchange by Henri Clausen." It lay at the corner of Old Levee and Barrack streets, and we soon agreed on terms with the innkeeper, a friendly and pleasing German, at half a dollar per head per day for bed and three meals. The hour for "supper" had arrived, and we had to seat ourselves at once at the great table, where about twenty boarders were being served. We had been dreadfully starved during the recent period of short rations on the ship, so it is no wonder that we threw ourselves at the plentiful food presented. Still, it was not without some disturbing surprises, especially for us decadent Parisians. First of all, all the food was served at once, and everything was eaten from the same plate, whether sweet, salty, or sour. Pork and bacon were the main ingredient: roasted pork and fried bacon, bratwurst and other sausages, in short, pork and bacon in all possible permutations. In between there would be fried eggs and buckwheat pancakes, hominy and cornbread and the inevitable molasses. A meal was served which would have sufficed for fifty hungry people rather than the twenty present. A couple of starved emigrants from our ship who had joined us devoured huge quantities of the stuff, but they could not master it. They ate the fresh-baked, hot cornbread as if it were cake, taking huge quantities of molasses along with it. When they learned that one gets this "cake" at every meal in America, they expressed their unbridled joy, believing they had reached the Promised Land.

An old Negro woman continually passed among the guests with two pots and asked repeatedly, "Please, sir! Tea or coffee?" I was lucky enough to say, "Coffee," and so a cup was filled with a brown liquid, a server with golden-yellow sugar was offered, and a pitcher with milk stood on the table. When I took the first sip, a line from the *Fliegende Blätter* occurred to me, where a guest in the same situation told the waitress, "If that's coffee, then I want tea, but if that's supposed to be tea, I would prefer coffee." This was precisely how I felt. The stuff smelled so nasty and tasted so dubious that I was not certain whether it was bad tea or bad coffee. It was in fact coffee, that miserable Brazilian sort which is known as Rio, then selling sixteen to twenty pounds for a dollar while twenty or twenty-two pounds of brown sugar cost only a dollar in those days. This Rio coffee we would not even recognize as real coffee alongside the splendid coffee of Paris, where only the finest varieties were used—Mocha, Java, and Ceylon. Rather this Rio is a variety that makes its presence known more than three blocks away through its penetrating, burning odor when roasted or brewed. I tried the tea, but it had the same taste, perhaps even more dreadful than the coffee, reminiscent of sarsaparilla. These were the cheapest possible varieties of the two refreshments, and I understood that our host, who only took half a dollar for a room and three meals, could not serve anything better. Our companions maintained old German custom and ordered a glass of beer, but beer was still a rarity then in New Orleans, and they declared ginger-pop to be dreadful medicine once they had tried a bottle. I asked for water, and it was brought with ice, but my host quickly came to warn me of drinking Mississippi water, which usually caused diarrhea in newcomers and which was doubly dangerous in times of cholera. That was a lovely prospect. I could not gag down the coffee or tea, the water had been declared dangerous, and so I paid extra for a bottle of claret. But this supposed Bordeaux was an artificially produced liquid from the New Orleans wine factory, consisting of water, brandy, sugar syrup and dyewood. So this route also proved impractical for a palate trained in Paris.[1] Only with time would I learn to drink brandy and water, always adding a little alcohol to the water to moderate its purgative qualities.

After we had talked a great deal and it had grown late, we were led to our sleeping quarters. It was a large room like a salon in which there were ten beds with mattresses stuffed with cornstraw. Five of them had already been occupied by other passengers; the others were given to us. There were two common washbasins for the ten inmates, and two towels on rollers on the wall had to serve for all ten residents. There followed a night that was entirely sleepless for us novices. Because we had been the first to go upstairs, we had burned a light for a while by an open window in the heat, attracting clouds of mosquitoes (*Gelsen* in Austria) into the room. We did not yet know how to use "mosquito bars" (gauze curtains that completely enclosed the bed), and numerous mosquitoes slipped under the curtains to commence their hellish whining, occasionally leading to a blood-sucking bite. We had to spend the entire night defending ourselves. Then our other companions in sleep arrived home, each one later than the other, disturbing our own attempts to get to sleep. Being more experienced, they did not use any light, but as a result, as they undressed in the night they made all the more bumping and noise until they were safely under their mosquito bars. That was a dreadful night I shall remember as long as I live, and we longed to be back on our good ship, where we had always slept so sweetly and peacefully under the spell of its rocking motion.

Suddenly, in the middle of the night, another dreadful racket arose in the house. People ran back and forth in the hallways, doors opened and slammed shut and loud conversations came to our ears. Due to the way American houses are built, the running back and forth set the entire house to shaking. A traveler in one of the other rooms had come down with cholera. Involved friends rushed to help him, a physician was called and came, all possible efforts were made to help, but the poor man did not live to see the dawn. We only learned this the next morning at breakfast, along with the distressing news that four or five had died in boarding houses in the neighborhood. Deeply shaken by this news and already in a bad mood due to the sleepless night, we decided then and there not to pass another night in the boarding house at any price. We further determined to take our meals there, but to return our beds to our host and spend the nights aboard our

---

1. Such adulterated or artificial products were common in nineteenth-century America, and the process was humorously described in Jakob Mueller, *Memoirs of a Forty-Eighter: Sketches from the German-American Period of Storm and Stress in the 1850s*, Steven Rowan, tr. (Cleveland: The Western Reserve Historical Society, 1997), 55, recounting the experience of Cleveland Germans making bogus liquor.

ship, in our bunks. Herr Clausen's boarding house was no worse, but also no better, than all the other boarding houses for immigrants. Our host was pleasant and helpful beyond all measure, all his people were competent and friendly, and for the price one could expect no more than what was offered in abundance. But we had been dreadfully softened by the refinement of Paris life, and to us everything was dreadful and horrifying. We wanted to get out of New Orleans as quickly as possible, and so long as we stayed there we would sleep on board.

After breakfast, which was as rich and substantial as supper, we rushed to the *Espindola*, where we learned that the French consul would not come to his office before ten. And what an unpleasant surprise met us on our ship. A crowd of carpenters was hard at work making the ship "clean and clear." The dividing wall of the 'tween decks, the emigrants' sleeping quarters, even our own bunks had already been demolished. The 'tween decks was clear the entire length of the boat, and heaps of planks were being sold to the highest bidder on the riverbank. The captain made quite a business of this, for he had purchased the planks for a song in Le Havre, and here he was making three to four cents a square foot. Innumerable carts had already drawn up on the riverbank, bringing enormous bales of cotton that were immediately loaded onto the ship.

The customs agents had already arrived to do their inspection, and the baggage had to be removed in the course of the day or would be dumped on the riverbank, where it could not be guaranteed against damage or theft. The review of our goods was rather casual. The customs agents were of French origin, Creoles as they are called, and they spoke good French. They all greeted us as *compatriotes* and were so circumspect that we did not even have to open most of the closed chests. What could be fastened was opened and quickly reviewed, and there was no problem.

We made our petition to the captain to stay one or two more nights on board, but he felt it was almost impossible. The cabins had already been occupied by his officers, who had to be continually present to load and stow cargo, and the sleeping quarters on the 'tween decks were already gone and before evening would be stuffed full of cotton. After long discussion he permitted us to sleep through the warm night on the deck in our own bedding, in view of the fact that the boarding house must have seemed dreadful to us. We accepted this suggestion with enthusiasm, and he pointed out a spot on the foredeck where we could pitch our camp.

While we were engaged in conversation, I witnessed my first "accident," as Americans call such not-unusual events. A steam tug that lay on the riverbank barely a hundred feet from us was making ready to depart to fetch ships from the river's mouth. The anchor was being raised with the monotonous ahoy songs of a number of the Negroes who made up the crew, and at the instant the ship was about to launch, steam was released into the cylinders. At this crucial moment there followed a destructive boiler explosion. There was a hollow thud, which shook the air all around. A thick, white cloud of steam was driven into the heights with dreadful force, a cloud which could be seen to contain various pieces of machinery as well as several human bodies. All was then showered on the decks or into the water. There was tumult and screaming on the riverbank, the bells of the nearest pump houses sounded alarm and innumerable groups of people gathered at the riverbank from all quarters, forming a single vast, gesticulating and screaming mass of humanity. A flotilla of barges rowed to the scene of the disaster to fish out the unfortunate and to help dowse the burning ship. Then it gradually grew quieter and stiller. The cloud of steam subsided, and the dreadfully ruined wreck lay smoking away. As soon as the fire was out the wounded and scalded were taken to the nearest hospital on stretchers. The dead were laid out on the ground on the riverbank so the coroner and his jurors could investigate them. Eventually the curious crowds dispersed, it grew peaceful, and another steam tug was quickly warmed up to take the place of the one that had exploded. I must confess that the episode shook me, making me anxious throughout my entire journey on the Mississippi. But as I have said, we could not go back; we had to go forward, to be with our loved ones.

By then it had long since passed ten, and we rushed to the French consul to get our long-desired letters and discover where we were to seek Bernays and our family. The French consul, Monsieur Roger, received us in the friendliest terms and delivered to me an entire packet of letters. One glance at the handwriting convinced me that our loved ones were still alive, at least at the time the letters were written. The first letter had been written by Bernays on the river voyage to New Orleans, while others were from New Orleans, and the very last were dated from St. Louis. A stone was removed from my heart, so that I could breathe freely again and face the many questions of the consul, who was naturally interested in hearing intimate, authentic information about the latest developments in France from an educated eye witness. He certainly felt as disappointed and uncomfortable about the election of Louis Napoléon as president as I did, and he believed he himself would soon be recalled from his post, which he had come to love. I consoled him with what was then the truth, which was that the new president was almost powerless and on weak footing. The newly elected legislative assembly was overwhelmingly conservative and monarchist, and the position of the Odillot-Barrot ministry was the weakest, lamed by the conservative majority in parliament. Because nothing decisive could be done, a massive recall of the diplomats installed by Louis-Philippe could not be considered for a time anyway. In fact the only new naming in the diplomatic corps had been for the

French ambassador in London, because the previous ambassador, Gustave de Beaumont, had resigned of his own free will. Further, there was a considerable lack of cash in the state treasury, and expenditures for unnecessary purposes such as *frais de voyage et d'installation*[2] for new appointees had to be avoided for the moment.

He gave me good advice for our continued residence, but he also advised us not to stay any longer than absolutely necessary in New Orleans, where cholera continued to increase and where the cases of yellow fever had also grown in the last few days. I would do best, he felt, to get places on a steamboat at once, for I could have my baggage, chests, and trunks taken directly from the ship to the steamer, and we could sleep, eat, and live on the steamer. We should make sure, however, that it was what was called a "crack boat," which charged a higher fare, but which made the voyage to St. Louis in five or six days. The older, cheaper and poorer boats often were underway for ten to fourteen days, bringing all sorts of additional risks, and while the price in 'tween decks with one's own provisions cost a passenger only two or three dollars, but he would not advise it. On the better boats a cabin cost twelve dollars, but with five persons, including two grown persons and two boys, an agreement could be made for no more than forty dollars, which later proved to be correct. He also applauded our decision to go to Missouri, which he praised as one of the most fortunate states, with the brightest future. This splendid, amiable man parted from us with the best wishes and the express desire to see us before departure, if time allowed, to have with him a real French dinner.

One may well imagine that I was no longer able to restrain my longing. Once I reached the street I set about tearing open all the letters and rushing through them. In my excitement I was unable to read them in an orderly and attentive manner, but I only comprehended that they all lived, and were well. For the moment that was all I wanted. Bernays and my loved ones did not come across in the 'tween decks as we had, but rather traveled in the cabins of the *Sea Lion*. Still, their voyage had been very unpleasant, as was to be expected in the wintry times of December and January. In the first letter I opened, which he wrote as the ship was being towed up the river to New Orleans, Bernays said:

> Our captain, a model man in every way, and my own openness to others, which sometimes descends to coarseness, combined to help make life on this voyage halfway tolerable. Without these two elements, my residence in the St.-Pélagie Prison would have been a paradise in comparison. Yet I write this only as history, for at this moment we are being towed up the marvelous

2. French, "costs of travel and establishment."

Marie Boernstein, wife of Henry Boernstein, surrounded by a wreath of her featured roles on the stage, lithographic frontispiece and title page of F. Kreuter and Carl Boernstein, Buhnen-Almanach des St. Louis Opern Hauses, 1861. Lithograph by Robyn & Co., St. Louis. Courtesy of the Missouri Historical Society.

Mississippi, and we have forgotten all sorrows and troubles. Soon we will only remember the pleasant or comic episodes, and the miserable and mean things will be forgotten. I must tell you in all honor that none of us lost courage even for a moment. We were not fearful even in the most extreme stage of seasickness, in the most dreadful storms, and I only saw anxiety on our Leon's face. There was not a moment of dissent among us, and if we bear troubles so well together in the future, and enjoy everything good and beautiful as we did on this trip, then we are entering on a pleasant time.

He then let me know that he was following the consul's advice and that of other experienced men, by not settling in Cape Girardeau and awaiting us there. Rather going directly to St. Louis, where we were to follow without delay.

As mentioned, I only reviewed the letters rapidly, enough to convince myself that all of my loved ones were not only alive but well and happy. I quickly read through the letters of my wife, who appeared to be in good courage, but put off studying them and weighing the letters' contents until the first available quiet hour. I did write at once to St. Louis, announcing to our loved ones our fortunate arrival and declaring we would follow without delay and soon be reunited with them.

Several people had recommended the "crack boat" *Sarah*, which was then being loaded for departure. It lay on the levee, and I went on board immediately. Captain Young had his own family—wife, daughter and son—with him on board, which made me more confident about trusting him. With one's own family on board, one is reluctant to engage in races and is doubly careful about fire and explosions. I had a pleasant reception, and our agreement was quickly settled just as the consul had predicted. Our baggage, consisting of twenty-four trunks and chests, could be brought aboard the *Sarah* at once; however, we ourselves could only come aboard the next day, for the cabins were being systematically cleaned and put in order. Hence we had to pass one more night aboard the *Espindola*, sleeping on the deck, which we thought better than repeating the hellish torments of our sleepless night in the boarding house. I inspected the entire boat, and I must confess that it was extremely impressive even when compared to European steamers on the Danube, the Rhine and the Seine. The *Sarah* was one of the loveliest and largest of the Mississippi boats, uniting comfort and elegance with solidity and competent leadership. Everything I saw made the most positive impression, and I could not wait to get on board.

Before that could happen we had to return to our boarding house and take dinner there. This midday meal was a precise copy of both supper and breakfast, with just as much "plenty" and as rich a supply of pork in all its forms. The unavoidable "Tea or coffee?" were there, along with the corn bread and molasses in which our ship companions had wallowed. After the meal I oversaw the transfer of our voluminous baggage on board the *Espindola* to the *Sarah*, and the day dwindled to its end without our having seen anything of New Orleans. We only had time to take supper in the boarding house, and then we returned to the *Espindola* to establish our camp on deck. Now I was able to study my letters in peace and leisure. We made ourselves comfortable on deck and smoked our cigars. The warm, beautiful evening, which never quite went dark, placed us in a happy mood. Without a breath of air moving, the wonderful river lay in a broad, glittering mirror before us. We surrendered ourselves to the endless comfort we felt, freed from anxiety and care. We congratulated one another for finally having escaped the nightly terrors of the boarding house.

In my prevailing mood of satisfaction I took my letters in hand and deepened myself in their details. Because I intend to report on my first impressions of America, I want to reproduce here the impressions Bernays received and expressed in his own letters, for they were correct evaluations and were later confirmed in reality a hundred times. They had arrived in New Orleans on 30 January, and after three days they continued on to St. Louis. Bernays's third letter was sent from St. Louis on 27 February, after he had been in St. Louis sixteen days. He wrote me that he had already made many acquaintances among the Germans of the city, and everywhere he had found the most friendly reception. Everywhere, however, he had also encountered rejection of our project to go to the country and become farmers. He wrote:

With the exception of a single person, they all discourage us from becoming farmers. They say we would be overcome by the burden of labor and in the end, as with hundreds like us, would have to come to the city and start from the beginning. Surely these people do know the situation on the spot, although they do not know our situation, and so judge our own intentions from the wrong point of view. A single man, the bookseller Detharding—who incidentally failed at farming himself—still recommends it. He pictures the life of a farmer as the most independent, attractive and happy existence possible. Certainly many have failed at farming, but only because they have had to hire the labor of others, and there was not enough money. Even though there is a great deal of money in St. Louis, there is extraordinarily little in the countryside. Detharding also believes there can be no doubt that we would succeed at any new business in St. Louis, for we have enough people so as not to need to hire the labor of others. But he doubts (as do I) whether we could tolerate the banal, obsessive, driven business life for long. Further, no one doubts that the summer climate in St. Louis is very perilous for foreigners. On the other hand, St. Louis is growing in a miraculous way into a world-class city. It has over 65,000 inhabitants. Six or seven houses are built every day, and where we live now (on Carondelet Avenue) they were hunting game not ten years ago. Despite the negative advice of all the people, I am still in favor of rural life. Other than the chance of becoming rich very fast, what we find in the city we have already left behind us in Europe, where in fact it was vastly lovelier and more pleasant.

In a later letter of 4 March he wrote—But suddenly it had become quite dark. Night had descended without the prelude of twilight, and I could not read. We could not show any light on the ship, because it was laden with cotton. So all we could do was put off everything until morning, lay ourselves down on our mattresses and dream away our last night on the *Espindola.* And so our friendly reader will excuse me that I must adjourn our first impressions of America until the next chapter. Good night!

On *the* Mississippi Bound *for* St. Louis
(1849)

It was a splendid, gorgeous night as we lay ourselves down to rest on the deck of the *Espindola* such as one can only find and enjoy in those southern parallels. The air was mild and warm, moderately cooled by the flowing water of the river. Above us was a dark blue, starry heaven, troubled by not a single cloud, and around us was profound silence, broken only by the murmur of the waves, the calling and moaning of the birds, snatches of song, the tolling of the hour, the barking of a dog. For a while we chatted in the dark, congratulating ourselves for having escaped our hot, smelly boarding house and its bloodsucking mosquitoes. Then ever-longer pauses interrupted our conversation, our speech became less clear, and finally our eyes closed. We slipped softly away in comfort. We had expected a peaceful, solid sleep, and in this we were not disappointed. We had been put into such a state of tiredness and exhaustion by all that had happened to us—our sleepless agitation on the last nights of the voyage, the final dreadful night at Mr. Clausen's, the care and distraction over transferring our baggage from the *Espindola* to the *Sarah*, the surprising first impressions of the New World unfolding before us, the great heat of the daytime—that we fell into a deep, death-like sleep. We only awoke as the sun stood rather high over the horizon.

Our awakening was no joy, much less pleasant than our falling to sleep. We arose with pounding heads and a feeling that was anything except well and healthy. When we saw one another, we all gasped at once, "Look at you!" There was no mirror on the cotton-ship, but each could see the other's face, not the state of his own. With an extremely unpleasant, painful feeling, our hands and face soon began to itch and burn. A dull headache made itself felt, and everyone felt his head had swollen to double its usual size. In fact this was so, since the skin on both hands and faces was swollen and covered with blisters and small swellings. In short, we had paid a high price for our deep sleep on the deck. Because of our ignorance of American, and particularly southern, peculiarities, our overnight camp on the ship's deck that we had thought was such a coup was in truth a jump from the frying pan into the fire. During the night the moon had risen, illuminating our hands and faces. It is not madness that the rays of the moon have a very negative effect, especially in southern climes. They ordinarily stimulate significant swelling of the skin, and our archenemies, the mosquitoes, had also done their best to put us into this swollen condition. So long as we were still awake and chatting we had smoked our cigars, and the tobacco smoke had held the mosquitoes at a distance. But as soon as we had finished smoking and gone to sleep, we fell victims to the murderous little insects. Hundreds of mosquitoes set upon our faces, necks and hands, sucking themselves full of our blood without our having the strength to resist them. So we awoke in the morning with heads fat, swollen, in which our eyes lay as if at the bottom of caves, while the little red swellings left behind by mosquito bites made us look like the victims of smallpox. Only now did we understand that our splendid idea to sleep on the deck was not a good one, and that we would have done better to remain yet another night in our boarding house.

But what was to be done? What happened had happened and could not be wished away. So we had to put up with our swollen state. First of all we had a good laugh over each others' appearance. But then came the irritation. The stinging and burning became continually more intolerable, and soon the laughing was at an end. In order to get at least some cooling, we drew one bucket after another out of the river, washing and bathing without pause, and the pain gradually relented and the swelling subsided. After long, continuous use of this washing had finally managed to get us looking half human, we had no further desire than to get aboard the *Sarah* to find protection, comfort and quiet nights. The mattresses were rolled up and given to a porter, along with our hand baggage. We trooped along at his side toward the steamer that was to take us to St. Louis, where we received immediate acceptance and a friendly reception. We were shown at once to our cabins, and because the ship was only partly filled, I was fortunate enough to have a cabin for myself alone. My companions were each two in a cabin. That was an entirely different and more pleasant time than on the *Espindola* or in the boarding house, and we felt we were in paradise. Our narrow but adequate cabins, the beds with their mattresses stuffed with cotton, the gallery which ran all around the ship like a verandah in front of the cabins, the grand salon with its sofas and other luxuries, the airy hurricane deck with its splendid panorama and innumerable other things were the objects of our constant marveling in the first hours. Once we had made ourselves at home, we took our places in our rocking chairs—the first we had ever seen, and which pleased us greatly—on the gallery and wallowed in a pleasant *dolce far niente*.

Now the letters of my loved ones were again brought out, frequently read and repeatedly analyzed. What they had to say tended to contradict the plans and project we had made. In his last letter of 4 March, Bernays wrote after having been a good twenty days in St. Louis, when he had come to know the place and its people to some degree:

We are cheerful, and we are staying close together. So far as I am concerned, I had not expected America to be other than what I find her to be. Here they think of nothing but making money. Despite the friendliest possible reception and the heartiest reciprocation I have received, and which you will receive in yet greater degree because you are known and popular due to your columns in the *Schnellpost*, we are still absolutely on our own. Here the only thing that counts is what the individual can do for himself. Everyone gives good advice, but I have found that no one is ready to lend a hand. But I have not the slightest doubt that if we persist, we would become prosperous persons in five or six years in any business. Because here it is only people who are expensive in a business, and we have hands enough.

. . . I beg and implore you to come here without any preconceived decision, without a set view, without a binding opinion, just as I have done. Keep the eyes and ears open, hear and see everything for yourself. Now even the last voice in favor of rural life has been stilled. Once our housemate Detharding, so enthusiastic for farming, saw our sixteen great crates, he shook his head and said to me, "Dear friend, even if you pay four thousand dollars for a farm, you will never find a house big enough to pile your crates one on top of the other, even unopened."

All experienced people here agree with him, and their corroborating descriptions have allowed us to see the farming life in all its details. It is admirable in its simplicity; but people like us are absolutely incapable of such simplicity, for in Paris we prepared ourselves for all possible human needs. There is not the slightest trace of romanticism here, nothing but want and labor, which farmers themselves describe as dreadful. As soon as you are here, Detharding will go with us to the Meramec River, where people are selling their property cheaply out of a madness to go to California. We will see and decide then.

Now we will look at St. Louis and consider our prospects here. I have written a dozen articles for the *Anzeiger des Westens*[1] in order to become better known and to win the support of the paper for any future undertaking. This has been a success. I know just about everyone who

---

1. Karl Ludwig Bernays, "Briefe eines in den Vereinigten Staaten reisenden französischen Diplomaten" ["Letters of a French Diplomat Traveling in the United States"], *AW,* weekly, vol. 14, no. 19, 24 February 1849, pp. 1, 2, 4; and vol. 14, no. 20, 3 March 1849, pp. 1-3, with the last (no. 12) signed and dated 1 March 1849. Bernays also authored five installments of "Die Revolution vom Jahre 1848 in Deutschland" ["The Revolution of 1848 in Germany"], *AW,* weekly, vol. 14, no. 22, 10 March 1849, pp. 2, 3; and vol. 14, no. 22, 17 March 1849, pp. 1, 2, 4.

Karl Ludwig Bernays, longtime collaborator of the Boernstein family. Photograph courtesy of the Missouri Historical Society.

speaks German and is of any importance. Journalism here is a thousand times grubbier than what we did over there, so we should not consider it. [Yet both of us did become American journalists in the end.]

With the exception of bookselling, carpentry and pharmacy, however, all businesses here are goldmines, and every sort of mercantile business will richly support a man. St. Louis is on the way to becoming the greatest city of the Union, it progresses with such giant strides. The greatest trading centers in Europe—Hamburg, Marseilles and Le Havre—are trifles in comparison with St. Louis and its future. People who started three years ago with sixty dollars now have four to five thousand dollars. Our next-door neighbor Herr Abeles, who has a large general store selling piece goods, ironware, just about anything, tells me he came to St. Louis with $100. Now he owns two houses and a flourishing business with ten young people as clerks. This is not just his story, but that of every active, prudent and thrifty person. Every day, in the sight of everyone, several people start businesses; all of them prosper, inevitably, because even if you move half an hour out of town and set up there, the town has extended to meet you within half a year, and a new neighborhood soon surrounds the business. All European standards cease to apply, and a person needs entirely new eyes and ears to evaluate things. Here, Carondelet Avenue, where we live, is called Frenchtown, and about two thousand persons of French descent live in the area. Nearby Carondelet is an entirely French village, and all Frenchmen like to go to shops where Germans or Americans can at least say *oui* or *non* and know that sugar is *sucre* in French. In our immediate vicinity there are people who have become stinking rich mangling the French language. Trade and usury are the source of all wealth here. All one has to do is to work hard and live rather thriftily himself until he is out of the worst of it, and to trade only in what people need every day. We have enormous advantages here; all that is expensive here is rent for housing and wages for people in business. Food and the ordinary necessities of life, purchased at the right time, cost here a twentieth, sometimes a thirtieth, of what they cost in Europe. If we could learn the technique of purchasing and live only a quarter as modestly as the Americans, we can survive on a dollar, at most a dollar and a half a day. Our people, whom others would have to pay thirty to forty dollars per month, cost us nothing, and we have no extraordinary expenditures, at least at the beginning. If we can learn purchasing well, we could combine all our forces, including the women, and experienced persons assure me that we will increase our capital at least tenfold in five or six years. We can always go live in the countryside afterwards, but then we could build a humane house, worthy of human habitation, and we would not have to live in a horse barn. I know what you will say—that we did not come to America to become rich but in order to be able to live independently and to establish a future for our children. At this point I genuinely doubt this can be accomplished by farming. In conclusion, I only ask you to keep your eyes open and not to be blind to anything. Here everyone is doing well, but in each case in a way other than he expected. Only ne'er-do-wells or layabouts, miserable, decadent people, are without fortune here. We cannot fail, and this conviction has given me great courage and cheer. I have not been out of sorts for a second, and that is saying something for a man of my character.

Bernays wrote this thirty-two years ago, and his verdict on the whole is still valid today. This information gave us much material for thought and mutual discussion, and I found a great deal that was true and worthy of respect there. My first impressions in New Orleans, as well as Bernays's portrayal of a farmer's life, shook my European project-making to some degree, considerably cooling my enthusiasm for farming. My brother continued to insist that we should stick to our plans. He did not want to hear a word about living in town or running a business; rather, he was committed to leading a simple and independent life in the country as a farmer. Our long debate culminated in his determined declaration that if I wished to live in town, he would move with his wife and Gunziker to a small farm and live in the country. I knew the firmness of his decision and knew he was not to be shaken from it. Through many years, from youth onwards, he had always remained loyal to me in his brotherly love; I could not bring myself to consider separating from him. So we decided to persist in our original plans and become farmers, despite Bernays's warning.

It was on board the *Sarah* that the servant of the French consul found us and delivered the invitation of Monsieur and Madame Roger to dine with them the next day at their villa, for which he would send his carriage. At almost the same moment, Captain Young advised us that the *Sarah* would depart tomorrow for St. Louis. Hence we had to decline this gracious invitation, and we paid a visit on the lovable man to express our thanks for his friendliness. He wished us the best on our journey, and we parted from this splendid man not without being touched. As I later heard, Monsieur Roger remained a while at his post. But after Louis Napoléon had solidified his position, he was recalled, as we had foreseen, and replaced by a Bonapartist, the Marquis of Montholon. I also bade farewell to Boulet, who had become particularly dear to me as a result of his charming and pleasing character. He had already found a good job in a painting shop, and because he was very adept at imitating wood-grain and marble, which was quite new then, he made continual progress. When I saw him again ten years later, he was already an independent man heading a flourishing, profitable business.

The *Sarah* did actually leave the next morning. We had been in New Orleans four days and had seen nothing of the city, our affairs having been so demanding. Now our attention was entirely absorbed by the giant river up which we were steaming. We came to know the truly American world of steamboating, which brought us new impressions every day. The majestic river streamed on, with its peculiar landscape on both sides. The web of moss and vines often entirely covered the trees. On the sandbanks sunned numerous alligators, which at first glance looked like rotting tree trunks due to their immobility. We landed at various towns and localities to drop passengers and take on new ones, and there was also the genuinely romantic nighttime loading of wood fuel. After frequent exchanges of signals, the boat would suddenly swerve toward the riverbank, close to edge of the forest. Masses of fir burning in iron grates would illuminate the river, the bank and the boat in a ghostly light while a gang of Negroes threw great logs aboard, all the while laughing and chatting. Then we would proceed upstream. As the fire on the riverbank was dowsed, the noise subsided, and the still, dark night once more enfolded us. There was also the overcoming of such manifold obstacles as sandbanks, tree trunks impaled in the bottom ("snags"), which often posed a genuine danger. In short, there was variety of life aboard an American river steamer, a unique mixture of culture and elegance with backwoods life and the wildness of nature. All of this was new to us and could not fail to awaken in us the liveliest interest.

Along the way the seasons rolled backwards. The further we went up the river, the colder and more hostile it became. We had left New Orleans in the glowing heat of summer, and we had worn the lightest possible summer clothing. In time, however, it became much cooler and more unpleasant. The lush vegetation receded, and above the mouth of the Ohio we found the trees leafless. A light snow flurry greeted us there, and we had to seek out our warm winter garments. The *dolce far niente* on the gallery that we had so treasured was soon gone. Outside it grew quite unpleasant, and we gladly flocked to the salon. In time the journey became monotonous and boring, and one hardly knew what to do with the day. The greatest relief was offered by the penetrating and surprising sounds of the gong ("tam-tam"), when it announced one of the various meals. Unfortunately this interruption was of very brief duration, for the meal was consumed and stowed away within half an hour. Here I learned the American haste at eating, which leaves one no time to chew but just to bolt it down. There was nothing else to do and there was nothing else to miss, yet the feeding was done in thirty minutes. The food was good and plentiful, but the character of the meals was the same as in the boarding house in New Orleans. Pork in all its forms and corn in the most various guises prevailed, only everything was better and more refined. All the food was once again eaten from a single plate, the knife was also used as a spoon, and the inevitable "Tea or coffee?" was served. Meals also had the most complete identity with one another, and breakfast, lunch and supper differentiated themselves in no way except that they took place at different times.

Here I learned another of America's peculiarities, which is the frequent questioning and examination of travelers by their companions. I had never encountered any people so ready to ask questions, so curious, so inquisitive as the company on this boat. When the people heard we came from Paris, we were almost tormented to death with questions—about all possible things, about the revolution, the Republic, about Louis Napoléon, social and industrial situations, religious conditions in France, all depending on the questioner's position and orientation. Ladies even asked about the latest fashions. We were also asked where we were going, whether we were married and had families, whether we had left our wives and children temporarily in Europe, etc., etc., without end. When we had answered all the questions of one, another came to be told the same thing, and we really did not have a quiet hour.

For example, I had a splendid Parisian travel valise in my cabin that I had received as a gift for a journalistic good turn. It was open when one of my fellow travelers entered from the gallery. After he had thoroughly examined the thing, he tirelessly grilled me on the purpose and use of the hundred different objects in such a valise. Once he was finished, a second came whom he had told of the thing, and eventually all the passengers on the entire boat came. They so examined and questioned me that in the end I felt like the owner of a menagerie or a curiosity cabinet. I had to explain every item and its use, everything was taken out and tested, one even sipped the contents of a bottle of cologne, remarking that it was hellishly strong brandy and had a dreadful "flavor." The most curious one wanted to use my toothbrush and toothpowder to whiten his teeth, stained black with chewing tobacco. Another wanted to trade the valise for a splendid riding horse. All of them were of the opinion that one would lose a dreadful amount of time with such a thing, and that it was foolish to make one's life more complicated with such machinery. They probably believed that one would have to use all of the hundred items every day. Even the ladies asked me to bring the valise into the ladies' salon so they could see it, which they did with the liveliest interest and zeal for learning, and so the game of question and answer lasted several days more. A lovely King Charles dog, which I had brought from Paris, also excited general interest and became the object of new examination. I was supposed to sell it, and numerous offers were made, continually increasing in size. I of course declined. The travelers consisted almost exclusively of Kentuckians and Tennesseeans, who had not been much touched by culture thirty-two years ago and who still had some primitive views. Most of them left us in Memphis or Cairo, but more came on board, asking their irritating questions in a new and revised edition.

So we steamed by Cape Girardeau, which I fixed with a rueful gaze of regret, although it looked somewhat different than it had appeared in the dreams of my lush imagination. On the evening of 20 April we finally lay at the levee of St. Louis, on the eighth day of our journey.[2] No one awaited us, for the letter I had sent to my people announcing the day of departure of the *Sarah* only came two days after we arrived. That was how good the postal connections with the South were in those days, and a letter from New Orleans to St. Louis took ten days.

We had arrived, and leaving the entire baggage aboard under Gunziker's control, my first priority was to seek out my people. That was no easy task, for it was growing dark. The street lighting was very poor in those days, and street names and house numbers could not be found. With great trouble we finally worked our way out of the crowds at the levee up to Second Street. Here it went better, for no one but Germans lived there. Our questions led us ever to the south, and the way never seemed to have an end. At last we ended up in Carondelet Avenue and asked for Künzel the smith, where our people were living. A cooperative neighbor led us to the house, where we flew up the stairs. With beating heart we opened the door indicated, entering. There was a general cry of shock and surprise, then joy, and we lay in their arms. Weeping tears of joy, we were together again after a hard, difficult separation of more than four months.

---

2. *AW*, weekly, vol. 14, no. 27, 21 April 1849, p. 2, from the daily edition of Wednesday, 18 April, declared that the *Sarah* had arrived the previous day, containing no cholera victims, "which can be taken as a good sign of the disappearance of the illness in the South." Boernstein thus errs on his arrival date; he has the fictional Boettcher family arrive on the *Sarah* on Sunday, 15 April, see Boernstein, *Mysteries*, 4-5.

First Impressions *in* St. Louis

The first days of our reunion were taken up exclusively with recounting everyone's travel experiences and with exchanging views about our first impressions of the new world we had entered. Bernays was able to give a much more thorough account than possible in a letter, including everything he had seen, heard and experienced in connection with our project. He told us of the new friends awaiting us, informing us their views and suggestions. The result was always the same, which was that we should do anything but farming, because neither born nor raised for such hard labor, we would soon be overcome by it. In opposition to this, my brother and I raised strong objection. In keeping with the old proverb, "Trying it is better than studying it," we stuck by our original plan, even if only to try it out on an experimental basis.

Our American friends had told Bernays that if we really wanted to become farmers, we should rent an existing farm, not buy it and bind ourselves to the soil without recourse. In the conditions prevailing then, everyone was trying to sell his farm in order to go to California, but no one wanted to buy one. We could always lease a farm of that sort without paying any cash, for in those days it was normal to pay the owner only ten bushels of corn per acre. In a good year an acre would produce forty bushels of corn, and even in bad harvests at least twenty or thirty. If we determined that the labor and trouble exceeded our strength, we could give up the leased farm and retire with minimal losses.

While these discussions were going on, we visited our new friends. I was presented to them, and we were received with great warmth and friendship. These new acquaintances were Arthur Olshausen[1] and Carl Mügge, who were amenable in every way and always helpful in advice and deed. Every day the circle of our acquaintances grew, and we continuously won new friends, but they were as one in recommending we avoid farming. A few days after my arrival, I wrote an article for the *Anzeiger des Westens*[2] explaining why I had come to America in disgust over Europe, and how it was now my firm decision to renounce politics and journalism forever, for they disgusted me

---

1. Arthur Olshausen (1819-?) was a brother of Theodor Olshausen of Schleswig-Holstein, later of Davenport, Iowa, and St. Louis. Arthur Olshausen emigrated to America in 1837, where he managed a bookstore in St. Louis; he was co-owner of the *Anzeiger des Westens* from 1844 to 1851. Körner, *Element*, 320; Cazden, *Social History*, 157, n. 89.

2. "Ein Brief von Heinrich Börnstein, ehemaligem Pariser Correspondenten der New Yorker Deutschen Schnellpost" ["A Letter from Heinrich Börnstein, Former Paris Correspondent of the New York *Deutsche Schnellpost*"], dated St. Louis, 18 April 1849, *AW*, weekly, vol. 14, no. 27, 21 April 1849, p. 4, from the daily edition of 19 April 1849.

totally. I wished to lead a peaceful and independent life in the country and dedicate myself totally to the education of my children. This article was intended to be my farewell to life as a publicist, and I wanted to live from then on only for myself and my dependents. I should say right here that I held this earnest commitment for a full year without interruption. But then conditions and events threw me back into a journalistic career, and I became more involved in journalism and politics than I ever had been in Europe. It is sad to say I have not been able to shake it even up to the present day. But in those days I had not a thought of ever resuming my old yoke.

Bernays had prepared things with care, renting an apartment with three rooms in which we all had a comfortable place. We had a cooking stove, beds and basic furniture obtained in the simplest and cheapest way, all to suit a farm. We intended to move at once to a farm as soon as the right one could be found. My brother had already found a large furnished room in the floor above us, and so we were spared the tiresome life of hotels. We were able to live as we had been accustomed to in Europe, cooking our French *pot au feu* of soup, meat, and vegetables. By all means we avoided the American practice of the many meals in a day, all dominated by meat in excess, particularly pork. Rather, we remained true to our old customs. We did not visit inns or public places, and despite all warnings about the perils of Mississippi water, we continued to have water as our ordinary drink.

Certainly it took a while to overcome our qualms and get to like the water as it was then offered in St. Louis. It really had an alarming appearance, and at first we drank it only with misgivings, with a few drops of spirit of fennel or rum. In those days the water works in St. Louis were still of a very limited sort. There was still no talk of clarification or filtration, and when a glass was filled from a hydrant, it looked like chocolate. It had to be let stand for a quarter hour before there was a half glass on top of reasonably clear water, the other half filled with mud sinking to the bottom. I recalled the old saying that every person had to eat seven pounds of mire and filth, but in St. Louis it was even worse, for we downed our seven pounds of mud every month. In later times we came to do well with Mississippi water, finding all alcoholic addition unnecessary, and we always felt well, although part of this was due to improvements in the water works with clarification basins and filtration. By continuing our simple European ways in years to come, we all remained healthy. I know that I was only sick in bed once in the first year, but otherwise always healthy and strong, and the same was the case with my entire family. We acclimatized ourselves rapidly, and despite many hardships and new, unexpected situations, we had no reason to complain of our condition in America.

The first impression St. Louis made on me was not very positive. The town was already in rapid expansion into a great center of trade, but to me, a spoiled Parisian who was at home on the asphalt of the boulevards, it struck me like a large village. To be sure the main streets had sidewalks paved with bricks placed on end. But the middle of the street was only macadamized, and there was as yet no spraying at city expense. The result was that the streets were like the Sahara in dry weather with thick, swirling clouds of dust, while in rainy weather they became bottomless seas of mire. In wet weather it became an art and a matter of some courage to cross from one side of the street to another without getting stuck in the mire. Granted there were crossing stones at a certain distance from one another, rectangular stones running right across the street so that the wheels of carriages ran between them. This was precisely the same primitive arrangement the Romans had used two millennia before, and which can be discovered in Pompeii, excavated from the ashes of Vesuvius.

A certain dexterity was always called for to get to the opposite side via these stones. One could not make a misstep or his foot would sink into the mire, and continuous rainy weather sometimes brought the mud so high that even crossing stones were covered. Then a person had to step into the unknown, trusting to luck to step in the place where a stone should be. This did not exclude many an error. Once in those days I was in the broad Carondelet Avenue, which then resembled a backwater of the Pontine Marshes in the relentless rain. I made a bad step, landing alongside a crossing stone rather than on it, and my right foot sank up to the calf in mire. I managed to work myself out, but with the loss of my boot, which remained stuck in the mud and was irretrievably lost. The result was that I had to hop on one foot to my apartment, which fortunately was nearby. Such was the condition of the main streets. But in most of the other streets there were neither sidewalks nor crossing stones, and in bad weather one sank in on stepping out of one's own house door. In the streets which ran behind Fourth parallel to the river, there were still no entirely uninterrupted streets constructed, with the exception of Seventh. Instead, large areas of grass, sand or clay lay between scattered groups of houses, the building lots of the future. Who was supposed to be building sidewalks there? Even the streets running to the west from the river were in the same miserable, interrupted condition. Street illumination was in its infancy, and the farther one came from the city's center the poorer it grew, ceasing altogether in the streets running near the outer edge.

There were only a few stone houses. The majority of homes were built with thin brick walls, strongly intermingled with frame houses, and the more one advanced from the center, the more log cabins were to be seen. The bricks for the brick houses, usually only a stone and a half in weight, made the interiors of these houses intolerably hot in the summer, and the heat absorbed in daytime was radiated by the walls at night, making the heat of rooms even worse after nightfall. Frame houses, since they were poor conductors of heat, were at least better in this regard. Here and there were even a few old houses of raw logs, as they had been erected by the first settlers. Such could be found at the corner of Spruce Street, as well as at the corner of Third and Plum. These were relics of the old French period, when St. Louis only had a few hundred inhabitants. Would it be believed today that only thirty-one years ago, in the liveliest part of the town—the point where the two chief streets, Second and Seventh, join, right next to Adolph Abeles—in the midst of the houses of the living, there were two cemeteries, one Jewish and one Christian, and that among the weathered gravestones cows and goats grazed?

In those days the town had 65,000 inhabitants. It was divided into six wards, that began at the U.S. Arsenal and reached to New Bremen. In those days the growth to 65,000 was taken to be huge, because when Pierre Laclède Liguest founded St. Louis on 15 February 1764 and erected the first log cabins, the entire population of his new colony, including those brought from Cahokia and Kaskaskia, was 120 persons. Despite their advantageous situation on the shore of the Mississippi near the mouths of the Missouri and the Ohio, the population took thirty-six years to rise to 900. Americans still had far too much disposable land available to find it worthwhile to cross the river to the new territories, and in 1835 the population was only something over 8,000 heads. Then it rose more rapidly, so that in 1840 it had already doubled, then quadrupled by the time we arrived. The great stream of European immigration came in 1849, and the census of 1850 showed a population of more than 74,000. From that point the growth took giant strides, and in the current census of 1880 the population of St. Louis is well above three-quarters of a million. Currently, St. Louis measures fourteen English miles from south to north, hence almost three German miles long, while it extends nine English miles to the west from the river, hence almost two German miles. So it will continue with giant strides, and I have not the least doubt that in the next century, the twentieth, it and its equally favored rival Chicago will far overshadow London, the largest city of Europe in population and size. Even if everything in those days, thirty-one years ago, was so lacking and unfinished as I portrayed it, still that was both entirely natural and easy to explain.

The new cities of America, to achieve continued importance, had to start out at once with those very facilities that are the accomplishment of a thousand years of culture and civilization in European cities. Water works, gas lighting, good paving and a hundred other things have to be brought into being immediately for a population that is rapidly increasing. But municipal income is still limited and inadequate. This helps to explain a chronic cultural deficit, the continually growing burden of municipal debt, which must heap loans on loans and bears down on the American urban population. The present generation has no idea what the earlier generation did without, tolerated and bore, what superhuman efforts were made, and most of all what giant taxes and contributions were paid to create even a relatively comfortable existence for present residents. Those living now see this as a given without sparing a thought for the ones who established this comfort.

This enormous rise of towns in America is unique. Let us look for a moment at a town in Europe such as Mannheim, founded in 1606, hence 275 years ago. The town has as advantageous a location as any America town, on the confluence of two trade arteries, the Neckar and the Rhine, and it was established not in a wilderness but in a densely populated region, on the spot where a large village already stood. The Elector established his court there, and it is still the second residence of the Grand Duke of Baden. It is one of the most important trading centers of Germany and a terminal for five railways. But despite all of that the population after 274 years has only reached 46,000 persons. Two hundred seventy-five years after their founding, St. Louis and Chicago will have reached a population of several million each, and St. Louis was founded 116 years ago, Chicago 85 years ago.

In material terms, we were quite pleased with St. Louis. All the necessities of life were astonishingly cheap, with only luxuries very expensive, and our simple way of life meant that we only needed the former, not the latter. In those days a pound of beef cost 5¢ or 22 *Pfennige* (an American cent is about 4 $^{1}/_{2}$ German *Pfennige*), veal cost 8¢, butter 1¢, chickens 15¢ to 20¢. Ham cost 5¢ a pound, and there were times when it could be bought for 2¢. A barrel of flour containing almost two hundred pounds cost $4 to $5. A bushel of corn (a bushel is 36 $^{1}/_{3}$ liters) cost 20¢, a bushel of potatoes 25¢ to 30¢, a pound of coffee 15¢, sugar 9¢, refined sugar 15¢. In fact, if a person preferred buying in bulk and tolerated lesser brands, a dollar would get you twenty pounds of Melis-sugar and sixteen pounds of Rio coffee for the same price. In the slaughterhouses, where they would pickle or smoke twenty-five thousand pigs a year (now it is more than five hundred thousand a year), the heads, lungs, hearts and feet of the pigs were thrown on a heap, and poor people could take as much of this refuse as they could carry away for the price of a good word. In short, plenty ruled everywhere, and no one had to go hungry. In his letters, Bernays had been absolutely right when he had said that we six could cover all our needs for a dollar, a dollar and a half at most. By now things have changed. When I left St. Louis in 1861, the cost of food had doubled, and now costs are probably three times what they were. On the other hand, luxury items are more available to all, hence cheaper.

But now that our domestic arrangements had been completed and our way of life stabilized, we had to think about our primary goal, which was

getting a farm. Our friend Detharding offered to take us on a tour into the
region beyond the Meramec in the first days of May, which we did. My
brother and Detharding rented horses from a livery stable, and my friend
Abeles lent me a fine gray horse with his usual hospitality. So off we rode
into the fastness in good cheer, chatting and spinning plans. On coming to
the Meramec river, we were taken to the opposite shore along with our horses
on a ferry run by two extremely comic old Negroes. Then we rode on, ever
farther and deeper into the country, until we finally reached the first farms
designated for sale several hours after noon. A powerfully built farmer's wife,
an Irishwoman whose husband had already gone on to California, received us
as welcome guests. Because we had been greatly tired by the ride in the heat
and were hungry, our friendly hostess prepared a quite tasty meal within half
an hour, following the famous American method of fast cooking. It consisted
of five dishes, including salt pork, ham and fresh pork playing the primary
role, with fresh-baked hot muffins and corn cakes playing support. After we
had suitably recovered, not spurning the brandy and water presented as
dessert, we viewed the farm. The house, a nice frame house, consisted of two
rooms, one containing the stove, the other a double bed. A small cellar and
attic with two rooms for the servants completed the house. There was also a
log cabin, the farmer's home before he built the frame house, which was now
used as a stall. The house and farm were well maintained, the cattle in the
best condition. It could be seen from the cleanliness and order that prevailed
that the woman was Protestant Irish. She and her husband were among the
Orangemen who had left Ireland, she told me, because the papists and their
priests had persecuted and tormented them.[3]

I liked the farm, but friend Detharding had been right in saying that our
forty chests could not have been sheltered in the house, not to mention
ourselves. We noted down the conditions of sale, made a quick inventory of
what was there, and then followed Detharding, who advised us not to rush
into anything but to look at the other farms as well. Because the farmer's
wife decisively refused to accept any payment for her feeding us, we could
only thank her sincerely for her hospitality and set forth again.

Detharding told us that if the night overtook us and it was impossible
to get back to St. Louis today, we would find the same sort of hospitality on
every farm we visited; we would be able to spend the night there and use the
following day for more visiting of farms. So we mounted our horses
refreshed. When we first broke into a trot, however, I discovered to my dread

---

3. This remark reflects the intense prejudice against Catholic Irish on the part of non-
Catholic Germans, which expressed itself both as sympathy with Protestant Irish and as
hostility to the Catholic Church. Shared prejudices gave German radicals an opportunity
to cooperate with Nativists in attacking Catholics.

that I had already ridden myself raw, a condition called "Wolf" in popular speech. This was both because I had grown stiff from not having mounted a horse in years, and because I had worn inadequate breeches. I perceived at once that continuous forcing on my part would only intensify the problem and make me totally incapable of returning; in fact, it would make me seriously ill, for I was already miserable. The upshot was that I made a quick decision and told my companions that I would return at once to St. Louis, preferably with them, but alone if they preferred to go on to the other farms without me. It was up to them. Detharding believed that turning back now would be a loss of time and money, since we would have to make the same journey another day, so it was better to do it thoroughly now. My brother, who had been seized with enthusiasm for farming and who had been impressed by the one farm we had seen, agreed with him. So we parted. I turned my horse back and they rode on, returning only the next day after seeing a dozen farms and making a thorough acquaintance with farming conditions.

I mournfully rode back toward St. Louis, letting the horse set the pace, for every time he broke into a trot I had intolerable pain. I have no idea how I ever got home. I left the whole thing up to the astonishing instinct of American horses, of which I had already seen and heard so much. My trust was not misdirected, for it was thanks to the horse that I got back home to my loved ones. The horse managed to find the right way to the ferry, and the two Negroes, whose joking no longer amused me, brought me across. When I climbed up the opposite shore, the pain became literally intolerable. I had numbness and drowsiness, and I was overcome with a boundless lack of resolution. I was strongly tempted to tie my horse to a post and lay me down in the grass, resigning myself to my fate, come what might. Only summoning up my entire energy allowed me to resist this temptation, and at the price of hard psychological struggles I steeled myself and made the solid decision to return to St. Louis whatever the cost. In vain I searched the entire area around to find a farmer's wagon going in my direction, so I could lie down in it and hitch the horse behind. But there was none to be found. There were certainly many going in the opposite direction, away from St. Louis, but none were going toward St. Louis. I did not stop to think that farmers would be going to St. Louis early in the morning, but not late in the evening. And so I limped forward alongside my horse, hurting a great deal. When I was too tired, I crawled back into the saddle, but because sitting astride was simply impossible for me I sat side-saddle like a woman, always risking falling over backwards if the horse bolted or made a misstep. The clever beast seemed to understand my condition, proceeding along its way at a careful, slow pace. There was no question of my leading the animal, for I had paid no attention to the route on the way out, and in any case I was now in misery.

Hour upon hour passed without my seeing the towers of St. Louis. I began to fear that I was on the wrong route, and my situation seemed more hopeless by the minute. I was utterly alien and understood little of the language, and I was becoming more physically tormented as I went along. So long as it was day, everything remained tolerable. The weak traces of wheels on the woodland paths could still be seen, and one could figure out that this way led somewhere, probably to St. Louis. But gradually it grew darker, until I was riding in pitch-black night without knowing whether I was on the road or simply going around in circles on the prairie. I consigned myself to my fate, tied the bridle to the saddlehorn and let the horse go wherever he wanted. On the distant horizon there were flashes of serious weather, and it appeared that a severe storm was blowing in. I had given up all hope of reaching St. Louis. Then my horse took a sudden turn to the right, stepping more confidently, and a row of lights arose out the darkness. These soon proved to be the streetlights in the southern part of town. Now my courage revived, and new hope returned. I had been right, and the clever beast had found the way back to his stable. Soon I was in Carondelet Avenue, and the gray led me to the door of Abeles' barn. I slid moaning from the saddle. The servant took the animal in, and I dragged myself gingerly toward my home, which fortunately was only a few steps away.

It was ten when I entered my home, and my anxious family heaped me with questions. It had been four when I left my companions, so that the return had taken six tormenting hours, a time I will remember with horror for the rest of my life. Still, the feeling of being back with my loved ones, along with an hour's worth of a cold sitting bath, stilled the worst pain. I could finally enjoy something, and after several hours of continuous cold compresses I finally slept gently and peacefully. Arising in the late morning after a sound sleep, I was fresh and cheerful, even somewhat well and mobile. It could have been so much worse, for it was a time when cholera raged in St. Louis with overwhelming intensity, and it particularly befell persons exhausted by great exertions.

Bad Times

(1849)

Bad times came upon St. Louis now, harsh tests indeed, and we were given no inviting reception from our newly chosen homeland. If the old French settlers, who founded St. Louis and formed the population of the town for forty years, had still existed, they would inevitably have used their curious, original style of dating to call 1849 *l'année terrible* or *l'année des grands malheurs.*[1] Those founders and original inhabitants of St. Louis, who tried their luck by marching into the trackless wilderness with Laclède Liguest to settle and lead a life filled with want, were all old-style French fur hunters, trappers and other adventurers from the lowest level of the people. They were used to journeys into wilderness and desert. They were accustomed to fighting wild animals and even wilder Indians, and to trade with them on occasion. They were hardened to the rawest way of life and the grossest shortages. But they were without education, even the most elementary schooling. It was very rare to find any of them who could read or write, and in figuring they did not get above their ten fingers. The result was that none of them knew which year he was born in, for counting in four figures was a magnitude beyond their grasp. The few clerics who lived in the broad territory, most of them Jesuit missionaries, and the few officials sent to administer the most minimal legal needs did know the numbers of the year and used them in the documents they issued as *anno Domini* such and such. But the population itself had not the least understanding of these numbers or their meaning. They were happy to name each year after the most significant events that had struck their small group; with this name they knew precisely the year in question, and they needed no more information.

So when St. Louis was attacked by wild Indian hordes urged on by an English commander in the sixteenth year of the colony's existence, and the settlers were saved from annihilation only by the help rushed in by the American Colonel Clark from Illinois on the opposite shore, the year 1780 became *l'année du grand coup.*[2] Again, when the Mississippi ran over its banks and not only turned the Illinois Bottoms into a great lake, but also flooded part of St. Louis in 1785, they called the year *l'année des grandes eaux.*[3]

---

1. French, "The Terrible Year," or "The Year of the Great Misfortunes."
2. French, "The Year of the Great Attack." George Rogers Clark (1752-1818) of Virginia relieved Cahokia, Illinois, and defended St. Louis against a British and Indian force in 1780.
3. French, "The Year of High Waters."

When the river pirates who had made boat traffic on the Mississippi unsafe by raiding several boats, robbing them and killing their crews, were finally neutralized in 1788 after great efforts, and ten loaded flatboats arrived in St. Louis within the space of a few months, this joyous year became *l'année des dix bateaux.*[4] A dreadfully severe winter in which people and animals perished caused the year 1799 to be called *l'année du grand hiver,*[5] and a terrifying smallpox epidemic caused 1801 to be called *l'année de la picote.*[6] These few titles remain to us; the others, which probably were to preserve events of less importance, have been lost and forgotten.

With annexation by the United States, the population was steadily Americanized. In part the old French died out, and in part they made way for the Anglo-American population from the East, emigrating either to Canada or to New Orleans and other places in Louisiana. The rich French property owners—the Chouteaus, Soulards, Prattes, Labaumes and others—remained in St. Louis. Through their properties of thousands upon thousands of acres, often purchased for a bottle of whiskey, they became millionaires and the most influential citizens of the territory. The small remnant of poor Frenchmen, lacking the means to emigrate to Canada or Louisiana, moved back to the little village of Carondelet, which then lay a good six English miles from St. Louis. Here they led a meager existence from day to day, deteriorating continuously, so that Carondelet became known popularly as *Videpoche*[7] because of its poverty. This usage took such deep roots that even in my time the name *Videpoche* was more common than Carondelet, and even the Germans, particularly North Germans, knew it only as *Widbusch*, perhaps believing that it meant "White Bush." Now everything has changed, and the poor village of Carondelet, which was then more than six miles away from old St. Louis, has long been overtaken by the expanding city and united with it. Since 1870 it constitutes the First District of the city of St. Louis. Where once lived a bare one thousand Frenchmen in the most miserable circumstances, now this First Ward houses fifteen thousand inhabitants, of whom more than half are Germans. The few descendants of the French continue to dwindle, and the smokestacks of great iron works and factories have given the place a prosperous appearance. Industriousness and wealth dominate what was once an old Creole village, and a flotilla of steamboats comes, goes, and lies at its levee. Such is American life.

St. Louis also received its own nickname from the old French. When they were among themselves, they would never call it St. Louis, but rather

---

4. French, "The Year of Ten Boats."
5. French, "The Year of the Great Winter."
6. French, "The Year of the Pox."
7. French, "Empty Pocket."

Pain-court,[8] and the little town was known by that name not only in the vicinity, but as far as Ohio and Indiana. This term arose from the frequent shortage of bread grain and flour, so that the inhabitants often had to rely on shipments from Ohio or New Orleans. There might have been a few agriculturists among the first colonists brought by Laclède, but far too few, and the fur hunters, trappers and adventurers had no taste for the labor of working the soil. Anyone who knows the primitive methods of agriculture practiced even today in new American settlements, despite massive immigration and the presence of modern agricultural machinery, has an idea how agriculture was pursued around St. Louis in those days. The trees of the primeval forest would first be girdled with an ax, then the dried-out trees burned and the soil plowed in a zigzag pattern between the tree stumps, whose removal would demand too much time and money. The soil was then seeded for corn, and only after decades did the tree roots finally rot in the ground and grow soft, finally turning to humus.

There were some fields being worked by residents just beyond Third Street, where the fashionable main streets of the modern city now run, but usually this was painstakingly worked with shovel and hoe for the needs of the household itself. Only enough was raised to support the household, and often a great deal less than it needed. The result was that there were often temporary shortages of bread grain in St. Louis, so that it was justly called *Pain-court*.

The fact that settlers avoided the use of the name St. Louis as much as possible could also have its foundation in the fact that they spoke very ill of their own *roi Louis-Quinze*,[9] who rudely abandoned them and sloughed them off to a foreign state. Up to the start of our own century the inhabitants of St. Louis for years at a time had no idea who their king might be. Laclède Liguest received a charter in 1760 from King Louis XV to found a fur company and a settlement in Upper Louisiana, as they called the entire region north of the mouth of the Ohio. He outfitted his expedition in New Orleans in 1763 and founded St. Louis, as he tells us, on 17 February 1764, naming the settlement after his king. Yet Louis XV had already ceded to the King of Spain the entire region west of the Mississippi to an uncertain northern border, together with the city of New Orleans, in a secret treaty almost two years before, on 3 November 1762. More properly it should be said that he betrayed Louisiana for an unknown amount of blood money. Great shock and bitterness reigned in New Orleans and the entire French region when this despicable cession became known in April 1764, for it was a sale of his own compatriots to an alien power. Everyone

---

8. French, "Little Bread."
9. French, "King Louis XV."

decided to resist Spanish occupation with force, and the Spanish government thought it better to postpone possession. Later, when this did occur, the first Spanish governor of New Orleans, Don Alloa, was received with curses and threats at his first landing and forced to embark again.

Several more years passed in this uncertain situation, during which French commanders continued to hold their posts and exercise their governmental powers. The Spanish government sent a new governor in 1764, Don O'Reilly, with three thousand men armed with cannon. O'Reilly's reception in New Orleans was also extremely unpleasant and hostile, and a general rebellion nearly broke out. But the new governor had strict instructions and carried them out energetically. He had twelve of the most respected citizens of New Orleans arrested and brought before a court martial; five were shot and seven sent in galleys to Cuba, where they perished miserably. This tribunal of blood spread terror and revulsion, and gradually there was subordination to the new circumstances. O'Reilly sent one of his officers, Don Piernas, as lieutenant governor to St. Louis, where he arrived with a strong military force in the spring of 1770. There Piernas lowered the French flag which had been displayed and hoisted the Spanish banner. The colonists, horrified by the bloodbath in New Orleans, submitted to the new rule with grumbling. Spanish rule turned out to be better than French. The new commanders, O'Reilly as well as Piernas, were reasonable and humane people and more was done for the region than had been the case under French rule, when no concern was shown for the colonists at all. But in 1800 the iron fist of Napoléon compelled the king of Spain to cede the entire region to France, and the colonists once more became unwilling Frenchmen. Napoléon, who understood that he could not maintain this vast area in the face of England's sea power, then sold it in May 1803 to the United States for 60 million francs and the acceptance of 20 million francs in debts. The United States already ruled the area east of the Mississippi, and for the insignificant sum of $16 million they came into possession of an area almost as large as all of Europe without Russia. Here a dozen new states were founded. In a prophetic spirit, Napoléon said to the representative of the United States, [Robert R.] Livingston, "This growth of territory makes the United States the principal power in the New World, and by doing this I have created a competitor with England that shall sooner or later humble its pride."

All of these changes in rule were made known on the Mississippi much later, and this situation of uncertainty persisted for as long. It was only in March 1804 that the formal cession to the United States took place. The actual taking of possession occurred immediately afterwards. From that moment on was there permanent security and a consciousness of the new status, under which St. Louis would bloom.

I should be forgiven this digression, for the early history of St. Louis has always held the greatest interest for me, and it could claim the attention of most readers. When I earnestly set to work researching for my novel *The Mysteries of St. Louis* in 1850, I concerned myself a great deal with these old times, looking for documents as well as the few persons from those days who were still alive. There were few documents, save for the journal of Laclède's companion Auguste Chouteau; Auguste Chouteau himself died in 1829, like his brother Pierre. Remaining alive was only a grandson, also named Pierre Chouteau, but I was never able to meet him.[10] Nothing could be learned from the oldest German settlers, because German immigration only dated from the years after 1830. The French had virtually died out, and only in Carondelet could I find a few old Creoles, comic old geezers. Dating mostly from the last decades of the previous century, they could tell me little worth knowing, but they chattered on with a great deal of dumb nonsense and petty detail. In St. Louis, I did meet a woman, Madame Elizabeth Ortes,[11] who was born in Vincennes in the same year St. Louis was founded and had been brought to St. Louis at the age of four with her parents, living there without interruption from 1768 to 1850. She had observed all the changes, and at the time she was eighty-six years old. The old lady was still in possession of her physical and mental faculties, saw and heard well, ate with gusto, and slept soundly (although only for a few hours). She was a passionate taker of snuff, and when she was brought around to her theme, which was old times in St. Louis, she was quite talkative. Her maiden name was Barada. At fifteen she was married to one of Laclède's companions, Jean Ortes. Her husband died in 1813, after which she lived quietly and without care in the house of her son-in-law, Joseph Philibert. She was still living in 1860 at the age of ninety-six. She has surely died since. The good lady, who had experienced all these mutations herself, could talk at length and eloquently, and with her good memory she was an invaluable source for the early history of St. Louis.

Now I return to the story of my own experiences. Terrible times indeed broke over St. Louis, and the old settlers would certainly have been justified in calling 1849 *l'année terrible*. Cholera, which had already greeted me in New Orleans, had broken out sporadically at the end of 1848 in St. Louis, disappearing again after but a few deaths. In early 1849, almost at the moment of our arrival, it broke out once more with great virulence, rising

---

10. Auguste Chouteau's journal, which was extensive, was destroyed save for fourteen pages. It was returned to St. Louis and deposited in the Mercantile Library in 1857 and published in an English translation in 1858. See the article, "Chouteau's Journal," in *EHSL*, I: 366.

11. Elizabeth Ortes (1764-1867), was born in Fort Vincennes, Indiana, daughter of Antoine Barada, married Jean B. Ortes (died 1813). See *EHSL*, 3: 1678, also a portrait and description in *Edwards's*, 527 (portrait), 529-30.

ever higher and allowing us to fear the worst. In 1832 cholera, which then first visited Europe, appeared for the first time in St. Louis, and 30 persons a day had died in a population of 7,000. At that time it lasted only a month, but a good seventh of the population fell to it. This time it appeared destined to reach even more fearful dimensions. The numbers rose from the end of April from 131 to 903 per week. This time the epidemic lasted a full four months, in which time 6,000 deaths occurred in a population of 65,000. Hence almost a tenth of the population was lost to the dreadful disease. Anxiety, terror, helplessness and confusion achieved the highest degree. More than other towns, the St. Louis of those days was ideally suited as a breeding ground of cholera. There were still no sewers. The alleys behind the houses, into which all the yards emptied, served to collect all manner of trash thrown out of the houses to rot, and they were never or only very seldom cleaned. In several parts of town, cellars were continually flooded with water seeping from underground, and this stagnant water produced pestilential mists. Street cleaning was pitiful, and it was only once cholera had seized the entire town and reached a high intensity that efforts were seriously made to clean the streets, clear the alleys of their two feet of filth, and disinfect the thoroughfares—unfortunately too late.

Officials completely lost their heads, and physicians had no means to fight the disease. This is no marvel, for thirty-two years later, medicine today knows nothing certain about the nature and origin of cholera, nor is there any specific remedy for this dreadful sickness. What has been learned in thirty-two years of intense research, particularly in Europe, rests on hypotheses and assumptions, and both these and the medicines proposed have proved undependable. So the physicians of St. Louis could be excused for being helpless in the face of the epidemic, and they could make no recommendations to the officials who appealed to them. The most important physicians of St. Louis, after gathering for a long discussion, finally delivered the opinion that for the duration of the epidemic they advised against eating fruits and vegetables, preferring the consumption of meat alone. The officials had nothing more important to do than to raise this opinion into law, and they strictly forbade the sale of fruits and vegetables in the markets by city ordinance. The controller of markets confiscated all of these vegetal materials when they arrived for sale, either destroying them or, as it was believed at the time, consuming them at home. That was a telling blow to the farmers around St. Louis, who had committed themselves largely to the production of vegetables. The products they could not sell in St. Louis rotted in the fields while butchers did a wonderful business. This was because the population misunderstood the instructions of the medical gathering, believing that eating meat was a protection, even a cure for cholera. Ten times as much meat was then eaten in St. Louis as in ordinary times.

Despite the diet of meat, despite the thorough cleaning of streets and the use of disinfectant, the severity of the illness rose by the day until it was reported that 160 had died in a single day. Now other physicians met and condemned the eating of meat as too stimulating, inclining to the disease. They warmly supported a completely vegetarian diet. The city council hence rescinded its ordinance forbidding the sale of vegetables and fruit, and the public consumed incredible amounts of vegetables, rejecting the meat diet it had once praised. Despite this, the epidemic persisted with undiminished intensity.

For me, who had experienced the great cholera epidemic in Vienna in 1832, survived the epidemic in Paris and finally in New Orleans, the illness held no terror. I led a regular life, followed a reasonable diet and believed in observing all the personal practices that had been shown to be advantageous and proven. In short, practicing moderation and avoiding all injurious excess was the best preventative. The most dependable cure seemed to me to be with water and ice, such as wrapping in wet linen cloths and other hydropathic methods. I have followed my views in all the cholera epidemics I have lived through and have passed through them unscathed. In St. Louis as well, I observed that whoever lived reasonably and modestly, preserving his ordinary pattern of life and scrupulously avoiding excesses of all sorts—most of all avoiding cholera preservatives, cholera bitters and cholera drops then advertised by the hundreds in the papers—would survive the cholera season untouched and healthy. Even if one or another of such people might catch a light dose of cholera, the constitution of the patient, strengthened through a regular and simple life, would successfully resist the illness.

Yet the number of such reasonable people was very small. The great majority believed in all sorts of medicines to protect or heal themselves rather than the advice of a simple and moderate life, and the hunt for medicines in a bottle led to the idea that the germ of the illness was in the air, which would have to be purified. The result was that the highest authorities commanded that great fires be built at crossroads to cleanse the air. The population cheerfully dragged in old crates, tar barrels and other incendiary materials and set them afire, whereupon the youths of the street jumped around and did their dances. The result was that smoke and mist swirled through the open windows into all homes, and everyone inhaled the dust of ashes and coal with every breath. Many an overexcited boy who had been jumping joyfully around the fire would suddenly turn pale as death and drag himself miserably away, to be stricken by cholera and die on the way or at home. Occasionally a sudden gust of wind would send sparks and flames onto the shingle roofs of the frame houses, and a row of homes would burn down. But that did not matter, for the air had to be purified.

St. Louisans received the best demonstration how of useless 'this purification of the air' by fire was a few days later. On 19 May, the great St. Louis Fire broke out. Lasting several days, it consumed 483 houses, 23 steamboats, 3 other ships and an enormous amount of wares piled on the levee. That was a great deal bigger fire than the burning of a few crates and barrels, but it still did not purify the air. After the fire, cholera increased to ever greater heights, to the point where a thousand deaths per week were being counted in late July. As fearsome as this rise in the epidemic might be, the terror and horror of the population was even worse. Formal funeral processions no longer took place. The dead were simply and silently taken to the cemetery with the greatest possible haste, where the coffins often sat for several days, there being a shortage of hands to dig graves. Fortunate was he who died in the bosom of a loving family, for he was brought to the cemetery quietly and quickly to be sure, but at least with decorum. It was worse with the residents of boarding houses and hotels, who were mostly single persons, workers, clerks or other subordinates, always several in a room, spreading infection rapidly among themselves. They found little help or care, and they died in droves, so that during the worst period of the epidemic ten to twelve residents of a boarding house might die in a day. If people cared little about them while they lived, once they were dead their burials also proceeded in an extremely summary manner. Some of the Negroes who had been pressed into service during this time sought reinforcement from brandy for a hard task. Half drunk or totally drunk, they came by night with a wagon, hauling the dead out of bed by their feet and dragging them down the stairs, thumping from step to step. Then they threw them on the wagon and once they had half a dozen corpses, galloped to the cemetery, where they emptied the vehicle into a common trench before returning to get more dead.

At that time, at the start of May, the epidemic had not yet grown so severe. We concerned ourselves little about it, but soon we were forcefully reminded. We were preparing to make a new expedition to see farms when I was suddenly awakened on the night of 8-9 May. My sister-in-law informed me that her husband, my brother, was dangerously ill. I rushed there at once and found my worst fears realized. My brother had his own views about illness; he wanted to hear nothing about cold water, while my family and I took a cold bath every morning. Further, he made gross errors in his diet, and the night before he had eaten a large bowl of salad despite the fact he was suffering from diarrhea. The exertions on his expedition to the Meramec had exhausted him, and so I found him on my arrival suffering a severe attack of cholera, which caused me to fear the worst. We tried everything to save him, and two physicians came at once. Whatever could be done was done, but already with the break of day came a complete plummeting of his strength, what is called *collapsus*, and my brother passed away on 9 May at midday. His last hours were without pain, gentle and peaceful, without his ever becoming aware of his situation. This was a hard blow for his wife, and for us all, and my presence in St. Louis was now completely embittered.

I decided to leave this unhappy city and to seek my peace in the countryside. My St. Louis friends completely approved my decision. They recommended to me the entirely German community of Highland in Madison County, Illinois, as the most proper country settlement. There I could become acquainted with farming first hand and decide whether I was suited for it. I rushed to make arrangements to move, solid in my decision never to return to ill-fated St. Louis. Our crates and trunks could be sent via returning farmers from Illinois who had brought their products to St. Louis and would take our baggage as return freight. We rented adequate carriages, and on 15 May we went to Highland. It was not many days too soon, for four days later, on 19 May, the great fire broke out that laid half of St. Louis, its richest and busiest part, in ashes and ruins, considerably outbidding the cholera in horror. My brother's widow remained behind in St. Louis, for she had always disliked country life. We, on the contrary, although badly shaken by a bitter blow that disrupted all our plans and calculations, turned with courage toward the new home we hoped to find in Highland. We were filled with the hope and the elasticity of maturity.

American Country Life

In those days the journey from St. Louis to Highland still took a full day. There was a great deal of talk about a railroad that would pass through Highland, but the undertaking still lay in an imprecise, nebulous distance. There was not even a regular highway but only a country road that no one maintained and that became a bottomless swamp when there was rain or thaw. The many creeks we had to pass along the way had no bridges, and so we had to go through the water. This almost always caused trouble for heavily loaded wagons, which would remain stuck in some underwater hole. When the snow was melting, and these creeks were swollen over their banks, it was often actually dangerous to cross them in this way. The colonists of Highland had built a lovely road running twenty English miles, using their own money and hands without any assistance from the county, in order at least to keep the postal service going. This assured that at least the postal coaches ran through Highland once this improvement was made, which was only in 1843. However, although this road was heavily used, no one but the Highlanders would maintain it, and it deteriorated continuously. In short, if a farmer of Highland wanted to take his harvest to St. Louis, he had to hitch two or three yoke of oxen in front of his wagon, and for the trip there and back he needed five whole days. Today everything is different and better. There is a railroad, to which the Highlanders contributed heavily, running from St. Louis through Highland to Vandalia and Terre Haute. One can get from St. Louis to Highland in an hour and a quarter, and from there he can ride the rails to Chicago and New York, as well as to Mobile and New Orleans.

In those days we were stuck with the old country road, and by the time we reached Highland the sun was setting. We had taken the slow, dangerous ferry across the Mississippi, hauled the wagons up the steep Illinois riverbank with the help of several people, overcome many obstacles in passing creeks, and we rested and foddered for a total of two hours along the way. But what an unforgettably beautiful view compensated us for all the efforts and cares of the last few days! Below our position on a gentle height was the most moving landscape we had yet seen in America. As we emerged from a group of trees, splendid Looking Glass Prairie lay before our eyes. The wavy plain spread as far as the eye could see, with the loveliest bluegrass and lush flowers. A few hills rose above it, and the whole prairie was edged with primeval forest. In the midst of this charming region stood the little town of Highland, with its broad, straight streets set at right angles to one another. Its houses were of blinding whiteness, with dark shingle roofs, or an occasional roof of red tiles. Everywhere were vegetable patches and gardens, behind which ranged a few small towers indicating a chapel. Further beyond the town in the prairie, in the embrace of woodland and on hills could be seen friendly farms with great spreads of plowland, herds of cows grazing on the prairie. The afternoon ennobled the whole pretty picture with its sun's red-gold coloration of the landscape. Peace and quiet appeared to rest upon the entire settlement, and following our sorrowful days in St. Louis we breathed afresh and renewed our spirits.

Enjoying the beautiful view, we had our coachman proceed at a slow pace. We finally came to the large house of the postmaster, Jacob Blattner, who combined his office with a sort of wayside inn. He had already been recommended to us in St. Louis, and we received the heartiest and friendliest reception. A couple rooms were ready for us, and after we had washed away the dust and cares of the day, we sat down in the public room for an excellent dinner that was half Swiss, half American. After we had Blattner and several Highland citizens tell all that was worth knowing about the settlement, we went to our rest with the cheerful awareness that our choice for a new home had been correct. Highland was entirely in keeping with our desires and expectations.

When we arrived in Highland, the friendly little town had only existed for thirteen years. The first colonists from Europe had erected their huts there eighteen years ago. Hence everything was new, new and primitive, but despite that the community made a positive and pleasing impression. A Swiss physician, Dr. Kaspar Köpfli, whose liberal and enlightened spirit could not be at peace with the conservative system that ruled then in Switzerland—particularly not with the domination of priests in his own canton of Lucerne, who oppressed every liberal tendency until they were broken in the *Sonderbund* War.[1] Dr. Köpfli had long harbored the thought of emigrating to America, and this idea ripened over years, during which obstacles of various sorts prevented carrying it out. It was only when Dr. Köpfli was all of fifty-seven years, nearing old age, that he was able to realize his long-treasured plan. He was not simply thinking of himself and his family as he said in a printed farewell letter to his fellow citizens. He also intended to clear a path for many heads of family who were vigorous but unemployed in Switzerland, oppressed by care there, to make for themselves a happier, more promising future. The colony of these pioneers consisted of old Dr. Köpfli and his equally elderly wife, four sons and a daughter, joined by Joseph Suppiger and his brother. Along with the group came five peasants

---

1. The Swiss Sonderbund War of 1847 was a confrontation between the Catholic cantons, which had formed a "special league" or *Sonderbund*, and the other cantons under the federal government. It ended in the defeat of the Catholic cantons and the abolition of the league.

and a maid. It was thus a total of fifteen persons taking a large wagon for baggage and equipment for the colony, several carriages and seven of their own horses. In those days there were still no railways in Europe, so that they had to rely on the old, traditional means of movement. The new colonists set out from Sursee on 21 April 1831, and arrived their new home of Highland after six months full of endless troubles and deprivations. They needed sixteen days just to get to Paris. There they sold horses and wagons, which had proved impractical, and proceeded to Le Havre along the Seine. Departure from Le Havre was delayed until 21 June, and it was only after a stormy crossing of six weeks that they arrived in New York on 10 August. There they were openly laughed at when they declared their intention to go to the Mississippi Valley, which was twelve hundred English miles away, to which there was still no such thing as a direct road. They simply did not allow themselves to be talked out of their decision, however, and they decisively rejected all suggestions that they stay in the East. After a twelve-day journey filled with troubles of all sorts using steamboats and canal boats and the most various means of transportation they finally arrived in St. Louis, which was then a little nest of five thousand inhabitants.[2] Here they made a temporary halt and sent out many exploratory expeditions to find a suitable place for a new settlement. Negro slavery, which was offensive to the liberal Swiss, ruled out Missouri itself. Iowa and Wisconsin were still in the possession of wild Indians, and so they turned their attentions to the interior of Illinois. They were offered Looking Glass Prairie, an area of about 460 acres, and some members of the colony were sent there to inspect it. When they first set foot on the splendid prairie, they were overjoyed by the charming sight. They determined to send their unanimous report to the others at once, saying, "It is good here. Let us build our houses!"

The purchase was completed and on 15 October, six months after their departure from Switzerland, they departed for Highland. On 16 October they took possession of their new property. They managed to buy an additional 400 acres, partly from the state and partly from private sources, and before the year had finished they were in possession of a complex of land amounting to 1,000 acres which they had obtained at an average price of $2.50 an acre. Farms were placed on this virgin soil, which was almost untouched by the plow or the hoe. Log cabins were built, and low-density

---

2. Boernstein's narrative follows Solomon Köpfli's "Die Geschichte der Ansiedlung von Highland" published in the *Highland Bote* in 1859, which has been published as *The Story of the Settling of Highland*, Jennie Latzer Koeser, tr., Raymond J. Spahn, ed. (Edwardsville: Lovejoy Library, Southern Illinois University, 1970), 3-9. Boernstein has several of the dates wrong. The departure from Le Havre was 2 June 1831, and the arrival in New York was in July. They arrived in St. Louis on 28 August 1831. Solomon Köpfli died in Zürich in 1869; Körner, *Element*, 272-4.

planting was pursued. In the course of the next few years, old Suppiger and their other children followed, and several acquaintances and some of their former factory employees joined up. During the following years, new recruits appeared, encouraged by Joseph Suppiger's accounts sent to Switzerland, so that the area continually grew in population. It still remained an affair of scattered farms without any connecting tie between them, and it lacked a community of goals or interests.

Then one beautiful morning in 1836 an American stranger rode in. He observed the fine, industrious life of the settlement with joyous astonishment. Interested in it for reasons that were easy to grasp, he inspected everything, asking many questions. This was General James Semple, an active, driven man who had bought large stretches of land in this part of Illinois. Together with other Eastern speculators, he anticipated the railroad connecting the East with the upper Mississippi, a feat which had long been projected and would sooner or later come to pass. Semple was a man who did much on behalf of central Illinois, then a region neglected and despised. This immigrant settlement, provisionally called New Switzerland, bordered his own property, and it interested him in the highest degree. He made the practical proposal to the Köpflis and Suppigers that founding a town here, halfway between the chief settlements of three counties and along the projected railway, would inevitably prosper. The leaders of the colony joyfully agreed with the proposal, and on 23 September 1836, a contract was signed. A property of 80 acres was divided into 600 lots by broad streets at right angles to one another, and so the town was founded. In honor of the Scot, Semple, and on his suggestion, the town was named Highland. In the next few years 51 lots were sold for prices between $5 and $40, and in every following year more were sold and built upon. When the town corporation was dissolved in 1861, there were only a little over 100 lots yet unsold; these were divided among the shareholders, who achieved a clear profit of $25,000 from the sale of lots after deducting their purchasing costs. Dr. Ryhiner from Basel, a thoroughly trained physician and a man of enterprise, erected the first steam mill with a sawmill in the same year, 1837. Hard-working Swiss and German immigrants, including skillful and active artisans, settled, and soon the town could supply its own wants without having to fetch everything from St. Louis or other places. Today, Highland stands on its own two feet, and it has grown to be one of the most prosperous, successful settlements in the West. On 16 October 1881 the residents of Highland proudly celebrated the fiftieth anniversary of settlement on Looking Glass Prairie. On 23 September 1886 they will celebrate the fiftieth anniversary of the founding of the town.

If our first look at Highland was a happy surprise, closer acquaintance caused our appreciation to grow. We decided to remain there and establish our new home. Bernays and I visited the fathers of the little town, Messrs. Köpfli and Suppiger. We were received there in the friendliest manner and were encouraged to remain there and join the settlement. A momentary impediment to doing so was posed by the shortage of housing, which then prevailed. As energetically as houses were being built, they could not keep pace with the rapid rise in population, for the town had received new streams of additions from Germany and Switzerland, particularly since 1848. When I came to Highland, the population was no longer exclusively from Lucerne; there already were people from Bern, Aargau, St. Gallen, Schwyz and Glarus. There was even an entire community from Valais in French Switzerland, who had emigrated with their pastor at their head. There were also many settlers from Baden, the Palatinate and Swabia. Then Waldensians came from the Piedmont, and now several small villages have formed around Highland and in its orbit, relying upon it, all about a German mile away. These include the French settlement of Sebastopol; Salina, founded by people from Grisons; as well as St. Jacob and Oakdale. The French-speaking immigration from Valais brought an ultra-pietist coloration into the colony, which was otherwise liberal. These were the so-called "Monier," though they were for the most part upstanding, active and hard-working people who were a credit to the town. Among them were some very well-educated and liberal men such as Messieurs Cortambert, Rillier,[3] Bandalier, and others, whose acquaintance and learned conversation I recall even today with pleasure. In short, Highland became ever more a polyglot settlement with a decidedly Swiss-American character.

The Anglo-American population, never represented by more than a few, either vanished or accommodated themselves eventually to the character and life of the Swiss and German population. The few Americans present here and there in the woods at the time of the settlement did not increase, and they either died out or wandered away. In my time there were only a few of them left, living more from hunting than from working the soil. I often bought a whole deer for two dollars from one of them living in the middle of the woods, on Silver Creek. When demand was low, I could buy a deer for one dollar. In a single week of a particularly severe winter this new Leatherstocking shot down more than fifty deer and, because he had trouble hauling them, tied them up high in the trees. After he had finished his hunt, he went into the woods with his wagon, brought down the solid-frozen, preserved deer from their trees, and went house to house in Highland selling them, mostly with success. What he could not sell was salted down, and the

---

3. For a French-Swiss treatment of Highland of the period, see *Extraits de correspondance d'un colon americain sur la Colonie suisse à Highland près de Saint-Louis* par M. Rilliet de Constant, colonel fédéral (Berne: Imprimérie Haller, 1849).

deer haunches were smoked into ham. A less successful version of the same speculation was that of another Anglo-American, who caught a whole wagonload of fish in the watery regions of Illinois and Indiana and tried to sell them in the fish-poor region of Highland's environs on his return. Business was good for the first few days, and he was able to sell some of the fish, but in the end the summer heat caused them to begin to stink. Finally the man had to dump the rest of his freight somewhere on the prairie, where the fish rotted away in peace and became fertilizer.

As I have already said, the rapid growth of the population in Highland produced a severe housing shortage in the town, and many attempts with Blattner's help to rent a house had no result. With so many in our party we could not remain for long in an inn, partly due to the large expenditure and partly due to our longing for a home of our own. When I complained to the two Köpflis, they informed me in confidence that their younger brother Dr. Kaspar Köpfli, a rather restless spirit, would be leaving Highland in a few days to go to Ohio. His house would then be standing empty, and they would have it to rent. They would be happy to let us have it, but it would not suffice due to the peculiar legal arrangements in that country. Several persons were already speculating on the house, and if one of them moved in immediately after the doctor's departure and took possession *de facto*, it would be a difficult and tedious business dislodging him. A formal trial would have to take place in a court in Edwardsville, eighteen miles away, and with delays and appeals, we could not rely on taking possession until the middle or even the end of winter. They promised to let me know the precise day and hour of their brother's departure, whereupon I was to send one member of my family along with a portion of my baggage to take possession of the house. It would then be very hard to dislodge me, more even than if the house were formally leased to me. I suspect they had already promised the house to several other parties, but that they wanted to win us for their settlement and now were embarrassed over how to cancel the earlier agreements. If I just took possession of the house, they would have a good excuse, and so I consulted with Joseph Suppiger, who was justice of the peace. He approved this procedure, and I decided to follow the advice. We lay in wait, and no sooner was Dr. Köpfli the younger in his wagon and on his way than our Léon and our trunks were in the empty house. We took possession, which was formally confirmed later by the Köpflis.

Now we threw ourselves head over heels into setting up the house. Country carpenters supplied the simplest furniture, but the primary matter—what always came first with me—was to put up a shower in its own enclosure. This was pretty primitive, a large barrel as reservoir that Léon filled every day, with a large nozzle that the town tinner added to it. As soon as a water drain was installed, we could resume our usual morning baths. The house had two rooms and a storage chamber on the ground floor, in addition to two large attic rooms. I occupied the rooms below, while Bernays resided upstairs until he could find his own home. As is normal in the American West, the cookstove stood in the courtyard in an open wooden shed in the summer; in the winter it would be moved to the living room, where it became a heating stove as well. My sons and Léon slept in a sort of barn behind the house. And so our household matters were in the best order. Completing our arrangements occupied us totally for a considerable time, whether it was organizing the garden (which included a small vineyard), unpacking our things, or becoming acquainted with the area and people.

Finally we came to the big question, which was what we were to do to earn some money. Bernays and I had deposited our capital of $500 each in the Bank of Missouri, but the money we had brought to Highland had begun to melt away, particularly because I bought two parcels of Congress Land of forty acres each on the edge of town at the government price of $1.25 an acre. Once this money was at an end and we had to draw on our deposit in the bank, our means came to be painfully reduced, particularly if we expected to start a business after getting to know the local situation. We now passed our free evening hours discussing how we were to earn money.

Bernays remained with his first idea, which was to start a general store. I pursued the idea developed on the sea voyage and since then dramatically developed, which was to establish a medical spa. This was something entirely lacking in the West in those days, although it had been so successful in the East in the case of Dr. Karl Munde in Florence, and Wesselhöft in Battleboro.[4] When I proposed this idea to the Köpflis, they were enthusiastic; seeing it as a great thing for the settlement, they declared themselves ready to do anything possible for the new undertaking, promising they would participate themselves. After long discussion, a draft contract to erect a medical spa was drawn up between the Köpflis and me. It is still in my papers. In this draft, the Köpflis obligated themselves to contribute a property of ten acres located on the same beautifully wooded hill where they had their own home. They also committed themselves to build within two years and at their own expense a building for the spa according to my instructions and plans, and to drill an artesian well for it. Further, they were to see to clearing the lot in order to turn it into a park and to make four cows available to the institution. For my part, I was to take care of all the interior facilities of the spa, both in terms of apparatus and furniture, and I

4. Dr. Robert Wesselhöft had studied at Jena University and emigrated to America in the early 1830s. In 1841 he moved to the Boston area, where he became a homeopathic physician in Cambridge. He established a water-cure spa in Brattleboro, Vermont, which Boernstein mistakenly calls "Battleboro." See Körner, *Element,* 33, 37, 176; Cazden, *Social History.*

had to commit myself to manage the spa for eight years. All payments for servants, bath attendants, care of patients and the like was to be shared equally through a common fund. The entire property was declared equal property of the two partners, and at the end of eight years it was to be auctioned off to one of them at the highest bid. The profits of the first three years were to be dedicated to enlarging and decorating the spa, but from the fourth year on the two partners were to divide the profits. Further, I received a free apartment in the spa for my family and myself.

We were entirely in agreement over these primary points, and an architect proceeded to draw up plans for the construction. My Léon and two workers set to work clearing and marking the paths of the park. Test boring began on the well, which gave us no grounds for concern, for one always hit fresh, cold water at the depth of twenty-five or thirty feet. All prospects were extremely positive, and as soon as the newspapers reported on it, the idea received general applause, particularly in St. Louis. In Highland the population appeared ready to make considerable contributions for our venture to be possible, because the benefits of success for the community were generally understood. However, on the very day when we were to sign the contract and seriously undertake to make the enterprise succeed, a sad turn of events occurred that would alter the destiny of Highland and postpone all our plans until the indefinite future. There was a sudden outbreak of cholera, which had hitherto spared Highland. The concerns and terrors of the moment claimed the full attention, of both the community and its individuals.

Medical Intermezzo

The outbreak of cholera in Highland had an important impact on me, upsetting my immediate plans and reminding me of the old proverb, "*On révient toujours à ses premiers amours.*"[1] It was just too remarkable for words. Never, among all the plans and projects discussed so intensely in Europe and on the crossing, had it ever occurred to me to see my knowledge as a physician and my medical studies as a means of advancement in America. I was hostile to the medical business, at least as it was practiced by members of the physicians' coterie, and as I had absorbed it during my own medical studies. Further, the minimal results that the art of healing had to offer, after all that study, awoke a doubtful spirit in me. I no longer believed in the *verba magistri*[2] or the infallibility of the academy. It was for precisely this reason that I had given up a medical career and taken up drama and journalism, which promised me more.

Despite this distaste, I had retained a lively interest in medicine as a science to whose study I had devoted so many years. Even when I was immersed in an entirely different profession, I continued to keep abreast of the more significant developments of medical science through reading and personal contacts with active physicians. Then, as the first idea of emigration to America was developing, and we discussed our plans to settle somewhere in the wilderness and lead an independent existence as farmers, I grasped the necessity of reviving my rather rusty medical knowledge. In order to help as a physician in advice and deed for my family and neighbors, I used my last year in Paris to supplement and complete my medical library. I was the most enthusiastic user of the reading room of the *Palais Royal,* where I earnestly studied the splendid Parisian holdings of professional journals of medicine. When I had committed myself to emigration, I set about gathering a compendious and thorough pharmacy for home and travel, adding to it a fine surgical valise. During the twenty years I had been married, I had always handled members of the family when they were sick, always with success, and so I hoped to be more than equal to this task.

During my negotiations over the spa, the Köpflis had encouraged me to take their brother's place as a family physician when he left Highland. The only German physician within a range of twenty miles and more, Dr. Ryhiner, could not possibly meet the demand. I had repeatedly declined on the grounds that I would not want to compete with a physician so

---

1. French, "One always returns to his first loves."
2. Latin, "The words of the master."

scholarly, energetic and beloved as Dr. Ryhiner. In response the Köpflis declared that there could be no talk of competition in this situation; although competition is the very soul of American business, Dr. Ryhiner would see it as a relief, for he often lacked the time to fill the demands placed on him. How often it was he would be called deep into Illinois, even to Indiana, due to his great renown. To make these journeys would require two, three and more days, and during this time the settlement and the area were bereft of all medical assistance. Further, while the spa was being built, I would become better known in the region and win a circle of customers who would later benefit the spa. At first my hostility to a usual physician's practice in keeping with the old academic clichés was stronger than all these temptations. I stuck to my refusal and only conceded that I was ready to practice in my home, and then only for sick persons willing to be treated hydropathically. A tin sign advertising this was placed on my door, and the malady, as they say, took its own course.

Other than an old Swiss by the name of Kuler, whose persistent swamp fever resisted the highest doses of quinine and arsenic and who was cured by a water treatment, I had no patients. The reason was that the Highlanders were good friends of a glass of wine or beer, but they had no interest in water, and they had a very low opinion of it as a healing agent. So I was sitting, smoking a cigar in my garden one fine summer evening and discussing plans for the future spa with Bernays, when two farm wagons accompanied by Highlanders drew up to our house at a slow pace, halting at our door. A deputation entered and announced that a farmer had been in St. Louis with his produce, and on the trip back he fell ill of cholera and could go no further. His neighbor, the owner of the other wagon, wanted to remain with him in Highland and seek medical help. He would have been at Dr. Ryhiner's, but the doctor had been called to Edwardsville and would only return in two days, so he turned to me for help, as I was also a physician.

I went out to the wagon, where a crowd of curious had gathered at the instantly, spreading news of the first case of cholera in the locality. I found the sick man fully conscious but already in collapse, with rapidly sinking life forces. I told his companion that there was little hope, but I was ready to do an act of kindness and take the sick man into my home, doing what I could for him. The poor man was taken carefully into the house and laid down to rest on my son's bed in the barn, after which his companion departed with thanks. I watched at the sickbed through the night with my sons, using the methods we had used in the Vienna and Paris epidemics. Everything was done to save the man, but his decline in strength was already so general and rapid that all attempts at help were in vain. The poor man had left St. Louis early in the morning, the illness had broken out right after crossing the river in the Illinois Bottoms. He had been hauled in an uncovered wagon in the burning sun for eight full hours, without medical help, without massage or movement, without even a glass of water. As a result it was easy to explain why his life force was almost entirely exhausted when he arrived. Still, his end was painless, and he slipped away softly and peacefully, with only a deep sigh indicating his last breath. His friend and neighbor came at sunrise to receive the sad news. I issued a certificate of death for the family, and a justice of the peace countersigned it. The friend bought a simple coffin, the dead man was laid in it, and he was carried off in the very wagon that brought him. The sad caravan departed Highland toward the distant farm where the wife and children of the man anxiously awaited him, their sole provider. Now they were to receive news of his death as well as his corpse with no forewarning.

In view of the family's loss I did not have the heart to ask anything for care and handling, having discovered that the man was not prosperous. So I had to bear the costs incurred when I took the bedding, linen and everything that had touched the sick man out into a clear place behind the house the next day and burn it. The episode had aroused a good deal of attention in such a small place as Highland, however, and when cases of cholera and virulent diarrhea broke out a few days later, I had a substantial practice for the first time. It is probable that it was my resolute conduct with Highland's first cholera victim that caused people to trust me. Then, when the first true case of Asiatic cholera appeared in Highland, I was called in preference, and I had as much to do as Dr. Ryhiner. Soon my little portable pharmacy no longer sufficed. I had to call for medicines from St. Louis, for there was no pharmacy for miles around, and what physicians produced themselves was unreliable. My sons ground the drugs in large mortars, brewed extracts and decocts, rolled pills, divided powders into doses and so on, so that we all had plenty to do. Soon cholera began to break out in the farms of the area and in neighboring settlements, and I was so repeatedly called out that I had to get myself a horse and buggy. My practice rose to unexpected heights in no time, and when I left Highland I had earned a clear profit of two thousand dollars in the course of a year of residence.

Most of this, to be sure, was not in cash but partly in services, partly in due bills. A due bill was a small slip of paper like the I.O.U.s that play such a role in English novels. On them the debtor writes the amount and payment date of his debt, and it is used as a sort of paper money for the payment of debts to others. In those days cash was a rarity in the countryside of the American West, only appearing sporadically after harvest or following the arrival of many immigrant groups. What little cash existed was usually saved to pay taxes, so that ordinary sales relied on due bills. These rested on a solid foundation in Highland, for all residents were sedentary, held land, and were honorable, upright people. I paid my shoemaker, tailor, butcher and all craftsmen with the notes I received in payment, and all accepted them without protest. This was because there were variety stores, inns and such all over Highland whose owners would pay cash for these notes at a small discount. To the credit of the Highlanders I must stress that, when I later left Highland and I still had $1,500 of these notes, I left them with Justice of the Peace Suppiger and good old Eggen to settle, and I did not lose $5 of the whole. That was when Highland was still in its golden age; mutual trust and goodwill still prevailed, and one had hardly heard of a theft or any other crime against property. Only a very few house doors had anything like a lock or a latch, and when one went out, he leaned a scrap of wood across the door to say, "No one is at home." This was respected by everyone. Strangers, crooks and wandering tramps found no reception anywhere; rather they were quickly and energetically encouraged to move on, so that Highland preserved a character of rural repose and untroubled peace. I wish and hope that modern Highland, which has made much progress, has at least preserved most of this honorable character.

There was now no doubt whatsoever that we would remain in Highland, and both Bernays and I set about to assure ourselves a permanent home. I bought a very pretty house with a garden from Kinne the saddler, and Bernays bought a house for himself, where he opened a general store for items of all sorts. Called "variety stores" in the country, these were where sugar and coffee, dry goods and iron goods, boots and hats, perfume and patent medicines, even ready-made clothes and cleaning materials were sold. Bernays had gone to St. Louis and had bought a great stock of all of these articles at the cheapest possible price with the support of his many friends there. He was hence well supplied, and his cultivated, cosmopolitan manner made him many customers. It was particularly the French Swiss who came to him only, because he could chat with them in their native tongue. In short, Bernays did excellent business, and in a little time he had overcome all the cares and troubles of a beginner. Further, he had built other relations with St. Louis and could use these to buy such agricultural products as butter, eggs and cheese from farmers in and around Highland, send these to St. Louis in large shipments, and sell them there at a profit. Because the farmers would often take goods from him in the place of cash, he had a double profit. Later he also established a brewery, which did a very good business. He would infallibly have been on his way to becoming a rich man had his brewery not burned down one night, uninsured, so that he lost the fruits of a year of hard work. It is only after this hard blow that he gave up on Highland, responding to my pressing call to come to St. Louis and dedicate himself again to journalism.

I had decided at that time never again to leave Highland. Having come to know farming from close range, I had proved to myself what all my friends had told me, which was that it was not only unsuitable, but even intolerable and irritating to people such as us, who had been spoiled by the hyper-civilization of Paris. On the other hand, my life as an independent American country physician among this sympathetic and friendly population was highly attractive, all the more so once I had become acquainted with my colleague Dr. Ryhiner. He was an amiable, pleasing, noble and humane man, free of any trace of envy over money. The duties of a country physician in such a community as Highland, with its rather uniform population, were also by no means difficult or exhausting. There are only a few frequently appearing illnesses endemic to an area to which a physician has to give full attention and thoroughly study, such as active or latent malarial fever, dysentery, and so on.

I had extraordinary luck in the course of the cholera epidemic. Out of 119 persons sick with cholera, only 22 died, which is an extremely positive result either then or now. These 22 were nearly all persons who came for treatment when they were more or less in a state of terminal collapse. I call this luck, which is what it was, because all treatment by physicians of this illness was then and is now at best only empirical and symptomatic. I noticed that the epidemic that year had an essentially bilious character, and that the influence of malaria on the moist prairie also made itself known. I thus followed the example of English physicians in India, who used strong doses of calomel and quinine in similar circumstances.[3] This was a procedure used by Dr. Edward Jörg in Belleville, who had lived long years in the South and the tropics and who recommended this dosage in his great work on tropical medicine; unfortunately his advice was largely ignored at the time.[4] When called to a sick person whose strength had not yet failed, I would have him take twelve grains of calomel and twelve grains of quinine, repeating the dosage in a quarter hour. Then followed a grain of calomel and a grain of quinine every quarter hour until the stool was firm and yellow in color, vomit and cramps had ceased, and the temperature of the body had returned to normal, which almost always happened. Further, to calm the vomiting I would give him an effervescent powder, and when the situation in the house permitted it, there

---

3. Calomel was mercuric oxide, frequently used in the nineteenth century as a result of Dr. Benjamin Rush's "heroic medicine." It frequently poisoned the patient, leading to loss of teeth, hair, and life.

4. On Dr. Eduard Jörg (1808-1864) in Belleville, Illinois, see Körner, *Element*, 265; *NUC*, vol. 281, 240, has three books by Jörg on tropical fevers, *Darstellung des nachteiligen Einflusses des Tropenklima's und der Behandlung der Tropenkrankheiten, des gelben Fiebers und der asiatischen Cholera* (Leipzig, 1851); *Anweisung die Tropenkrankheiten, die asiatische Cholera und das gelbe Fieber zu verhüten oder sicher zu heilen . . .* (Leipzig, 1854), and *Die gänzliche Unterdrückung der asiatischen Cholera, den europäischen Staatsregierungen als aufführbahr dargetan . . .* (Leipzig, 1855). Jörg also anonymously published *Briefe aus den Vereinigten Staaten von Nord-Amerika* (Leipzig, 1853).

would be a hydropathic treatment consisting of strong rubbing with wet linen cloths, followed by aggressive toweling with a woolen blanket. By these means, I achieved the positive results described, using large doses of calomel without causing salivation. At the beginning, when I was still working cautiously with small doses of calomel, salivation was inevitable and excruciating.

In the midst of my activities, after the epidemic had almost run its course, I myself had to pay my dues both for my intense agitation as well as for being in the unaccustomed American climate. I fell ill with a massive, painful case of diarrhea, during which my colleague Dr. Ryhiner treated me with friendly collegiality and self-sacrifice, even taking over my patients. He had me back on my feet in a week.

I was barely recovered when I wanted to go out riding; I had my horse saddled and rode out the back entrance to the yard. The brief, intense illness had greatly weakened me, however, and I had hardly ridden fifty paces and brought the horse to a gallop when I suffered a fainting spell. All went black before my eyes, and I lost consciousness, sliding backwards off the horse and landing on the back of my head. This is how passers-by found me, my dear horse standing over me snorting with anxiety. I was lifted up and taken into my house, and Dr. Ryhiner was called by my anxious family. I only returned to consciousness several hours later, but I could not recall a thing which happened, neither that I had been ill nor that I had gone riding and fallen from a horse. It was only gradually, days later, that everything gradually returned to my consciousness. Physically, I had stiff limbs and some pain, but my head had struck soft ground, so that I had no injury to my skull. I had to remain another week in bed, but this period paid my price of entry to America in full. Through the next thirteen years I was never again ill and spent not a day in bed.

Hardly had I recovered than I was surprised by news of my own death. My friend Olshausen sent me an Eastern paper in which it was reported that I had died in St. Louis of cholera, appending to the bare report of death a positive obituary. Naturally I immediately sent the *Anzeiger des Westens* a humorous correction in which I thanked the Eastern paper for giving me the rare pleasure of being able to read my obituary while still alive;[5] as uncomfortable as it might be for me, however, I had to declare to them that I was indeed alive, that my numerous patients could not do without me, and that I would be even more necessary for the spa that we would soon open. Many papers reprinted the report of my death, just as many printed my

---

5. "Ein Brief von einem Verstorbenem" ["Letter from a Dead Man"], letter dated from Highland, 2 June 1849, *AW,* weekly, vol. 14, no. 34, 9 June 1849, p. 4, from the daily edition of 5 June 1849. He took the opportunity to sing the praises of Highland, Illinois, and to tout his forthcoming water-cure spa.

recall of it, and I received messages of affection from friends all over both Europe and America on this occasion. Still, for people who did not keep good track of things, I was indeed dead, for it had been reported in the papers. Later I would be able to read my biographical entry in the first edition of *Meyer's Conversations-Lexikon*, which ended, "Died in 1849 of cholera in St. Louis." There is an old folk saying, "Whoever is falsely reported dead will have a long life." This has proved to be true in my case, for I have survived the report of my death by thirty-two years.

I was extremely alive and active in Highland in those days, for besides my strong practice as a physician, I intensely studied American history and politics and supported the formation of a Reading Society. This was a sort of social club to which Blattner contributed two large rooms, one as a reading room, the other as a room for games. We had many newspapers, both American and European, as well as the newest brochures and pamphlets. We also intended to create a small library. We had meetings, read and discussed the news, debated the events of the day and in short fulfilled our purpose to entertain and educate one another. I am told that after my departure the game room won out over the reading room, so that the Reading Society was finally dissolved. It was reconstituted in 1858, however, and still flourishes. I also created an amateur theater. A temporary stage was erected in Blattner's large salon, where my wife and I, Mrs. Bernays and several gifted amateurs had great success performing the *Strassenjungen von Paris*[6] and other pieces to great crowds of Highland residents and farmers from the area.

Along with theatrical performances came winter, with all its difficult conditions on the prairie. The roads in the town became bottomless, for although hard frosts were rare, either rain or snow predominated, quickly followed by thaws. There were, of course, no sidewalks along the unpaved streets. If one took a step beyond his threshold, he sank deep in the mire. Even with high boots reaching to the knee, it was a work of art to cross the street to the post office and get one's mail. The Reading Society and all social gatherings suffered from this interruption of communication, and it became increasingly eerie in the town, as if all were under involuntary house-arrest. My lovely idyll of American country life lost its fresh color, becoming ever grayer. My medical practice began to become unpleasant, even burdensome. Patients who came for office visits brought mountains of mud and filth into my office on their boots and left a good deal of it behind when they left, so that my quarters had to be scrubbed every day. The rounds I had to make became dangerous for horse and buggy, often placing me in mortal danger, especially when I went out on the prairie to scattered farms. In the end I had to send my eldest son ahead on a second horse to check the

6. German, *The Street Boys of Paris*.

solidity of the ground so that we wouldn't fall into a swampy hole, particularly at night. Such holes could lead to the buggy being stuck until help could be fetched from the next farm.

The winter so passed in a manner less than pleasing, and I began to long for spring and summer. This is no marvel, given that a year earlier I had been still enjoying Paris, with its luxurious civilization. The contrast was all too crass.

So I stood in a bad mood one March morning under the roof of my house's porch, which formed a sort of balcony, and I looked out on the bleak scene. It had been snowing for a week, and suddenly there was a thaw with warm rain. The entire prairie was flooded. As far as the eye could see there was water, with houses merely sticking out. No mail had reached Highland for four days, neither a post coach nor a two-wheeled post-chaise. We were cut off from the world. Then I suddenly saw the familiar post-chaise, carefully rolling toward us with a span of three horse, splashing through the water. Defying death, I drew on my boots of Russian leather and waded to the post office. There I found my delayed mail, including a letter from Arthur Olshausen informing me that his editor of years, Wilhelm Weber, had been elected justice of the peace in the southern part of St. Louis and that he had to take up his office immediately.[7] Olshausen asked, in fact he conjured me on the basis of our friendship, to come and help him in his time of need. I must come to St. Louis at once to take over the editorship of the *Anzeiger des Westens.* What was I to do? Only a short time before I had graciously declined a very advantageous offer from Horace Greeley[8] to head a new Whig paper to be established in New York. But Olshausen appealed to our friendship, and I could not leave him in the lurch. So I decided then and there to go to St. Louis, although even today I regard the year I spent in Highland as one of the most enjoyable of my life. I retain even now a pleasant memory of fair Highland.

---

7. Wilhelm Weber (1808-1852), son of a government official in Altenburg, Saxony, studied at Jena University 1828-31, but was compromised by sympathies with the Polish uprising of late 1830. In 1834 he emigrated to St. Clair County, Illinois, serving as librarian of the collection which would be the core of the later Mercantile Library in St. Louis. He became the editor of the *Anzeiger des Westens* in February 1836, which he continued until 1850. He withdrew both because of illness at home and because of his own indifferent business management. See Körner, *Element*, 317-21. For his nomination and election as justice of the peace, see *AW,* vol. 15, no. 97, 12 February 1850, p. 2; *AW,* vol. 15, no. 105, 21 February 1850, p. 3. He was mentioned as a justice of the peace in the final chapter of Boernstein, *Mysteries*, 301.

8. Horace Greeley (1811-1872) was one of the principal journalists of the mid-nineteenth century, and noted for his support of leftist writers, including Fourier, Marx, and Engels. His *New York Tribune* was a leading mouthpiece of antislavery Whigs, then Republicans. He was defeated as presidential candidate for the Liberal Republicans and the Democrats against Grant in 1872. See *ACAB*, 3: 734-41.

Back *in* St. Louis
(1850)

There were only three closely written pages in Arthur Olshausen's letter, and yet they exercised a decisive influence on the direction of my life, leading me to take a novel path without long consideration or hesitation. Even today I cannot understand how rashly and decisively I went along with Olshausen's proposal, and how I threw away all the plans I had made for the rest of my life without a second thought and without looking back. I had departed St. Louis after the most unhappy of experiences, vowing never to return. I had been almost a full year in Highland, and during this entire time I had never felt any desire or need to visit St. Louis. I had fully expected to remain in Highland, for otherwise I would not have bought a house or made myself a comfortable home there. I had a pretty house that was comfortable and well furnished, a charming garden that gave me a great deal of joy, and a household with comfortable equipment, a horse and buggy, a cow, chickens, dogs and cats—in short all the elements of a good country life. On top of that I had an income that was more than adequate, and I was loved and respected in the settlement. Despite all of this, Olshausen's letter was enough to cause me to give it all up without regret and take a position in St. Louis that offered a lower income, much effort, and even more trouble and distress. It was the old story of the retired war-horse who throws back his head, whinnies and breaks into a gallop with his stiffening legs when he hears the bugle sounding charge! Whoever has once dedicated himself to journalism or the theater is never free again, for those two professions never release their hostages.

Discussions with my wife lasted barely half an hour, and the decision to go to St. Louis was irrevocably made. A letter went off to Olshausen within the hour announcing that I would be coming, and coming right away. Olshausen had enjoined me to move instantaneously, for Weber had to take up his own office at once. We wrote on 3 March, so I had to leave by 5 March at the latest. And so there was an entire household to dissolve at once: the house had to be sold, along with horse and buggy, all the equipment and a cow; all the unnecessary material brought from Europe had to be auctioned off; the due bills received had to be turned into cash and a mass of debts collected; and debts of my own paid, and obligations fulfilled. I had to pass this entire tedious business, which would have claimed the full attention of any man, to my wife, who carried out the whole difficult assignment with surprising dispatch. With that inborn talent women have of resolving impasses, she put my departure from Highland into much better order than I could ever have done myself.

I had to make arrangements to depart at once, so I went to Postmaster Blattner to get his good advice. The information he had to impart, however, was most distressing. We could not rely on the postal coach that passed through Highland three times a week, because the concessionaire had written Blattner that he would not provide a change of horses so long as the prairie was completely flooded and the Illinois Bottoms a bottomless swamp. The concessionaire had decided to suspend the postal coach, which would return in a better season when the roads were passable again. I also could not expect a farmer to take me there, either, for no one would risk his horse and wagon in the present state of the roads. If I absolutely had to go to St. Louis, there was no alternative to the two-wheeled post-chaise due to pass through Highland on 5 March on its return from Edwardsville. If I did not mind some discomfort, it was sure to get me to St. Louis. There being no choice, I had to agree to this proposal, and the matter was settled.

I then threw myself into preparations. I wrote out all necessary instructions for my wife to liquidate our household in Highland, packed absolute necessities into a bag, and awaited the arrival of the post-chaise on the morning of 5 March, ready to travel. Finally, it slowly rolled into Highland. The postman, who also performed the tasks of a conductor, was informed that he had to take two passengers along, my Gustav and me, for I did not trust myself alone in perilous St. Louis. One horse more was harnessed up, and we were to leave within the hour. The hardest part was finding a place for Gustav and me in the two-wheeled cart. The cart consisted of a basket of wood and wicker about five feet square, resting on an axle with two wheels. It was joined to a wagon shaft to which a saddled horse was hitched, on which the postman rode. The other three horses—we were traveling with four horses—were joined to the cart with temporary leads and reins. The large postal sack contained three days of delayed letters from at least twenty post offices in Illinois and even more in Ohio, Indiana, and so on, going to St. Louis. This sack had swollen to such a size that it overflowed the rim of the basket. Sitting on it was a great gymnastic accomplishment, unless one wanted to fall out every hundred paces and fly into the mire of the road, because there was nothing to hang onto. Something had to be done, so I rammed a couple of short boards vertically between the sack and the rear of the basket. I wrapped each of the boards with a strong rope, which I anchored with a pair of nails, and each of us tied ourselves to it after we had taken our seats so that we would not be thrown out with every jounce. Our bags were lashed in front, and at last we were off. But within the very first hour we had established that this manner of sitting was intolerable over the long term. We had to hold our legs stretched straight ahead of us, so that they became so stiff that they went numb or produced leg cramps. If one sat toward the front in order to let his feet hang outside the basket, he risked having his shins shattered by the hooves of the horses, which flew with every crack of the whip. But when we remained in the rear, the horses tossed back such a mass of road mire and filth on us passengers that after the first hour we were completely drenched and could hardly see out of our eyes. Soon the cloudbursts of the last several days resumed with full force, washing the dirt off of us but soaking us to the skin, so that even today I marvel that I did not catch a mortal illness then.

I need not go further on the other adventures of this dreadful journey, our getting stuck or our crossing swollen streams. We were thrown out twice, fortunately falling in very soft mud. To make a long story short, after innumerable problems, we had only managed to reach Troy by the time it grew dark. There the postman declared we had to stay the night, for he did not want to continue along the swampy roads in the dark. I was glad to agree, for we needed reinforcement, recovery and peace, too. The inn where we stayed was by no means the worst of its kind. A very substantial dinner was bolted down rather than eaten, and then we went to bed, allowing our clothing to dry out overnight in the kitchen. Our sleeping room, which held six beds, was shared with four other travelers, cattle traders returning from St. Louis who talked about their transactions there late into the night.

This would not have prevented me from sleeping, however, because I was deathly tired and thoroughly exhausted by the terrible jolting of the cart and our superhuman efforts to stay in. It was another element that made sleeping impossible. As soon as the lights were put out, all the nooks and crannies of the room came noisily and weirdly alive. Legions of rats emerged from their holes and hiding places, running here and there, eagerly seeking something to eat. You could hear them clambering up the table and jumping down from it. You heard them rattling about and gnawing in the half-hollow walls and above the ceiling of the room. In the end they regarded my well-oiled Russian leather boots as welcome booty indeed. I vainly tried to shoo them away, but they commenced gnawing and eating the boots. There was nothing left for me to do than to take the filthy boots into bed with me so as to render them a more effective defense. My other roommates had the same experience, so the night passed in continuous combat and defense, without sleep. We were glad when the servant called us before the break of day and delivered our dried clothing. A huge American breakfast was quickly eaten, and we resumed our journey at dawn.

It rained in streams, as it had the previous day, and all the previous horrors were repeated with double force. Finally we descended from the bluffs into the Illinois Bottoms, which were a sea of muck and mud as far as the eye could see. Not a trace of a road could be discovered, and we had to rely totally on the instinct and feelings of the wise horse. At last, when we had traveled a full twenty-eight hours from Highland, we arrived on the bank of the Mississippi. By five o'clock we were in St. Louis. You can imagine our condition, and at least for my part, I shall recall this 5-6 March with a shudder my entire life long.

Of course I had to register in a hotel of the second rank, for it was impossible in those days to rent a furnished room, but I took my meals at Olshausen's table. I was invited to do this until I had a household of my own. Mügge also came right away to greet me, and we passed the evening at Olshausen's, as tired and worn as we were. We sat with them until well past midnight, eagerly talking about everything past and future. With Mügge as with Olshausen the friendly, cozy tone of a North German home was elevated and rendered more beautiful by the American sense of independence. There were readings, music was played, the events of the day were earnestly discussed, and over everything there reigned a cheerful and hospitable spirit binding everything together. I had missed this sense of German family life during my residence in Paris, but I felt good and at home here.

Now the serious part of my life began. On 8 March 1850, I took over the editing of the *Anzeiger des Westens*.[1] The conditions of my employment were anything but splendid, but they corresponded to the conditions of the day. My monthly salary was $60, but I had the assurance that every 100 new subscriptions would raise my salary by $2, so that a rise of 1,000 new subscribers would bring my salary from $60 to $80. That was by no means the equivalent of what I had been earning in Highland, but I had such a firm faith in my star, such a solid conviction that I would make a great future for myself in St. Louis, that I never looked back with regret on what I had given up.

I can confess here that, at the beginning of my career as an American editor, I felt quite out of place, and I would probably have been happy to go back if it had been possible. There I sat, a thorough greenhorn. I was hardly aware of the general outline of American history and politics, entirely ignorant of the situation in the state of Missouri, and even more ignorant of the local party situation in St. Louis. I was only imperfectly acquainted with the English language, and I knew little or nothing about the political jargon, the slogans and symbols of the various parties. And now a municipal election was coming up, and I was supposed to carry the banner of our party for the most important German paper in town.

---

1. *AW,* vol. 15, no. 118, 8 March 1850, p. 2, has a departure notice from Wilhelm Weber as well as a programmatic statement from Boernstein. A contrast between Weber's unfocused liberalism and Boernstein's aggressiveness is given in two rare copies of the annual calendar poster delivered to subscribers at New Year's Day, for 1850 (under Weber) and 1854 (under Boernstein), preserved at the Institut für Auslandsbeziehungen, Stuttgart, copies in WHM-SL, exhibit collection "Mit Feder und Hammer! Die Deutschen in St. Louis, Missouri." Boernstein's "prophetic" poem there looks forward to a time when Queen Victoria and the other crowned heads of Europe are deposed and trying to make a living as theatrical performers before a raucous crowd of their former subjects.

Masthead of the Anzeiger des Westens *in the 1850s. Courtesy of the Missouri Historical Society.*

At least I did not have to worry about our political denomination, because in those days there were only two political parties in the United States, the Democratic Party and the Whig Party. The entire German population of St. Louis (amounting to about twenty-five thousand) belonged to the Democratic Party, as was generally the case in the West. This is because the Whig Party was then too deeply involved in temperance, fanaticism and nativism, so that it was loathed by German Americans. In all of St. Louis there were only three Germans in the Whig Party: the wholesale merchant Adolphus Meier, the merchant Adolph Abeles, and the linen merchant Friedrich Reichard, who was called "Shirt-Reichard" to distinguish himself from others of the name. These three were regarded by the mass of the German population as monsters and apostates and were attacked in every possible manner, although they had a very honorable position among American Whigs. My program was thus predetermined, and I did not have to worry myself about it. The *Anzeiger des Westens* was a Democratic paper and had to remain that way if I did not want to lose all my readers.

I was in much worse shape when it came to my lack of local knowledge. I did not know a single one of the many candidates for municipal office. Knowing nothing of their antecedents, I had to rely on what people told me. This included the American wire-pullers and party leaders, who would sit in my office for hours chewing tobacco, spitting in my stove and talking me to death. Then there were the petty ward politicians who wanted to put in their protégés as aldermen or delegates. Then came the various candidates themselves, recommending themselves to my support. I endured dreadful days. Now I can admit without restraint what I let myself be talked into in those weeks without understanding the first thing about it; how many times I was reduced to saying "Yes, sir," or "Of course, sir," and the like; how helpless I would feel at the end of those long, hot days. Finally I reared up and made a solid decision. I had always had too much of a conscience to praise or recommend candidates who were unknown to me. So I declared in my paper with a naïveté rather rare for an American editor that, due to my lack of knowledge of local situations and persons, the *Anzeiger des Westens* would endorse no party in the municipal election but remain neutral. The paper would stand equally open for the tickets and statements of both parties and would not take a partisan stand; it would leave the decision to the people itself, the citizens of St. Louis. I stuck to this, so that afterward I had the time to learn something about the place and people.[2]

---

2. *AW,* vol. 15, no. 136, 22 March 1850, p. 2; and vol. 15, no. 138, 31 March 1850, p. 2, stating that the removal of Thomas Hart Benton from the Senate did not necessitate division in local elections.

This was a time of transition in the political life of America when the old parties were in the process of breaking up. Both the Democratic and Whig parties had their factions. In the Democratic Party there were Barnburners, who laid the foundation for the later Free Soil Party with their platform of "Free Soil, Free Speech, Free Labor, Free Men!"[3] In the Whig party, which did not want to continue to be dominated by Southern Fire-Eaters, a large part of the Northern Whigs inclined to the Free Soil Party while another part made common cause with the nativists. The split in the Democratic Party was more important, for it cast its shadow over the slave states as well, so that in the presidential election of 1848, the Whig ticket was elected with General Zachary Taylor and Millard Fillmore. This was the last victory of the Whig Party, for from that moment they went downhill, and a few years later they had completely vanished. Some of them went to the Republican Party, some to the Know-Nothings. In Missouri, in those years the Benton Democrats were also formed, and although restricted to a slave state, they inclined to the Free Soil Party. The combination was very attractive to me as it was to Germans in general.

Still, I do not want to deal with events before their time, and so I will restrict myself to my own experiences. I passed through a hard, bitter time of testing in the editorial office of the *Anzeiger,* and it was a considerable while before I recovered my faith in myself. On top of that there was the custom at that time in the German American press—or rather abuse—which required one to treat journalistic opponents in a violent tone. As a result I was heaped with the meanest abuse, cursing and libel, and my hands were full dealing with only the most infamous attacks.

My wife and children were still in Highland while I lived alone in St. Louis in the most uncomfortable circumstances, pursuing an occupation that gradually grew intolerable. Still, even for me there was an hour of deliverance. My wife took almost two months to liquidate our household in a satisfactory manner, resolving everything for the best. The house was sold without loss to Captain Woldemar Fischer, the horse and buggy to Dr. John Olshausen, and everything else at public auction. On 20 April my wife and children were finally able to join me. In the meantime I had established a new home. Although it was of the simplest, my means allowed nothing better. The greatest problem was finding a small house for us that was not too far from the printing shop of the *Anzeiger* and the business district of the city. Small, cheap cottages in such central locations were very hard to find and

---

3. Eric Foner, *Free Soil, Free Labor, Free Men: The Ideology of the Republican Party before the Civil War* (Oxford University Press, 1970) deals extensively with these and other elements of what would become the Republican Party. The peculiar contribution of Benton Democracy to the formation of the Missouri Republican Party is an epic which has not found its bard.

Frontispiece of the English-language edition of Boernstein's novel, The Mysteries of St. Louis. *Lithograph by E. & C. Robyn, St. Louis, 1852. Photograph of Steven Rowan's own copy.*

lease. A small cottage stood on the southeast corner of Third and Cedar, probably built in the first quarter of the century. It contained a room and a salon on an elevated ground floor, a room and salon on the second floor, and a large kitchen in the basement. In addition, as a luxury item, it had a wooden summer kitchen in a little courtyard and a hydrant hooked up to the water supply. The cottage was small, but for us and our modest needs it was large enough. It was also clean and in good condition, and what was most important, we had no alternative. So I rented the cottage for seventeen dollars a month, and I lived there a year and a half and was quite content. On the neighboring cottage there grew a lush Mexican vine whose fire-red, tulip-like flowers swarmed with innumerable hummingbirds, who sipped their nectar there. In what little free time I had, this charming spectacle occupied me for hours, and this single blooming plant on a neighbor's building was our garden, our recreation and our joy. In those days St. Louis was no Paris, with public gardens where one could refresh himself with a quiet walk. Really, in those days in St. Louis there was no time to take walks. The cottage at the corner of Third and Cedar has surely long since vanished, making way for a large apartment building, but I still think of it with pleasure as my first modest beginning in St. Louis.

So the first year of my time as an editor passed in continuous battle with bitter, reckless opponents. Eventually I won more friends and adherents in the population, and soon I was the leader of the Germans, at first in Missouri, then in the entire upper Mississippi valley. A novel contributed materially to my winning this popularity, a novel which I wrote and published in the *Anzeiger,* and which took place in the past and present of St. Louis. The novel received its title, *Die Geheimnisse von St. Louis [The Mysteries of St. Louis],*[4] from my publisher, because my competing newspaper, the *Deutsche Tribüne,*[5] had planned to publish a novel with that title. The original title was *Die Raben des Westens [The Ravens of the West].*

This novel, to which I attribute a considerable portion of my advancement in America, has since had an unusually fortunate destiny. It was originally published as a serial in the *Anzeiger* in 1850 and 1851,[6] and it elevated the number of subscriptions by more than a thousand in a matter of

---

4. Boernstein, *Mysteries;* Cazden, *Social History,* 391-2, translates this passage.

5. *Die deutsche Tribüne* appeared from 15 July 1844 to May 1852 in various editions (daily, weekly, semiweekly, triweekly) It began as a Whig paper but became Democratic; Arndt/Olsen, 255. Boernstein had a particularly bitter feud with the *Tribüne* at the start of his editorship, see *AW,* vol. 15, no. 145, 9 April 1850, p. 2; vol. 15, no. 151, 16 April 1850, p. 2. See his facetious "burial oration" for the *Tribüne, AW,* weekly, vol. 17, no. 31, 22 May 1852, p. 2, for 17 May.

6. *AW,* vol. 16, no. 100, 16 February 1851, p. 2, first installment; last installment, vol. 16, no. 206, 20 June 1851, and a parallel publication in the weekly edition. Reprints of the

a few months. Ten years later it was published in the *Anzeiger* once more in response to demands from the younger and newly immigrated generation. Beyond that the demand was so large that the book version experienced six editions, and although each consisted of fifteen hundred to two thousand copies they were soon exhausted. Further, many German American journals reprinted the novel with my permission, and on the initiative of Dr. H. W. Gempp it was translated into English.[7] It appeared in a French paper in New Orleans in a French translation, and it was published in a Bohemian translation in a Bohemian newspaper in St. Louis. Further, three editions appeared in Germany: the first in 1851 by H. Hotop in Kassel, the second in 1868 in the illegal manner of a reprint without permission by H. Prinz in Altona, and the third in 1871 with my permission and under the original title of *Die Raben des Westens* with Röhlig and Co. in Berlin. These three editions also are completely sold out, and I myself have only one copy. That was my first great success in America, and it leveled the way for my further advancement.

four parts were issued using newspaper galleys as they were completed; see Boernstein, *Mysteries*, ix-x. The book had exhausted three printings by the end of July 1851; see *AW,* weekly, vol. 16, no. 41, 26 July 1851, p. 3, for 24 July 1851. On 18 June, Boernstein protested that the *Deutsche Journal* of Dayton, Ohio, was printing the novel without permission, *AW,* weekly, vol. 16, no. 36, 21 June 1851, p. 3, for 19 June 1851.

7. A serialization of the English translation of *The Mysteries of St. Louis* was begun in *The German American* on 4 May 1851, though it is doubtful publication was completed before the paper closed; see *AW,* weekly, vol. 16, no. 30, 10 May 1851, p. 1, for 4 May 1851. The English edition, boasting an engraved title page and frontispiece, was published in sections in 1851 and 1852 as Henry Boernstein, *The Mysteries of St. Louis, Or, The Jesuits on the Prairie des Noyers, A Western Tale* (St. Louis: Anzeiger des Westens, 1851-52). See Boernstein, *Mysteries*, x, xiv-xv on Friedrich Münch as the translator.

The Aftershocks of 1848
(1850-1852)

Now I am coming to a period that was not only crucial for the development of Germans in America, but that also exercised a decisive influence on me and my destiny in my new home. I mean that great intellectual movement created in the United States by an extraordinary number of political refugees of all countries, particularly Germany. The results and influence of that group are palpable today, even though weakened or moderated. Thousands upon thousands of refugees who had compromised themselves in Germany and Austria in the movement of stormy 1848, now pursued and threatened by the iron fist of victorious reaction, had been fortunate enough to escape to America. Most of them had not only given up positions, professions or income, but also lost all they possessed, saving nothing but their naked lives. The United States teemed with refugees, particularly in the East from New York to Baltimore, as well as in the West in states with large German populations such as Ohio, Illinois, Indiana, Missouri, Wisconsin and Iowa. The first to come over were received as heroes, freedom-fighters, and martyrs of the people's cause by the German Americans who had long been resident in the country. They were offered every possible assistance, and everyone tried to find them support, a position or craft. Unfortunately, most of the refugees were professors, scholars, students, officials, journalists and other professionals of no use in America. Almost none of them could speak English, and in the course of the struggles of the stormy years they had acquired a sanctimonious, commanding, all-knowing and dictatorial style of speech. Soon they found themselves in open conflict with the older settled German Americans, whom they denounced as "pigtails" or "old compromisers" and "reactionaries." In response, the long-settled German Americans—who knew land and people and who understood American history and politics—accused the new refugees of bottomless ignorance. Established Germans denounced them as being raw professional revolutionaries completely lacking in knowledge of American conditions.

The new arrivals were called "Greens," while these older German Americans were mocked as "Grays." As a result, enthusiasm for the increasingly numerous refugees cooled, and far too many of them arrived for it to be possible for each to be accommodated or even supported effectively. The earlier refugees, who had more or less got their feet on the ground, took the matter in hand. They established refugee societies whose first purpose was to help the new arrivals as they themselves had been helped. Whatever refugee had learned a craft was quickly assisted. Those who belonged to the class of peasant or gardener could also be placed on the land in no time by having him lease a small farm. The rest had to make their peace with learning a new skill, so that they became cigar makers, housepainters, innkeepers or waiters. In those days one could see intellectually gifted teachers and journalists, former professors and scientists, high officials and lawyers—in short, people who belonged to the privileged classes in Germany—practicing the most ordinary trades, often not the cleanest, in order to earn their daily bread. Those who did this, who did not reject any honest work, were always better off than those who did not have enough courage or self-denial, or just the strength, to stand on their own feet. When support from others ended, these would waste away miserably and go to their ruin in need and want. Such was the lot of innumerable refugees.

As a result it was natural that most of these refugees had nothing good to say about America. They scourged the diffidence and ingratitude, the indifference and apathy of established German Americans. These "Greens" regarded their residence in America as only a temporary exile, from which they would return as soon as the momentarily repressed revolution broke out again in Germany. They would return at the first call to bring their beloved old Fatherland help and liberation. These refugees were active not only in America but also in England, Switzerland, even in Turkey, preoccupied with the coming revolution and how this was to be prepared, precipitated and carried through. The more pacific "Grays" opposed this obsession, which degenerated to the point that Eastern activists seriously proposed to organize the assassination of princes and the setting of rewards for murdering all emperors, kings and other rulers. The "Grays" believed the new arrivals would do better to learn something here, earn their bread through their own labor, and make themselves useful citizens of their new homeland. So the struggle between the "Greens" and the "Grays" grew ever more intense and bitter.

Even though I was one of the "Greens," in this respect I shared the views of the "Grays." For me a fact confirmed by the experience of all times and countries, that every emigration overseas eventually loses any understanding for developments in its old homeland and sacrifices all influence over events there. This has been repeatedly demonstrated in the Spanish, Italian, French and other emigrations in the course of our century. The position of my paper, which I expressed in my first article in the *Anzeiger* immediately after my arrival in St. Louis, was my own. I declared that I had emigrated from Europe not because of the tyranny of rulers, but because of the opportunities of [American] liberty, however misunderstood.[1] This made me

---

1. *AW,* vol. 15, no. 118, 8 March 1850, p. 2.

the deadly enemy of all refugees, and I was heavily attacked, fortunately without success since the German population had already come to quiet reconsideration. Now they had come to disapprove of the fanatical, one-sided efforts of the refugees.

During this time, precisely because of my novel, *The Mysteries of St. Louis,* I came to know a gentleman who was one of the older Germans, a so-called "Gray," who had considerable influence over me. This was Dr. Heinrich Wilhelm Gempp, an elderly, much-loved, and talented physician.[2] He had been personal physician of one of the minor princes in Germany of the old German League, and he had been celebrated for his fortunate cures and his thorough knowledge of medicine. His openness and directness, as well as his liberal political views, drew on him the hostility and hatred of this mini-court, and the result was petty friction and irritation. In the end this painful association became intolerable, so that Dr. Gempp conceived the manly decision of rejecting princely servility completely and becoming a free man. He emigrated to America, creating a better, more independent future for his children. He carried this decision through with courage despite the entreaties of the prince, who did not want to release him, and despite the disapproval of his friends and relatives. And he came to St. Louis, where his knowledge, long clinical experience and friendly, humane character quickly won recognition. He became the most beloved German physician in town. Soon in possession of a large practice and considerable wealth, obtained honorably, he was generally respected and honored. Yet he still found time and inclination to interest himself for all philanthropic and humanitarian undertakings outside his medical calling.

One of his favorite efforts was bringing about understanding, cooperation and collaboration between German Americans and Anglo-Americans, who then regarded one another with hostility across a broad gap. Both populations pursued common goals, and they were only separated by external appearances. The Anglo-American took care to appear as a gentleman, always with a stovepipe hat, in black whenever possible, with a smooth-shaved face and clean boots. He was rendered uncomfortable by the peasant character of the earlier German immigrants,

2. Dr. Heinrich Wilhelm Gempp (1798-1851) obituary in *AW,* vol. 16, no. 190, 1 June 1851; see also Elizabeth Gempp, "Henry Gempp—Pioneer Doctor," *BMHS 18* (1961-2): 260-4. After studying medicine at Marburg, he was court physician in the mini-principality of Reuss-Lobenstein-Ebersdorf in Saxony. He arrived in America in 1836 and was a notable supporter of the Old Lutheran refugees, having the Lutheran bishop Martin Stephan baptize his two sons. He helped arrange the sale of property in Perry County to the community. See also Walter O. Forster, *Zion on the Mississippi: The Settlement of the Saxon Lutherans in Missouri 1839-1841* (St. Louis: Concordia, 1953; repr., 1977; 1983), 347-50, 360.

with their caps, their long pipes, their sauerkraut and beer, and all the other peculiarities. Now came the refugees with their moustaches and long beards, their bohemian appearance, their revolutionary emblems and slogans, and especially their denigration of the church and its ordained servants. They managed to offend the feelings of Anglo-Americans even more than the others. A large gap emerged between the two nationalities, despite their being citizens of the same country, dedicated alike to that country and its institutions. Germans had no understanding for Anglo-Americans, and they in turn had none for the Germans. Alienation grew between two peoples who neither knew nor understood one another, and this led in the end to the regrettable fact that the majority of Anglo-Americans supported the Know-Nothings during the next few years. Dr. Gempp regarded it as a political and social necessity to bring the two nationalities to know one another so that alienation would soon disappear. He made it his task in life.

What was said and written in English-American newspapers was usually communicated to German Americans through their own papers, but the reverse was not the case. Anglo-Americans learned almost nothing of what appeared in German papers, for no English newspaper found it worth the trouble to pay attention to a German paper, or to publish a translated article for their readers. I proudly regarded it as a great success, a result of years of effort when I managed at last to compel the English papers not to ignore the German press but to have "The Spirit of the German Press" as a perennial title. There they would publish the most important articles from German American papers, although usually only in excerpts, distorted, and almost always with hostility. In 1851, however, we were by no means so advanced. And so Dr. Gempp established a newspaper written in English to advance understanding. The *German-American* consisted entirely of excerpts and translations of the most remarkable articles of the German American press, intending to bring Anglo-Americans to understand the views and nature of German America.[3] I came to know Dr. Gempp in this context, for he sought me out and asked me to permit a translation of my novel, *The Mysteries of St. Louis*, which was then being published, to appear as a serial in

---

3. Gempp stated his principles for the newspaper in an exchange of letters with Boernstein, *AW,* weekly, vol. 16, no. 19, 22 February 1851, p. 1 for 16 February, and 4, letter dated 31 January. An announcement of the first issue of the *German-American* is made in *AW,* weekly, vol. 16, no. 21, 8 March 1851, p. 1, for 4 March 1851. Boernstein actually published a weekly English-language edition of the *Anzeiger des Westens,* of which two numbers are included with the *AW,* weekly edition microfilmed at the State Historical Society of Missouri, vol. 1, no. 1, 15 July 1853, and vol. 1, no. 16, 16 October 1853. Boernstein's argument for the newspaper is found in *AW,* weekly, vol. 18, no. 37, 16 June 1853, p. 3.

his *German-American.* Naturally, I was glad to consent.[4] Soon the *German-American.* was being printed in the *Anzeiger* printing shop, so that we came into daily contact.[5] This soon grew to mutual respect and affection, developing in the end into a true friendship with this man who was twenty years my senior.

Among the German refugees with which St. Louis teemed in those days was a former member of the Frankfurt Parliament, Franz Schmidt. Called "Schmidt of Löwenberg" after his place of election to distinguish him from all the other Schmidts in the parliament,[6] he was a thoroughly educated, highly gifted man, a former theologian who had broken with the traditions of the Church to play a major role in the "German Catholic" movement. In those days the aggression of the Catholic hierarchy in the United States was represented everywhere by the Jesuits. Abetted by influencing political elections through bigoted Irishmen, evangelism, legacy-hunting and other abuses, this movement had begun to excite general alarm. It led to bitter attacks by Anglo-Americans, partly from Protestants, partly from nativists. This was a struggle that German Americans took up in a humanitarian and libertarian sense. Samuel Ludvigh, a Hungarian German, founded his *Fackel*[7] and traveled throughout the Union as its editor and agent, holding lectures and making propaganda. Friedrich Hassaurek in Cincinnati established the *Hochwächter*,[8] a combative journal written with great talent but also with the wild intensity of its editor, barely in his twenties. Heinrich Koch published

4.   The translation was by Friedrich Münch (1799-1881) of Marthasville, Missouri, noted as a viticulturist and newspaper columnist; see Boernstein, *Mysteries*, xiv-xv.

5.   See the large advertisement for job-printing and serial publications by Boernstein and Gempp in German, English, and French, including three editions of the *AW*, the *German-American, Freie Blätter*, and *Le Moniteur de l'Ouest*, in *AW*, weekly, vol. 16, no. 31, 17 May 1851, p. 3.

6.   Franz Schmidt (1818-1853) was a "German Catholic" follower of Johannes Ronge, but he was also a radical socialist and a sympathizer of Polish nationality rights as a member of the Frankfurt Parliament. What Boernstein did not know was that Schmidt also remained in communication with the Communist Central Committee in Brussels, using the code-name of "Theseus." See Steven Rowan, "Franz Schmidt and the *Freie Blätter* of St. Louis," in Elliott Shore, Ken Fones-Wolf, James Danke, eds., *The German-American Radical Press: The Shaping of a Left Political Culture* (Urbana and Chicago: University of Illinois Press, 1992), 31-48; Steven Rowan, "Anticlericalism, Atheism and Socialism in German St. Louis, 1850-1853: Heinrich Börnstein and Franz Schmidt," in Henry Geitz, ed., *The German-American Press* (Madison, Wis.: Max Kade Institute, 1992), 43-56.

7.   German, "The Torch," published 1843-69 with interruptions, originally in Baltimore, but also in New York and Cincinnati. See Arndt/Olson, 189.

8.   German, "The Guardian." Friedrich Hassaurek (1831-1885) of Vienna, was wounded fighting in the Vienna Student Legion against regular troops. He arrived in America in 1849, settling in Cincinnati and publishing the radical socialist *Hochwächter*. United States Minister to Ecuador from 1861 to 1864, he became editor of the Cincinnati

his *Antipfaff,*[9] and in St. Louis Franz Schmidt founded the *Freie Blätter,*[10] a paper written in a decent tone, and which was both courageous and scholarly. The Jesuits, who slyly ignored the Anglo-American movement directed against them, sensed danger once Germans had joined up. The order sought to bring Germans into discredit with Americans by portraying the opposition as a group of freethinkers, blasphemers and atheists. Wherever they could, they sought to turn the Americans, who hated excess, against Germans by provoking riots and tumults. Thus it was that the black brethren managed to conjure up a street scandal in Cincinnati on the occasion of the visit of the papal nuncio for America, Monsignore Bodini. The incident was stimulated not by the fulminating articles of the *Hochwächter,* but by the activities of secret clerical agents. What began as a *shiveree* with the smashing of a few windows at the residence of nuncio Bodini was raised to a general brawl between freethinkers and a mass of agitated Catholics who rushed in. This led to police intervention and many trials, which greatly discredited Hassaurek and his paper in the eyes of Americans.

A similar explosion was supposed to take place in St. Louis as well, and a similar fate was planned for the *Anzeiger.* In the middle of March 1851, I suddenly received a note in which a young German named Bosshard, who told me that he had been enticed to an unknown place one night due to his freethinking talk, then assaulted. His eyes had been covered, and he had been placed in a wagon and carried off. He now knew he was in the Jesuit monastery in Florissant,[11] where he was being held prisoner in order to be converted to piety through fasting and bodily chastisement. By bribing a groundskeeper, he had managed to send this letter, and he called on me and my German fellow citizens to save him from his dreadful situation.

This letter, which I at first took seriously, was published in the *Anzeiger* the next day. It stimulated the greatest uproar among the Germans of St. Louis, and a German mass meeting was called at once. In those days,

Volksblatt in 1865. He wrote travel memoirs, a novel, and a book of verse. See Zucker, 300-301. The *Hochwächter* of Cincinnati was published 1850-59, with Hassaurek as the editor from 1852. See Arndt/Olson, 446.

9. German, "Anti-Priest." The journal was published 1843-5, 1847-8 by Heinrich Koch (1800-1879), a working-class polemicist from Bayreuth, who fled Germany after the Hambach Festival of 1832. Koch was the first open communist in St. Louis. He led a military unit in the Mexican War and pooled his unit's land grants received for service to establish a socialist community in Iowa. See Cazden, *Social History,* 139, 141; Arndt/Olson, 250.

10. German, "Free Pages," primarily a mouthpiece of Schmidt and Boernstein himself, partly on behalf of the '*Freimänner Verein,*' 18 March 1851 to 5 March 1853. See Arndt/Olson, 258, and articles by Rowan on Schmidt cited above.

11. St. Stanislaus Seminary in Florissant, now a museum of Jesuit activities.

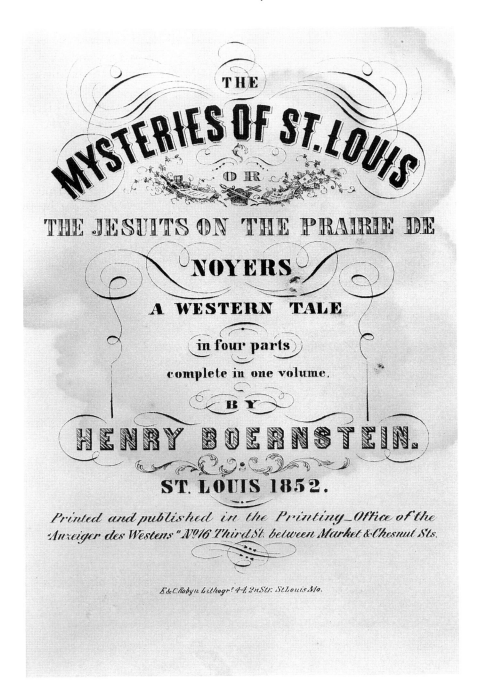

Title page of the English-language edition of Boernstein's novel, The Mysteries of St. Louis. *Lithograph by E. & C. Robyn, St. Louis, 1852. Photograph of Steven Rowan's own copy.*

under the influence of stormy 1848, such assemblies were as common as they have grown rare today, and almost every week there would be one or two German assemblies. The most violent, aggressive speeches were made at this assembly, and the hotspurs of the gathering even discussed a resolution for the Germans of St. Louis to arm themselves and undertake a volunteers' expedition against the Jesuit house in Florissant to free the imprisoned Bosshard. This or some similar stupidity was probably what the other side hoped to provoke in order not only to defend the house with forewarning, but also to demonstrate the house's complete innocence by suddenly discovering Bosshard on the way to California or some other place. These possibilities, together with some investigations I had made on Bosshard's past, caused me to hesitate and moved me to oppose the motion with my full influence and popularity. I proposed to refer the disappearance of a citizen of St. Louis to the lawful authorities and police, with his letter as evidence, and to demand that they take all necessary steps to free the prisoner. I called upon them to renounce any act of self-help, particularly in this specific case, which was not completely clear. Instead I moved the cooperation of all freethinkers to found a *"Freimänner Verein"* ["Society of Free Men"], whose purpose it would be to act through the founding of freethinking schools, the fighting of superstition and the exposure of all Jesuit efforts to hoodwink the populace. My speech had the desired success. The expedition to Florissant was rejected by a considerable majority, and the establishment of the Society of Free Men was adopted virtually unanimously. It should be remarked in passing that the mysterious Bosshard matter never was cleared up.[12] Despite investigations by the police, and efforts by the daily press, usually successful in such cases, Bosshard remained missing, and no one heard from him again.

In contrast, the Society of Free Men created on his behalf flourished. On the first evening 55 members joined the society, on the second 200, and on the third 306. So it went from evening to evening in a climbing progression, so that the society had several thousand members within a short period of time and had become one of the most important and influential German associations in St. Louis. Other chapters following the same goals as the St. Louis society were quickly established in Cincinnati, Louisville, and all the towns of Illinois, Wisconsin and Iowa where Germans made up most of the population. The principal society in St. Louis was soon in a position to pursue its goals in practice, partly through the regular or voluntary contributions of its membership, partly through festivals, picnics, concerts and theatrical presentations. The society constructed two large schoolhouses on leased land, each having four classrooms and a large hall. One school was

---

12. References on the Bosshard affair, see *AW,* 15-21 March 1851.

located in the north of town, and one in the south, and they were opened on
15 December of the same year. They offered the German population free
German schooling for their children, the tuition and all other costs being
paid by the society. The large hall in each building served for society
meetings for education or edification on Sunday morning. Nonmembers had
free admission, and these meetings were always well attended. When the
Society of Free Men dissolved after a few years thanks to the usual German
disunity, both the buildings and their equipment passed into the possession
of the municipal public schools and continued to serve the same socially
useful goals.

In those days, there reigned in the German population an earnestness
and readiness to sacrifice which would be inconceivable today given the
indifference and devil-may-care attitude that now prevails. This earnestness,
enthusiasm and self-sacrifice, which regarded everything in a dramatic sense,
persisted for years. Its last expression was the heroic rising of the
German Americans when the Union was threatened by secession in 1861. At
the first call, all Germans unanimously reached for their weapons, risking
family, position, fortune and all private interests. Going to battle for the
defense and preservation of a united republic, they succeeded. From what I
hear, this earnestness and enthusiasm is no longer to be found. But it is to be
hoped that this quality of German Americans will return in some great and
decisive cause, and that Germans remain worthy sons of the great star-
spangled republic.

It was one morning in early 1851, during the period when the Free Men
movement was in full course, that Dr. Gempp sought me out, desiring a
serious talk about something important. He told me that Olshausen did not
agree with the radical position of the *Anzeiger*. He feared bad results for his
paper, and he was considering selling the *Anzeiger* and retiring. Gempp
proposed that I take this opportunity to make myself independent and buy
the *Anzeiger*, together with him. We would then lead the paper ourselves,
making it into the dominant mouthpiece of Germans in the West. Once he
had put to rest my objections about lack of money, assuring that he would
cover it, I was glad to agree. Gempp commenced negotiations with
Olshausen, and it went exactly as we expected. Not only was Olshausen tired
of running a newspaper; he also loved peace, and foresaw the paper's
involvement in revolutionary struggles. Perhaps he was also afraid that
sooner or later I would make myself independent and found a competing
paper. In any case, we were soon in agreement. We bought the *Anzeiger* as it
was for what was then a considerable sum, six thousand dollars. Gempp paid
half of the contract at once for his share, and for my part I issued three
promissory notes, endorsed by Dr. Gempp. Through these I committed
myself to pay a thousand dollars after one, two and three years respectively,

with a yearly interest of 6 percent. So we were in agreement, and Dr. Gempp and I entered into possession of the paper on 22 April, even as it was daily gaining in subscriptions and influence. Great was our joy over the influential position we had won and the great field of activity opened to us. The plans we spun were even grander, and we advanced toward a promising future with hope and confidence.

Unfortunately our brave, true friend was not to share in these successes. Only a few days after we took over the *Anzeiger*, Dr. Gempp began to complain of feeling unwell. The discomfort increased to sickness, which grew ever more threatening despite the help of medical friends. As early as the middle of May, Dr. Gempp was taken from his family, his worshipping patients, the *Anzeiger* and me through a gentle, painless death.[13] The mourning at his funeral was universal, and this man of honor was painfully missed by the entire German population. Most of all he was missed by me. I had taken over a large, difficult business without means of my own, and now I had been suddenly deprived of my friend, my true support in the enterprise.

I did not allow my courage to sink. Instead, I told the widow that I would continue the business with my full efforts, protecting and preserving all her rights as heiress. Frau Gempp, however, who had not been fond of her husband's newspaper enterprises while he was alive, now had no desire to consider a continued partnership. She told me that she would accept no further risk, and that I should take over her husband's promissory note for $3,000 myself. I was to pay off the $3,000 cash her husband had paid in three annual installments, assured with corresponding notes. She wished to be free of all further responsibility, and she would transfer to me her husband's half-share in the *Anzeiger* without any further ado. This agreement was carried out. A proper document was drawn up with Olshausen's approval, and I took over sole payment of the three notes that were assured to Olshausen through a bond, as well as payment of the $3,000 to Frau Gempp. Thus I was the sole owner of the *Anzeiger* by the end of May. I paid all the notes at the proper times, so that for the payment of $6,000 I came into possession of a paper for which I was vainly offered $60,000 six years later. The actual founder of my fortunate career in St. Louis was thus the worthy Dr. Gempp, and I remain thankful to him and his memory to the present day.

---

13. Obituary for Gempp, *AW*, weekly, vol. 16, no. 34, 7 June 1851, p. 1, for 1 June 1851; burial, where Boernstein spoke along with Dr. Schöneich, is described on p. 4, for 3 June 1851.

From Stormy Times

It was a remarkably stormy, agitated time. Barely two years in America and little initiated in the special conditions of the country or its parties, I found myself in control—through the accidental coincidence of fortunate circumstances—of an influential newspaper and business. I also found that I had been made the political and social leader of my compatriots, who honored me with their trust and depended on me. I must confess that at the time I had not yet grasped the full importance of the slavery question. My very location in a slave state imposed a certain caution. On top of that, I was bound by the fact that my paper was a Democratic mouthpiece. My readers and subscribers all belonged to the Democratic Party, and the Democratic Party was none other than the slaveholders' party.

In the East and North of the Union, the struggle against the institution of slavery had already stimulated sharp division and violent differences of opinion. These had weakened and torn the Whig Party, which was then on its deathbed and in the process of dissolving. At the same time the Democratic Party, the party of slaveholders, had reached the conviction that there were no new slave states to be formed in the territories to the north. Hence the party had to turn its attention to expanding the Union to the south. It eyed new territories in Mexico, Cuba and Central America to be annexed as slave states, which would maintain the majority of the slaveholding states in Congress, and, more particularly, the Senate. The slaveholders' party masked its intentions with propaganda about freedom, and Young America. Their program was said to be the "manifest destiny" of the star-spangled republic. One southern region after another was to be conquered and annexed, and these new states would receive the blessings of slavery, along with freedom and independence. This was the purpose of the war with Mexico, after which California, Texas, New Mexico and Arizona were annexed straightaway. And just as the appetite grows only once eating commences, the lust of the Democratic Party for new annexations then began expanding to a distressing degree.

Against all the expectations of the slaveholders, California excluded slavery in its constitution, and the same was expected in Oregon. Hence the gaze of the party shifted ever more southward. There was speculation about taking Cuba, Nicaragua and the other small states of Central America, which would provide a bridge to conquer (and make amenable to slavery) New Granada, Guyana, Ecuador and other southern states as far as the Amazon. Filibuster expeditions—General Lopez to Cuba and of Walker to Nicaragua—were raised without the government hindering recruitment of these adventurers or the departure of the expeditions from American ports.[1] Finally, two years later a conference of American diplomats from Madrid, London, and Paris—Soulé, Buchanan, and Mason—published the results of their discussions in the so-called Ostend Manifesto. This document declared ". . . [T]hat, since the possession of Cuba is entirely necessary to the United States, [the United States] was justified in obtaining the island in any manner necessary if Spain was not amenable to a voluntary cession for adequate compensation." This Ostend Manifesto[2] combined with the Kansas-Nebraska question, which developed into a bloody struggle between proslavery and antislavery people, and the suspension of the Missouri Compromise through the Squatter Sovereignty formulated by Senator Douglas. The general shock that this expansion and fortification of the slaveholding power stimulated in the larger part of the Union were the actual cause of the rapid emergence and growth of the Republican Party. Thus the air was filled with political electricity, and a struggle began in secret between North and South that would be carried out on the battlefield ten years later.

Into this stormy atmosphere came Europe's political refugees, particularly the so-called Forty-Eighters from Germany. Although almost all set foot on the territory of the Union in 1849 or 1850, they still lived under the impression of what they had experienced in the stormy year of 1848, and they were still full of revolutionary projects and grandiose plans for improving the world. On American soil—where no police, state prosecutor or penal judge persecuted their efforts, where they could speak, write or make plans however they wished without hindrance or restriction— they did not have to face the notion that their revolutionary movement was at an end. Despite the fact that the pope was returning to Rome supported

---

1. See especially on the disastrous Lopez expedition, *AW,* weekly, vol. 16, no. 48, 20 September 1851, p. 4, where Boernstein provided an English translation of his major articles on Cuba in order to clarify a dispute with the *Missouri Republican:* "Cuba Affairs!! Keep it before the People!!! . . . Reply to the Missouri Republican of Sept. 11th, by the Anzeiger des Westens." Filibusters were a central concern of radical writers at this time, so that Boernstein himself advertised a sequel to *The Mysteries of St. Louis* entitled *Das Blutbad auf Cuba (The Bloodbath in Cuba).* See Boernstein, *Mysteries,* x. The Narciso Lopez expedition of 1851 was a major theme of American political fiction in the mid-fifties, featured in German (Emil Klauprecht, *Cincinnati*) as well as English (Ned Buntline, *The Mysteries and Miseries of New Orleans*). On William Walker (1824-1860), who staged attacks in Mexico and Nicaragua, actually becoming president of Nicaragua for a time, see *DAB,* 19: 363-5. Generally, see Robert E. May, *The Southern Dream of a Caribbean Empire, 1854-1861* (Baton Rouge: Louisiana State University Press, 1973).

2. The Ostend Manifesto, a statement of the American ministers to England, Spain, and France, was composed on 18 October 1854 and delivered to Secretary of State Marcy. See *DAB,* 12: 277.

by foreign bayonets, that Prussia and Denmark were making peace by sacrificing the brave Schleswig-Holsteiners, that the Federal Diet in Frankfurt was meeting once more, that the Austrians were making order in Hessia and Schleswig-Holstein, despite that the Prussians had endured the most despicable humiliation in Olmütz and Warsaw, and that Louis Napoléon's *coup d'état* had succeeded, overweening reaction was victorious on the entire Continent, the refugees saw the revolution as only momentarily suspended. They hoped and expected that the revolution would soon break out again, and that they would see victory over the throne. The refugee clubs soon became revolutionary societies concerned with how the revolution in Germany could be brought back to life from America. At the same time numerous reform societies were also formed whose aim it was to turn the American Constitution in a more radical direction. Workers' associations were almost as numerous, based partly on the doctrines of Wilhelm Weitling and partly on those of the Frenchman Cabet or the Englishman Owen.[3] These associations founded various communist colonies in their first enthusiasm, colonies which all quickly collapsed. Only a single accomplishment arose from these workers' associations and societies for land reform and worker's associations. This was carried out by the Republican Party, who solved the worker question by no longer selling public land but giving it away free to genuine settlers and farmers under certain conditions. Their policy was embodied in the Homestead Act, which is still in force.[4]

Using the enthusiasm of the year of revolution, these associations discussed much that was good and true. It was mixed with a great deal of

---

3. Wilhelm Weitling (1808-1871), a journeyman tailor from Magdeburg, was a member of the League of the Oppressed in 1835, 1837-45 a leading member of the League of the Just (the predecessor organization to the Communist Party) and a leading working-class utopian socialist. He was in America from 1846 to 1848, and after 1849, publishing the *Republik der Arbeiter* 1850-1855, in which he stridently opposed Marxian socialism. He supported the creation of worker cooperatives and labor-exchanges. *MEW*, 27, 744; see also Carl F. Wittke, *The Utopian Communist: A Biography of Wilhelm Weitling, Nineteenth-Century Reformer* (Baton Rouge: Louisiana State University Press, 1950). Robert Owen (1771-1858), English industrialist and utopian socialist, led the model New Lanark factory in Scotland, 1800-1829, supporting worker welfare and cooperation. He participated in the New Harmony, Indiana, community. *MEW*, 27, 733-4. Étienne Cabet (1788-1856), French jurist and publicist, came under the influence of Owen after 1834 while in exile in England; he edited *Le Populaire*, 1841-1849. His 1842 utopian novel, *Voyage en Icarie*, was used as the program for communist communities in America, *MEW*, 27, 713. Utopian communism was specifically criticized by Marx and Engels in the *Communist Manifesto* (1848), part III, section 3, *MEW*, 4, 489-92.

4. Boernstein himself published a great deal on workers' causes and on land reform in his first period with the *Anzeiger*, see *AW*, vol. 15, no. 137, 30 March 1850, on land reform; no. 232, 21 July 1850; no. 234, 24 July 1850; no. 235, 25 July 1850; no. 237, 27 July 1850, "An die Arbeiter!"

junk, however, and they discussed both to death. I regarded it as my mission energetically to expose this idealistic boilerplate, which could never have a practical result. If the Germans in America were ever really to win any influence over politics and take a position worthy of respect, it would be necessary to put aside all subsidiary questions, whether projects for a European revolution or freebooter expeditions by the slaveholders. They would have to avoid all division over secondary matters and gather themselves in unity behind their chosen leaders, organizing themselves according to strict party discipline. This simple doctrine, containing the basic elements of all political organizations, was accepted by the German population in the West. They began to count their own number and realize their strength if they would only unite. The Free Men organization, already numbering in the thousands, was the core around which the rest of the Germans solidly crystallized. In a short period of time I was happy to see the German population united and disciplined, following the *Anzeiger.*

I now saw it to be my first and highest purpose to place this united German community on its own feet, making it independent of the Anglo-American wire-pullers and party hacks. It had been shocking to see how Germans had been handled by Anglo-American leaders in the Democratic Party like a passive herd, rounded up for the ballot boxes without being asked their own opinion. There was no question of giving Germans their due when it came to the distribution of the offices of city, county or state. A small caucus of a dozen Americans and Irishmen put together the ticket, the list of candidates for election on which Germans had no more place than at most as overseer of a municipal market. This situation quickly changed once Germans became unified and disciplined, and they were ever more highly regarded, acting as one with their votes. I was twice forced to put up an independent ticket in opposition to the regular one of the party convention, and since Germans cast several thousand votes for that ticket, we sent a painful message to defeated party leaders to respect Germans and give them equal rights in the future. That is how it remained as long as Germans were unified, and it was only after their split, at the time of the formation of the Blair and Frémont factions in 1862, that they began their decline. May the Germans always keep in mind that their strength, influence and power lie in unity and discipline, beset as they are by hostile nationalism, confessionalism, temperance, and similar enemies. It is the old story of the bundle of arrows on the Dutch ducat: individually each of these arrows can be broken, but when united in a bundle they are invincible.

I have to vouch that the Germans of that time completely grasped this truth. They were not confused, despite all the attacks by mouthpieces of Jesuits and muckrakers, despite all the threats of nativists, despite hateful vendettas of the slaveholders' party and despite all the suspicions and denunciations continuously being directed against my paper and my name. Instead, they stood together and remained true to both my paper and me.

It appeared to me that a further mission was just as important, that of lifting and ennobling the tone of the German American press. The present generation cannot conceive of the tone in the German American press then. The order of the day was to ape the tone of low-down fishwives and barflies, preoccupied with throwing muck. Even the simplest, most careful comment or objection against a newspaper and its position was routinely answered with a salvo from a muck-battery of the lowest words with cursing and abuse. Libels, groundless accusations, and common lies were the weapons of choice. These always benefited the most conscienceless journalistic rowdy or the rudest newshound, while a decent person shrank from using such filthy weapons. Fortunately, there were many decent, educated publicists who came to America with the emigration of 1849. These gradually won admission to the various German editorial offices, where they were disgusted by the prevailing plebeian tone. I began exchanging letters with some of them, and I suggested to them that one means of solving this was to form a league of better newspapers which would ban this low libel from our columns, avoid personalities and exercise only objective criticism. I received friendly agreement from all quarters, and cooperation and support were promised. Others doubted it could be done, among them Emil Klauprecht of Cincinnati,[5] believing I would alter nothing and would get only trouble for my pains. I did not waver, publishing a series of letters on the German American press in the *Anzeiger.* Friedrich Schnake wrote the following about my letters in his "History of the German Population and of the German Press in St. Louis":[6]

> On 3 October Börnstein began a series of masterfully written letters on the German newspaper press in America.[7] With great ability he portrayed the faults and excesses that generally degraded the journals of that time.

---

5. Emil Klauprecht (1815-1896), born in Mainz, came to America in 1832, making a career as an engraver, journalist, and writer as an antislavery Whig. Like Boernstein, he became a U.S. Consul early in the Lincoln Administration, in Stuttgart, and like Boernstein, he gravitated to Vienna after his service was ended. He authored an extensive *German Chronicle in the History of the Ohio Valley and its Capital City Cincinnati in Particular,* Dale V. Lally, tr., Don Heinrich Tolzmann, ed. (Bowie, Md.: Heritage Books, 1992), originally published in 1864, and a mammoth novel, *Cincinnati; or the Mysteries of the West,* Steven Rowan, tr., Don Heinrich Tolzmann, ed. (New York: Peter Lang, 1996), originally published in 1852-53.

6. Friedrich Schnake, "Geschichte der deutschen Bevölkerung und der deutschen Presse von St. Louis und Umgebung," *Der deutsche Pionier,* vol. 3 (1871-2) to 5 (1873-4).

7. *AW,* vol. 15, no. 295, 3 October 1850; and vol. 15, no. 307, 17 October 1850; *AW,* weekly, vol. 16, no. 3, 2 November 1850, p. 4, "Offene Briefe über die deutsche

He demanded a higher, nobler manner of speech, the end of fishwives chatter and an effective commitment to the political situation of the new homeland. These letters not only excited general respect, but were also the first step in emancipating the German American press from their dependence on the large American journals. Eventually it took the respected position it now holds, and Börnstein raised a monument with these letters he may look back on with pride.

As kind and positive as Schnake's evaluation is, I still must confess that the success of my efforts was largely due to the fact that so many of my journalistic colleagues joined with me and worked in the same direction. Yet I can assert without praising myself that there was at that point a decided turn for the better, and the language and attitude of German American newspapers improved from year to year, a few atavistic backslides excepted. Whoever needs to convince himself of this should look at an old annual file of a German American newspaper from the end of the forties and compare it with a German newspaper appearing today. He will quickly discover the tremendous difference.

Even while I was working to introduce a decent, educated tone to German American journalism, I had to keep in mind how relations between German American citizens and the old fatherland were to be maintained and intensified, how interest in political conditions, science, art, literature and music in Germany were to be kept fresh. As a result, I placed a high premium on the most complete and understandable delivery of news available from Europe under the prevailing conditions. In those days there was still no electric telegraph to keep Americans up to date with European developments by the day and hour, and only the largest English papers had European correspondents, with these only in Paris and London. One or two steamers would arrive in New York from Europe, bringing a packet of the latest European papers from which editors culled the most interesting items, publishing this colorfully jumbled collection the next morning under the title, "Latest European News." These newspapers were almost all English, however. Only the stewards of German steamers brought an additional packet of German materials to the German papers, which also hurriedly culled a mélange from it. The situation of papers in the interior of the country was even worse, particularly in the Far West, where we received no

---

Zeitungspresse in Amerika." Related responses and discussions can be found in *AW,* vol. 15, no. 299, 8 October 1850, "Die deutsche Zeitungspresse in den Vereinigten Staaten," and *AW,* weekly, vol. 16, no. 6, 23 November 1850, p. 2, for 19 November 1850, "Die deutsche Zeitungspresse in Amerika," and ibid., vol. 16, no. 10, 21 December 1850, p. 2, for 18 December 1850, "Noch ein Wort über die deutsche Zeitungspresse in Amerika. (Offener Brief an Wilhelm Weitling)."

such deliveries and thus had to reprint the planless, unselective dispatches of the New York papers. Needless to say, none of the German newspapers in the West had a correspondent in Europe.

It thus became my mission to make my paper and myself independent in this matter. I not only subscribed to the most important German papers, which I then began getting regularly and completely so that I could make my own selection, but I also sought to win a European correspondent, which was not all that easy in Germany in those days. At first Franz Pulszky wrote interesting European reports for my paper from London, but he soon became so involved in active daily politics that he had to give up his correspondence. Taking his place was Moritz Mahler, a refugee from Vienna who was one of the most hard working and conscientious correspondents. Poor Mahler, who had been severely compromised in the March revolution and the October Days in Vienna, had barely escaped the pitiless court-martial of Prince Windischgrätz. In expensive London, he had no source of support but his pen. Hence he had to work tirelessly day and night writing for English, German and American newspapers—writing and nothing but writing. His eyes, weak in any case, could not tolerate this enormous strain over the long haul. He became nearly blind and was finally compelled to give up his work as a correspondent. He told me of this sad necessity, commending as the best replacements Arnold Ruge[8] and Lothar Bucher,[9] men also living in London as political refugees. I willingly went along with Mahler's recommendation, and I won both of these gifted men as continuing collaborators with my paper. Arnold Ruge remained the European correspondent for my paper until I went to Europe myself and began my work as a correspondent in the *Westliche Post.* I soon lost Lothar Bucher, however, due to a difference of political opinion.

The year 1859 arrived, and with it the French and Italian War against Austria in Italy. The Pan-German Party in Germany stormily demanded that Prussia and all of Germany stand at Austria's side, supporting it militarily against the French hereditary enemy. The patriotic and liberal majority of the German people opposed this, declaring the Austrian oppression of Italy to be no German concern, and they pressed Prussia to remain neutral. The latter view won out in the Prussian cabinet, and Prussia remained neutral despite Austria's warnings and pleas. North Germany entirely agreed with

---

8. Arnold Ruge (1802-1880), collaborator with Boernstein in the Paris *Vorwarts!*; leftist in the Frankfurt Parliament, leader of democratic revolutionaries in London opposed to Marx and the Communists. See *MEW,* vol. 27, 737.

9. Lothar Bucher (1817-1892) was a member of the center-left at the Frankfurt Parliament, later National Liberal and collaborator with Bismarck in the Reich Foreign Office.

this position, and eventually the excited tempers in South Germany—that was where they were excited about rushing to Austria's aid and wished, until the defeats at Magenta and Solferino, to precipitate an immediate war with France—were calmed.[10] This same division between the Great-German and the national German factions was also sharply present in the German American press, and it precipitated a lively, bitter polemic. It was a mere plurality of the German American press and public that opposed any intervention of Prussia or Germany in matters concerning Austria alone. Arnold Ruge wrote in this vein, and the editorship of the *Anzeiger* also took the German nationalist position. We declared it was a matter of indifference to the German people whether or not Austria possessed a couple Italian provinces, because no German interest was involved, and so on. In addition to this, absolutist Austria was very unpopular in America, and German Americans—influenced by Austrian refugees and the many Hungarians, Italians and Poles—did everything in their power to turn public opinion against Austria and its government.

Lothar Bucher, however, continued to belong to the Great German faction, advocating the cause of Austria and Germany's duty to help militarily. As a result I received the following denunciation from him on 22 June—hence before the bloody decision of the matter at Solferino. The letter said:

London, Chabrol Terrace, 22 June 1859
Esteemed sir!

There exists such a great and growing difference between my views and the perception of European affairs held by you and by Ruge that it would little satisfy all parties were I to continue my correspondence, which is essentially predicated on reason. Hence I have requested Herr Mahler to find a replacement, and I will surrender the small payment which I am still owed.

With respect, your servant
L. Bucher

The result of the French and Italian War spoke against Bucher, and yet this gifted man was ultimately right over the course of time. His favorite idea, which was that Germany and Austria should join together to form a powerful Central Europe, determined and strong enough to keep the peace

---

10. The battles of Magenta and Solferino, both taking place in June 1859, caused the Austrians to concede control over much of northern Italy to the Kingdom of Piedmont, leading to the creation of an Italian Kingdom under Piedmontese leadership.

in Europe and hinder any disturbance by French or Russian aggression, was brought to pass by Prince Bismarck. This was simply achieved by different paths and in different ways from those Bucher expected in 1859. Five years after the letter printed above, Bismarck, a man who knew how to find and keep real talent, called the former tax-protester and political refugee Lothar Bucher to the Foreign Office in Berlin. He placed him at his own right hand, and now Legation Counsel Lothar Bucher is Bismarck's closest aide and best resource, initiated into all the grand political plans occupying the German Reich Chancellor. When Prince Bismarck came to Vienna in 1879 and concluded the alliance between Germany and Austria to achieve and secure European peace, twenty years had passed since Bucher's letter, and Bucher had been proven right. The antagonism between Prussia and Austria had vanished from the world, and the Great-German idea was reality.

German Seriousness

(1850-1852)

When I think back on that time and leaf through old papers from that period of my career, what particularly impresses me is the high moral seriousness that filled the entire German population in those days, the upright enthusiasm with which they joined together to pursue the goals they had set for themselves. I wish to consider here a small example. In the year in question, as is the case this year, the Fourth of July fell on a Sunday.[1] The sleazy sensationalist and Pharisee press gave out the line that had been generally followed until then, which was that the festival of the Fourth of July could be celebrated on the fifth in order to avoid desecrating the Sabbath. I opposed this in the *Anzeiger*, remarking that Sunday was only now rendered sacred by the celebration of our national holiday of independence. Germans would not bother to follow the silly practice of waiting for the fifth to celebrate the Fourth, but they would hold the celebrations of the Fourth of July on the day itself. I presented the matter to the Society of Free Men, and the resolution passed unanimously. This moved all the other German associations and militia companies to celebrate the Fourth of July on Sunday as well. Statements of participation came from all sides, and a conference of delegates of all societies and militia companies agreed on a program for the festival. All the societies with their flags and bands were to gather in the northern part of the city and proceed in festive procession through the entire town to Lindell's Grove, a charming copse on the southern border of the city. At the assembly of the festival, the Declaration of Independence would be read out and a number of speeches presented on the importance of the day. Then there would be a great popular festival with song, music and dancing, games, enjoyments and fireworks.

When this program was published, the entire American press rose in shock, just as was the case with the Jesuit and sensationalist press. They stormed against German blasphemers and atheists who wished to desecrate Sunday, the Day of the Lord. It was declared in the most energetic fashion that the festival should not and would not take place. They would oppose the Germans by all legal means and, if that did not suffice, with force to prevent them from celebrating the holiday on Sunday. At the same time,

---

1. The Fourth of July fell on a Sunday in 1852, as it did in 1858 and in 1880, when Boernstein was completing the memoirs published in 1881.

disturbing rumors spread in the town that ten thousand Americans and Irishmen would disperse the procession and stop the celebration. At the least German resistance, German neighborhoods would be set aflame. Similar silly threats abounded. The German societies were alarmed, but in a general assembly of their delegates, my opinion was adopted that it would now be double cowardice to turn back or cancel the festivities. In such a situation, Germans would be reducing themselves to the status of helots and slaves; it was high time to demonstrate the strength of the German population, asserting our rights and liberties. There was no law against observing such a holiday on Sunday, and an arbitrary exercise of police power would be ignored. In the extreme case of brutal force, we decided to show manly resistance. It was unanimously agreed to observe and completely carry out the planned program, although to avoid irritating our opponents, we would hold the march out at six in the morning, when there were not yet any church services. All noise was to be avoided, and the bands were to march through the city silently; only outside city limits were they to begin playing their marches.

When these plans of the Germans were announced, the bitterness and threats of opponents spun into madness. The papers raged without measure, red placards demanded the extermination of the blasphemous Germans, and anonymous letters declared that none of the participants in the procession would return alive. The Germans did not allow themselves to be terrified by these mad threats, although we were perfectly aware of the seriousness of the situation and were quite aware of the excesses of which an American mob was capable.

It was a sleepless night that ended with the morning of the Fourth of July. The associations were fully present and made preparations for every eventuality. At four in the morning the associations and militia companies had already gathered at the mustering place, all present. Not a one had been frightened away by the threats. All had appeared, and each of them was armed. The German militia companies, which opened and closed the procession, had their weapons loaded and cocked. Among the civilian societies, almost everyone had a revolver, a pistol or a Bowie knife in his vest, and whoever could not lay hands on a weapon had at least two pounds of hard gravel packed in a stocking in his pocket to use as a weapon of offense or defense. So the procession set out, each row with six men in it, going arm in arm, silently moving forward and marching through the city in silence. There must have been about eight thousand Germans in procession, and the Society of Free Men alone had two thousand. All of them carried oak leaves on their hats as a mark of recognition, and rosettes in the American colors, the colors which dominated the procession in the form of the star-spangled banner. So the procession marched through the center of the town, past a thickly pressed gauntlet of Americans and Irishmen who looked on with hostility. There was no lack of hateful and hurtful comments, but our people did not grant the slightest attention, let alone respond, in keeping with the order of the day. No one dared disturb the procession, as they were impressed by German seriousness, and even professional troublemakers and rowdies kept themselves in the background. So it was eight o'clock when the procession reached the southern part of the city, where the Germans living there greeted us with jubilation. When we finally left the city limits and the bands struck up stirring triumphal marches, every person felt that Germans had won a great victory and overawed our opponents. And so we had. The festival was completed without disturbance. Attempts of a few trouble-makers to penetrate the grounds and excite excesses were rejected with stormy popular justice and palpable lessons. In the afternoon, many unprejudiced Americans even came and participated in the Germans' general festivities, and it was only the following morning that the celebrants got home, precisely when the Americans were commencing their celebration of the Fourth of July—on the fifth. This day, which certainly could have turned out for the worse, was a splendid success due to the peace, calm and decisiveness of the Germans. Germans won the respect of the rest of the population forever, and there would never again be any disturbance of a German festival or any question about observing the Fourth of July on a Sunday. Germans had emancipated themselves from their prior subservience, which they now aimed to do politically as well. Even the most perverse opponent or bitter nativist now recognized the Germans' strength and power, even if unwillingly. The moral seriousness of that time, with its high enthusiasm, filled everyone; but it was particularly the Germans' unity, solidarity, unanimity and discipline, that won this victory and propitious victories to come.

Passing *the* Plate *for the* Revolution
(1850-1852)

In this period it grew ever quieter in almost all the lands of Europe, where victorious reactionaries suppressed every free effort with an iron hand. But things grew all the livelier in America, England, France, Switzerland and everywhere else where refugees who had been fortunate enough to escape and find asylum. There they organized themselves as the revolutionary emigration. All of them believed the revolution was not yet over. They had been expelled and hunted from their fatherland, separated from family and friends, and they had no prospect for a happier future. Many had even been condemned to death or to life in prison in their absence. Yet they hoped for an imminent new outbreak, a victorious rising in France, Italy, Germany or anywhere. All their efforts upon emigration were concentrated on calling the uprising into life as soon as possible. As a result, a Supreme Revolutionary Committee was formed in London. It consisted of the leading refugees of all nations, including Ledru-Rollin and Louis Blanc for France, Mazzini for Italy, Karl Marx for Germany and others who could claim general leadership of national revolutionary associations and wished to act as a supreme instance. But the revolutionary associations themselves each went their own way, and as it has been since the formation of human society, there were contradictory concepts and conflicting views. Soon there were moderates and ultra-radicals fighting one another. Around the Russian Bakunin, some French anarchists and Italian *Carbonari*, there formed a new Revolutionary Central Committee, opposing the old Revolutionary Committee and pursuing its goals in its own way.

The revolutionary committees in America, which arose from the refugee associations, soon came into contact with their counterpart associations in France, England and Switzerland. They also carried on an intense correspondence with the supreme Revolutionary Committee in London. The sympathetic reception generally accorded refugees in the United States, the warm sympathy and lively demonstrations with which the Germans in the Union followed the developments in 1848, the great empathy shown for the struggles of freedom against spreading reaction—all of these led German refugees in particular to harbor exaggerated hopes and unjustified illusions. Soon the idea developed that the way to revolutionize Germany and create a German Republic would come from America, where so many compatriots and sympathizers lived in comfortable circumstances. Kossuth, the former dictator of Hungary, published a plan to raise the means for a renewed revolt and separation from Austria with a Hungarian national loan.[1] Kossuth himself had already crossed the ocean to apply the full weight of his popularity and the considerable power of his eloquence to carry out this plan. If Hungarians, only a small branch of the European family, could accomplish this, then the Germans would have a much easier time of it, for they already had millions of their compatriots in America.

Today, with the experience of the last thirty years, one smiles in pity at the fantastic idea of begging together money by passing a plate in order to make a great revolution happen. We have seen what it cost for the last great revolution, in which a unified, strong Germany was created. France alone paid five billion francs in war reparations and suffered disruption of private and public property, as well as an interruption of business amounting to ten billion francs. But Germany itself had to pay a heavy charge for unification, and despite the five billion francs from France, it suffered a drop in national wealth, as was seen in the years after 1873. But in those days, in the aftermath of the 1848 movement, everyone was still quite sanguine and believed everything he wanted to believe. In that way, the German Revolutionary Committee in London actually believed that if they could gather a couple of million Taler they would not fail to revolutionize all of Germany and carry through the rebellion victoriously. The entire emigration shared this faith, and the decision of the Revolution Committee to raise a revolutionary national loan of two million Taler in America was greeted and supported by all refugees. Particularly enthusiastic were those staying in America, who longed for activity and return and (incidentally) suffered dreadful homesickness for the old homeland. Letters of support flowed in from all portions of America; the refugees portrayed the loan project as certain of success and promised active support. For this purpose, Gottfried Kinkel was named to travel to America and get the German loan started there.[2] He was given Dr. Georg Hillgärtner as an escort.[3]

---

1. Lajos (Louis) Kossuth (1802-1894), a Protestant from what is now Slovakia, played a major role in a Hungarian national government in 1848, serving as governor of an openly insurrectionary administration in 1849. He was released from captivity in Turkey partly as a result of American pressure. He visited America from 1851 to 1852; described by John H. Komlos, *Louis Kossuth in America, 1851-1852* (Buffalo, N. Y.: East European Institute, 1973).

2. Gottfried Kinkel (1815-1882) returned to England after his American tour, and he eventually took a professorship in Zürich. See Zucker, 310-11.

3. Georg Hillgärtner (1824-1865), a lawyer in Heidelberg before the revolution, fled Germany under sentence of death. He worked as a lawyer in Chicago, then as a journalist in Chicago and St. Louis. He was a major supporter of Frémont against Lincoln in 1864, and he is buried in Bellefontaine Cemetery, St. Louis. Zucker, 305.

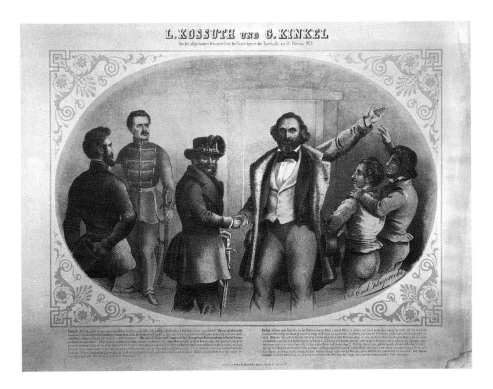

The Hungarian revolutionary leader Lajos Kossuth and the German revolutionary Gottfried Kinkel speaking at a general gathering of German Americans at the Cincinnati Turner Hall, 14 February 1852. Lithograph drawn by the German American artist, writer, and diplomat Emil Klauprecht, published by Klauprecht & Menzel, Cincinnati, Ohio. Courtesy of the Missouri Historical Society.

The choice of Kinkel was very fortunate, for Kinkel, Professor of Art History at the University of Bonn, was one of the most accomplished and outstanding men of 1848. Personally active in the Baden uprising, he had been captured there and condemned to penitentiary for life. He had been freed from Spandau by the bold efforts of Carl Schurz[4] and brought to England in a Mecklenburg ship, where he took a prominent position among the refugees. Beyond that he was a man of thorough honor of whom no one could say anything negative, and he enjoyed the general respect and trust of his countrymen. In the end, however, what was decisive in this undertaking was that he possessed great gifts as a speaker, so that he was just the man to carry out the planned project in America with success.

Following Kinkel's liberation in November 1850, I had discussed with other men in the associations the idea of a national subscription to gather money to offer Kinkel a nice home and adequate support in the United States. The appeal, which was published in all the German newspapers, was generally welcomed, and in an unbelievably short time we had gathered a substantial fund which would have sufficed to buy Kinkel the loveliest farm, fully equipped, and leave him with a substantial capital besides. Dr. Gempp and Carl Mügge interested themselves in the project, contributing considerably to its success, so they were commissioned to notify Kinkel of it and place this national gift of esteem from his American friends at his disposal. But Kinkel was still too involved in the storm and stress of 1848, and he also believed the revolution would soon break out again in Germany. As a result he declined our offer, although he thanked us deeply with his full eloquence for this sign of love and concern from his compatriots in America.[5] He also declared that he could not retire now, but rather had decided to place his full and as yet undiminished strength in the service of Germany, of freedom and of the imminent revolution.

Soon after this came the first news of the projected National Loan and of Kinkel's journey to America, stories that were soon confirmed as fact.

---

4. Carl Schurz (1829-1906) was a doctoral candidate at Bonn when the 1848 revolution broke out, during which he was a follower of his professor, Gottfried Kinkel. Schurz managed to escape to Switzerland after the collapse of the revolution, but Kinkel was imprisoned in Spandau near Berlin. Schurz rescued Kinkel on 6-7 November 1850. Schurz arrived in America in 1852, settling in Wisconsin in 1856. He was U.S. Minister to Spain, 1861-2, then served in the Union army, reaching the rank of major general. In 1866 he became coeditor of the *Westliche Post* in St. Louis. He was U.S. Senator from Missouri 1869-1875, U.S. Secretary of the Interior under Rutherford B. Hayes, 1877-81. *DAB*, 16: 466-71. Hans Trefousse, *Carl Schurz: A Biography* (Knoxville: University of Tennessee Press, 1982).

5. Appeal for subscriptions, *AW*, weekly, vol. 16, no. 11, 28 December 1850, p. 4, for 25 December 1850; Kinkel's response, letter dated London, 20 February 1851, *AW*, weekly, vol. 6, no. 25, 5 April 1851, p. 4, for 30 March 1851.

Views on this project were naturally divided. Refugees and younger German Americans greeted the project with jubilation and enthusiasm, making intense propaganda for it. On the other hand, the quieter and more reflective, particularly the "Grays," were decisively against it. My paper and I were among the opponents of the project, although I preserved personal sympathy for Kinkel. I was decisively against it from the beginning because I had no faith or trust in a revolution brought about by money gathered in begging. I was convinced that revolutions could only be brought into being by an enlightened ruler or a great statesman, as had been the case with the Emperor Joseph [II], or from below through a powerful idea permeating the entire people, an irresistible pressure for liberation from an intolerable situation as had happened in France in 1789. Nowhere in history had a great revolution moving all mankind ever been brought into being with money, particularly money that had to be collected by begging.

Kinkel arrived in person in New York in the first days of September 1851. From there he announced his arrival to me in the following letter:

New York, 16 September 1851

Citizen! I arrived last Sunday, and I intend to make a journey through America on behalf of and in agreement with the most important men of the revolutionary party in Europe, whose names I will be happy to tell you in person. I will seek to win the most influential leaders here on behalf of a plan for a German National Loan, and also to gather enough money through personal agitation to have a definitive committee for the revolution elected on the basis of the loan. This project, which would end the splintering of the entire emigration, is the key for our entire position toward Europe. I trust surely in the success of our plan.

The death of Dr. Gempp filled me with true pain. I had hoped to be able personally to shake the hand of this man of honor, who has shown me such goodness. But now he has found his death here in America!

My journey takes me first to Philadelphia and Cincinnati. In Cincinnati I will go to the post office and ask if there are any letters for me, and I would appreciate a brief response. From there I am going north to the Lakes, after which I will coming down the Mississippi to you. This would be in the last week of October. From you I will continue, if time allows, to New Orleans, and I shall return to Europe before New Year's.

Due to the powerful position that you, citizen, have in the press of the West, I beseech you to prepare the way for my arrival. Advocate the loan, and make it popular in the press. You should make preliminary contact concerning the loan with sympathetic persons, particularly those who approached me with such dignity in December.

Retain me in your good graces and have the goodness to send your weekly edition to my friends in London, who are continuing their lithographic correspondence, under their previous address.

> Greetings and a handshake.
> Gottfried Kinkel

I answered him at once with the open, honest declaration that I would not support the project of a national loan, but rather that I would oppose it. I gave him a full account of my guiding perception of the situation, and although I assured him of my personal respect and sympathy, I said that I had to oppose what he was representing. In the meantime, the refugees and their friends staged vast demonstrations in Kinkel's honor. This artificially created enthusiasm transplanted itself from town to town in the East, and both large and small notes of the German National Loan found takers. Balls, theatrical presentations, song evenings and bazaars were held to benefit the German National Loan, and quite considerable amounts of money were gathered, even if nowhere near the two million hoped for. This money was all sent to London and made available to the revolutionary committee.

The further Kinkel penetrated the interior of the Union, the stronger and livelier the dispute grew between promoters and opponents of the National Loan.[6] Eventually Kinkel arrived in St. Louis around Christmas. His friends figured that because the principal resistance to the project was centered in St. Louis, this opposition could be overcome through his personal appearance.[7] Kinkel's friends and the guarantors of the loan were all honorable men full of upright convictions, but their guarantees on behalf of the loan were meaningless, for an American court would not have recognized them as guarantors for a thousand Taler. These bold men were risking everything to make Kinkel's mission a success. A noisy newspaper polemic unrolled, one that had to be resolved by a decision of the German people of St. Louis.

---

6. *AW,* weekly, vol. 17, no. 12, 10 January 1852, p. 3, for 6 January, a series of negative arguments on Kinkel's National Loan from Cincinnati. Karl Heinzen in particular argued strenuously against the National Loan.

7. *AW,* weekly, vol. 17, no. 9, 20 December 1851, p. 2, for 16 December. He arrived on Sunday, 14 December, and there was a plan that he address a mass meeting on Thursday, 18 December.

I have already mentioned that everything, even the unimportant, was done in those days with solemn seriousness and righteous enthusiasm. It was all the more so with a situation that dealt with the good or pain of the old homeland, the liberation of millions of Germans from the bonds and chains of reaction.

A German popular assembly was called for 28 December, a Sunday, in the large hall of the southern Free Men school. There Kinkel and I were to hold a public debate on the projected National Loan, the assembly would vote for or against the project. Days before it was to take place, this assembly became the common subject of conversation, and public attention was almost exclusively drawn to it. Attendance was enormous. Not only was the large hall of the school overfilled with people, but all the schoolrooms on the ground floor were also stuffed. Thousands more Germans stood all around the schoolhouse who could not find a place in the building, and they were kept informed of the progress of the debate by messengers going in and out. Franz Schmidt was unanimously elected president of the assembly. He was given a board of vice presidents and secretaries chosen equally from the two sides, and the oratorical duel commenced.

After a strictly objective introduction by the president, Kinkel took the podium. Describing the project for a National Loan and its expected great influence on the liberation of Germany, he spoke for almost an hour, accompanied by the loudest applause and shouts of support from his friends and adherents. I really did not have an easy task before me in following Kinkel, who was a sympathetic personality and powerful speaker. But I had to step forward as an opponent of the project and refute his arguments one by one.

My profound conviction strengthened me, and I found words to communicate this conviction to the assembly in a penetrating way. In this way the battle proceeded back and forth for almost five hours. Each of us took the podium four times under the rapt attention of the assembly, until the president declared the debate at a close following our respective summations. The resolutions presented by the opposing sides were presented, and the resolution in favor of the National Loan was rejected by a great majority. The other resolution, which denounced the loan as incapable of being accomplished and incompatible with its goals, was passed by a two-thirds majority. The proceedings were carried on with the greatest decency and respect by the speakers, and the assembly followed them in strictest order and decorum.

After the end of the assembly I went to Kinkel. I presented my hand, repeating that although my personal respect for him remained unchanged, it had been my duty as leader of my compatriots to oppose the cause he was defending. He heartily responded to my handshake and only expressed his true regret that I could not have worked with him arm in arm on the undertaking. So we parted from one another, personal friends, but irreconcilable opponents as far as this matter went. This public discussion, which was taken down by the recording secretaries and published the next day, was the beginning of the end for the National Loan. In those days St. Louis set the tone for Germans in the West, and the debate as well as the voting had an effect. Kinkel was no longer received with the same enthusiasm. The bonds of the National Loan found ever fewer takers, and before three months were out, the societies that were supposed to lead the revolutionary loan were gradually dissolved. Indifference took the place of earlier enthusiasm, so that when Kinkel returned to Europe, the entire National Loan flickered away like a waning candle.

This affair was beautiful in its own way, as was the enthusiasm that prevailed on both sides. Even today I look back with pleasure on those ideally enthused, beautiful times, times that will never return in the face of our latter-day practical obsession with business.

As proof of the seriousness which possessed us all in those days, I will give a couple typical letters from that period. The first Kinkel wrote to me on the day before his departure. I preserve it as a worthy souvenir of this bold man:

St. Louis, 29 December 1851
Mr. H. Boernstein
Esteemed Sir!

A scheduling question has kept us apart, and it will only be after my departure from the city that I will be able to send you the letter from your sister-in-law, given me by the esteemed Frau Dr. Hoffmann in Pittsburgh, which was to serve as a letter of introduction. Please excuse this oversight and allow me to thank you for the courtesy you showed in taking and forwarding my correspondence.

The Homeric heroes had a joy in combat with opponents whom they had to recognize as powerful. Despite the pain your defeating me in this matter caused me, I have still had this same feeling toward you last Sunday.

Accept from me the respect that neither of us has ever denied the other in the midst of battle. I bid farewell to you and your city, which was once to be a home for me through your efforts. I treasure the relationship of personal esteem that your offered hand last Sunday sealed.

Gottfried Kinkel[8]

---

8. Published in *AW,* weekly, vol. 17, no. 13, 17 January 1852, p. 1, for 9 January, delivery having been delayed in the mails for eleven days. Boernstein also wrote a conciliatory

The second letter Kinkel wrote to Bernays in Highland:

St. Louis, 30 December 1851

I have been denied my wish of a pleasant half-hour with you, dear Bernays. I had looked forward to it since London, and yet I did not think I would be held here for fourteen days. Hillgärtner has been very sick, and our ways must part here. I am going tomorrow to New Orleans and he goes ahead of me to Cincinnati.

Boernstein has become an opponent to my cause. I know that his loss is a great loss one to the cause, and I wished for him and for myself that we could go forward together. Two powers in one party cannot dispute without causing both to lose power.

Live well and hold me in your affection. I greet you in parting with respect and hearty good wishes.

Gottfried Kinkel

Fourteen days later there was a silly epilogue. In those days the Prussian consul in St. Louis was the merchant E. C. Angelrodt,[9] an amiable, educated man and splendid businessman. Although he was not a professional (hence not a Prussian official) but only a trade representative, he still allowed the extreme reaction in Prussia to influence his attitudes. I was hence not a little amazed suddenly to receive the following letter from this man, with whom I was only superficially acquainted. This letter is also characteristic of the times:

Esteemed Mr. Boernstein!

No sooner had I recovered sufficiently from my very painful illness of four weeks duration (facial neuralgia, or gout of the head) to be able to think and read a bit, than I reached for the *Anzeiger des Westens,* of which a few

---

letter to Dr. Georg Hillgärtner, Kinkel's aide and Boernstein's future assistant, *AW,* weekly, vol. 17, no. 12, 10 January 1852, p. 3, for 7 January.

9. Ernst Carl Angelrodt (1799-1869) was born in Mühlhausen, Thuringia, and owned a spinning mill before emigration. He departed Germany due to his outspoken liberalism, although he served in the provincial estates of the Prussian province of Saxony. In St. Louis, where he made a name as a merchant and entrepreneur, Angelrodt became consul for Prussia, Saxony, Bavaria, Württemberg, Electoral Hessia, Brunswick, the Saxon Duchies, Oldenburg, and Mecklenburg. He was also deputy consul for Austria. He returned to Germany in 1864, dying in Karlsruhe. See Körner, *Element,* 307-8.

copies lay about my sickroom. These included number 74 of the day before yesterday, with Herr F. Schmidt's "Confession"[10] and your endorsement of it, and a part of the issue with the interesting discussion between you and Kinkel. During my illness I heard so much without any coherence about Mr. Kinkel's arrival and presence that I would like to know completely about the interesting discussion between him and you. Since I was unable to find the papers dealing with this, could you please send me all the issues dealing with Kinkel from the day of his arrival, particularly those dealing with your disputation with him?

It does my spirit good to read such a clear and correct evaluation on the refugee nonsense, as well as on the position a man should take in this country. It is good to read about a brave and spirited man such as I find portrayed in your presentations.

Dr. Engelmann[11] said Mr. Kinkel had letters of introduction to me, but he did not use them nor did he visit me. Well! A Prussian consul, even if only a trade representative, must appear in the eyes of many to be a servile subject. That can be understood. But one expects that an educated man will be able to distinguish between office and person. Kinkel should always be able to visit Angelrodt, and I am really sorry not to have met him. It would be interesting to me to meet a man of such scholarly education who stands so high, even if our views on politics and the loan might be quite different.

Excuse my scribbling—my hand and my head are too weak.

> With respect and friendship,
> Your
> E. C. Angelrodt

---

10. Franz Schmidt's "confession" was a statement of principles published in the first issue of *Freie Blätter,* 18 March 1851; see Rowan, "Anticlericalism, Atheism and Socialism," 47.

11. Dr. Georg Engelmann (1809-1884) was a physician by profession and botanist by avocation, one of the premier American scientists of the era. He came to St. Louis in the 1830s, and in the 1850s he convinced Henry Shaw to make his gardens (now the Missouri Botanical Garden) into a research-oriented institution. See Patricia P. Timberlake, *George Engelmann: Scientist at the Gateway to the American West, 1809-1860,* Master's thesis, University of Missouri-Columbia, 1984. Although a strong supporter of the 1848 revolutions, Engelmann joined with Christian Kribben, Ernst C. Angelrodt, and other educated Germans, whom Boernstein contemptuously called "Latins" or the "Clique," to support the regular Democrats against Boernstein and the Benton Democrats in 1852 and after. See Boernstein's attack on the "Latins" in *AW,* weekly, vol. 17, no. 26, 17 April 1852, p. 4, for 11 April.

It is possible that this letter was meant well, but in those days my blood was not so cold nor my judgment so placid as it is now. I felt injured by this letter, and it irritated me. In those days, one in my position had to be very careful. Whoever did not throw in his lot with the refugees was denounced as a servile lackey of princes. Whoever had even the slightest social contact, or even friendship, with a representative of the European governments was mercilessly pilloried and forever branded a spy of the Prussian or Austrian governments. A laudatory letter from the Prussian consul on my opposition to Kinkel and the revolutionary loan hit me as a mockery, a malignant perversion of my views. At the first opportunity I sat down and wrote a response to Consul Angelrodt. It was very proper in form, but injurious in content, for I had not thought that to oppose Kinkel was *"de travailler pour le roi de Prusse."*[12] Rather, I desired a revolution in Germany with my whole heart in order to end the miserable conditions there. Although I differed with Kinkel only over the proper means, as well as over a few details that would seem laughable today if I were not actually ashamed of them. From the time of this letter forward Consul Angelrodt, who had previously been pleasant to me, became my enemy and opponent. I was to endure long, bitter struggles with him and his friends, until time—which heals all wounds—and the experience of riper years brought about a peaceful understanding between the two of us.

---

12. French, "To work for the King of Prussia," a phrase used ironically by King Frederick the Great about himself.

The Revolutionary Collection *for* Hungary
(1852)

The history of revolutionary begging was not completed with Kinkel's argosy to win the American golden fleece. Kinkel's alleged triumphs and the initial success of the German National Loan—announced by refugees in all portions of the Union, but especially in the East, through overwrought correspondence articles—did not allow others to sleep. They too wanted their part of this German revolutionary California that was supposedly to be found in the United States. And so the leftist red wing of the German emigration in London, which considered itself the Supreme Revolutionary Central Committee, decided to collect money in America as well. As its apostle it sent the Baden refugee Amand Goegg[1] to the United States to fetch back a few million for revolutionary purposes. Richly supplied with instructions and powers, pamphlets and proclamations, Goegg also found his adherents. Also like Kinkel, he toured all the towns and settlements of the Union. Everywhere assemblies were called, speeches made, resolutions composed and revolutionary societies founded where they did not already exist in order to organize a great German American Revolutionary League across the entire Union. It was a grandiose idea, and Goegg was to organize it.

A basic fund for the future revolution was to be created, and there was also an effort to emancipate German Americans intellectually. In America, a German revolutionary literature was to be created whose products were to be smuggled to Germany by any possible means; this would maintain hope for a future revolution and keep intellectual preparation for it alive and ready. In order to raise the necessary funds for these purposes, a German Revolutionary League was to be established with a very large, budgeted income. It was estimated that three million Germans were living in the Union, all of whom were to join the Revolutionary League.[2] Each member

---

1. Amand Goegg (1820-1897), member of the Baden Provisional Government in 1849 and correspondent of Friedrich Hecker, was a Social Democrat in the 1870s. See *MEW,* vol. 27, p. 721; Zucker, 297.

2. *AW,* weekly, vol. 17, no. 27, 24 April 1852, p. 4, for 17 April, minutes of a meeting held on 12 April to establish a St. Louis branch of the American Revolutionary League, attended by Amand Goegg; ibid., vol. 17, no. 28, 1 May 1852, p. 2, for 27 April, the bylaws of the "Revolutions-Verein in St. Louis." The revolutionary Friedrich Hecker wrote an open letter to his old correspondent Goegg, *AW,* weekly, vol. 17, no. 26, 17 April 1852, p. 2, for 13 April, letter dated 10 April, Lebanon, Illinois.

was obliged to pay the pittance of 5¢ a month, which came to only 60¢ per member per year, but which amounted to nearly $2 million as an annual income. If the Revolutionary League had only existed for ten years, the League's wealth would have amounted to $18 million, or 90 million francs. With that sort of money it could have staged a nice little revolution. The idealistic side of Goegg's mission, which was that revolution was the first civil obligation of all Germans, made sense to German mass assemblies called everywhere. At least it made sense so long as they were still under the pressure of the inspired speeches of the revolutionary apostle and his disciples. The financial side seemed plausible to them as well, and everyone said, "We'll just drink one glass of beer less each week!" This was at the outset, and the first payment of 5¢ was willingly made. It was far easier than the National Loan, for that was supposed to be repaid by the future German Republic with interest, as the guarantors assured them. The revolutionary fund was an enterprise based on a sinking fund that demanded no accounting, and as a result it was much more popular with the masses.

Amand Goegg was as enthused and tireless at his assigned task as Kinkel, but there was a great difference between the two. Kinkel was an inspired speaker with great powers of persuasion, classically educated and yet understandable to anyone. Goegg, however, was a South German who made use of the language of the London Refugee Club. He would make a forceful entrance and set to work humorlessly. The efforts of the two resembled one another insofar as they both had momentary success, but neither could achieve anything lasting. Like meteors they came and were gone, without leaving a trace. Three months after Kinkel's tour of the United States, no one remembered the National Loan. The second payment of 5¢ was never made to Goegg's Revolutionary League. The revolutionary societies dissolved benignly. Most of the guarantors of the National Loan sought and found some way to support themselves, and the German Revolutionary League fell to quarreling. If anything was occasionally said of these groups, it was done with a smile of disbelief and a significant shrug of the shoulders.

In taking a position on this matter, I found it wiser to display no opposition to Goegg's mission; this conceded him no importance, at least among my personal opponents. On the other hand, I saw his efforts as only one of many possible means to achieving the primary goal I had in mind, which was to bring about a unity and solidarity among German Americans in order to win influence and significance in the internal situation of our new homeland. Hence I supported Goegg's efforts so far as it was in my powers, and so far as my own established position permitted. Goegg thus had a much friendlier reception in St. Louis, and he wrote me the following revealing letter on his departure:

Dear Mr. Boernstein!

I would have loved to have seen you once more before the steamship's departure.

My mission commands me to depart quickly and to renounce the desire to stay more days in St. Louis.

Receive my thanks for the selfless, helpful support you offered me in my difficult mission.

I also feel myself duty bound once more to wish you luck in your successes, brought about by your consistency, activity and spirited execution, to make Germans count for more with Americans than they have in St. Louis until now.

This your success will exercise a positive influence on the other parts of the Union in the direction indicated.

With a friendly greeting, your
A. Goegg
St. Louis, 15 April 1852

While these specifically German efforts at revolution were playing themselves out, Louis Kossuth, the former dictator of Hungary, came to the United States at almost the same time as Kinkel. He, too, was passing the plate, this time for Russian- and Austrian-oppressed Hungary. Unlike Kinkel and Goegg, Kossuth did not concentrate on the Germans; rather, he turned to the whole of America. He was not shy about addressing German and Irish assemblies, as well as Anglo-Americans, making propaganda for the cause of Hungary. Kossuth also displayed a much larger entourage than his German predecessors, and he appeared in greater pomp. He was usually preceded by old Ujházy, the former governor of Komorn,[3] who defended that fortress together with General Klapka until long after the disaster of Világos and the obliteration of all of Hungary's hope. He had surrendered Komorn to the Austrians only after all were granted free withdrawal and honorable conditions.

As a result, Governor Ujházy and a small escort of *Hunved* officers arrived in St. Louis as Kossuth's vanguard. A great mass meeting was called

---

3. "Lászlo Ujházy, civilian governor (kormánybiztos) of the fortress of Komorn," Komlos, *Louis Kossuth,* 35.

in the rotunda of the Courthouse,[4] into which the entire population streamed. I received the task of introducing our Hungarian guest to the meeting, which I did by giving a brief description of the Hungarian revolution, particularly the defense of Komorn. Then Ujházy announced in German the expected arrival of Kossuth and the purpose of his journey, which was to raise new financial aid for the momentarily repressed Hungarian revolution.

They had developed a much more practical method of raising money than either Kinkel or Goegg had pursued. Instead of shares in a National Loan or monthly dues to a Revolutionary League, the money was to be raised for Hungary once and for all, the surest way to success given the rapid dissipation of first enthusiasms. For this purpose Kossuth had brought along very beautifully engraved bank notes, the so-called Kossuth Notes. They were worth one, five, ten, or one hundred dollars, and were sold for their full nominal amount. After the victory of the revolution and the constitution of an independent Hungary, the notes would be accepted by all government authorities of the new state at face value, in gold if requested.[5] This was a very successful financial operation, for by these means there was created a national loan realized at once, without any interest. In the first enthusiasm of Kossuth's reception, Kossuth Notes found a large demand. Anglo-Americans, especially the ladies, literally made a sport of it, and the first Kossuth Notes to arrive in St. Louis were bought at a premium over their nominal value. One person known to me bought so many Kossuth Notes that she could paper her sewing room with them, as well as those her friends had collected when the dreams of Hungarian independence later exhausted themselves.

Soon after Governor Ujházy, Louis Kossuth himself came to St. Louis with a great entourage of Hungarian commanders and officers, accompanied by Franz Pulszky. All the clubs and militia companies received him in parade and went with him to his hotel, where a deputation of the city greeted him. In short, he received all the honors of a sovereign. Although these delegations were really nothing but a protest by Americans against the reaction then prevailing in Europe.

It was only natural that many insignificant people gathered about Kossuth to win notoriety through him. In the East particularly, many went

---

4. The Old Courthouse, a domed structure occupying the block between Fourth and Fifth Streets and between Market and Chestnut Streets, was begun in 1839 and completed in 1862. It is now part of the Jefferson National Expansion Memorial historical park.

5. "Kossuth Bank Notes were issued in one, five, ten, twenty-five, fifty, and one hundred dollar denominations. The notes above twenty-five dollars accumulated interest at 6 percent from the date of purchase. . . . Kossuth offered the Hungarian salt mines as collateral for the notes, which were due one year after Kossuth's government took office." Komlos, *Louis Kossuth*, 154.

beyond the limit. Thus a deputation of Germans in Newark assured Kossuth that the Germans threw themselves at his feet and were ready to die for him and his cause. Kossuth replied to this expression of servility with great tact, declining the offer by saying that "he did not believe that the speaker represented the views of the German people, but he could only desire that the Germans would place this readiness to sacrifice to their free principles and their fatherland. He could not expect them to do that either for his person or for the cause of Hungary."

It was even worse in Baltimore, where Schnauffer held an address to Kossuth on behalf of a festival committee and said, "The Germans are perennially divided, and only at the name of Kossuth are they united and ready to follow him if he should unfold his banner." At that time Kossuth responded, concluding by saying, "If the German people should choose him as their leader, he would be ready to answer that call." This was too much for many spirited Germans, and Dr. Wiss, who was present in a delegation at the reception put aside his planned message to make the following impromptu statement:

> Pardon me, Mr. Governor, if I exceed my mandate. But words have been spoken here that deeply shock me, for they belittle my people. My people, too, is oppressed under the same tyranny as Hungary. We well know that the united peoples must fight the united princes. But first of all each people has its own matters to settle, and it is not necessary to have a foreign leader dealing on its behalf. Otherwise the much-praised solidarity of all peoples would be an insult to an individual people. The German people will find the means from its own strength to make a revolution and lead Germany to unity and freedom. We pay full tribute to the brave deeds and greatness of Hungary without lowering ourselves in Hungary's regard. I ask you, Mr. Governor, not to misunderstand Germany's republican pride and self-reliance.

Kossuth was visibly moved by these words and replied with tact, saying, "Gentlemen, I know the German people, and it does not allow itself to be led. I do not need this warning. But it remains true that the Germans, at least up to now, have not learned how to lead themselves."

I am recounting this little episode, because it best illustrates the seriousness and pathos with which everything was done in those days.

I saw it to be my first obligation to hinder such excesses and servile demonstrations in the West, or at least in St. Louis. It would have been easy for me to have obtained control over German participation in Kossuth's reception and residence. Instead I took a very independent position in my paper, as well as in my discussions with Kossuth and

Pulszky. I stressed the German position both in dealings with the Hungarian and in public speeches.

It was precisely then, when Kossuth was in St. Louis (March 1852), that the struggle of the Society of Free Men was at its greatest intensity, and I was very interested in getting Kossuth to support a freethinking position. Up to that point Kossuth had remained entirely neutral in this regard, and he had carefully avoided the religious question. I now explained to him that this was now the most pressing matter of all, setting all other questions in the background. I explained that he would have to show his colors for certain and take a clear position in an upcoming German mass meeting. Kossuth had nothing good to say about the clergy, which agitated against him in Hungary and was in the first row of his enemies in Vienna. It was so that he agreed to deliver a thundering address against the papacy and the Jesuits at a mass meeting at Soulard Market.[6] This speech was widely applauded, but it had the result that the Irish, who had until then participated enthusiastically in every anti-monarchical demonstration, now were strictly forbidden by their priests to attend Kossuth gatherings. The entire ultramontane element turned against him.

After a longer visit than in other towns,[7] Kossuth finally departed St. Louis, bidding me farewell with the following lines:

St. Louis, 16 March 1852
Esteemed sir!

Allow me, before I depart, to recognize in the warmest terms the active zeal with which you have taken a stand for the sacred cause of civil and religious freedom in Europe. Talented men such as you can do much for the spread of freethinking principles, which I also support; I hence urge you repeatedly to hold in your heart the cause of Hungary, which is so closely tied to the interests of the United States. Proceed as you have been doing and allow me to hope that my presence has reduced neither your zeal nor the sympathy of the great circle of your friends and adherents. I remain, esteemed sir, your devoted

L. Kossuth

6. Soulard Market is an open-air farmers' market in the southern part of St. Louis which is still in operation.

7. Kossuth's visit to St. Louis was from 9 to 16 March 1852, see Leslie Konnyu, "Two Kossuth Letters in the Archives of the Missouri Historical Society," *BMHS* 18 (October 1961): 49. I owe this reference to Peter Acsay, then a graduate student at the University of Missouri–St. Louis. See also *AW,* weekly, vol. 17, no. 22, 20 March 1852, p. 1, for

Kossuth remained in the United States until the end of June, only then returning to Europe. He was significantly disappointed in both his financial and political expectations. The sale of Kossuth Notes had continuously declined until it fell to nil, and material assistance for Hungary from the American republic would not be realized. The Hungarians had been led to expect aid for a number of reasons—the recognition of Hungary by the United States, the zealous efforts of the American minister to free Kossuth and his entourage when they were interned in Turkey, the manly efforts of Captain Ingraham on behalf of the Hungarian refugee Martin Koszta in Smyrna, as well as the rude note of Secretary of State Marcy to the Austrian *chargé d'affairs* Hülsemann, had caused them to hope.[8]

This was precisely time for a presidential election in the United States, and no one could predict with certainty whether the Democrats might return to power. (This actually did happen with the election of Franklin Pierce.) Kossuth sought to couple the cause of Hungary with the American presidential election, making the support of Hungary by the United States into a plank of the party platform in order to win German votes. For this purpose he called a great mass meeting in New York, and in his farewell address he explained his central ideas. For the first time, attention was turned to the importance of the German vote in the Union; for the first time it was made a rallying point for all German Americans. Until then, Germans had always voted with the slaveholders, through thick and thin. Even if the cause of Hungary was only a subordinate interest for the Germans in America, used to protest the absolutism prevailing in Austria, even if enthusiasm for Hungary gradually declined after Kossuth's departure until it ceased, the issue still gave the first push for Germans of the Union to take count of themselves. They recognized their own strength and began to close ranks to deal with others in common. This movement made slow but steady progress from that moment on. Germans separated themselves ever more from the existing political parties, emancipating themselves from the paternalism of the wire-pullers.

Here is the letter Kossuth sent me from New York before his departure, published as an interesting document for judging the times:

---

16 March; p. 3, for 14 March; and p. 4, for 17 March. His "farewell" letter to the Germans of St. Louis is in *AW,* weekly, vol. 17, no. 23, 27 March 1852, p. 1, for 18 March, letter dated 16 March.

8. In July 1853, Captain Duncan Nathaniel Ingraham, commander of the *St. Louis,* confronted an Austrian warship in Smyrna (Izmir) harbor over the custody of a Hungarian refugee named Martin Koszta who had claimed American rights. The incident led to negotiations and a compromise in which Koszta was held by the French consul until the matter was resolved and Koszta released. *DAB,* 9: 477; 12: 277.

New York, 28 June 1852, 52 East 16th Street
My dear sir!

I hope that you have already read my German farewell address in the Tabernacle, New York, on 23 June, as well as the resolutions passed in the meeting.

I also hope that the impression that this occasion excited in the two political parties has not escaped your attention.

Truly, it is impossible not to see that America's German citizens with the vote the controlling power have in their hands when they are united in a single agreed direction, in keeping with the principles outlined in my speech.

They can determine the direction of foreign policy for the coming administration of the United States, and with that the triumph or collapse of liberty in Europe.

America's German citizens have never before been in this decisive position of power. The leaders of the parties have become aware of this power, and they are alarmed; they know that even in the worst case Germans will at least render every combination, every calculation of the parties uncertain.

Will German citizens grasp the importance of their position, which will not return in a century?

I hope so! May God the Almighty, Protector of Liberty, forfend that they should neglect this moment.

Will they not regard principles higher than names and party titles?

I hope they shall! The power of America, the liberty of Europe, of Germany, of Hungary and Italy, lies in your hand!

For God's sake, work to make your German brothers take this position. Endorse the principles outlined in my speech through meeting resolutions. Have them declare the way pointed out there to be their own.

Deal boldly! Hold the power of your position in your hand until one or the other party offers you real guarantees. That is of the greatest importance for you!

If I should be so fortunate that the German citizens of various parts of the United States publicly endorse my principles and the direction pointed out in them—openly proving that they are making this their policy—it would place me in a position to undertake effective negotiations with the parties and offer them guarantees corresponding to the principles and sympathies of German hearts.

God sees my inmost thoughts, and He knows that my heart is not moved by self-importance. No, it is the consciousness that the liberty of Europe depends on the unanimous support of America's German citizens that causes me to make this communication.

My requests are as follows:

    1) Call a German meeting at once to discuss which way America's German citizens wish to go in the presidential election.

    2) Have a committee of influential men (of both parties, if possible) prepare resolutions, including the following:

        a) That the German citizens of St. Louis able to vote should endorse the principles I declared in my New York speech of 23 June, making the political position given there their own. This will be because they recognize the true interests of the United States to be identical with those of the liberty of Europe, and hence these interests should serve every German citizen as a guideline.

        b) That they should publicly demand of me that I not depart the United States before I inform the German citizens of St. Louis which party has given the proper assurances, indeed the proper guarantees, to determine on this basis how to act in the question of the presidential election.

        c) That they particularly regard the revocation of the Neutrality Laws of 1818, or at least an interpretation in keeping with the individual rights of citizens of the United States guaranteed by the Constitution, to be a specially desired issue.

        d) That they call upon their fellow citizens of other ethnic identities to unite with them on this principled basis of world liberty and the honor and prosperity of the United States.

This way would be of permanent importance. Open acts and secret intrigues are at work to paralyze such success. But the Germans have become a power. Alas if we neglect this nod of providence! We must crystallize the movement so that its strength is not dissipated. The more it is publicly known that my politics and I can rely on the support of

German citizens, the more I can do for the cause so dear to your hearts. In the name of the esteem I hold for America, in the name of the oppressed peoples of Europe I beseech you to give me your hand in the direction indicated. Let me hear soon of an action I have desired!

With respect, the greeting of a brother, and a handshake

Your devoted
L. Kossuth
Henry Boernstein, Esq.[9]

Kossuth returned to Europe, and in the pressures of commercial and political life in America he and his efforts were as quickly forgotten as those of Kinkel and Goegg. But the political testament he left to German Americans in the letter above gradually came to pass, albeit neither in Kossuth's sense nor with any advantage for Hungary. Developments turned very much to the advantage of the Germans, who would have won an even more complete success if they had been freed of their primary disease, the proverbial German disunity, and closed together into a powerful whole.

---

9. A letter with virtually identical text, addressed by Kossuth on the same day to Wilhelm Stengel in Louisville, Kentucky, is published in English translation by Konnyu, "Two Kossuth Letters," *BMHS* 18 (October 1961), 50-51.

Congresses, Conventions *and* Platforms

While so much noise and tumult was being expended in America on the German revolution, things were gradually growing quieter in Germany itself. There no one thought to revive the orgies of 1848. The Federal Diet sat once more in its palace in the Eschenheimer Gasse in Frankfurt, waging revenge for the terrors the revolutionaries had given them. In Austria, old Metternich did not return, but others ruled even more despotically, and they were much worse if not nearly as clever as the sacked Prince Chancellor. In Prussia, the reaction ruled recklessly, and the government made its own people pay for the humiliations of Olmütz and Warsaw by oppressing every free expression of opinion and independent thought with an iron fist. In the rest of Germany there was competition to follow the Prussian example as closely as possible. As a result it grew continuously quieter in Germany, and one hope after another proved a sad disappointment. General relaxation spread, and the nation wallowed in indifference and decay. In fact it was years until Germans began again to arise spiritually, showing the first signs of life, of restored strength and activity in the establishment of the German National Society in 1859.

With this snuffing out, or rather falling to sleep, of the liberal movement in Germany, it was only natural that people in America began to take notice. They could no longer deceive themselves but finally overcame their homesickness for the old fatherland. In some halfway plausible fashion they must seek an escape from the excesses the "Greens" had committed. All the people who had leveled their gaze on Germany for three continuous years, basing all their calculations on the revival of the German revolution, now began to recall that they had indeed become American citizens. Their new home and its interests, they realized, were now more important to them than the distant old fatherland. They saw that they could be far more useful in their new theater of action, and do better things for themselves and their fellow citizens than chasing fantastic delusions, building castles in the air, or fighting with windmills à la Don Quixote. So ended the German American revolutionary epoch. And in a manner typical of the spirit of overexcitement which ruled then, it did so with a new extravagance topping everything that had come before.

The number of revolutionary societies in the United States in those days was already over a thousand, and the leading spirits of these associations consulted with one another over the fact that Germany would or could do nothing for its own liberation, and the question of how their American brothers might help. A few of the most outstanding leaders came to the ingenious idea that the liberation of Germany could be accomplished by having the United States of America declare itself a World Republic. Concentrating the entire region from the northern polar seas to Tierra del Fuego and Patagonia into a single vast republic, it could then annex old Europe to this World Republic. This also left open the possibility of later absorbing Asia, Africa and Australia into the new world state, establishing the Universal Republic of United Mankind for eternal peace on earth. This colossal idea, about which our present extremely prosaic time can only smile and shrug its shoulders, was then adopted with enthusiasm by the overheated spirits of refugees and greeted with stormy applause.

Then came the notorious congress called at Wheeling, where all German American revolutionary societies would be represented and where the measures would be discussed and passed to realize this grandiose idea. The congress was called for 12 September 1852, and 1,112 revolutionary societies announced their participation. Wheeling made the most elaborate preparations to receive the 1,112 delegates in a worthy, friendly manner, and the eyes of all Germans were directed with great suspense on the tiny, then little-known town of Wheeling. Anxiously, German Americans awaited what the great assembly would pass for the benefit of German humanity.

Either the treasuries of the revolutionary societies were very short, so they could not raise the travel costs and per diem expenses for their delegates, or the first enthusiasm had already evaporated, and everyone calmly expected what the other would do by laying his own hands in his lap.

In any case, on 16 September there were only thirteen registrations of actual delegates, to which were joined three delegates from Wheeling. The congress hence actually consisted of sixteen delegates, on whom 1,112 revolutionary associations had bestowed their representation by proxy. The history of that time has preserved for us the names of these sixteen, these brave freedom fighters, who gathered on this American *Rütli* to declare America a World Republic that would annex little Europe.[1] They were the president, Dr. Conradin Homburg; his secretary, Eduard Schläger of Boston, the most inexhaustible of all stump speakers; L. Meyer was also from Boston; C. Göpp and W. Rosenthal from Philadelphia; Roth and E. Hoffmann from Pittsburgh; A. Gerwig from Cincinnati; L. Roos from Newark; J. Müller from Cleveland; L. Kirchner from Troy; G. Baczko from Albany; and the three Wheeling delegates, R. Fischer, C. Strobel and J. N. Winkler. Joining these fifteen delegates was a sixteenth, the revolutionary traveling salesman W. Rothacker from London, and the congress was complete. These "brave

---

1. The *Rütli* is a meadow in the center of Switzerland where the original cantons of Uri, Schwyz, and Unterwalden gathered in 1291 to form the confederation which became Switzerland.

men but poor political musicians" were filled with the best and most honorable intentions, righteously enthused for the great idea.

As a further backdrop, the theme of annexation was in the air. Texas, California, and New Mexico had just been acquired, enterprises were continually being armed to annex Cuba and Central America, and the hope was always being nurtured sooner or later to incorporate the English holdings in Canada into the star-spangled republic. Further, Secretary of State Webster had used language against Austria in the affair of Martin Koszta that the powerful Czar Nicholas of Russia would not have allowed himself to use in Europe, even against the Prince of Reuss-Schleiz-Greiz.[2] Immigration streamed in from Europe, bringing continual growth in the working force and national wealth, and hence in power. In short, the mood in the Union was ebullient and overweening, and everything seemed possible, even the most unlikely. Whoever wants to get an idea of how the idea of America's world mission was discussed and developed in those days should read the book written then by C. Göpp and Theodor Pösche, dedicated to the new President Franklin Pierce, *The New Rome*.[3] In this book, written in a truly enthusiastic language, the immediate future of a united mankind is portrayed in a glittering manner, with the United States as its central sun. Copies of this work, which is entirely gone from the bookstores, could certainly still be found in the Library of Congress or the Smithsonian Institution. C. Göpp thoroughly developed these ideas at the congress himself, stressing how the contradiction between the monarchical paternalism of old Europe and the independent self-reliance of individuals, communities and states in young America would find its fortunate resolution through an American world-republic and the annexation of Europe. Resolutions to achieve this end were adopted by this congress of sixteen men. Boston was designated as the central bureau, and a Peoples' League for the Old and New World was organized, at least on paper. An address was also issued which, translated into all languages, was to be sent to all the peoples of the world to inform them of what had taken place and to exhort them to collaborate. Among other things, this overwrought address says:

> America's welfare requires the unchaining of European life; the freedom of America requires the liberation of our European brothers; the American Union requires its extension to the states of Europe: the time has come when the motto, *E pluribus unum* must cross the Atlantic. We demand the expansion of American liberty. It can be victorious without American

---

2. Reuss-Schleiz-Greiz was a miniscule principality in Thuringia.
3. Charles Goepp and Theodore Poesche, *The New Rome; or, The United States of the World* (New York: G. P. Putnam & Co., 1853); see Cazden, *Social History*, 603-4.

blood or money. But thanks to the god of battles, it is probable that—just as Greece had its Trojan war, which transformed a fishermen's state into the beacon of civilization; just as the crusades awoke Western Europe from the night of that epoch—America will also have its Iliad and its crusade, winning its place among the peoples as the focus of mankind! A war to spread our institutions is not a war of conquest; because the spirit of our government is the principle of self-government, or rather non-government, its expansion is not the introduction of a system, but the abolition of force and violence. Its goal is to establish the sovereignty of the individual by striking off bonds against which the individual has fought in vain.

The American continent divides the ocean as Italy does the Mediterranean. And just as the old Rome gazed down on a circle of lands, so the United States of the New World casts its eyes on the world. The universal realm of the future belongs to it. It is a realm not of conquest and subjection, not of origins, not of national tensions and hate, but of brotherhood, unity and liberty. We swear to complete its mission and to make one world out of many.

The grand work of republicanizing the world and annexing Europe was finished in three days, and the Congress adjourned with the exalted feeling of having delivered a clever blow and brought about a great deed. Unfortunately the end did not correspond to this promising beginning. In the presidential election and the great agitation of the entire country that went along with it, the Wheeling Congress vanished without a trace. The Peoples' League for the Old and New World never came into existence, and the central bureau in Boston had as much as nothing to do. Three months later, even before the new year of 1853, all the revolutionary societies had quietly dissolved. "The Address to All the Peoples and in All Languages" was sold cheap to a cheese merchant, who used it for a more material purpose. With these glittering idealistic fireworks, which were the last salvo of the "Greens," the German American revolutionary period ended, never to be revived.

Yet these active, unpeaceful natures, still living under the effects of the Forty-Eighter movement, could not damn themselves to absolute peace. Something had to be done. They had to have associations. And so suddenly they recalled that they were actually in America; they had obligations to their new homeland, which they could enlighten and grace with the exalted ideas of 1848. In Germany, and in Europe in general since Napoléon's coup d'état, there was nothing more to do. So they busied themselves with America, beginning to learn something about American history and politics, to study the Constitution of the United States. There our Forty-

Eighters discovered that in this best of all republics there was still a great deal that was not splendid and much, in fact an enormous amount, that was very needful of improvement. When the microscopic loupe and the sharp analysis of criticism were applied to the Constitution and institutions of the United States, one soon discovered that the republic and its constitution, in fact all American conditions, were a mass of incoherencies and contradictions. Abuses and inconsequentialities had resulted, and all of these crying injustices needed pressing reform. There arose a mass of new movements, characterized by new reform societies that sprouted like mushrooms out of the ground. The slogan of the day was reform, political reform, religious reform, socialist reform. In short, everything should be made other than it presently was. In the sessions of the associations and in the newspapers, continuing proposals were made and discussed on how the Constitution of the United States—which had been brewed up by a bunch of old fogies way back at the end of the last century with no notion whatsoever of modernity—was best to be altered in a contemporary way so as to conform with the relations and demands of the enlightened nineteenth century, particularly of the eternally venerated year 1848.

The only strong, positive voice among Germans was for the necessity of abolishing slavery. On all other questions, whether it was the president of the republic, the legislature, the judiciary or state sovereignty, there were as many opinions as there were heads. The exalted socialists and communists even rose to the point of proposing the abolition of money, declaring all possessions to be state property, abolishing marriage, introducing free love, eliminating the family and raising children by the state at state expense. Conventions of the most various sort were called, among them the Convention of Free Germans, which first met in Louisville, with a platform by Karl Heinzen.[4] Similar conventions followed in Ohio, Indiana and other states. An English language paper was established to make these earth-shaking ideas available to the Americans. But many of these movements went predictably and quickly lame, and the beginning enthusiasm went up in smoke. In its place came indifference, and the power of lethargy, the "masterly inactivity" of American conditions won out over the volcanic movement of Germans. Nothing in the Constitution was changed, the various reform associations gradually dissipated, and everything remained as it had been until the great events of 1861-65.

---

4. Karl Heinzen (1809-1880), born at Gravenboich near Düsseldorf, arrived in America in early 1848. He returned for the Baden revolt of 1849, finally settling in America in 1850. His radical socialist *Pionier* was published in various places from 1854 to 1879. *DAB*, 8: 508-9.

I kept myself far away from these monstrosities, at the same time using my influence with Germans in the West to warn my friends and readers of the *Anzeiger* against these futile efforts. In fact, neither the Wheeling Congress nor the American reform movement that followed found any response or following in the West, particularly in the Mississippi Valley. On the other hand, I consistently pursued my set goal, which was to organize the Germans in the West into a large, strong unity in order to help them attain power and influence in the internal matters of their new homeland.

One episode in particular helped my efforts in this direction, although it placed me in some danger and caused some Germans to pity me; on the whole, however, it had only the best results and considerably accelerated bringing the Germans together. The so-called Nativist Party later engendered the Know-Nothings and was more or less a satellite of the Whig Party, returned to greater significance after long quiescence. As early as the presidency of the elder Adams and the Hartford Convention, they had been at work, using the election slogan, "Only Americans should rule America." Not helped by the circumstances of the times, the Nativist Party had shrunk into the background. Under the Whig administration of Fillmore, however, they regained courage and boldness, believing they had a chance of winning before the complete breakup and disappearance of the Whig Party which was already underway. Their efforts were ostensibly aimed against Catholicism, which was winning ever more property, power and influence. In fact they hated all foreigners without distinction, wanting all public offices to go only to born Americans and advocating the granting of citizenship to immigrants only after they had lived here twenty-one years without interruption. The nativists were the Janissaries and Mammalukes of the Whig party, performing the crude work of disrupting and stealing elections, of inciting election riots and falsifying votes.

The rising influence of Germans in the West was a horror to both the Whigs and the nativists, and because the German organization in St. Louis had faded away, they decided in secret caucus to give us a lesson then and there. The city government of St. Louis was in the hands of the Whigs, and one of the chiefs of the party, Luther M. Kennett, was Mayor of St. Louis.[5] He was to be reelected at all costs and the Democratic candidate defeated, but because the Democratic Party had a large majority from German votes, this could only take place through brutal force. For this purpose, the

---

5. Luther Martin Kennett (1807-1873), born in Kentucky, moved to Missouri in 1824 and was deeply involved in railroad investment; alderman 1843-6; mayor 1850-53; president of the St. Louis and Iron Mountain Railway, 1853; elected as a Whig to Congress over Thomas Hart Benton in 1854, serving 1855-57 and failing reelection. See *EHSL*, 2: 1167-68, and *Edwards's*, portrait, 151, text 153-54, *BDUSC*, 1301-02.

notorious Ned Buntline (actually named Judson),[6] one of the most disreputable nativist rowdies, was called to St. Louis. He joined with his cohorts and soon began disrupting Democratic rallies. The election was to take place on 5 April, and the preparatory rallies began in the last days of March. One rally of German Democrats was attacked by the nativists, and it was dispersed because the municipal police helped the attackers, instead of defending the assembly.[7] The rally had been called by Alexander Kayser, a German lawyer and a gifted, ardent man, who unfortunately suffered from overexcited eccentricity, harming more than he helped.[8] There were the most dreadful threats in the American papers against me, against the *Anzeiger*, against Kayser and against all Germans whomsoever. At Whig election rallies, nativists and Irishmen, egged on by the Jesuits, who had hitherto united with the Democratic Party, were actually encouraged to strike down the Germans, hang the editor of the *Anzeiger*, wreck the printing shop of the paper. They went systematically to work to organize a mob against the Germans, and the language of both the papers and the orators provoked serious concern.

As early as 3 April, two nights before the election, another assault was carried out on the last Democratic rally, but the Germans were better prepared than before, and the nativist rowdies were sent away with bloody heads.[9] On the Sunday that followed, the mob was further drilled. Then came Monday morning, election day. In those days the First Ward was called "the Banner Ward," because almost all ballots were cast for the Democratic ticket, with at most half a dozen votes for the Whig ticket. Because of this, the First Ward, which was primarily German, was to be severely disciplined. Immediately after the opening of the ballot box, many rowdies and members of Ned Buntline's gang arrived in the First Ward, insulting the election judges and the Germans gathered to vote. They fired pistols in the air and did everything to provoke the Germans to some excess.

---

6. Edward Zane Carroll Judson (1823-1886), also known as Ned Buntline, was a disreputable adventurer, rioter, popular journalist, and founder of the American dime-novel as a genre. Many of his works celebrated his own dubious activities as "Ned Buntline," and after the Civil War he promoted the image of "Buffalo Bill" Cody. Boernstein's account, bizarre as it seems, agrees with other reliable accounts of Buntline's career. See *DAB*, 10: 237-39.

7. *AW*, weekly, vol. 17, no. 24, 3 April 1852, p. 4, for 1 April.

8. Alexander Kayser (1815-before 1865), born 1815 at St. Goarshausen on the Rhine, brother of Henry Kayser, longtime St. Louis engineer, arrived in St. Louis in 1833. He was a practicing lawyer in St. Louis after 1841, serving as a lieutenant in the Mexican War. He later split with Boernstein over the question of the abolition of slavery, siding with secessionists, and he was attacked by a German mob in south St. Louis in 1861. See Rowan/Primm, 271-3; *Edwards's*, 564-5 with portrait; Körner, *Element*, 342-4.

9. See *AW*, weekly, vol. 17, no. 25, 10 April 1852, p. 3, for 6 April.

The Germans, however, who had been warned in time, remained calm. They coolly disarmed the disturbers of the peace and sent them home with the warning not to be seen there again. The rowdies then rushed to the Fourth and Fifth Wards, spreading the rumor that the Germans in the south of the city had taken possession of the ballot boxes, had driven off all the Whigs who wished to vote, were admitting no Americans to vote, etc. This false rumor raised tremendous excitement among the Americans. A mob formed, and Ned Buntline appeared on horseback in their midst to hold one of his eccentric speeches, entreating the people to maintain the liberty of elections and to mob the "damned Dutch." While this was going on, leaders of numerous nativist gangs were gathering in various groups, firing them up with unbridled speeches calling for murder and plunder of the Germans, for the destruction of the *Anzeiger,* and the murder of Boernstein and Kayser. Soon the mob had grown to more than a thousand persons, who now headed down to the First Ward under Ned Buntline's leadership. Gathering their courage and hurriedly arming themselves, they were joined by a number of plundering Irishmen.

The First Ward had no warning of impending trouble, and because the Germans were completely unprepared, the first attack on the house where the voting was taking place was a complete success. The ballot box was smashed and the German votes already cast were destroyed. Now the mob set about destroying and plundering neighboring German taverns. The first was the German tavern of Niemeier, in whose courtyard stood the cannon of Captain Almstedt's German volunteer artillery company. The cool-headed Niemeier defended his property with the help of his people, and he managed to keep the rowdies at a respectful distance for a while. But Niemeier only had two guns, while Ned Buntline and his cohorts all had revolvers with which they shot continuously at the Germans. At the same time, a fire company that had brought up its pumper turned its hose against anyone trying to help Niemeier, throwing his defenders to the ground with a strong blast. Niemeier bravely held his ground, shooting down a leader of the rowdies named Stevens and wounding several others. But in the end he had to give in to superior forces and flee out the rear of the building. Now the mob broke into the house, demolished and plundered it, and set it afire, so that the neighboring house burned down as well. They loaded the cannon and promised to fire it at anyone who sought to hinder them in their revenge.

In the meantime, the Germans had recovered from the first shock, assembled and armed themselves. Growing ever stronger and more numerous, they soon attacked the rowdies in return. First of all, as a number of Germans drove the plundering rowdies from the burning Niemeier tavern, other bold men entered the back of the building and rescued the now-wounded Niemeier and his wife, who had given birth the day before. Then the Germans turned on the vile attackers, who had run out of ammunition, sending them home with bloody heads and broken ribs.

Throughout this entire time, the Whig municipal administration of Luther M. Kennett took not the slightest measure to establish peace and order. Only when the Germans were in the majority and were flocking in, well armed, and the rowdies had no hope of progress did sundown at last bring peace. The German militia companies, which had gathered in the meantime, remained under weapons in the First Ward, throughout the night, and even through the following day, when the rowdy Stevens, who had been shot, was to be buried. In the meantime, Ned Buntline issued a printed proclamation, which said:

> Americans, the events of yesterday must teach you that the institutions of our republic cannot be maintained if you do not do your duty. Yesterday at the ballot boxes it was Germans and foreigners against Americans! This despicable crime cannot be tolerated, and it will not be tolerated. This story has only just begun; what happened yesterday was only the beginning of the end, and no one can say what the end shall be. The American spirit has been awakened, and the blood of our murdered brother will not go unrevenged . . . (etc., etc.)

I was soon informed that there was to be a general attack on the German parts of town on return from the cemetery, after the burial, and that the prepared and armed nativists intended to destroy my printing shop along with the German neighborhoods. There was no time to lose, and so I attended the session of the district court with my lawyer, Thomas C. Reynolds.[10] Before the judges I demanded that Sheriff Belt, who was present,

---

10. Thomas Lyttleton Caute Reynolds (1821-1887) was born in Charleston, S.C., graduating from the University of Virginia in 1838, and receiving a doctorate "in both laws" from Heidelberg in 1842. He served in Europe as secretary of the U.S. legation in Madrid, 1846-48, and settled in St. Louis in 1850, working as a lawyer. He was United States District Attorney, 1853-57. He was elected lieutenant governor of Missouri as a Douglas Democrat in 1860. He fled Jefferson City in June 1861, and the death of Claiborne F. Jackson made him acting head of the Confederate Missouri government in exile in Texas. After the war he went to Mexico, returning to St. Louis in 1869, where he ended his life by throwing himself down an elevator shaft in 1887. See William E. Parrish in *EC*, 3: 1323, but also Stella Drumm, Isaac C. Lionberger, eds., "Letters of Thomas C. Reynolds 1847-1885," *Glimpses of the Past*, vol. 10, no. 1 (1943). On his efforts to engineer the secession of Missouri from the Union, see Arthur Roy Kirkpatrick, "Missouri in the Early Months of the Civil War," *MHR* 55 (1960-61): 235-66, and "The Admission of Missouri to the Confederacy"; ibid., 366-86. Questions about Reynolds's identity are mentioned and dismissed by Boernstein later in this book.

take the necessary measures to keep peace and order, securing persons and property. This demand in a public court had the desired effect. Judge Treat[11] supported my demand and urged the greatest energy on the sheriff. He in turn called out all the militia companies, even the American ones, to place themselves in proper locations with live ammunition. The entire police force was placed in readiness, and two hundred citizens were sworn in as special constables. On my pressing appeal in the morning paper, Germans were also gathered, properly armed and united, swearing to stand one for all, all for one. Germans made up three-quarters of the volunteer companies, so that one could look forward to the afternoon with confidence. They were solidly determined to treat the attackers as they deserved and to send them home with a "German push."

The burial of Stevens took place in the afternoon. Ned Buntline led the entire procession, badly dressed and still on horseback. Next to him were carried two large banners on which the following texts appeared:

Americans!
We bury our brother!
Remember, how he was slain!

and on the other banner was:

Our brother was murdered,
While we mourn our loss,
We remember his worth.

The coffin was covered with the American flag and behind it, as the first mourner, was the Mayor of St. Louis, Luther M. Kennett!!! During the

---

11. Samuel Treat was judge of the Common Pleas Court under St. Louis County in the *Directory,* 1854-5, 244.

procession, various gentlemen occasionally leaped up and reported as *agents provocateurs* that some Americans had just been attacked by Germans and mishandled, but in part they were not believed, and in part the measures taken by the sheriff and the decision of the Germans to tolerate nothing had so impressed the rowdies that they did not attempt to take revenge. The evening of the burial passed without serious disturbance, although a threatening crowd gathered in front of the printing shop of the *Anzeiger* and some stones were thrown at windows.[12] This episode brought the Germans of St. Louis together, and this inner solidarity was the primary element of their power and strength for the following years.[13]

12. For a "man on the street" view of these events, see MHS, Tiffany Family Papers, box I, folder 16, Pardon Dexter Tiffany (1812-1861) to Hannah Kerr Tiffany, Planter's House, St. Louis, 6 April 1852: " . . . I told you it was election day & such an one as St. Louis never before saw & I sincerely hope never will see again. Reports were circulated that the Dutch in Soulards addition had taken the Polls & would not allow any one to vote who was an American. This aroused the Natives and the result I would not go into details was that one man was shot dead a dozen or more were wounded by being shot, many more by being struck by stones & two Dutch Houses were burnt up by the excited Mob. The young man named Stevens one of the firemen was buried to day by the firemen and all Kinds of Mottoes and banners were carried in procession to excite their sympathy and arouse to vengeance. Boernstein & Alex Kayser are denounced for having stimulated by the newspapers the Germans to their outrageous proceedings and many of the better class of Germans are as much incensed against them as the Americans are. It is said that Boernstein has been notified to leave the State & Kayser yesterday applied to the Court of Com. Pleas & the Sheriff for protection for himself & family & that of Boernstein against the threats of a mob."

13. *AW,* weekly, vol. 17, no. 25, 10 April 1852, p. 2, for 7 April, "Der fünfte April 1852."

Thomas H. Benton

(1852)

The electoral uprising of 5 April 1852 not only caused the Germans in the West to draw ever closer together, but also opened their eyes to the question of whether and from what quarter they (and all other adoptive citizens) were threatened. To be sure, this electoral rebellion had been carried out by nativist ruffians; but its true, deeper motivation had been the slaveholders and their desire to rule unhindered. The Germans had always been a thorn in the side of the southern slaveholders, who watched the power of the German element grow with misgivings and bitterness; immigrant Germans played a decisive political role even in a slave state, Missouri. As a result, nothing was done during the election riots by the Whig Party or its mayor, Luther M. Kennett, to protect threatened Germans and to keep peace and order. Although intervention would have been very easy at the start of the upheaval, it was only after blood had flowed and property had been destroyed, after the Germans had precipitously organized and armed themselves completely—that the courts (not the municipal administration and its police) took courage and acted with energy.

In any case the result of the election was another victory for the Whig Party. With the ballots from the First Ward destroyed, the larger part of the German votes had been lost, and Luther M. Kennett was once again elected mayor of St. Louis. But this victory proved very expensive for the city, because according to the laws of Missouri, towns and communities are responsible for the full value of damage to persons and property through tumult or revolt as soon as they have neglected to repress these tumults or revolts with the legal means at their disposal. This had been the case in St. Louis, and many suits for damages, destruction, looting and arson by nativist gangs were brought against the city. All were decided in the courts for the plaintiffs.[1] Further, penal prosecutions were begun against the worst plotter of the riots, a Whig leader by the name of Dr. Moses, who was sentenced to fifty dollars or three months in prison for violent attacks on Germans. A warrant for the arrest of Ned Buntline was issued, but it could not be executed because he was warned by friends and managed to avoid it by rapid flight.[2]

---

1. *AW,* weekly, vol. 17, no. 24, 3 April 1852, p. 4, in which Boernstein published affidavits of witnesses, along with lists of damaged property and their owners; ibid., vol. 17, no. 25, 10 April 1852, p. 2, for 7 April.
2. *AW,* weekly, vol. 17, no. 27, 24 April 1852, p. 3, for 22 April, chiding the *Evening Dispatch* for announcing the forthcoming publication of a Ned Buntline novel.

Thomas Hart Benton, United States Senator for Missouri, 1821-1851, and member of the House of Representatives, 1853-55. Photograph c. 1856. Courtesy of the Missouri Historical Society.

Ned Buntline was a true representative of American rowdies, making murder and homicide his profession, drunkenness and gambling his enjoyment. To him a human life had no value at all, and he and his followers always had a hair-splitting Bowie knife and a pair of six-shooters for use in a minute. This low-down scum has already lost much of its earlier dangerousness, and with the advance of civilization and the assumptions of its rights by humanity, they will in time entirely die out.

Ned Buntline (or Edward Judson as his real name was) came, so far as I know, from New York, and in fact from the most dreadful and disreputable part of that great world-city. Not much is known of his youth. He first made a public appearance in Nashville, where he seduced a married woman and straightaway shot down her husband when he discovered them *in flagranti.* He was arrested for trial, but an aroused mob seized him from the bailiffs, held a short lynch trial over him, and hanged him from a tree outside town. Dragging him out of town, holding court and obtaining a rope took some time, and in the interim the bailiffs alarmed local officials; a strong troop of police, aided by order-loving citizens, rushed the lynchers, arriving at precisely the moment when Ned Buntline was yanked up into the tree with the rope around his neck. A brawl took place between the two parties, and Buntline's friends the rowdies used the confusion to cut him loose. He soon regained consciousness, and he was about to be taken away when the police received reinforcements and renewed their battle, driving the rescuers away. But then the lynchers received strong reinforcements from crowds running from the town, and Buntline was grabbed again and hanged for the second time from the same tree. This time the police, the supporters of order, and Buntline's friends, the rowdies, made a desperate charge at the lynchers, and once more they managed to cut the hanged man loose. He was thrown over a horse and, surrounded by his friends, sent off at a gallop to safety.

He then disappeared from the state of Tennessee, only resurfacing a few years later in New York as the publisher and editor of a rude, shameless boulevard paper. The residents of the most disreputable part of New York, Five Points, were its readers and subscribers. The paper was the mouthpiece of rowdyism and blackmail, such as we in Europe call the "revolver press" nowadays, and with it, Buntline provoked the notorious Astor Place riot, which cost fifty lives. The occasion was the guest performance of the famous English tragedian, Macready, who visited New York in 1849 and performed his most famous roles as Hamlet, Macbeth, Richard III, etc., at the Astor Theater. Despite the splendid reception Macready received from the New York public, Buntline (said to be in the pay of the American actor Forrest) managed to get the lower classes of the people enraged at the "alien infiltrator," the "infiltrating Englishman," and the result of this sensationalism was the gathering of a huge mob in front of the Astor Theater on the evening of Macready's benefit. The crowd was encouraged by Buntline to mob the hated foreigner; beginning with threats, howls and screams, they proceeded to deeds, and in the end the theater was stormed and demolished. The authorities gained control of the situation only after using military force, including artillery. More than a hundred persons were killed or seriously wounded. About twenty rowdies fell in battle against the military, and Buntline himself was arrested and later sentenced to a year in the penitentiary.

After surviving imprisonment, he was called to St. Louis by Luther M. Kennett's Whig friends, there to revive his glorious activities as already described. When he vanished from St. Louis in order to avoid arrest, he became a leader of the Know-Nothings; then in the process of organizing under the name of the "American Party," they would reach their high point in 1854 and 1855. They marked their emergence through bloody electoral riots in Louisville, Baltimore, Washington, and New Orleans. They had their demise in the presidential election of 1856, when they vanished as a political party. During this brief period, when Know-Nothingism was in fashion, Buntline was so bold as to return to St. Louis and attempt to resume his dirty game of 1852. The city had a Nativist municipal government, but at that time the *Anzeiger des Westens* had become an influential paper. It denounced in the sharpest language the reappearance of the bold rowdy, for whom there was still an outstanding warrant of arrest. Further, several respected German citizens and I went before the grand jury then in session and presented the matter to them. The grand jury took up the matter at once and directed the sheriff to execute his warrant. Ned Buntline vanished, and since then he has virtually disappeared. At least he has not played any outstanding role. Since the decline of the Whigs as well as of the Know-Nothing Party, he had no employers or protectors. I never heard what finally became of him.

August of 1852 brought the congressional election for Missouri, and with it a decision over the influence of the *Anzeiger* and the strength of the German element. Thomas Hart Benton,[3] one of the most important statesmen of America, had been the most intimate friend of General Jackson, his adjutant-general during the War of 1812, and he came to St. Louis after the end of the war in 1815 and established himself there as a lawyer. During this time he also published a Democratic weekly. When

---

3. Thomas Hart Benton (1782-1858) was born in North Carolina. Attending Chapel Hill College and William and Mary, he settled in Tennessee in 1806, being a member of the state senate, 1809-11. After service as a colonel of volunteers and as General Jackson's aide, he moved to St. Louis in 1815, entering the U.S. Senate in 1821 with the admission of Missouri to the Union, serving until 1851. He was elected as a Democrat to the 33rd Congress (1853-55), failed reelection in 1854 for Congress and losing election as governor in 1856. He died in Washington, D.C., and is buried at Bellefontaine Cemetery in St. Louis. *BDUSC,* 612.

Missouri was admitted as a state, Benton was sent as Missouri's representative to the Senate. He held this office for thirty years, during which he moved from being a supporter of slavery to being its opponent—or at least speaking in favor of restricting its further expansion into new territories. Then Calhoun argued his new doctrine that each sovereign state had the right to declare measures of the federal government to be null and void if these appeared, in the view of the state, to exceed the powers of the federal government.[4] Calhoun was even then thinking of a division of the federation, and Benton opposed him, describing both Calhoun and his adherents as "Nullifiers." This division within the Democratic Party was at first limited to the state of Missouri, where a third political party emerged, called Benton Democracy, opposing the Whigs as well as the proslavery Democrats or Nullifiers. This Benton Democracy, five-sixths of which consisted of Germans, was the first forerunner of the later Republican Party. The so-called Free Soil Party, whose first origins date from 1848, had only been able to strike roots in the East. Benton Democracy, which opposed any expansion of slavery, was the first phenomenon of this sort in the Southwest, and in a slave state to boot. When the Calhounites and Nullifiers finally brought down old Benton after thirty years of honorable service as senator, sending one of their own to take his place in the Senate, Benton Democracy took a completely hostile stance toward the proslavery wing of the Democratic Party, condemning it to complete impotence in St. Louis and all other communities where Germans formed a majority.

At the head of Benton Democracy stood "the four bad B's," as the Whig and Nullifier press always complained, meaning Benton, Blair (Frank P.),[5]

---

4. John C. Calhoun of South Carolina (1782-1850), who served as Vice President as well as in the House and Senate, was the tactical as well as the ideological leader of the movement for Southern autonomy during his lifetime and an inspiration to "fire-breathers" after his death.

5. Francis Preston Blair, Jr. (1821-1875), youngest son of Francis Preston Blair, Sr., graduated from Princeton in 1841, studied law at Transylvania University in Lexington, Kentucky, and settled in St. Louis in 1842. Blair served in the Mexican War under Kearny and was appointed attorney general of New Mexico Territory. He married Appoline Alexander in 1847. An early advocate of the Free Soil Party in 1848, he served in the Missouri legislature 1852-56 and was elected to Congress in 1856, serving 4 March 1857 to 3 March 1859. He successfully contested the election of John R. Barrett to Congress and served 8 June to 25 June 1860, when he resigned, but he was elected again, serving 4 March 1861 until resignation in July 1862 to become a military officer. After the 1862 elections, he was seated from 4 March 1863 until removed on 10 June 1864, when Samuel Knox was recognized as the legitimate representative. Before the war, he advocated the compensated, gradual abolition of slavery and the colonizing of ex-slaves outside the United States. He served as a major general in the army, particularly as a corps commander under General Sherman. On being driven out of the Republican

Brown (B. Gratz)[6] and Boernstein. The city of St. Louis at that time had to elect a representative to the House of Representatives for four years,[7] and for this position Benton Democracy nominated their proven leader and statesman Thomas H. Benton. This was to be compensation for the distinguished statesman, who had been removed from the Senate by the Nullifiers, but it was also to be a test of the strength of the party.

The election campaign commenced, and it was carried on by our opponents with the greatest bitterness. The Whig Party hoped to win with their candidate due to the splitting of the Democratic party,[8] and they went to work with enthusiasm. The proslavery Democrats, on the other hand, were embittered; recognizing well how much their domination in Missouri was in danger, they did everything to hinder Benton's election and thwart his triumph, sparing neither money nor effort. Immediately after the opening of the campaign, all of the papers of St. Louis appeared to stand on the side of Benton's opponents. This was natural for the Whig papers, due to their concern for their own party, and the Democratic papers did so because none of the publishers in those days would dare to oppose the powerful slaveholder party or attract its enmity. But the other German papers took sides against Benton, simply out of hostility to the *Anzeiger.* As a result, the election campaign offered a remarkable and unheard-of drama: in a city of almost one hundred thousand residents, all of the newspapers (English and German), as well as the various weeklies, wrote savagely against one candidate (Benton), while this same candidacy was supported and represented by a single German paper, the *Anzeiger des Westens.*[9]

Party by the Radicals, Blair aided in the resurrection of the Democratic Party in Missouri, becoming their national vice-presidential candidate in 1868. He supported the Liberal Republicans in 1872, helping them to oust the Radical régime in Missouri. He was U.S. Senator from Missouri, 1871-73, and state insurance commissioner in 1874. *DAB*, 2: 332-34; *BDUSC*, 629.

6. Benjamin Gratz Brown (1826-1885), born in Lexington, Kentucky, graduated from Yale University in 1847 and moved to St. Louis in 1849. Brown was a Free Soil member of the Missouri legislature, 1852-59, favoring gradual emancipation of slaves. He edited the *Missouri Democrat* and was wounded in a duel with Thomas C. Reynolds in 1856. Brown served as U.S. Senator from Missouri, 1863-67, and he advocated votes for women. He was the governor of Missouri, 1871-73, and vice presidential candidate on the Liberal Republican ticket with Horace Greeley. *DAB*, 3: 105-07; *BDUSC*, 680.

7. Boernstein is, of course, in error here, since representatives are always elected to Congress for two-year terms. Benton was defeated in 1854 by Luther M. Kennett when he ran for reelection, and he was defeated again in 1856 as a candidate for governor, after which he retired from politics, dying in 1858.

8. The Whig candidate was one Samuel Carruthers, who received most of the votes cast against Benton.

9. *AW*, weekly, vol. 17, no. 32, 29 May 1852, p. 4, for 23 May, presents the Benton Democracy ticket.

The proslavery Democracy had nominated the rich banker Lewis V. Bogy as its candidate,[10] and he shrank from no expenditure to achieve the highest goal of his ambition. Bogy's supporters made a special effort to separate the *Anzeiger* from Benton's candidacy in order to rob him of all journalistic support, and a person standing close to Mr. Bogy came to me in order to sound me out and win me. This intermediary offered me a high sum of money, many thousands of dollars, if I would give up my support of Benton and at least remain neutral. I rejected with decisiveness and offense, and it only intensified my original position. Something about this offer and my rejection reached the public—although not through my fault, since I observed complete discretion—and there ensued a tiresome newspaper polemic particularly free in suspicions and libels against me. Naturally this forced me to disclose the entire matter in detail and in an irrefutable manner; the facts could not be refuted or their believability in any way shaken, and the electoral campaign was carried on under their true impression. I spoke at all the rallies. Once more there was no shortage of threats against me, my paper, my printing shop and Germans in general. It was to be feared that the bloody scenes of the municipal election would be repeated, all the more so because one did not have to go far back in the history to see how opponents of slavery and colored people themselves were handled in St. Louis.

In 1836, for example, a free Negro who had helped an arrested steamboat worker flee was himself arrested. With a knife he wounded two officials escorting him to jail. Taken from prison by a mob roused by the slaveholders, he was chained to a tree at the corner of Seventh and Chestnut. Chests, barrels and lumber were piled about him. This was then lit, and the unfortunate man was slowly roasted to death.[11]

One year earlier the Presbyterian preacher [Elijah] P. Lovejoy, who published an antislavery religious weekly called the *St. Louis Observer*, was assaulted at night. His printing shop was stormed, and he escaped death only through rapid flight. Lovejoy then moved to Alton, in the free state of Illinois. There he resumed publication of his paper, in which he demanded the immediate emancipation of all Negro slaves. The slaveholders of Missouri could not abide that, and with the help of Democrats in Illinois

---

10. Lewis Vital Bogy (1813-1877), born in Ste. Genevieve, graduated from Transylvania University in Lexington, Kentucky, and became a St. Louis alderman in 1838. He served several terms in the Missouri legislature and was U.S. Commissioner for Indian Affairs, 1867-68, and U.S. Senator from Missouri as a Democrat, 1873-77. See *Edwards's* for a portrait and article, also *EHSL*, I: 190; *BDUSC*, 638.

11. The lynching of Francis J. McIntosh on 28 April 1836, gruesome even by prevailing local standards, precipitated a strong protest by Wilhelm Weber, editor of the newly launched *Anzeiger des Westens*. This protest was regarded as a bold act at the time.

they organized the persecution of Lovejoy. Even at the landing of his press in September 1836, a lawless mob was waiting on the levee, falling on the press and destroying everything. Freethinking citizens sent him a new press and type, and the weekly appeared regularly for eleven months. On 21 August 1837, the mob once more stormed the printing shop and destroyed everything. Lovejoy himself could only be rescued by his friends with great difficulty. Again, well-intentioned citizens raised the money to supply him with a new press and type, but the slaveholders in Missouri were also not inactive; the mob seized this new press on its landing and destroyed it again. Once more a new press was found, sent by land to Alton, and established in a solid, stone house, where Lovejoy and his friends guarded it. But before it was even in operation, its arrival was being denounced in Missouri. The mob was roused, and on the evening of 7 November a gang from Missouri surrounded the building in which the press stood, demanding its surrender. The rowdies and scum of Alton joined the gang in a wild lust for destruction, and attempts were made to storm the building. Lovejoy's supporters were prepared for the attack, having barred all the doors and shuttered the windows, and the attackers could accomplish nothing. Burnable material was brought, placed around the house and set aflame at all four corners. When the burning roof fell in, Lovejoy and his friends tried to save themselves. They opened a door to get out, but they were received by the mob with revolver shots and killed or wounded. Lovejoy himself was pierced by five bullets and died instantly. The authorities did nothing, as usual, to prevent this gross butchery.[12]

Such episodes were not exactly calculated to encourage the friends of Benton, and enemy papers openly threatened my paper and me with the fate of Lovejoy and the *St. Louis Observer*. But we did not allow ourselves to be intimidated; we remained solid, thinking only how to increase our capacity to resist and to fight. New German militia companies were organized, despite every possible hindrance placed in the way of these enterprises by the state government in Jefferson City. For example, a new militia company organized under Captain Rottermann asked Missouri's governor, King,[13] for weapons from the state armory, to which they were entitled according to the

---

12. Elijah Parish Lovejoy (1802-1837), see *DAB*, 11: 434-5; also Robert Tabscott, "Elijah Parish Lovejoy: Portrait of a Radical. The St. Louis Years, 1827-1835," *GH* 8, no. 3 (Winter 1987-8): 32-46.

13. Boernstein correctly recalled the day, but not the month, so that he transposed an event of fall 1851, to summer, 1852. For the exchange over the delivery of weapons, see *AW*, weekly, vol. 16, no. 49, 27 September 1851, p. 2, for 24 September 1851. The dispute prompted several rallies by military companies. Austin A. King, a Democrat of Ray County, was governor of Missouri 1849-53. See *Official Manual State of Missouri 1991-1992* (Jefferson City, Mo., 1991), 29.

militia law. Unfortunately, Captain Rottermann asked for immediate issuance of the weapons, since the new militia company intended to muster on 24 July. Now it happened that 24 July fell on a Sunday, and instead of the expected weapons, a message came from Jefferson City rejecting the request because the company planned to muster and drill on a Sunday! At the same time, the governor remarked that he was advising the Germans to Americanize themselves as quickly as possible, particularly by holding Sunday holy in the American fashion. What was to be done? Might makes right. But despite that, the company got its weapons by buying them.

As the feared election day approached, election rallies provoked bitter irritation and raw disturbances. The Germans were determined not to allow their right to vote to be altered by one iota. Their experience had been so considerably enriched by the events of the municipal election in April that they drew even closer together, and they were resigned and prepared even for the worst. The election itself was carried out with the most extreme tension, although without any material disturbance worth mentioning. Frank P. Blair's personal courage and the solid, determined attitude of the Germans impressed our opponents, who did not dare attack.

As long as I remained in St. Louis, there was only one other election riot, and that at the time of the election of Luther M. Kennett to Congress. That was directed not against Germans, but against Catholic Irish, of whom several were shot by the mob, and many houses were destroyed.[14] On that occasion, the mob did attempt to attack the hated *Anzeiger* printing shop, but they were easily dispersed by a few friendly militia companies. As soon as the command was given to load, the mob rapidly scattered in all directions.

The election of 2 August 1852 ran relatively smoothly, and when the votes were counted that evening, Thomas H. Benton was elected as a member of Congress by a large majority.[15] Our opponents, both Whigs and slaveholders, greeted this result with wild curses. Benton Democracy gained a solid niche and a reinforcement of its numbers, while the reputation and influence of the *Anzeiger* rose to new heights. This is because one German paper had brought about Benton's election against all the other papers. From now on, the way was cleared for the *Anzeiger des Westens* to become the leading paper not only in St. Louis, but also in the entire Mississippi Valley. The number of subscribers climbed every day.

---

14. *AW,* weekly, vol. 19, no. 42, 19 August 1854, p. 1, describing the riots. Comparisons between 1852 and 1854, ibid., vol. 19, no. 41, 12 August, p. 3. See also John C. Schneider, "Riot and Reaction in St. Louis, 1854-1856," *MHR* 68 (1973-4): 171-85.

15. *AW,* weekly, vol. 17, no. 42, 7 August 1852, p. 3, for 5 August, gives the detailed election results for St. Louis and environs. An explication of the victory is given in ibid., vol. 17, no. 43, 14 August 1852, for 6 August, "Der Sieg. Vergangenheit—Gegenwart—Zukunft."

Benton himself personally expressed his thanks and esteem to me in the heartiest way, inviting Alexander Kayser and me to dinner. (Kayser had stood out during the campaign as a stump speaker.) Being invited to dine with the old man was seen in the same light as being commanded to dine with the Emperor Franz Joseph here in Vienna or with the German Emperor in Berlin. But this dinner which Kayser and I took with old Benton remains a humorous memory to me because of the hordes of mice who dined with us.

This is because the old man had passed thirty years of his life as a senator in Washington. He had his family with him there, maintaining a fine household, while his house in St. Louis stood empty, in the control of an elderly Negro couple. When Benton had to resume legal residence in St. Louis for the election, he supplied the house with what was necessary. The problem was that the caretakers of the house, the old Negro and his wife, had taken thought only for their own comfort during their lord's absence. Vermin had gained an upper hand, and they thwarted all attempts to exterminate them.

Benton received us in his office, where we chatted for a short hour. We then went to the table. We had hardly taken our place and commenced being served by Negroes with a rich but truly American dinner, than there came a suspicious rustle from all corners of the room. I sneaked a peek around to see the source of the noise and observed hordes of mice emerging from all the corners, drawn by the aroma of food. They bustled back and forth in a businesslike manner, finally gathering under the table to snap up the crumbs that fell to them from the table. The dear little beasts were so bold that I surprised a couple of them on my lap, where they were munching bread crumbs that had fallen on my napkin. I nudged Kayser, who also made a surprised face, and both of us had trouble keeping from laughing. Old Benton, however, in his Olympian repose and dignity, did not appear to be aware of the activities of the little quadrupeds; he continued to expound his political views. When we finally departed, both of us broke down on the sidewalk in loud laughter, compensating us for the long repression we had been forced to observe.

I must ever recall the old man with thanks, however, for the fact that he was always very benevolently inclined toward me. Whether earlier as senator, later as representative, or after 1856, when he renounced a political career, he was helpful and pleasing on every occasion.[16] I still possess numerous letters

---

16. Shortly before the 1854 election, a German translation of Benton's senatorial memoirs was published to be distributed at a nominal price; see *AW*, weekly, vol. 19, no. 34, 24 June 1854. Boernstein did not always agree with Benton's proposals, particularly after Benton failed to be reelected in 1854, since he supported compromise on the Kansas-Nebraska bill during the "lame duck" session of Congress. Boernstein blandly declared that all political alliances had been ended with the August 1854 elections. See *AW*, weekly, vol. 20, no. 11, 6 January 1855, p. 1.

from him, and these as well as his entire attitude are clear witness that he was a man of the good old school, always honorable in intention and alien to mere convenience and social nicety. Missouri owes him a very great deal, and he and his efforts actually constituted the first stimulus to the emergence of the Republican Party, even if indirectly. Honor be to his memory, which will only come to its full estimation if the state of Missouri can ever be liberated from the claws of the former slaveholders, the Democratic Bourbons, who now rule again. Only then will Missouri becomes a happy, blooming, and truly free state. Then will the thankful people of Missouri erect to their great leader, Thomas H. Benton, a monument such as has always dwelt in the hearts of his thankful contemporaries.

Before *the* Grand Jury
(1853)

U p to this point in my memoirs of my first years in America, I have been rather thorough. Perhaps to the taste of some I have been all too thorough; but I regarded it as my duty to indicate why I succeeded in the relatively short period of less than three years to such an influential position. I was a leader of German Americans and of public opinion in the American West. I owed this unexpected success, which went far beyond my wildest expectations, partly to my own effort and persistence, but partly also to the intersection of many favorable circumstances and relations. What is in the process of coming to be engages our attention and commitment, while we treat what has come to pass with the cool detachment of something obvious; it is only when what has emerged commences to dissolve and enter into decline that it once more claims our attention and commitment. For that reason, in the case of significant phenomena in human history, we follow with the greatest intensity their development, their youth, their beginnings and their upward struggles. In a life as important and influential as that of Napoléon I, we are interested in his youth in Corsica, his development in the military school of Brienne and his experiences as a simple lieutenant. We follow with rapt commitment this beginning of his career until the siege of Toulon opens the gates of honor and fame, power and influence. On the other hand, his splendid career as consul and emperor, his campaigns of conquest throughout all of Europe, leave us rather cold and indifferent. Our compassion is only reawakened as this giant approaches his fall, when power falls to bits and the emperor, abandoned by self-centered friends and servile adherents, languishes hopelessly as a prisoner on the rock of St. Helena in the southern ocean.

In the same way, I am mainly interested in my own life in the beginning of the various careers I have undertaken, the start and first development of new undertakings—with one word, what was becoming. I have thrown myself into the chapters dealing with those events with gusto and love, while the story of what was created and what had come to pass remains rather cool even in memory. Hence I believe I am able to summarize the following years of my work in America, from 1852 to 1861, quickly and compactly. In fact, I would be just as happy to have it written by another, totally uninvolved, pen. This is because when one has come to terms with the passions of youth and manhood and has achieved a nonpartisan, objective vision, one remains somehow partisan even as an old man without wanting to be so, for it is a matter of telling his own experiences.

With Benton's election to Congress through the sole efforts of my paper (the only one to support him) and the votes of the united and disciplined Germans of St. Louis, there began a continuous, intense struggle for freedom and progress. This was a struggle for liberal principle against the reactionary, egoistic machinations of the slaveholding party. Carried on in newspapers, at rallies, and at the ballot boxes, it had a liveliness and enthusiasm that must seem adventurous and overwrought to the present, rather indifferent generation. Still, it was done at that time with righteous enthusiasm and the greatest self-sacrifice, bearing in itself the most complete assurance of being right. We Germans carried on this struggle against the dominating slaveholders with the greatest fearlessness and valor, especially in the West, until the battle of opinions worked to incandescent intensity in 1861 and passed into a battle with lethal weapons on genuine battlefields.

Again it was the Germans of the West who took up weapons for the Union when the matter was in bloody earnest, providing the largest and most persistent contingent for defense of the republic. I cannot outline here the long parliamentary struggle that led up to the War of Secession, but I played an active and leading role in it, and without boasting I can say that Frank P. Blair and I merit being called the founders of the Republican Party in the slave state of Missouri. If I wanted to describe all the struggles of these long years up to 1861, I would have to report a mass of things that have now long vanished and belong to a history that is forever past. I would have to tell about the Missouri Compromise and the Mason-Dixon Line, Henry Clay's Omnibus Bill, Bloody Kansas and Douglas's Squatters' Sovereignty, the Dred Scott case and the Fugitive Slave Law. These and a hundred other matters are long since dead and forgotten, although we newswriters of those days broke our heads over them and wrote until our fingers were bleeding. This lasted until Lincoln's election in 1860, when the Last Judgment fell on slavery and the evil took its course. It was a bitter, hot, exhausting struggle that we men of that period went through, particularly those of us living in a slave state who had to fight for the ideas of liberty and progress year in and year out. But it leveled the way for the later victory of the Union after 1861.

The German immigration of 1848 made a laudable contribution to that victory, willingly spilling blood and sweat, sorrow and renunciations of all sort. We did this in order to free the star-spangled republic from the curse of slavery that was attached to it, the brand of shame that had been affixed. Later historians of the republic, far removed from the partisan struggle and passions of that time, will look in a purely objective manner, and grant full recognition to those who carried on the spiritual preliminary battles from 1848 to 1861 with such success. Then the German immigration of 1848 and after, the so-called "Greens," will receive their full credit. Almost without exception they were the bearers and representatives of ideal republicanism, while the older German immigration, the so-called "Grays," had gradually come to live with slavery. It is true the institution was nowhere near as arrogant then as later. There were even a few who had come to like the peculiar institution or saw it as a necessary evil that one had to preserve and protect as a good conservative. It was precisely the contribution of the Forty-Eighters that they threw their enthusiasm, their idealism and their radical vision into the turbidly flowing stream of daily compromise and worn-out party slogans that was American political life. They stirred the waters to the bottom, bringing life and movement to the whole sodden mass. There is no one individual who merits credit for stimulating and freshening American party life, but the entire emigration of 1848, as individuals everywhere, brought new blood, new movement, new ideas into the old sourdough of the parties. The leaders had only the merit of throwing the igniting idea of the day into the mass, largely as a result of their education and European experiences. The masses themselves deserve the real recognition, for they grasped and absorbed liberal, progressive ideals with understanding and enthusiasm. Particularly in the West, these masses organized and disciplined themselves into a power with which American politicians and party leaders had to reckon, one that they had to regard as important.

If I were to enumerate all these intellectual skirmishes here, I would have to relate the history of the United States, and particularly the history of Missouri from 1848 to 1861. But that is not my mission here, because I wanted to tell only my personal experiences. I am also revulsed to be continually writing about myself and my own doings, and that would be inevitable here, because I was for years the leader of the antislavery movement in Missouri. I also do not wish to fall into the practice of Léon Gambetta, who when attacked from the radical side starts every sentence of an oration with *je* and ends it with *moi*.[1] Hence I will deal with the events before 1861 very briefly, only touching on a few outstanding facts. I do not intend to revive any sort of polemic with my numerous enemies of those days in the course of this narrative. Nor do I wish to rewarm any of these old disputes, although in those days I waged continued and bitter struggles with many opponents, and I had to withstand continuous attacks on my person and efforts. Time reconciles, and in the almost twenty years since my voluntary exile, "I have learned much and forgotten much." I now contemplate those heated, tense battles with the peace of age, without bitterness or personal offense. I have long since forgiven all my enemies, no matter how intensely they fought me or how many nasty hours they gave me.

---

1. Léon Gambetta (1838-1882) was an egotistical political leader of the revival of France after its defeat in the Franco-Prussian War.

In many cases I cannot recall their names, let alone what they did. Hence there shall be no recriminations and no warmed-over polemic from those days of the wrestling of spirits; *sono tempi passati.*[2]

Benton's election through the German vote brought the Germans of St. Louis to a position of influence. At the same time it strengthened Benton Democracy, which was on the rise, making possible its expansion and organization. I have already mentioned that not a single paper except the *Anzeiger*, neither English nor German, was found to support Benton's candidacy. So little faith did the newspapers have in the future of Benton Democracy. In those days the total support for Benton Democracy consisted of perhaps two hundred Anglo-Americans, a better sort of Irishmen, and Germans, who made up the main strength of the new party.

Following the surprising success of Benton's election, these proportions changed. All the American and Irish office hunters who sought positions and offices in city and county joined Benton Democracy, which had demonstrated it could get nominated candidates elected. As a result, Benton Democracy grew in numbers to a surprisingly large strength, so that even opponents of slavery from the Whig Party joined. A proslavery Democracy ticket presented in St. Louis was unable to get 150 votes for its candidates. The Whig Party was then in the process of dissolving, heading for its inevitable collapse, and the Know-Nothing Party was not yet organized. So Benton Democracy won all the elections of 1853 and 1854, making one of its leaders, John How,[3] mayor of St. Louis. The city council, as well as all city officials, also belonged to Benton Democracy. With the exception of one election, which we shall soon discuss, this pattern continued through 1856, when St. Louis elected Frank P. Blair as its representative in Congress, a decisive Free Soiler and enemy of any expansion of slavery. Finally, in 1860, Benton Democracy had become so strong that it could present a Republican ticket for the entire state and win seventeen thousand votes for Abraham Lincoln in a slave state. Germans always remained the center and main strength of Benton Democracy, and Germans made possible the transformation of Benton Democracy into the Republican Party. When the South withdrew from the Union and raised the secessionist palmetto flag, it was once again the Germans who rushed to their weapons; abandoning everything else, they prevented the secession of the slave state of Missouri and through their manly efforts kept it in the Union.

In those days as Benton Democracy, this predecessor and vanguard of the later Republican Party, began to form, the slaveholders and their

---

2. Italian, "They are times past."

3. John How (died 1888), elected mayor in 1853 and 1856, made his fortune in mining and lost it after the Civil War, dying in San Francisco. See *EHSL,* 2: 1065.

adherents had no inkling of the development and future of this new party. Despite this, both the slaveholder Democracy and the largely nativist Whig Party regarded German citizens with distrust and suspicion, placing all possible obstacles in their way. Petty persecution of Germans by temperance people, by advocates of the Sabbath, and by the police, which was dominated by Irishmen, eventually became the order of the day. It was one of these questions that involved me in a battle with the traditional, venerable institution of the grand jury.

I owed my little bit of influence in St. Louis primarily to the fact that I did not simply sit in my office and write articles, but rather on every occasion went out and exposed myself personally as an agitator and leader. Whether it was attending a public assembly promoting a charitable or useful purpose, combating evils and abuses to defend German citizens and their constitutional rights, I was always in front, active and in person. In short, I was always ready for that personal, active intervention that the French call *payer de sa person.*[4]

So it was that after the victorious municipal elections of 1853, the grand jury met for its semiannual session. The jury was so cleverly packed against the Germans that temperance men and Sabbath-bats had the majority. Now began a formal persecution of German innkeepers and their guests for desecrating Sundays by keeping their places open and serving alcoholic beverages on the Sabbath.

The beer question played a large role among German Americans, often too large a role, and there were times and places the Germans would rather have renounced one or several of their constitutional rights for the freedom to drink beer when, as often, and as much as they wished. German American editors always had to devote adequate care to the beer question, and many elections were decided entirely on this issue. In fact it often sufficed to assert or hint that this or that candidate was a temperance person to lose him the entire German vote.

The plan of the German citizens' enemies was to persecute German tavernkeepers and their German guests. This they would do by penalizing them severely, or at least involving them in costly, tedious trials through a mass of indictments. At the same time, I was to be brought into a false relationship with my German compatriots and portrayed as their accuser. German tavernkeepers had the practice of attracting a considerable public by special advertisements declaring free lunch, musical productions, folk singers, etc., and posting these "attractions" in the newspaper. I now received a summons to the grand jury as a witness, and there, after being sworn in, I

---

4. French, "Paying with his person."

was to answer faithfully the questions placed before me.[5] Among these questions was whether this or that invitation by a tavern for Sunday events had appeared in my newspaper. If I did not wish to commit perjury and expose myself to the consequences, I had to say yes to the questions, so that I appeared as a plaintiff and informer.

I had long been interested in the institution of the grand jury, and I was also not entirely free of the zeal of Forty-Eighters to reform old America in the spirit of the times. The institution of the grand jury is only found in English jurisprudence and in the criminal justice system of the United States of America, and it derives from old English Common Law, a collection of written and unwritten laws, customs and traditional institutions. No one knows the Solon or Lycurgus who issued or collected these laws in gray ancient times, but common law still exists, and its precedents are binding in jurisprudence. In England as in America there exists no chamber of prosecutors, no public persecutor who brings crimes or misdemeanors to light and places them before the court. Rather, according to the principle of the solidarity of the community—that the community would not keep silence over crimes committed within its bounds—the business of public accusation is given to a body of twenty-four citizens. They constitute a grand jury, whose duty is to investigate in secret all crimes or misdemeanors committed in the district, and to accuse those who had been seen as guilty on the testimony of believable witnesses. At least twelve members of the grand jury have to vote for an accusation. If there is no indictment, then the person in question cannot be pursued by the court. Even judges can only deliver supposed wrongdoers over to the grand jury. If they find for indictment, the accused comes before a criminal court and a petty jury of twelve jurors. If the grand jury does not rule for indictment, then the accused must be released at once.

The grand jury was a thoroughly justified institution in England, where it protected the people against oppression and judicial persecution by the king, his ministers and a powerful aristocracy. Because no one could be pursued criminally without the sentence of his fellow citizens in the grand jury, the grand jury was a weapon and shield for citizens against unjust or political prosecutions. Because their proceedings were and remain secret, even the powerful and the magnates of the realm could be accused when they committed crimes, being passed then to the grand jury. The institution of the grand jury thus moved to the American colonies, where it has been

---

5. According to *AW*, weekly, vol. 18, no. 43, 10 September 1853, p. 3, and ibid., no. 46, 17 September 1853, p. 1, A. B. Hofer of the *Demokratische Presse* was first to be grilled by the grand jury, and he fingered Boernstein as one who most aggressively advertised Sunday businesses.

preserved into the most recent times, as is the case with a mass of other old traditions. Under American conditions, however, this institution eventually decayed into misuse. It was delivered over to the abuse by the sheriff, who chose jurors of the grand jury whom he preferred for his own purposes. As a result, particularly in the South, innocent persons are in many cases persecuted, while wealthy and respected criminals with political influence slip through to avoid valid accusation, prosecution or punishment. I quickly decided to use this occasion to combat the antiquated, anachronistic institution of the grand jury, which no one else had dared undermine.

Hence on the day of the summons I appeared before the grand jury, which was enthroned with its president on a dais. I was told that the grand jury wished to present questions to me, and that I was to be sworn to answer these questions with "the truth, the whole truth, and nothing but the truth." I arose and declared that making such an oath in advance, without knowing the questions in advance, would violate my conscience and be against my conviction. Therefore, I had to decline to swear such an oath. There was general alarm and great uproar among the twenty-four jurors. Such reluctance had never before occurred. I was asked to withdraw for a moment so the grand jury could discuss this unusual case. I betook myself to the antechamber and listened as a lively, loud debate took place among the jurors. From the disjointed bits that reached me, it appeared that the majority of the jurors favored compelling me to take the oath and making the necessary statement. A minority, on the other hand, wanted to send me home as a totally unusable witness. In the end I was recalled and the foreman told me that I had to take the oath without condition or would be prosecuted and punished for contempt of court.

I answered by repeating that I would never swear such an open oath. First of all, questions could be presented to me that might lead me to incriminate myself, and according to our laws no one was bound to incriminate himself. I explained this possibility with the example that by printing a tavernkeeper's advertisement inviting people to a Sunday entertainment, I became a conspirator with the tavernkeeper and thus my own accuser, which was illegal. The president demanded once more that I take the oath and rely on the equity of the grand jury. When I once more decisively refused, I was declared a prisoner on the motion of the district attorney, who had been called in for the purpose. On the grounds of contempt of court, I was delivered to the custody of the sheriff and taken to the criminal court. We marched in solemn procession to the criminal court building, first of all the president of the grand jury and the district attorney, then the sheriff and me. The sheriff lay his hand on my shoulder, indicating symbolically that I was his prisoner. Behind us came the twenty-four jurors, two by two in worthy procession.

The session of the criminal court was immediately interrupted on our appearance, since the grand jury always has precedence. Judge Colt,[6] an amiable and humane man, was then criminal judge. He heard the matter with close attention from the district attorney, and he appeared to be placed in some embarrassment by this unheard-of development. He attempted to negotiate and encouraged me to take the oath, promising that I would be excused from all improper questions, but stating I could not give an example of open disobedience. I continued to insist on refusing to swear, and Judge Colt declared that though it distressed him, he had to follow the law. I was made a prisoner, and I would remain in custody until my defiance ended and I took the oath. He placed me in the custody of the sheriff and set the court date for my case on the next morning. Until then, he said, I had twenty-four hours to consider the matter with cooler blood and to come to a better conclusion. We paraded out of the criminal court, and the sheriff led me to the prisoners' room in the courthouse. I then demanded to be released on bail until the definitive disposition, so we returned to criminal court, where Judge Colt approved my request with the condition that two guarantors offer ten thousand dollars bail for my appearance. The matter had already spread in town, and not two but ten citizens came forward to offer bail. I was provisionally freed after the completion of legal formalities, but the episode drew considerable attention. The evening papers were full of it, and the morning papers the next day dealt with almost nothing else. When the session began at ten the next morning, the grand hall was crammed full, and all the lawyers of St. Louis were there to follow the development of this *cause célèbre*. I appeared, accompanied by my friend, Christian Kribben,[7] who was to make the juridical arguments.

There began a long trial in which my contempt of court was demonstrated through testimony of jurors, and then the defense was passed to me and my counsel. I remained solid in my statement that it was not contempt of the grand jury which led me to refuse the oath, but only my conscience and my conviction that compelled me against such an oath. A long debate followed, in which my lawyer made a convincing oration, and the case was adjourned until the following day. After an interval of twenty-seven

---

6. J. B. Colt is listed as an attorney residing on the south side of Pine between Eleventh and Twelfth Streets in *Directory* 1854-55, p. 35.

7. Christian Kribben (1821-1864) was born in Clevel near Cologne. He arrived in America with his parents in 1835 and began practicing law in St. Louis in 1843. He served as a lieutenant of artillery in the Mexican War under Col. Doniphan, publishing accounts of the war in the *Missouri Republican*. When the Democratic Party divided in 1854, Kribben remained with the regular party. He was speaker of the Missouri house of representatives in 1858. The start of the war caused him to withdraw from politics. Körner, *Element*, 346-48.

years the proceedings are not that clear in my memory, and I have a copy of neither the *Anzeiger* nor any other paper from this time to refresh my memory of the necessary dates and facts. I only know that in the end Judge Colt—who wavered between the letter of the law and his view of humanity and equity—finally ruled that, because making the preliminary oath was against my conscience and conviction, and because the constitution of Missouri guaranteed complete freedom of conscience and opinion, the grand jury would first present the questions and then have me sworn for each and every question. I had thus won the case, and I declared I was ready to obey this decision. There were plenty of people among the lawyers and the public who accused Judge Colt of weakness or extreme leniency, and who demanded that he should have had me sit in prison until I took the oath, for which the letter of the law gave him full power.

We now returned in procession to the hall of the grand jury, where the first question was presented to me and then the oath demanded. Because the question was entirely harmless, I swore and answered it, along with some of the others. When questions became more entangling and were directed exclusively against the German tavernkeepers and their desecration of the sabbath, I simply declared that I could not answer this question under oath. Much time passed this way, and either it was impossible for them to get me to confess anything clearly on the facts, or I directly refused to answer a question because I would incriminate myself, which was illegal. This procedure was repeated ten or twelve times within an hour, until my lords the grand jurors had had enough. There was nothing further to be gotten from me, and they released me. Yet my appearance had some good result, because the case was reported throughout the Union in many newspapers. The institution of the grand jury was thus brought up for critical discussion, which did not benefit this archaic institution. Through my decisive appearance, I had reinforced my position, and even Anglo-Americans gained respect for the leader of his German fellow citizens. In later years, I even had the satisfaction of seeing that various Western states such as Michigan and Wisconsin abolished the grand jury altogether when they revised their constitutions, deeming it archaic and useless.[8]

8. For the story of the grand jury episode, see *AW,* weekly, vol. 18, no. 46, 17 September 1853, p. 2: "Stimmen der Presse über die Grandjury-Angelenheiten . . . ," and p. 4, "Vor der Grand-Jury," and "Noch einmal vor der Grand Jury und vor der Criminal Court." A final attack on the grand jury as an institution is in ibid., vol. 18, no. 47, 24 September 1853, p. 1.

Through *the* Desert *of* Nativism
(1855)

I have already mentioned how the sudden emergence of Benton Democracy, the forerunner of the Republican Party in the Southwest, drew attention through its first surprising victory over the two older parties. I have also reviewed how it gained considerably in importance and how, as is usually the case, all of those who pursue any rising star streamed into the new party. As a result, the ranks of this new political creation were soon filled with office hunters and ambitious men, who hoped to achieve their desires more quickly with us because the older parties had already distributed all influential positions years in advance. It was certainly not the best element that now entered Benton Democracy; rather the expansion of the party brought with it domination by self-seeking interests, and the same sad spectacle which had disgusted us with the old parties was repeated in the new one. The goal of struggle was no longer the victory of principle but the achievement of office and influence.

Since the great successes of Benton Democracy in 1853 and 1854 had been primarily due to German votes, I was firm with the party leaders that German citizens, who were the true center of the party and who bore the largest part of the taxes and burdens, should also be assured a proper proportion of the offices. I found Frank P. Blair and his American friends always inclined and ready to do this; Irishmen, however, who had hitherto kept the privilege of income-producing jobs to themselves, resisted with vigorous protests any preference for Germans, as they called it. Most of all it was old Edward Walsh,[1] a rich and respected Irishman, who simply could not grasp why his dear and precious Irish brethren should be passed over to bring offices and positions to "stupid Dutchmen."

In the first years Blair did not allow himself to be misled by self-seeking Irish machinations, and in forming the ticket, offices were distributed among the three nationalities according to the principle of equity. Germans were elected to the city council and held city offices, and the municipal police that had been previously dominated by Irishmen and French Creoles experienced a transformation through the introduction of German citizens, to the benefit of that institution. In contrast, the Germans, who had previously not

---

1. Edward Walsh (1798-?) a wholesale grocer born in Tipperary County, Ireland, emigrated in 1818 and made his fortune in flour mills. His company in the 1850s was J. & E. Walsh. See *Edwards's*, 487 (portrait), 489-90; *Directory* for 1853, 111; 1854-55, 199.

held offices or positions, were awakened by the drive for offices. Interests of ward, coterie, and private persons won the upper hand, and there arose a sort of overweening pride, a rude insistence on their own majority. The result was that party discipline loosened ever more, while everything was done by American and Irish office hunters to shunt aside undesired German competition. I had always made it my firm principle never to seek an office for myself or a member of my family, and whenever these "party payoffs," as they were called, were offered me, I firmly declined. Yet I watched with increasing alienation the ongoing struggle for offices among the various nationalities within my own party. As private interests won out over questions of principle, I saw how this loosened party discipline in a destructive way. It appeared to me a commandment of necessity that the party undergo a catastrophe to put an end to this destructive direction. It was my conviction that the party had to experience a defeat in order to purify itself and be freed of a harmful element.

I could not expect my American and Irish party comrades to agree to such a rash act, so I had to do whatever I could on my own account alone. If I might be so bold, I seemed to myself like a sort of Moses. Leading his people across the wasteland, he subjected them to every sort of privation and trial for a full forty years in order to train them to obey the new commandments of Mount Horeb through this school of adversity. In this way he disciplined them without the distraction of alien influences. The occasion for me to do this was offered in the spring of the following year, 1855. The Whig Party had collapsed and out of its ruins had risen the Nativist or American Party, which also called itself Sons of the Sires and finally Know-Nothings. Their organization consisted of the favorite American form, lodges of a secret order in the possession of inviolable secrets. In response to any questions from a non-member, they were bound to reply, "I know nothing!" All of these Know-Nothing lodges sent delegates to the supreme council of the order, which created the list of candidates, and all members of the lodges were bound by oath to vote for these candidates. Through this mysterious organization, the Know-Nothings obtained the top positions in many individual states, and in the presidential election of 1856 they were able to present their own candidate, who received eight hundred thousand votes.

The national convention of the Know-Nothings demonstrated that the new party was composed of elements too various and contradictory to be capable of proceeding in one and the same direction for very long. The convention fell into major conflict over the slavery question, and as a result a significant number of Northern delegates withdrew from the Philadelphia convention and called their own convention in New York. There they proceeded to offer an alliance with the newly formed Republican Party. The

Republicans, however, rejected any negotiations until the Know-Nothings repealed articles 4 and 9 of the Philadelphia Platform of 21 February 1856, formulating other articles in a less alienating fashion. This fourth article said, "Americans must rule America, and for this purpose, before all others, only native-born citizens should be elected to all federal, state and municipal offices." The ninth article demanded that the naturalization laws be altered so that immigrants had to live twenty-one years in the United States without interruption to receive the rights of citizens and be able to vote in elections.

Once the Republican Party rejected the offers of the Know-Nothings, northern nativists had no choice but to vote for the Republican presidential candidate, John C. Frémont; southern nativists had already nominated Fillmore, and northerners could present no candidate of their own with any prospect of success. This meant their fate was sealed after their rule had only lasted one or two years in some states. Marked by petty, hateful persecution and mean torment of immigrant citizens, their rule left an indelible stain. The result was that despite all the nativist desires glimmering in the hearts of the population, the return of nativism as a party organization became quite impossible. With every year and every new growth of immigration it grows ever more impossible. Most remarkable however, is the fact that the worst Know-Nothings, the bitterest and most hateful persecutors of Germans, were mostly renegades, sons or descendants of immigrant German parents who changed their names from Meyer, Schmidt, Müller, Funkhauser, Dorscheimer, etc., into Myers, Smith, Miller, Funkhouser, Dorsheimer, etc. These persons turned themselves into the most embittered Know-Nothings which existed.

A year after the Nativist Party vanished in smoke and fumes, leaving only a stench behind, the same people who had desired to devour my paper and all Germans meekly crept to my editorial office, in the midst of a financial panic in 1857. Weeping and howling, they beseeched me with raised hands to use all my influence to prevent my compatriots from making a "run" on the savings institutions and banks. If German Americans withdrew all their capital, everything would collapse and go under. I first investigated the financial situation of their institutions through certain documents, and I demanded guarantees that Germans would not lose anything if they kept their confidence in such institutions. We worked halfway through the night, and I convinced myself that all the means to cover obligations were present, and that they were not just bargaining for time to cover them. At the same time the richest and most respected citizens—the Chouteaus, Lucas, Benoist, Soulard, Lindell[2] and so on—

---

2. Pierre Chouteau, Jr. (1784-1865), descendent of St. Louis's founder, Pierre Laclède, *EHSL*, 1: 363-65; James H. Lucas (1800-1873), *EHSL*, 3: 1317-18, *Edwards's*, 183,

guaranteed every depositor at any of the St. Louis banks against loss. So I requited the demands of these anxious gentlemen and wrote an appeal to my compatriots that very night. I called them to peace and quiet reflection, telling them this was the only way to achieve what they sought. Any upsetting or running on banks, I explained, would bring with it complete ruin and total loss of their money.[3] This appeal, which was followed by several days of similarly directed articles, had the desired effect. Germans, who were major depositors in banks, remained trusting and quiet, and there was no "run." This time the financial crisis passed St. Louis without severe results, although there were some aftershocks for trade and industry. A few suffered losses in their businesses or credit, but there was no general collapse, and a week later the banks were in a position to have money to spare in their drawers. They could have paid back all deposits if they had been demanded, but no one desired to do so any more.

But I return to my narrative and the year 1855. In keeping with the fashion, numerous Know-Nothing lodges formed in St. Louis. These gatherings, guided by their supreme council, saw that the time had arrived to present a ticket of their own for the municipal elections in April comprised entirely of native-born citizens. The Whig Party, in full dissolution, had not the slightest prospect of electing its list, and the proslavery Democracy was barely able to get two hundred votes in these years for its candidates. Still powerful in the interior of the state, however, where the slaveholders lived, and where it remains powerful to the present day, when it continues to dominate the entire state of Missouri.

No one knew the strength of the Know-Nothing Party, because everything was done in secret in the lodges, but they were certainly underestimated. The Benton Democracy regarded electoral victory as easy and certain. The result was that our party's camp was overconfident and careless, and the wire-pullers of the party decided the time had come to pay less attention to the demands of the German citizens and more attention to American and Irish office hunters. When the municipal convention gathered, members of which were chosen in ward primaries through manipulation of wire-pullers and abetted by German indifference or sloppiness, it was so artfully packed that Germans were almost without representation. A ticket was

185-57; Louis H. Benoist (1803-1867), *EHSL*, I: 131-32; James G. Soulard (born 1798), *Edwards's*, 539, 542-43; Peter Lindell (1776-1861), born in Maryland, arriving in St. Louis in 1811, *EHSL*, 3: 1287-88, *Edwards's*, 419, 421-23. Except for Lindell, these were all Creoles whose family fortunes predated the sale of Louisiana to the United States. On the 1857 panic, see James Neal Primm, *Lion of the Valley: St. Louis, Missouri, 1764-1980* (Boulder, Colo.: Pruett, 1981), 208-09.

3. *AW,* weekly, vol. 22, no. 50, 1 October 1857, pp. 1, 3; ibid., vol. 22, no. 51, 8 October 1857, pp. 1, 3; ibid., vol. 22, no. 52, 13 October 1857, p. 4.

put together at this convention in which there were only Americans and Irishmen, with one exception, I believe, and Germans were entirely excluded. As soon as this result became known, I lodged a decisive protest, saying that I could not support such a ticket. Dissatisfaction among the German population, who comprised a good third of the electorate, grew by the hour, and I called an independent convention to compose a new ticket. Frank P. Blair was absent at the time in Washington with his father, and the lesser party leaders believed the victory of their ticket was assured despite German dissatisfaction, because Germans would vote for neither the slaveholders nor for the Know-Nothings. Many of these leaders also had a profound respect for the holy nimbus of a party convention, whose verdict was accorded unconditional respect. This is because a "bolter," or someone breaking with the party, was punished by lifelong political damnation. There was hence no alteration of the original ticket. The convention I had called gathered a few days later and passed an independent ticket, on which the three nationalities were equally represented.[4]

This schism of Benton Democracy won considerable ground for the Know-Nothings, and they redoubled their efforts to get their ticket elected. At the head of the Know-Nothing ticket stood Washington King,[5] a merchant of St. Louis and the son of an immigrant Englishman who was still alive to see his son waging bitter war against all immigrants, and hence himself. Washington King was also a kind of renegade, a Know-Nothing out of speculation or interest. He could not excuse his nativist efforts with ignorance of European conditions, because he had just returned from Europe after a stay of three years. But he wanted to achieve prestige and influence, and because he could demonstrate no other merit, he committed himself to the hatred of foreigners. German-eating thus was for him a success. After his mere one year of municipal government, he became Missouri director of the great Adam's Express Company, a position which would richly reward any man.

The election took place and passed rather quietly. The result was that the votes were roughly equal between the two factions of Benton Democracy and the Know-Nothing Party, but the Know-Nothing ticket had a small plurality, so it was elected.[6] Now there was howling and gnashing of teeth in the Benton Democracy. The party leaders and

---

4. *AW,* weekly, vol. 20, no. 21, 1 March 1855, p. 2: "Die nächste Stadtwahl," demands a "People's Ticket" in preference to the Know-Nothings, the Democrats, and the Benton Democrats. Boernstein caustically attacked what he called the "Kentucky Clique" ruling Benton Democracy, including Blair and B. Gratz Brown.

5. Washington King (1815-?), born in New York City, arrived in St. Louis in 1844 and was occupied as a merchant. He went on a long tour of Europe, 1850-52, and he was elected to one term as mayor in 1855. *Edwards's,* 432, portrait 433.

6. *AW,* weekly, vol. 20, no. 25, 12 April 1855.

wire-pullers recognized too late the errors they had committed. Blair came raging back from Washington, denouncing them mercilessly as "stupid blockheads," apologizing to the Germans and to me for the clumsiness and indecision of his myrmidons. But what had happened could not be undone; as the French say, *"Le vin est tiré, il faut le boire."*[7] The results had to be borne, and in the course of the year that Washington King was mayor and his friends the Know-Nothings ruled St. Louis, there were unpleasant, even bitter results. Crass nativism and intolerant temperance oppressed the entire population with an iron hand. The people were held in virtual slavery through restrictions in their freedom. The entire police force became a band of informers, and trial followed trial against German tavernkeepers and against any use of public establishments on Sunday. In those days the following biographical sketch of Washington King was published in a temperance howler and Sunday busybody paper:

> Washington King is the first mayor who has sought to sustain the respect of the law for the benefit of general well-being, by compelling obedience to the laws with a strict and powerful hand, banning and strictly punishing every excess and desecration of the Sabbath. His memory will be blessed by all friends of peace and good order.

The year of Know-Nothing government in St. Louis was certainly bad for many. But as much was drunk as ever, in fact perhaps more, because there was much drinking in secret. Taverns shuttered their windows on Sunday on the side toward the street, but the back doors in the alley were wide open. Finally, no one could keep people from taking home their needs in beer, wine and brandy on Saturday night, to consume within their four walls on Sunday. In fact, because everyone feared not having enough to drink at home on Sunday, all laid in a larger supply and hence became drunker than otherwise.

My own paper fought and damned this narrow-hearted madness without restraint, exposing all the inquisitorial and arbitrary trials, the spying and informing of the Know-Nothing Party. Despite dreadful threats, I hung all of it out to be seen by the public. Now there began hot days of struggle for Germans in general and for myself, but it had positive results when party leaders came to their senses and saw that neglecting or oppressing German citizens and reducing their rights had the most negative results for the party. At the same time, the previous arrogance and carelessness vanished from the ranks of practical Germans. Interests of private persons and coteries were

---

7. French, "The wine has been poured, it is necessary to drink it."

pushed into the background, and the Germans once more willingly took on party discipline.

Thanks to this reorganization, the party now gained in power and strength, and good results at once showed themselves. There would be only one more time when I would see myself compelled by similar circumstances to promote an independent ticket in a state or county election, giving the party leaders a much-deserved lesson. This also had good results, and such extreme measures would not be needed again as long as I was in St. Louis.

Within that same year, in August 1855, the Germans won a great victory despite the Know-Nothing regime. After years of effort, instruction in the German language was made an obligatory subject in city schools, fulfilling a long-term demand of the population. The Know-Nothing city administration did not play even the smallest role in this victory of Germans; on the contrary, they did their best to hinder it. Yet once they were defeated at the ballot box, they had to put a good face on a bad business.

On a later occasion the hatred of foreigners in fact proved to be an advantage to the Germans, for when the first segment of the Pacific Railroad was opened, the leading Know-Nothings saw to it that very few Germans were among the invited guests. It was precisely on this maiden journey that the newly built bridge over the Gasconade River collapsed on 1 November as the train was crossing it. Several train cars fell off the bridge, and many lives were lost. Among them was my old friend Adolph Abeles, one of the few Germans to receive an invitation to this death trip. I had not made any use of the invitation I received, for I was offended by the neglect of German citizens. I therefore stayed in St. Louis and thus avoided a dreadful demise, as did so many others of my compatriots. The catastrophe was so dreadful and so many families were stricken that a dark All Souls atmosphere prevailed over St. Louis and environs the next day.[8] The entire city was occupied with burying the bodies of those killed, which had been speedily returned.

This dreadful misfortune took place in 1856,[9] darkening to some degree our joy over the great success that a united Benton Democracy and the Germans won in municipal, county and congressional elections in that year. Our party was victorious in all of these elections, and Washington King and his Know-Nothing municipal administration were shown the door *sans compliments* in April, when John How and our entire ticket were elected. It

---

8. The second day of November is the Christian holy day of All Souls. See *AW*, weekly, vol. 21, no. 3, 8 November 1855, pp. 2-3.

9. Boernstein misremembers the year of the train disaster (but not the day), which was 1 November 1855.

was in August, however, that the decisive battle was fought, when a declared antislavery man, Frank P. Blair, was elected to Congress. Members of our party, including many Germans, were also elected to the state legislature, and all county officers were filled with Benton Democrats. In short, it was a victory along the entire line, the first victory of the Republican idea in the slave state of Missouri. The ice had been broken. Movement was underway, and from now on it advanced without pause until our efforts were crowned with Lincoln's election.

Under Protest[1]

(1856)

The splendid election victories of April and August were followed in November by the presidential election of 1856. The bitterness between defenders of slavery and opponents of any expansion of the "peculiar institution" had attained the highest degree. In the new state of Kansas there were bloody battles between the proslavery people and the newly immigrated Free Soil men. In Congress it took nine full weeks and innumerable votes to elect the antislavery man Nathaniel Banks as speaker against the southern fire-eater Aiken. Another of these ultra-slavedrivers, Preston Brooks of South Carolina, assaulted the liberal senator Charles Sumner from behind following a Congressional session, fearfully mistreating him with a walking stick weighted with lead. In short, the "irrepressible conflict" between slavery and free labor, as William H. Seward described the situation, was close to breaking out.

The presidential election of 1856 was held under these conditions. The Whigs had vanished from the political battlefield. The newly arisen Republican Party nominated John C. Frémont and W. C. Dayton as candidates for president and vice president, while the American or Know-Nothing Party nominated Millard Fillmore and Donelson for these high offices. Fillmore, who as vice president had taken the presidential seat after the death of General Taylor and had ruled the Union for three and one-half years, publicly approved the anti-foreign principles of the Know-Nothings and was otherwise thought to be "sound," as the jargon of the times said, on the slavery question. If this made him acceptable to southern nativists, that was no longer the case with northern Know-Nothings, who were mostly opponents of slavery. In fact, many northern Know-Nothings voted in November for the Republican candidate, Frémont. The Democratic National Convention of the friends of slavery finally presented James Buchanan and J. C. Breckinridge for president and vice president, and it spoke in its platform for the unlimited extension of slavery and nakedly even for the annexation of Cuba and Central America.

There were thus three tickets in the field, the Democratic, the Republican and the Know-Nothing. In the slave states alone there were only two tickets, because the presentation of a Republican ticket would be

---

1. This chapter was also translated and annotated by Elizabeth Gempp as Heinrich Börnstein, "Under Protest," *BMHS* 13 (1956-57): 25-29.

regarded as treason in a slave state, and anyone attempting to present a Republican ticket or trying to vote for one would have been threatened with murder or manslaughter. We leaders of Benton Democracy had long discussed whether we dared to unfold the Republican banner in Missouri and present the ticket with John C. Frémont and Dayton. Frank P. Blair and I were decidedly in favor of doing this, but our friends in the interior of the state warned against it. They cautioned that we should not upset things, for besides the fact that in all slaveholder-controlled counties there could be bloody acts by mobs, this strategy would also demonstrate the numerical weakness of the Republican Party in a frightening manner. The greater part of our friends would prefer to abstain from voting in order to avoid the threat of conflict. We could not raise any adequate answers to these arguments. The final ruling was given by the action and attitude of old Benton, who was still our leader, even if only nominally, even though Benton Democracy had long since passed beyond him and his views. Thomas Benton declared himself for Buchanan in the presidential campaign and against his own son-in-law John C. Frémont;[2] we had to respect this act of the old gentleman if we wished not to offend the large number of those in the ranks of our party who esteemed and followed him. As a result, a Republican ticket was not presented in Missouri. With the bitterest mockery the proslavery papers—especially the *Missouri Republican*—announced in triumph that the Germans and the Benton Democrats were now compelled to vote for the Democratic Buchanan ticket, it being impossible to vote for their mortal enemies, the Know-Nothings. There was no third ticket in Missouri for which they could vote. The Republican Germans would have to "eat their shoenails" this time, an elegant *bon mot* used in those days for voting against one's own principles.

I wracked my brains about how this triumph of the proslavery party could be frustrated and their mockery refuted, and in discussions with Blair I laid out my view. Although they could keep us from voting for Frémont and the Republican ticket, as no such ticket was available in Missouri, no power on earth could force us to cast our votes for Buchanan and the principle of slavery. Hence I proposed that Benton Democracy should unanimously vote for Fillmore and the Know-Nothing ticket, but only "under protest." Fillmore and the Know-Nothing ticket had no prospect of winning in any case, so that our votes would not make the difference. I went on to explain that it was more honorable not to abstain from voting out of cowardice, but rather to vote openly against the principle of slavery. This proposal, which

---

2. In 1856, Thomas Hart Benton was waging his last political campaign, for the office of governor of Missouri, so that he was trying to win votes throughout the state, beyond the St. Louis base of Benton Democracy.

was at first received with horror, was finally raised to a resolution after long debate. It took all the popularity and solid trust that Blair and I enjoyed with the people to make voting for the hated Know-Nothing ticket acceptable, particularly for Germans and Irish. The resolution was announced in the other party papers, and after some hesitation an understanding gradually dawned of the embarrassing situation we found ourselves in a slave state. Even Germans and Irish agreed, and rage and bitterness prevailed in the ranks of the proslavery party.[3]

The example Missouri gave in this situation was observed in other slave states where there was no Republican ticket, so that enemies of slavery—mostly Germans in Kentucky, Tennessee, Louisiana, Texas and other slave states—preferred voting as we did for Fillmore and the Know-Nothings rather than Buchanan and the proslavery principle. So it came about that of the 3 million votes cast in the presidential election in November, despite the mass of northern Know-Nothings who fell away from Fillmore and voted for Frémont, there were still 873,000 votes for Fillmore, while 1,834,000 voted for Buchanan and 1,342,000 for Frémont. Our ballots bore the words **"Under protest!"** in large letters at the top, followed by the names of the Fillmore electors. This telling demonstration attracted a great deal of attention from Anglo-Americans of all parties, and it contributed in no small degree to raising the Germans in their eyes and inspiring respect.

It would be another four years before Missouri would be ready for the presentation of a Republican ticket. The treasonous administration of President Buchanan had to open the eyes of even the blindest, favoring the South ever more and making it even more powerful. The corruption of officials, reaching as far as Buchanan's cabinet, rose from day to day. Rotten mismanagement stimulated disgust and dismay from honorable persons. Under the influence of these factors the ranks of the Republican Party filled. Even southern fire-eaters desired the election of a Republican presidential candidate in order to have a pretext for seceding and the tearing of the republic into two parts.

When the presidential election of 1860 approached, Blair, the chief party leaders and I had long since decided to present a Republican ticket in the slave state of Missouri. Unashamedly we would unfurl the banner of liberty and progress. We were all agreed that we could not win. The state government would undoubtedly remain in the hands of the proslavery people, and our effort would only have value as a Republican demonstration in a slave state. Nevertheless, we unanimously decided to take this crucial step with energy. As a result, we presented the first Republican ticket in the

---

3. *AW*, weekly, vol. 22, no. 2, 6 November 1856, p. 1.

slave state of Missouri at the state elections in August. The effort entailed great difficulty, it being endlessly difficult to find candidates for this ticket. Most of our friends declined the honor of parading as candidates on the Republican ticket; election would have been inconceivable, and it would only expose them to hatred and persecution by their slaveholding neighbors. At last we succeeded in filling the ticket with the names of self-sacrificing party people after one of the most respectable men in the party, the lawyer Gardenhire,[4] accepted the nomination for the office of governor. I had to do my part "for the success of the whole," as well, and although otherwise abstaining from seeking office, I was on this ticket as candidate for superintendent of common schools. We had long since given up any illusions about the prospects of our list of candidates, and so we were not a little surprised that six thousand votes were cast for the Republican ticket at a time when many of our friends and party members were kept from the ballot box by violent mobs and were prevented from voting. One of the ultra-slaveholders, Claiborne Fox Jackson,[5] (in his heart already a raving secessionist) was elected governor. His friends of a similar persuasion were elected to the other offices, and the preparations were begun in earnest to tear Missouri from the Union.

Although we had achieved no material result from presenting the Republican ticket in August, we had still had a fine moral victory. Convinced Republicans in Missouri conceived new courage as a result of our appearance, and in the presidential election in November a full sixteen thousand votes were cast for the Republican candidate Abraham Lincoln in the slave state of Missouri, or thrice as many votes as had been found in the entire state a few months earlier in August.

Chief credit for the growth and expansion of the Republican Party in Missouri is due to the energetic, bold, reckless efforts of Frank P. Blair, a man who never received anything like adequate credit from his

---

4. James B. Gardenhire (died 20 February 1862), a Whig from Buchanan County, was appointed state attorney general on the death of the incumbent in September 1851, and was elected to a full term in 1852, serving until January 1857. He died in Fayette, Missouri, of tuberculosis. See *Official Manual, State of Missouri* 1991-1992, p. 58; *MR*, 23 February 1862, p. 2.

5. Claiborne Fox Jackson (1806-1862), born in Kentucky, moved to Missouri at the age of twenty and settled in Arrow Rock. He was an ally and supporter of Benton in the state legislature until after the Mexican War, when he became a strong advocate of the expansion of slavery. His opposition to Benton's reelection to the Senate in 1850 helped end Benton's thirty years of service there. Jackson was elected governor in 1860 as a Douglas Democrat, but he took a strongly secessionist position after inauguration on 3 January 1861, though declaring a policy of neutrality in public. After the expulsion of his government from the state, he died of pneumonia in Little Rock, Arkansas in November 1862. See William E. Parrish, *EC*, 2: 828-9.

Francis Preston Blair, Jr. as a U.S. Army colonel. Photograph by E. Anthony, New York. Courtesy of the Missouri Historical Society.

contemporaries. In the end rejected and abandoned by the Germans, although he had been their truest friend and leader, and they drove him into the ranks of their opponents. I stood in intimacy with Frank P. Blair for many years, and I can permit myself to judge him. Blair's was a character that is unfortunately rarely found among American politicians. Although he was born a southerner—his ancestors having immigrated to Kentucky from Scotland—he was a decided enemy of slavery, as was his father, Francis P. Blair, Sr., the long-term friend and confidant of old General Jackson (eight years President of the United States), as well as his brother, Montgomery Blair,[6] a member of Lincoln's cabinet. As early as 1848 Frank P. Blair, Jr. was the first Anglo-American in Missouri to express himself energetically in word or print against the further expansion of slavery. From that point he became the leader of the Free Soil Party in Missouri, which consisted primarily of German citizens. It was Blair who had the largest role in the successes and accomplishments that Germans attained through years of manly struggle. Thanks to Blair and his efforts, the city of St. Louis and the greater part of Missouri was spared the terrors of civil war, and Missouri remained in the Union. It was later the practice to attribute all the credit for keeping Missouri in the Union to Lyon, but Infantry Captain Lyon was a man who had arrived in St. Louis weeks before, ignorant of local relationships and known by no one. He could have accomplished nothing if Blair had not supported and led him, and if the Germans had not stood at his side! Only the historiography of the future will give Blair's services full credit, and it was only after his premature death that the Germans in Missouri recognized what a true friend and protector of their interests they had lost in Frank P. Blair.

Yet it was the Germans who rejected and abandoned Blair. They turned against him to follow a new star, John C. Frémont, whose later deeds and development opened their eyes, showing them how they had rejected their truest friend in order to follow a misguiding light, all because of a few fine-sounding phrases and an adventurous appearance. But I can say here with pride that I remained true to him unto the last hour, as long as I still had a paper and a voice in Missouri. The fact that Blair—after preserving the Union, ending the Civil War, destroying secession and legally abolishing its cause, which was slavery—returned to the Democratic Party out of his

---

6. Montgomery Blair (1813-1883), the eldest son of Francis Preston Blair, Sr., graduated from West Point in 1835, studied law at Transylvania University in Lexington, Kentucky, and settled in St. Louis in 1837, where he was a protégé of Senator Benton. Elected mayor of St. Louis in 1842, he moved to Maryland in 1853. He was counsel for Dred Scott, and he was postmaster general 1861-64, but was removed by Lincoln as a result of Radical pressure. After the War he inclined to the Democratic Party as did Frank Blair. *DAB*, 2: 339-40.

distress over German hostility, that he wrote the notorious Broadhead Letter[7] and finally appeared on the Democratic ticket as candidate for vice president, all arose from his hot-blooded temperament. Despite that, he was elected United States Senator in 1871 and represented Missouri alongside Schurz in the most honorable manner. Later, in 1872, he allowed himself to commit another political error by participating in the Independent convention in Cincinnati, speaking and working there for the nomination of the utterly impossible Horace Greeley as candidate for president rather than the highly qualified Adams.

His end was sad. He was brought down by that national vice of American politicians, destructive drunkenness, which lamed his physical and mental capacities through a sudden stroke that later swept him away. It is unfortunately an American abuse that daily politics are usually carried on in the barroom at the bar, and that an influential party leader must not only drink more than he would like, but also drink more than his health permits. Approached by hundreds to join in a toast, he has to comply with each demand, even if he only has a nip each time, he bolts down a great deal of alcohol, of which the greater portion is bogus and damaging to health. No American politician can avoid this alcoholic poisoning, because refusing to toast someone, or even not emptying the entire glass, is regarded as belittling. Often such a refusal at a bar leads to bloody conflict. How many people have I seen in the bloom of their years decline and perish miserably of this American national vice? I myself avoided this common fate of American politicians by making it a strict law never to set foot in a tavern, a coffeehouse, a barroom or any other place where liquor is served, under any condition. This oath to myself I held faithfully and without violation through all thirteen years of my work in America, and it saved me many unpleasant and dangerous results.

Blair's was a powerful nature. He could bear a great deal, and he never lost his judgment; he was thereby able to reduce the burdens of his position, particularly popular toasting, to a minimum. It was only when I returned to St. Louis from Germany in 1862 to assist in the congressional and state elections that I was shocked to see that Blair was drinking more than before, so much more that it often ended in stupor. In an intimate moment I warned him about it and stated my fears of the probable results. He was silent for a while and listened with patience. Then, when I was finished, he spoke after pausing to collect painful memories: "You are right, dear friend," he told me,

---

7.   The Broadhead letter was a message written by Francis P. Blair, Jr. to James Overton Broadhead during the presidential campaign in 1868 declaring that Blair would advocate the suspension of all Reconstruction governments as unconstitutional if the Democrats were elected. See *DAB*, 2: 333-4.

"I do drink more now than I should, but your friends, the Germans, are at fault." And that was in fact the truth. He drank to kill the pain. The falling away of the Germans and their persecution of him, their true friend and leader, had profoundly injured and distressed him. He sought anesthetic and oblivion in brandy, the drink of Lethe.

He gathered his strength again when he worthily did his duty in the course of the War of Secession. As a general of the Union army, he ventured with General Sherman's columns on that bold campaign from the banks of the Potomac through the middle of the Southern enemy country, proceeding without a secure basis of operation all the way to Atlanta and on to the coast of the Atlantic Ocean.[8] Thus the rebels were deprived of their last resources and cut off from all supply and reinforcement, and the defeat of the South and the capitulation of its generals Lee and Johnston became inevitable. But his constitution was already ruined, and as an active politician back in Washington he once more paid his homage to the national vice of the barroom. Soon a stroke put an end to his political career, and he died not yet fifty-four years of age.

I have regarded it as my duty to dedicate these words of remembrance to my esteemed friend and leader, for I continue to hold him in honor. Allow me to add the evaluations of two more contemporaries whose opinions are in keeping with this capable man. Governor Gustav Körner[9] of Illinois said on Blair's death at the conclusion of a necrology paying full tribute to the merits of the departed:

> Frank Blair was ambitious and could sacrifice much to this passion, perhaps too much. But he was no demagogue. He committed himself without considering the results, going boldly into the breach for his principles and for his friends. He was carved of an entirely different wood than those who flattered and waited on the people, such as Morton, Logan and a hundred other so-called party leaders. In our time, when mediocrity prevails, when characters flatten out and form themselves according to

---

8. Sherman's campaign began from Chattanooga on the Tennessee River in 1864. Following his victory at Atlanta, he commenced the famous March to the Sea.

9. Gustav Körner or Koerner (1809-1896), a lawyer from Frankfurt am Main, was involved in the Frankfurt Putsch of 1833 and fled, settling in Belleville, Illinois, after finding Missouri less than billed by Gottfried Duden. He became an Illinois lawyer, and he was a member of the Illinois Supreme Court, 1845-50. He was lieutenant governor of Illinois, 1852-56. A close friend of Lincoln, Körner was a liaison to the government of Illinois in Missouri in 1861, then U.S. Minister for Spain, 1862-64. His English-language memoirs are excellent and revealing. See *DAB*, 10: 496-7, also *Memoirs of Gustave Körner 1809-1896, Life-Sketches Written at the Suggestion of His Children,* Thomas J. McCormack, ed. (Cedar Rapids, Iowa: Torch, 1909).

clichés, Frank Blair was a refreshing phenomenon. For that reason, if one knew him personally and came within the range of his personal magnetism, one was inclined only to think of his great qualities, and to happily forget his great shadowy side, which always occurs in such natures.

And the victorious leader of the Union army, the valorous General Sherman, expressed himself thus on learning of Blair's death:

I always held General Blair to be one of the best patriots, an honorable man through and through, and a courageous soldier. The services he did for the country at the outbreak of the war shall never be forgotten, and the country has his prompt dispatch, his nerve and solidity to thank for the fact that St. Louis was preserved as a strategic point and Missouri kept in the Union. Frank Blair was a noble, honorable and magnanimous man. He was valorous, open and selfless. His qualities will always be recognized and never forgotten, while his failings will be buried with him; they harmed no one but himself.

I shall preserve an honorable memory of my bold, energetic leader and dependable friend as long as these eyes remain open. I stood next to him and learned to value his character and merits in their full value. He was an able, honorable person and a whole man, whom many more failed than he himself had failings of which to be accused. For that reason, "Peace to his ashes, honor to his memory!"

Cultural Efforts

Now I come to the portion of my activities in the then neglected West of America that always gave me joy and provided me with my sole recreation after hard labor. I still regard this portion with pleasure and estimate it even higher than my political work. My political undertakings were, in fact, easier, because I quickly came into possession of the rather simple machinery of a party organization, and through this was able to guide thousands of my German fellow-citizens and lead their movement. It was an entirely different affair with my efforts to spread culture and education among the masses, lifting them to a higher intellectual level. When I was doing this, which I could not openly describe in those terms without offending their self-esteem and good opinion of themselves of individuals, I was thrown entirely on my own resources.

Whatever the gentle Gustav Körner and H. A. Rattermann and other praisers of "the good old days" might say on this matter, the truth is that the German element, especially in the Far West, stood at a very low educational level. In fact in some states it was utterly hopeless and savage. All the thousands of intelligent men who came over after 1848 said this. The earlier immigration of 1818 to 1848 consisted mostly of the poorest and most oppressed peasants and artisans of Germany, who had grown up almost entirely without education or training, in ignorance and narrowness, sometimes with prejudice and superstition of all sorts. They migrated from Germany to escape death by hunger, as well as the misery and sadness of the old homeland. Lacking all means, they had to bind themselves to the buyers of souls who were so numerous in those days. Packed on old ships as if they were herring and hauled to America, they had to work off their passage and other advances after arrival, so that they were leased as white slaves by the soul-sellers to farmers, factories and the like, usually for several years. Under these oppressive conditions there could be no talk of education or imparting knowledge, and most of the children of these people grew up without schooling or instruction of any sort. When they reached the age of seven or eight, they had to join the work on the farm or in the factory to earn the money to redeem themselves. The difference in the life of these people between their old homeland and America was the fact that in America they always had enough to eat, which was not always the case in Germany. As a result, a large portion of the German element in America grew up as a group without education or prospects. Once they had worked their way out of their enslavement to the salesmen of souls and became independent, they had to start from nothing all over again, establishing a home through their own hard labor and deprivation. Years passed with bad harvests, natural disasters, and other hindrances. These people grew old early, and their children grew into men and women. Many died before they could enjoy the fruits of their hard labor, which would only benefit their children. In such situations there could be no talk of education, intellectual stimulation or progress of any sort.

Even that portion of the immigrants who did not place themselves at the disposal of the salesmen of souls and came over with their own means, however limited, stood on a very low level of education. Broken and deteriorated by the subordination inherent in the European state system, they cared only for their daily bread, rejoicing like kings if they could eat meat every day. (Meat had been served rarely or only on holidays in Germany.) They had lost all intellectual rigor and independence, and they did not feel the slightest need to learn anything, to educate themselves or to send their children to good schools. As a result, the German immigrants before 1848 lived in large and small settlements intermingled with Anglo-Americans who looked down on these uneducated arrivals, laughed them to scorn and mocked them for their crude peculiarities.

This is because, as one must concede, the Americans almost without exception possessed a certain level of education. While not elevated, it was at least uniformly spread across the whole Anglo-American population. Reading, writing and arithmetic are assumed among them, and most of them know the history of their country and the geography of America. They take and read their newspapers, and they have a political opinion. This admittedly not very high level of education is, however, possessed uniformly by the entire Anglo-American population. Their denigration of German immigrants can be justified. They could not imagine how respectable heads of families owning farms of 80, 120 or more acres could not read a written or printed line, making three crosses in the place of a signature.

Plattdeutsch[1] immigrants were somewhat more resourceful than southern Germans. Due to the close association of their Low German idiom with the root of Anglo-Saxon, they learned English with startling rapidity, and by the second generation they were completely Americanized and lost forever to Germandom. German artisans and workers in towns, however, lived in circumstances similar to the illiterate peasants. They too were uneducated, and they had neither the time, the desire nor the opportunity to learn anything and educate themselves. They stood on the same intellectual level as the Irish, although they were better and more skilled workers; instead of doing homage to whiskey as the Irish did, they regarded the beer mug and the tobacco pipe as the highest goods of this earth. A book or a newspaper

---

1. *Plattdeutsch* is the "Low German" dialect spoken in northern Germany.

was regarded as something extremely superfluous. So an intellectual morass prevailed in the open countryside, and in towns the tone was set by the raw crassness of the *Kaffern*, the completely uneducated plebes, who dominated the educated minority of Germans.

Like many others, I found language among Germans in the American West to be raw and uncouth, punctuated with the most improper turns of speech. Rawness was taken as sincerity and crudeness as directness. Expressions such as *du Saukerl*[2] or *du Saumagen*[3] ranked as pleasantries, and almost every conversation between such souls included as a refrain the unappetizing invitation that Goethe has Götz von Berlinchingen say to the Imperial commander, of which the Kitchen Latin of students, *"Lex mihi ars"* ["Art is a law to me"] is the least offensive rendering.[4]

That was the average level of education and tone among the German masses. The political party leaders, the wholesale pipe-layers and wire-pullers, felt justified and encouraged by these conditions. To them it was perfectly proper that the mass of Germans remain as ignorant and uneducated as the Irish, for then they were easier to control and to lead about by the nose. It was not necessary to persuade the people's intelligence and understanding in political questions and at elections; rather, all one needed was to engage a few dozen "preeminent ward politicians" for so much per day. Consisting of taverners, barkeepers, deputy tax assessors, sheriffs, marshal, and other gentlemen loafers, they roamed about the ward. Storming the bars, buying beer for everyone, they went to bed at the end of the day with a few hundred German votes in their pocket.

To be sure there were some educated people among the German immigration then, as well. Gustav Körner in his *Deutsches Element vor 1848*[5] as well as the bold, tireless Rattermann in his *Deutscher Pionier,* made us acquainted with several dozen such Germans from the days before 1848.[6] Yet even if it had been several hundred, one would have to consider how a few hundred educated Germans would be distributed among an immigration that, from 1818 to 1848, numbered in the millions. On top of that, there were many of this educated elite who were more or less Americanized and completely alienated from Germandom.

---

2. German, "You porker!"

3. German, "You sow-belly!"

4. This is a pun on the German "Leck mich am Arsch!" which means (approximately) "Lick my posterior!"

5. Gustav Phillip Körner, *Das deutsche Element in den Vereinigten Staaten von Nordamerika 1818-1848* (Cincinnati, 1880), reprinted with an introduction by Patricia Herminghouse (New York: Peter Lang, 1986).

6. H. A. Rattermann, ed., *Der deutsche Pionier. Monatsschrift des deutschen Pionierlebens in Amerika,* 11 vols., published in Cincinnati, 1869-1879.

It was an entirely different matter with the immigration streaming to America after 1848. In the course of this migration, educated men were almost the most numerous category. Authors, journalists, painters, musicians, engineers, professors, teachers, men of science, artists of all the branches, and a more or less educated mass came by the thousands. They penetrated the American population as well as the old German immigration, once and for all. Rapidly they made their influence felt. Everywhere they brought with them intelligence and education, and after the first wild years of adjustment, they achieved such effectiveness that they brought Germans to a position of honor from once having been despised. Neither America nor any other land has ever experienced an immigration such as the German of 1848, and this grandiose phenomenon will certainly never be repeated. What a mass of educated minds, gifted disciples of the sciences and the arts, tested pedagogues and shapers of youth came to America in the space of a few years! What a plethora of knowledge, learning, intelligence and ability was poured out on the whole Union! The benefits of this transfusion of fresh blood soon showed themselves. In the next ten years, tremendous changes for the better were visible, not only among Germans but among Anglo-Americans as well. Surprisingly quickly, there was an enormous prospering of cultural and social areas. The people of future decades shall recall with thanks the blessed activity of the Forty-Eighter immigration.

A mass of talented and gifted men went to their ruin at the same time, however, failing to find activity suited to their talents, or able only to assure their personal survival. It was like a battle in which thousands were laid low and more thousands wounded and crippled for life. That was how it was in the great German migration of 1848. Hundreds of gifted men, trained in the sciences or in literature, came over in those days and perished alone, abandoned in want and misery. Others were rendered savage by the continual struggle for existence, losing their spark and their self-respect. Still others perished in a sense by seeking solace and forgetfulness in the whiskey bottle. In short, the sad victims were as many as in a great modern war. Their names have long since been forgotten, and their earlier activities are forgotten as well. No one recalls their existence or knows where they are buried. And yet they were fine men of conviction who had fought with words, and later on the barricades with weapons, for liberty and progress in Germany. Persecuted by victorious reaction, they fled to America; but without support for their existence, they perished in silent despair. Whoever lived through this period will confirm that I am not exaggerating.

Scholars and professors, authors and artists, educated men experienced in all branches of knowledge, were compelled to earn their bread with the coarsest labor. They worked as cigar rollers, waiters, servants, even as boot polishers or street sweepers. There were also those unable to support themselves in even this way, and they wasted away miserably. I once met a bartender in a second-rank hotel who had been a professor of philology at a German university; he could speak and write Latin, Greek, and Hebrew as fluently as his German mother tongue, but he could still find no better work because he did not know English. If he had been able to learn that, any American university would have been happy to take him as a professor of ancient languages. But he remained a bartender, serving up various cobblers and drinks to ignorant plebes. Finally blunted and rendered savage by this banal, numbing activity, he vanished in a few years without a trace.

Then there was my dear Ernst Violand,[7] the son of one of the principal shareholders of the great mercantile and banking house, Hausner and Violand in Lemberg. Educated at the University of Vienna, he was one of the best jurists, a member of the Frankfurt Parliament and of the Austrian *Reichsrat*. Severely compromised in the October Days in Vienna, he had been condemned to death *in absentia*, but was fortunate enough to escape to America. Unable to find adequate employment, he was lucky to find a German cigar maker who took him as an apprentice and taught him cigar rolling. At least he could earn his bread that way. And he lived in poverty in Peoria, Illinois, a cigar maker, who wrote something for the newspapers now and then, not for a fee but only when the theme interested him. Despite his highly restricted situation, he rigorously rejected all offers of help and support, feeling the need to support his independence, as he saw it. He was a true friend and collaborator on the *Anzeiger des Westens*, but he decisively rejected any fees or help offered, but since I knew of his poverty, I was compelled to have friends in Peoria buy his cigars, which I then distributed to my friends in St. Louis. In the course of years, Violand was able to work his way up a little, and he even hired a few workers himself. Eventually he married, but he was never able to get security in life. He died still in his prime, of the results of overwork and worry. I could give so many other examples were I not afraid of tiring my reader.

After having portrayed the intellectual situation of Germans in those days, I now return to the point of my narrative, which is how I personally undertook initiatives in culture and education. Parallel with the efforts of the educated portion of the Forty-Eighter movement, these were largely a recreation from my own hard labor.

First it is necessary to say a word here about my style of life in America after taking over the *Anzeiger*. I was overcome by the great responsibility that had descended upon me, and I understood that only tireless effort, restless

---

7. Ernst Violand (1820-1875) settled in Peoria in 1849. See Zucker, 350; Boernstein's defense of Violand, *AW,* weekly, vol. 19, no. 8, 17 December 1853, p. 2.

activity and reasonable thrift could allow me to carry out the mission assigned to me of supporting my enterprises with my meager means. My entire time was systematically dedicated to business alone, and my sole release was within the circle of my family, which had significantly expanded. My eldest son [August] Siegmund had married, and his wife gave me grandchildren. My wife's desire through many years to have a daughter was fulfilled, even if by adoption. A young German couple had come to America at about the same time we did, settling in Hermann. During the cholera epidemic the man, Mr. Kroh, was suddenly swept away by the disease, and the widow was left helpless and abandoned with a little daughter of five. A bold German, a neighbor who had known her as a good housewife and mother, made a proposal of marriage; he did not want a stepchild in the house, however, so he set as the sole condition that the child be cared for elsewhere. The man was prosperous, and the future of the poor widow appeared permanently assured if this condition were met. So Frau Detharding, a friend of the woman who also knew my own wife's desire for a daughter, became a go-between, proposing that we take the little girl. We wanted to see her first, and the mother brought her to us in St. Louis. This pretty, friendly child pleased us, and we took her into our home at once. The widow returned to Hermann, relieved and ready for her new marriage.

I then asked my lawyer, Mr. Thomas C. Reynolds, to take the necessary steps with the courts to adopt little Karoline as our daughter. To my amazement I learned from Reynolds that this was entirely impossible. The law code of Missouri had nothing about adopted children or adoptive parents, and adoption neither bestowed legal rights nor had any legal results. I could do nothing more than take the child in apprenticeship, which was understood and regulated in the Missouri code. As a result, I had to participate in a minor transaction before the county court, in which the guardian of the child transferred all rights in the name of himself and the mother to me. This was registered in a document, and little Karoline was bound to me as an apprentice, obligated to obey us until reaching majority. My wife and I obligated ourselves to educate her and release her on the day of her majority, giving her a complete bed, a Bible, a woman's saddle and a small trousseau of linen and clothing as her own property, just as had been required in the Missouri Code, composed at the time of the first settling of the state. Karoline was a good and lovable daughter to us, giving us much joy and richly repaying us for any trouble. In the course of years she grew to be a blooming maiden, a loyal support to my wife in housework. In 1861, after the outbreak of the Civil War, she married the talented music teacher, Adolf Wilharditz. A good, hard-working wife and true spouse to him, she was a loving mother to his children. She died a few years ago, sadly enough, still in her best years, of the complications of a miscarriage. This event painfully touched all of us, but particularly the parents who had adopted her.[8]

So I happily lived with my ever-growing family, finding in my home my best and sole recreation. I personally associated with only a few persons, and I avoided public places and taverns, first of all out of health considerations, but most of all because the mean, raw tone prevailing there repelled me. So it was that I was thrown back on my business and my family alone. Day after day I was at work at nine in the morning in the editorial office, and I worked there without interruption until midday. I returned to the circle of my family for two hours, only to be back at my office at three at the latest, remaining there until the last telegram had arrived and been translated, which ordinarily was between two and three in the morning. Only when the telegraphist wrote "Good night!" on the last page did I go home. In eventful times, when there were elections or important decisions, I remained in the printing plant until the paper had gone to press and I had corrected the first proof. In the last ten years of my American activity, I ordinarily never left the editorial offices or printing shop before two in the morning, but sometimes only at seven or eight o'clock, only returning a few hours later, ready and actively at work. Two hours in the morning and two hours at midday were the only times for relaxation which I allowed myself, in the circle of my family.

I lived only for my work, and I never managed to get to know even the close environs of St. Louis. I was in neither Belleville nor St. Charles, and I did not come to the little German town of Hermann, where I had so many fine German friends, until I led my regiment there at the beginning of the Civil War. I dedicated myself utterly and exclusively to my paper, and during the twelve years of my journalistic activity, I did not let its political, technical or financial control out of my hands even for a day, but always led it myself and alone. I did have coeditors, but I had little joy with them. It was a long time before I could bring them to understand my way of thinking and make my goals understandable to them. Once I had managed to train them to the point that they could have been useful to me, they thought they had figured out "how the old man whispers and spits." Leaving me to establish their own newspapers with the financial help of my opponent, they placed themselves in sharpest opposition to the *Anzeiger* and to me. This happened with all of my coeditors, from Louis Didier to my last deserter, Georg Hillgärtner. All of them dealt with me in the same noble manner. Remarkably enough, none of them had any success with their competing

---

8. For some reason Boernstein avoids mentioning his previous foster-daughter in France, Josephine Wolf, who married Karl Ludwig Bernays. As in so many matters in his professional career, Boernstein's personal life was a swirl of repetitions.

papers, which either collapsed or, if the paper survived, the fruits only fell into the laps of their successors.[9]

The German immigrants after 1848 found Germans in the United States in an entirely different situation from what they expected. Older immigrants had developed their own orientation contrasting with the descriptions in Franz Löher's *Geschichte der Deutschen in Amerika*[10] and similar books and newspaper articles about how the Germans in the United States had remained true to the customs and practices of the old fatherland. They spoke of the German immigration as sympathetically participating in Germany's progress and success, closely following the attainments of German scholarship and art. As a result, one expected to find the German settlements of America mere extensions of the old homeland, a true mirror image. The truth was very different. German America had become something essentially different, a people utterly contrasting with Germans in Germany. This occurred through the climatic, social and political influences arising from different purposes of life, as well as through living together with Anglo-Americans, Irishmen, Creoles, etc.

In material terms, the German Americans had essentially gained from this change. They had become practical, businesslike, active, progressive, and tireless in creating and doing. In the intellectual direction, however, they remained far behind when measured against compatriots in the old homeland. Arising from oppressed situations, they had only elementary education or none at all. With a few notable exceptions, they also had no training. They would always remain backward in cultural terms, for their entire time and activity were absorbed by physical labor. Their need for education had been ignored, and in those days there was never much opportunity to get an education had they the time or desire. The few books brought along from Germany were soon read to pieces, and to replace them never occurred to anyone, and it would have cost a great deal of money. German American newspapers in the first half of the century, again with a few exceptions, stood on a very low level. Their language, in an attempt to be popular, was nearly common, often with bad grammar. A significant proportion of German American papers were written in Pennsylvania Dutch, a jargon concocted of English and German words. The German books printed in America consisted mostly of cookbooks, prayer books, treatises on farming and veterinary medicine, etc. Our German classics, such as

---

9. Here Boernstein finesses the most important "break-away," which was the foundation of the *Westliche Post* by Carl Dänzer in 1857. This eventually became the chief German newspaper in Missouri, surviving until 1938, though Dänzer admittedly soon left it.

10. Franz von Löher, *Geschichte und Zustände der Deutschen in Amerika* (Cincinnati, 1847); see Robert Cazden, *Social History*, 216; Körner, *Element*, 17.

Goethe, Schiller, Lessing, and others, had fallen into oblivion, seldom found in the possession of a German family.

Further, the independence and autonomy of the individual—the self-government of communities and complete lack of petty police regulations—that usually had such positive results in America, had the opposite effect on Germans of the early migration to America. Coming to America to escape the oppressive conditions of their old homeland, they became a little too independent and autonomous, suffering a spirit of presumption and stubbornness. This expressed itself in rude expressions, a rejection of social conventions, and in a coarseness and rawness among adults. The youths, growing up in the free schools, were either Americanized or rendered entirely savage. That was the situation of most Germans the Forty-Eighter migration (consisting largely of educated persons) found, although I repeat that there were individual and honorable exceptions. The Forty-Eighters deeply felt a crass contrast between here and there.

As soon as the first cares about survival were past and the horns of the revolutionary epoch blunted, as soon as the tilting at idealistic windmills à la Don Quixote and other excesses of the first years were survived, there suddenly awoke without any urging a great intellectual need. Among the great mass of educated immigrants, there was a desire and solid will to elevate German Americans intellectually rather than to descend to their lower level. There was an effort to spread the intellectual achievements of recent times through word, letter and deed. This was indeed a remarkable movement among the five million Germans in America in the 1850s. The new additions to the German element worked like a ferment, bringing intellectual strength and clarification after quiet brewing. Everywhere heightened awareness was given to German schooling. Lectures on science, literature and general information, once the exclusive domain of Anglo-Americans, were given more and more often in German. People made an effort to keep their German pure and to cleanse it of the Anglicisms that had contaminated it. The tone and attitude of German newspapers improved, rising from year to year. German gymnastic societies and singing associations increased everywhere where Germans lived in large numbers, and they practiced their educational activity to a happy degree. German artists and musicians rose to general admiration. An enterprising publisher, Mr. Thomas in Philadelphia, produced cheap popular editions of the classical works of Goethe, Schiller and Lessing, of Humboldt's *Cosmos*, of Heine's and Börne's writings, and other jewels of German literature, which soon circulated among the German American population in thousands of copies. Since then the European tourist, when he is in the Far West, is astonished to find Goethe's *Faust*, Schiller's *Don Carlos*, Lessing's *Nathan the Wise* and similar masterworks of German poetry in a farmhouse, even in the living room of a log cabin. As said, there was neither any agreement nor any plan in these cultural efforts. Each of us who felt entitled to it through education and knowledge worked and pressed in this direction on his own and according to his own idea in his area of activity. And I can say without flattering myself that I did a good deal to carry out this cultural mission. In the beginning it was still unclear and with little sense of a goal, but later, in the course of years, it grew increasingly surer and more powerful.

My first attempt in this direction was a failure, being based on European assumptions not corresponding to American conditions. Certainly no one in St. Louis still recalls, but in 1851 I established a German Reading Room in St. Louis, modeled after the *cabinets de lecture* of Paris from which I had only recently come. I had noted that my German compatriots read little or nothing at all, and even those who took a newspaper only skimmed superficially over the new advertisements or local notices. Still in part based on my European viewpoint, however, I assumed that there would be a desire to read more, to know more, to expand knowledge.

On the second floor of a house on the north side of Market Street between Main and Second, I established this reading room in a long salon above Dr. Gempp's second pharmacy. It was quite centrally located and comfortably furnished, equipped with maps, encyclopedias and a small reference library. The long reading table offered a rich selection of English and German newspapers from all parts of the Union, European journals, reviews and the newest brochures and pamphlets. The price of entry for a sitting was fixed at the pittance of five cents, for I was not figuring on a profit. Despite this low price and the broad range of reading material, my enterprise found no response, for the Germans living in the southern part of town found it too far away, and the Germans in the northern part had the same complaint. In truth this was just a lazy excuse, because the same people did not hesitate walking several miles to where a particularly good beer was being tapped.

Only a few curious came, including some Americans who had learned German. The best customers were young apprentices in merchandising and others who had not been here long enough to find a position. They did not feel comfortable in crowded boarding houses, and for the price of five cents they could spend an entire day in the reading room. There they killed time reading all the newspapers, writing their letters and saving money for heat and light. Experience quickly taught me that there was as yet no need for a reading room in the German population. The best interpretation was that the effort was premature, and I allowed it to close quietly after six months, all the wiser for the experience.

In the meantime the Society of Free Men and its schools had been established. These had found a considerably greater response in the German population than my reading room and so I now dedicated my whole attention to these schools and their leadership. Hand in hand with Franz Schmidt and other fine men, we succeeded in winning capable teachers for them, and the number of students rose from semester to semester. In the course of the next year I had the joy and satisfaction of seeing the fruits of our labors ripen with a new, better-instructed and motivated generation in development. We also concerned ourselves with the adult portion of the population. Evening schools for adults were established, and lectures and presentations on literature, art history, ethnography, and history were given every Sunday morning. These events spread extraordinary information and soon replaced going to church for a large portion of the German population.

These efforts on our part had only benefited the male side of the population, because our schools were for boys and our Sunday presentations were largely attended only by men. If the training and education were to have genuine worth and success, it had to expand to the female sex, and women would have to concern themselves actively in it, being the first and best teachers of children. Here there was more hesitation than was the case with male instruction. With a few exceptions, most of the prosperous Germans were self-made men, even if in the best meaning of the term. All of them had more or less neglected their educations, coming to America as boys due to the depressed circumstances of their parents. They had all earned their bread through tireless labor, loyalty and persistence, punctuality and uprightness, order and thrift. Working their way up gradually, eventually they became prosperous, even rich or on the way to becoming so. Restlessly active and tireless in their labor, they had had little time to think of their own education. In addition, most of them had married young, when they were still traveling salesmen, helpers or similar subordinate positions. Their selection of mates was quite limited at that point, and they married the daughters of farmers and artisans, even maidens from the servant classes. If children came, neither mother nor father could do much for their education or training, partly because of the press of their own labors, partly because the parents lacked an education themselves.

The boys were soon taken care of, since there were both free schools and private schools, and after these came academies and higher institutions of learning. In the West, however, there was much to be desired in the education of young women. Girls could always attend the free schools, and there were here and there sectarian schools and female educational institutions taught by nuns in which more piety than knowledge was imparted. But in all of St. Louis, with a population of twenty-five thousand Germans, there was not a single higher daughters' school or female educational institution such as can be found in even small towns in Germany. This need increased from year to year, and mothers who deeply regretted the neglect of their own education desired nothing more than to make available to their daughters the education they had been denied by social conditions.

I cannot omit here the fact that some of our German self-made men, once they had assured themselves a secure existence, did dedicate themselves to learning what they had missed in youth through no fault of their own. So it was that one of the most respected Germans of those times in St. Louis, the merchant Andreas Krug,[11] was happy to tell the story of his life and development. He had come to America as an ignorant youngster, and on setting out to what was then the Far West, he was forced to rely totally on himself. For years he earned his own daily bread by hauling bricks and mortar for house construction as a day laborer, but every cent he could save was spent learning to read and write. In the end, a rich merchant named Braun became aware of the young man, who pleased him. Braun took him in as a servant in his large business, where Andreas demonstrated his great ability and reliability. He was so tirelessly active, honest and dependable that he grew steadily in the regard of his employer. When Brown learned that Andreas spent his free hours of Sunday and several hours every evening educating himself, he shifted the hard work to others and placed our Krug at one of the desks of his counting house as an assistant. In this position, as well, the young man demonstrated himself worthy of confidence, and his usefulness to the business grew along with his zeal for education. So it was that our Andreas eventually became the first clerk, then the executive officer, and finally the partner of old Braun. He married the man's sole daughter and became the heir of the entire property and business of the old man. When I came to know him in St. Louis, he was one of the most respected citizens in town. His name and firm were everywhere respected, and he was regarded as an educated, experienced man. In the course of his activities he had developed both a pleasing manner and wide, encyclopedic knowledge. That was what our German self-made men looked like in those days, although not all of them had the same desire for self-education.

I had frequent occasion to voice complaints about the lack of female educational institutions, and I urged my friend Franz Schmidt to establish an advanced school for girls. He was an energetic pedagogue from a good German school, rich in knowledge and experience. His young, amiable wife, whose maiden name was Schuster, had been educated as a teacher. The other teachers were easy to find, and support and encouragement came from all sides to assure this undertaking. Long desired, it was launched in the most promising manner. After a brief period of preparation, Schmidt was able to

---

11. Andrew Krug of the partnership Meyer, Krug & Meister lived at 25 Elm in *Directory* 1857, 128.

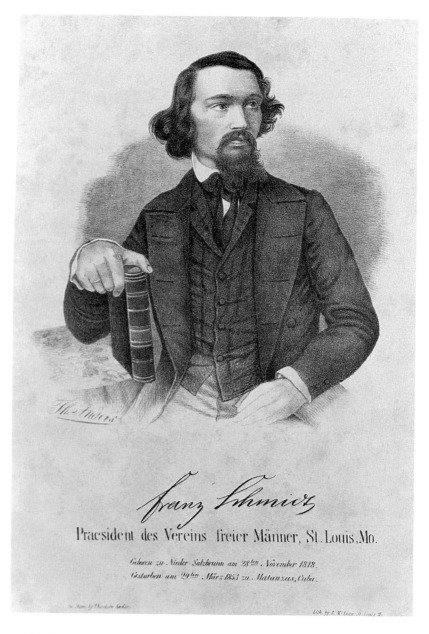

Praesident des Vereins freier Männer, St. Louis, Mo.

Franz Schmidt as president of the Society of Free Men. Schmidt had been a member of the German national parliament in Frankfurt. Using the code name Theseus, he corresponded with the Communist Party Central Committee in Brussels while in St. Louis. Lithograph by Theodore Anders published by A. McLean, St. Louis, after Schmidt's death in 1853. Courtesy of the St. Louis Public Library.

open his advanced girls' school. The pressure of applicants was so great that despite the large size of the available location, enrollment had to be closed. In addition to two young Austrians, A. Lenz and Gustav Klier, two other teachers and the gifted music teacher Robyn were won. The institution grew to considerable importance, and the pupils and teachers were pleased with the best of success.

Yet, as our poet says, "There is no eternal league to be made with the powers of fate!" That is how it came to pass here as well. The institution had reached its second year when Schmidt, the tireless doer, suddenly fell ill with a severe malady of the throat. This illness grew from week to week, expressing itself in hoarseness and a tormenting cough and soon making all personal activity as a teacher impossible for Schmidt. I was happy to help my sick friend and, despite my many obligations, took over teaching German poetry, reading and declamation, to which I dedicated two hours a day. Thus passed the autumn months, and for a while Schmidt felt better. As soon as he wanted to take up teaching again, however, he had a relapse which left him more miserable than before. With the onset of winter his situation grew worse, and before Christmas his physician Dr. A. Hammer[12] consulted with leading medical authorities, advising Schmidt not to spend the winter in St. Louis. Instead, he should be taken to a warm, moist climate such as in the tropics, where there would be relief and, if healing were possible, also healing. This was a killing blow for the new enterprise. The means for the sick man to travel to Cuba were gathered by his friends in an instant. The wealthy sugar refiner Ch. Belcher offered lodging to Schmidt on his large plantation in Matanzas, together with food and all the comforts, as long as he wished to stay there, but how was the school to survive without his teaching? His friends would certainly be able to act on his behalf while he was sick, but their own professional obligations made it impossible for them to replace him permanently as a teacher. It was necessary to search for a replacement.

Poor Schmidt traveled to Cuba, accompanied by our good wishes and hopes. There he was received heartily by the employees of Mr. Belcher,

---

12. Dr. Adam von Hammer (1813-1878) fought in the Swiss *Sonderbund* wars, then as a partisan of Friedrich Hecker in Baden in 1848. In St. Louis, he organized the Humboldt Institute, a German medical college, and he used his house opposite the U.S. Arsenal as an armed guardpost, with faculty and students as troops. In 1861 he was lieutenant colonel of the Fourth Missouri Volunteer Regiment, under Col. Schüttner, and he organized military hospitals. After the war he was a professor of the revived Humboldt Medical College (to 1869) and then the St. Louis Medical College. He returned to Germany in disgust after the corrupt election of Rutherford B. Hayes in 1877. See Kaufmann, 506-07; Zucker, 300; James Moores Ball, *Dr. Adam Hammer, Surgeon and Apostle of Higher Medical Education* (St. Louis, 1909).

Messrs. Plagge and Biranyi. Although he arrived in January, which is the severe rainy season of the Cuban tropics, it seemed that the uniform, mild and warm temperature had a good influence on his malady. I soon received a letter from him written in Matanzas on 31 January 1853, in which he gave a spirited, humorous account of his travels and first impressions of Cuba. The beginning of this hopeful, interesting letter reads:

Dearest friend!

Yes indeed, now I have finally reached that splendid point on earth of which Humboldt says, "All around the tropics, this is the sole place on earth where one can pass the entire year and never feel a need for a coal fire." No one in the world seeks to dispute the title of this fortunate isle as Queen of the West-Indian Islands! It is true that I feel revived in this air and this temperature. Even though those who live here complain about the unusual raininess, it is still warm (70-75° F). It is summer, and everywhere flowers and trees bloom, everywhere the fruits ripen, everywhere are clouds of mosquitoes. What more do I want? I am finally free of winter and I no longer need to stoke a fire. I have arisen as if to a new life. [And so on]

The last part of the letter, in which Schmidt cheerfully described his brief visit to Havana and his way of life on the plantation in Matanzas, ended with the hopeful words, "And now a thousand hearty greetings to you and all my friends in St. Louis, and I hope for a happy reunion soon!"[13]

This lovely hope would not be fulfilled. This letter was the first and last I received from him in Cuba. A few weeks later a letter arrived from our friend Biranyi announcing Schmidt's death. Biranyi, a splendid man and a thoroughly amiable character, had been a Hungarian *Hunved* officer with Kossuth in Turkey and had accompanied him to St. Louis, where he remained and was sent to the plantation in Matanzas as an employee of the Belcher house. Together with Mr. Plagge he had done everything to make Schmidt's residence in Cuba as comfortable as possible. At the outset the sick man revived and gave reasons for the best hope. He was ardent in pursuing the sugar therapy advised to him, drinking the warm molasses and breathing in the aroma and steam of the sugar kettles. Yet the malady appeared to have deep roots, and after the momentary respite there was a relapse. The tuberculosis in his throat began to rise, and one lovely morning in February, after reading with great excitement a letter from his wife

---

13. Three letters by Schmidt, dated 31 January, 2 February, and 4 February 1853, were published by the *AW,* weekly, vol. 18, no. 19, 12 March 1853, p. 1, for 4 March.

brought him by Biranyi, he drank milk brought warm from the cow by a Negro, and said he wished to rest a bit. He reclined on his pillow. There were a few short breaths, then a deep sigh, and he slumbered forever. It was gentle, painless, without agony. Biranyi had him buried on the plantation, in the favorite place where he had loved to sit and lounge those days under the palms. As a Protestant he could not be buried in the Catholic cemetery of Matanzas. His money, clothing, books and everything he had brought from St. Louis were confiscated and kept by the royal treasury, despite the protests of the American consul. This was because Spanish law assigned to the Treasury goods of all foreigners who died in Cuba.[14]

With Schmidt's death, which deeply distressed his friends and the entire German population of St. Louis, there vanished every chance to maintain his school. His widow had to give up the enterprise, and the school was closed. It was later revived by the experienced pedagogue Theodor Plate, who launched the operation on an even larger scale and continued it for many years with success. The present generation of women and mothers of St. Louis can thank their education to this school, recalling with thanks their earlier teachers Franz Schmidt and Theodor Plate.

Schmidt's young widow remarried quickly. This is the practice in America, where it is very rare to meet a widow who has not remarried. Mrs. Schmidt married her husband's chief teacher, Mr. Lenz (his real name was Knafflenz) from Graz in Styria. Lenz was an educated, gifted young man, but the school had to be given up, as mentioned. As a result, Lenz got a position with the North Missouri Railroad, where he became chief of a train station several miles from St. Louis. Here in the impenetrable forest primeval, cut off from the old civilization and all comfort, denied all company, this young couple passed their first year. With the start of the next winter, the fragile woman, unused to the primitive, harsh life in the woods, began to show distressing symptoms. Soon she developed the same illness which had taken away dear Schmidt. Poor Lenz told me later with tears in his eyes the story of his wife's suffering. Tormented by the horrors of a hard winter, without the help of a physician or any assistance except that of her husband, distracted by his job, she fought long and painfully for survival over months. She slowly died inch by inch, finally taking her last breath just as nature awoke in spring. He told me his painful memory of those dreadful hours when he washed and dressed the corpse alone and abandoned in the woods. Then how by night, when no train was to pass, he shoveled a grave by moonlight in the midst of the woods, bore the corpse

---

14. Death notice for Schmidt in *AW*, weekly, vol. 18, no. 24, 23 April 1853. Description of his burial, which required the presence of Catholic clergy, in ibid., vol. 18, no. 28, 14 May 1853, p. 4, letter from Cuba dated 12 April.

there, bedded her down and filled the grave with dirt. All of the horror of these dreadful hours returned in his narrative, and the effects that remained with him were unmistakable. He gave up his job and returned to Europe. We bade farewell, and I never saw him again, never even heard of him again, not even here in Europe.

But away with these sad memories. I now come to happier experiences, to the role I played in another field in which I had an opportunity to work, a school for adults. More of that in the next chapter.

The School for Adults
(1856-1858)

Education is power! I have chosen this proverb as my motto, and I have always acted under its influence as far as my poor powers have reached, spreading knowledge and education among my compatriots. For growing children, a good deal was often done by the excellent free schools, and much besides was done by individuals. Still, it was not enough to educate youth. Adults as well, particularly the parents of children, have to take interest in these cultural efforts in order to help and lead their children in their development and education where possible, or at the least stand at their side with sympathy and support. Of course it is no longer possible to place adults on schoolbenches, and for those trying to make up what was neglected in youth there is no time for self-education in the press of American business and the restless drive of daily life. For most people, there is also no desire to learn anything in their riper years. Efforts in this direction can be made only indirectly and very slowly, and the friend of education who wishes to spread to a wider circle must always try indirect paths to reach his goals. He carefully has to hide his intentions and pretend only to entertain or divert. This is how it was with me and my friends of the same persuasion. We could not look German Americans in the face and tell them, "My dear compatriots, you are rather deficient in education and knowledge, but education is power, and you must recover lost ground, learn what is missing, and go to school once more." The preacher in the wilderness who spoke in this manner to the people would have been laughed to scorn, and they would have turned their backs on him with a resounding no. But by an indirect path, under the mask of entertainment, the same people are quite accessible. They will soon gain a taste for better literature and become interested in many an intellectual effort. By this means I made my attempt, and it was successful.

Honestly, it is uncomfortable and even painful for me to be saying so much about myself and my activities, since it almost seems that I am praising myself or ascribing great things to myself. Yet there is nothing else I can do. I am trying to write my memoirs, and I must speak of myself, if not too much, rather often too little. If I speak so much in the first person and let myself appear a great deal, then the sympathetic reader should forgive me; I am doing this not to praise myself, but rather because I carry in myself the conviction and the elevated awareness of having desired the good and also having accomplished good.

I had in my hands a powerful, effective means for education, a great newspaper with an extensive circle of readers. It was not restricted to St. Louis or Missouri alone, but spread across Illinois, Indiana, Iowa, Wisconsin and the entire Mississippi valley. I have already spoken of my efforts to raise the tone of the German American press, and I made it my conscientious duty to set a good example for colleagues. By cooperating with those who were well disposed, I had visible success. I dedicated particular care to the serial portion of my paper, and through the reprinting of better works of modern German literature—particularly historical novels such as *Emperor Joseph and His Court, Frederick the Great, Napoléon I,* and the like—historical knowledge was spread among the mass of the population.[1] These historical novels found such an intense, dedicated public that I published special book editions of each of them, and they found an excellent market. Besides that, I established a Sunday supplement for *belles lettres, Westliche Blätter.*[2] This was something quite new in those days, and I called upon the noted novelist Otto Ruppius,[3] who was well-known in Germany as well, to edit it. In order to stimulate the productivity of German American authors, I posted a prize contest for the best German American novella. In the first of these contests, the prize was received by Adolph Douai for his *Fata Morgana.*[4] In the second,

---

1. The novels he describes were written by Luise Mühlbach, the pen name for Klara Mundt, née Müller (1814-73), author of wildly popular novels on historical figures; see *NUC,* vol. 401, 282-310. On Boernstein's program of serial novels, see Steven Rowan, "The Cultural Program of Heinrich Börnstein in St. Louis, 1850-1861," *In Their Own Words,* vol. 3, no. 2 (1986), 186-206. Besides the *feuilleton* publications, Boernstein also published a book subscription called the *Hausbibliothek des Anzeigers des Westens,* which provided plays, novellas, and—often quite scandalous—vignettes from history. A subscriber to his newspaper could receive several volumes as a prize for signing up.

2. *Westliche Blätter* begun April 1859, was the Sunday edition of the *Anzeiger des Westens.* The title was continued when the paper was revived under other management in 1863, and it was used until 1912. See Arndt/Olson, 274. Boernstein had a Sunday supplement, *Der Salon,* which was published from October 1857, to at least 1859, and could be subscribed to separately; Arndt/Olson, 269.

3. Otto Ruppius (1819-1864), from Saxony, participated in the 1848 revolt in Baden, worked in the 1850s as a cultural journalist and musician, and returned to Germany after amnesty in 1862. "He ranks with Sealsfield and Gerstäcker as a writer of German novels with settings in the U.S.," Zucker, 333-4. Boernstein allowed him to write what was to be the only sequel to *The Mysteries of St. Louis, Der Prairieteufel* (St. Louis, 1861).

4. Carl Daniel Adolf Douai (1819-1888), from Altenburg, Saxony, arrived in Texas in 1852, settling in New Braunfels. He was run out of Texas for supporting black rights, and he was a popularizer of Marxist views as well as of the Kindergarten movement. His "prize" novel, *Fata Morgana* (St. Louis, 1857) has been called the earliest American proletarian novel. See Zucker, 288-9; Cazden, *Social History,* 390.

F. W. Arming received it for his *General Kalb*.[5] There was no lack of effort by others to spread enlightenment. A small circle of active, like-minded persons formed, of whom I only mention Franz Schmidt, Lüdeking,[6] Gustav Klier and Dr. Dreis. They sought to work in this direction and make themselves useful through speeches, presentations and popular courses. During one winter, I presented a cycle of twenty dramatic lectures, in which I presented in speaking roles both classic masterworks and more recent examples of our modern German dramatic literature. Prefacing each of them with an explanatory introduction on the poet or author, I explained the origin and importance of the piece. These lectures, which had a large response, produced a considerable profit that went to the German Women's Association.

I promoted the founding of the *deutscher Frauenverein* [German Women's Association] partly in order to give the German female population the opportunity to meet one another, partly to unite them for common useful efforts. The association, whose helpful activities I followed for many years, was quickly organized, with the tireless Mrs. Kreutzbauer as chair and the educated Mrs. Emelie Krähe as corresponding secretary. The most respectable German ladies joined the Association, and it soon numbered members in the hundreds. I happily did what I could drafting its statutes and, once the Association was in full operation, raising sufficient money through garden festivals, balls, theater productions and lectures to permit it to operate with success. The German Women's Association did a great deal of good, and if I am not wrong it still exists as the *deutscher Frauen-Hilfsverein* [German Women's Assistance Association].

Still, the best school for adults, the true education for the people, remains the dramatic stage. There the truths that reach the awareness of only a few through books press rapidly and deeply from the podium of a theater into the knowledge of the masses, taking solid root. The best school of the people is and remains a good theater, and a performance of Lessing's *Nathan the Wise*, Schiller's *Don Carlos*, Goethe's *Faust* or *Egmont* spreads more ingenious ideas, raising and ennobling the masses, than all the books, professorial assertions or glib sermons in the world.

5. Friedrich Wilhelm Arming, an Austrian author living in Brooklyn, won the prize competition for *Ein deutscher Baron* (St. Louis, 1860), about General De Kalb in the American Revolution. See Cazden, *Social History*, 390.

6. Carl Lüdeking (1819-1885), born in Giessen, emigrated to America in 1851, and from 1852 he was "speaker" of the *freie Gemeinde von Nord-St. Louis*. He spoke and wrote extensively on moral and political issues, and he was the American delegate to the Congress of Freethinkers in Naples in 1869. Zucker, 317. The papers of the *Freie Gemeinde*, which Boernstein joined after the demise of the "Free Men," are in WHM St. Louis.

Marie Boernstein, wife of Henry Boernstein, in stage costume, c. 1856. Carte de visite photograph. Courtesy of the Missouri Historical Society.

The situation of the German theater in America was still very poor in those days. What was done in drama smacked more of actors' wagons or portable stages than of a moral, ennobling spectacle. In the vast area of the United States, occupied by five million Germans, there was not a single German theater deserving the name. The best situation was in New York, where, when I came to America, a German director named Eduard Haman performed with his troupe. They performed first in the drill hall of a militia regiment, then in the salon of an inn, then in a circus or a desecrated church, until finally, after many visits to small English theaters, he managed in 1855 to build a *deutsche Stadttheater* (German City Theater). In other towns with a strong German population it was usually the Turners or singing societies that would occasionally make amateur presentations, in which there was usually a great deal of trouble finding women to take roles, and the men's efforts witnessed more to good will than to dramatic talent. There were also some traveling theater directors, such as Messrs. Bötzow, Wolf and others, who would visit this or that town for a few months, seldom finding much return for their efforts. There was a severe lack of German actors in America, and only rarely was one washed up there by a perverse fate. Such guest performers as later went to America, such as Davison, Hendrichs, Mrs. von Baerndorf, F. Haase, Marie Seebach, Madame Janauscheck, etc., had not yet arrived. The only great European artists to come to America in those days were all from either the opera or the concert hall, such as Jenny Lind, Thalberg, Ole Bull and a few Italian opera companies. It was my warmest wish to establish a German theater in St. Louis, but the difficulties just described, particularly the lack of actors, thwarted my desires. Many years would have to pass before I could consider a really stable German theater. The best that could be done at that time were amateur performances, which could at least be better prepared, more artistically led amateur performances than people were then accustomed to. For this purpose I founded the *philodramatische Gesellschaft* [Philodramatic Society], discovering much potential for training among my friends and acquaintances. These people joined with enthusiasm and love, and what they lacked in higher inspiration was made up for by their energy and good will.

With our good dramatic training, my wife and I naturally bore the chief burden of the enterprise, and I had plenty to do as an actor as well as producer and director. I had the greatest difficulty with male romantic gentlemen leads, which were almost non existent, for German American life had nothing gentlemanly about it. It was easier to find female romantic leads, because all women are born actresses. The best male romantic leads I was able to raise were the gifted lawyer Christian Kribben and the merchant Hermann Schröder. Both of them had the bearing, manner and style, but the extensiveness of the roles made a thorough memory a primary requirement for good performance. As a result I had an awful time, particularly with the men, because the restless, wearing drive of American life really leaves people with very little time for quiet reflection or undivided attention for any one undertaking. By innumerable rehearsals and tireless drill, I did manage to bring the performances into order. And if small gaps occurred on the first evening, my wife or I resolutely sprang in, often delivering the speeches others were to deliver, so that the public suspected no interruption.

I wrote two pieces for the first evening; a comedy in five acts called *Der betrogene Betrüger* [*The Cheat Cheated*], which was later performed more than twenty times in Vienna with great success and became a favorite in the German stage repertoire, and a local jape called *Deutsche Einwanderung und deutsche Gesellschaft!* [*German Immigration and German Society*], a picture of the German American world that quickly made the rounds of all America, becoming a support and fallback for all German amateur stages. The success of the evening was magnificent. The largest theater in town, the Variétés Theater, was filled to the rafters, and even Americans came to see the so-called "Dutch play." The actors were pleased with the jubilant applause and the innumerable calls for bows. The future of the Philodramatic Society was assured by this opening, and it continued for several years with growing support from the German population, until its place was taken in 1859 by the genuinely permanent German theater I founded. The profits from opening night went to the *Deutsche Einwanderungsgesellschaft* [German Immigration Society], which brought this useful institution all of twelve hundred dollars. The profits of the second performance went to the German Women's Association, and the third to the *Freie Gemeinde* [Free Congregation] of New Bremen. So it went in these as in subsequent years, and the profits of every production, seldom below one thousand dollars, either went to a German enterprise of general usefulness or to charity.

Things went much better for the Philodramatic Society in the second winter. My old members had learned a great deal in the first season, and I undertook to get fresh talent. A very capable professional actor, the character actor Stein, had come to St. Louis with his very talented wife (later director of the German theater in San Francisco), and sought me out. The company they had been in had dissolved as a result of the director's bankruptcy, and the Steins had sought another engagement in vain. It appeared they had no prospects, and the terror of winter was at the door. These people were just what I needed, but I could hardly ask them to work for nothing like us amateurs. So I engaged them for the winter for a moderate but decent salary, which I paid out of the basic costs of individual performances. Both of them did me excellent service, and the result was that the work of the Philodramatic Society gained both individually and as an ensemble.

There continued to be a problem with romantic leads, particularly roles as gentlemen and ladies. Young people I tested as romantic leads moved about like apprentice tailors at a Sunday gala. It got so bad that I even considered taking the stage as a romantic lead myself, although I had only played *bon vivants*, clowns and comic character roles in my dramatic career. I did recall, however, that I had played the noble Meinau in Kotzebue's *Menschenhass und Reue [Misanthropy and Regret]*, which is still a regular feature of the repertoire in England and America as *The Stranger*. I had also played a young lover once in a comedy by Weissenthurn.

Then, before the start of the second season, a friend made me aware of a recruit whom he pressed me to get. He told me that there lived in the First Ward a young German physician from Vienna, a highly educated man with pleasing appearance and poetic gifts. Almost utterly shy of people, he lived withdrawn, and his haughty and elitist manner did not make him particularly popular. I was to seek the man out, my friend urged, making his acquaintance and winning him for the Philodramatic Society. I decided to make the visit, and the very next day I went down to the First Ward. At the start of Carondelet Avenue there then stood a small, low frame house consisting of one room and an entry, or rather a kitchen. On the door of this little house, designated as my goal, was a tin sign with the inscription, "Dr. Rudolf Guszmann, German Physician, Surgeon and Obstetrician."[7] I entered and was astounded. There were heavy damask curtains on the windows, rich table coverings, beautiful bronzes, numerous nick-nacks, a small library bound in fine leather, and pictures and copper engravings of artistic merit. Other marks of European elegance and comfort were to be found in this unprepossessing room of a humble frame house. I later learned that these were gifts from his family in Vienna sent to enhance his exile. Dr. Guszmann was not permitted to return to Austria, being one of the politically compromised refugees of 1848.

The doctor, who assumed I was a new patient, received me in the friendliest manner. With a few words I explained that I had not come to receive his advice as a physician but to make the acquaintance of an educated man. We soon fell into a lively conversation, and he proved indeed to be a highly educated man, experienced in many fields of knowledge, whose idealistic orientation made him ill-fitted for practical America. We were pleased with one another, and a closer acquaintance flowed out of this first visit, followed by intimate friendship, and after some hesitation Dr. Guszmann fulfilled my wish and joined the Philodramatic Society as an active member. With him I had found the romantic lead I needed. He became a strong support for the enterprise and was soon the favorite of the public, as well, which greatly increased his practice as a physician. He remained a true friend and collaborator both on the stage and in journalism, for he was a gifted poet and practiced writer of serial pieces.

---

7. Rudolph Guszman, M.D., lived at "336 S. 5th" in the *Directory* 1854-55, 74.

In my last year in St. Louis he suddenly left town and went East. Later I heard that he returned to Europe in disappointment, like poor Lenau, and "tired of America," like the embittered Kürnberger.[8] Grass had grown over the memory of his participation in the events of 1848, and the amnesty of Emperor Franz Joseph reopened the gates of his homeland to Guszmann as to others. He was again able to live in Vienna. Yet his embittered mood grew with the passing years. He could never quite adjust to the new people and situation in Vienna, and he became ever more withdrawn and estranged from friends and acquaintances. It is remarkable that when I reestablished my residence in Vienna in 1870, I lived several years in the same district as Dr. Rudolf Guszmann without having the slightest hint that my worthy friend was in Vienna. I thought him still in America. It was only two years ago, when he died, that I learned from the laudatory obituaries in all the Viennese newspapers that we had lived so near for so long. I was only able to follow his coffin to burial, accompanying my friend's earthly remains to their final rest. I shall keep his memory in honor as long as my old eyes remain open.

I believe the best way to end this chapter is to append the prologue that Dr. Guszmann wrote and performed for the opening performance of the second season of the Philodramatic Society. This beautiful poetry can describe in a much more effective manner than I the doctor's high poetic gift, as well as the spirit that then filled German groups.

The text of the prologue was:

Once there lay in deepest mourning a woman,
The loveliest by far for unmeasured distance;
About her body waved a garment all of flowers
And on her head a diadem of stars.

And I myself addressed the woman of beauty,
"What profits you this fine face?
What profits you the starlight of your eyes?
What profits you the clarity of your spirit?
What profits you the truth of your love?
No one may see your face,
No one may implore your stars,
And no one understand your spirit.
No one in the throes of love

---

8. Ferdinand Kürnberger published the classic novel of disenchantment with America in the late 1850s entitled *Der Amerika-Müde (The Man Tired of America)*, a play on the common immigrant phrase of being "tired of Europe" (*Europa-Müde*). See Cazden, *Social History*, 452, n. 24.

Rises or succumbs for you.
I do not wish it remain so,
And what my spirit conceives
Will now be quickly brought to deed."

And there appeared a marvelous being,
So beautiful, as divine as a mother.
Who could that woman be?
Who that child, the mother's reflection?
This woman is Nature; you, however, were this as well
You yourself, o person, through whose birth
The mother has at last recovered from her woes.

And ever more prospers the race
Of mankind through the love of Nature.
A tender, weak suckling child depends for a moment
On the holy name of his mother;
Yet time restlessly rushes past him
And only with millennia it matures
And feels joy when he discovers who his mother is
And what divinity has done for him.
And yet the great woman is never sad,
For he holds her body in close embrace
And gazes lovingly into her fine face,
For now he understands what her eyes say,
He is clear himself in her clarity,
He becomes true through her truth!
And this consciousness of his divine power
Is realized in him only through art and science.

Yet who thinks of art and science
Without also thinking of German creativity?
Never spurn the land that raised you;
There art and science are cultivated.
Even if the hatred of princes has expelled you,
Robbed you of your homeland, yours, beloved, German,
You still have German art and science to call your own!
Let it propagate now on free soil!
Let free schools be its protectors!
And tolerate not that here, in this land,
Another despot swings his club,
That through self-indulgence's brazen slavery

We bind ourselves about the neck!
Reach into your breast and tear the poisonous worm
Of prejudice from your suffering hearts.
Only so can you still the fever
Of passion, and its deepest pain.
Seek no God in heaven, filled with glory,
Seek him here on earth, where we dwell.
It is the God wrapped in your own bodies.
He can only be enthroned in human hearts.
And if you long for prayers of consolation,
Then look piously into the face of a mother,
Or into the sun, high in the firmament,
Speaking warm consolation into your soul.
Look to the spring that longs tirelessly
To reach the mighty ocean,
The great goal that enlivens it.
The whole must have its being in individuals.
The smallest power is welcome
Where it is needed to approach the truth,
And however loudly the lie might maunder,
In the end the victory must go to the truth.
But what is truth? It is nature!
Oft misunderstood in its doctrines,
Mocked, mistreated and crucified, only
By its own children, born of its own womb.

Still, let us not gaze here on a scene of sadness.
Let us rather with worthily massed strength
Now build a temple to truth
And raise above it the sacred starry banner!
Let us in art and science
See the columns of this structure;
What anyone adds to this
Is recognized by all with thanks.
And if our little festival of muses
This evening does not fulfill all its promise
Forget not the good of the whole
Or our good will!

St. Louis, 17 January 1854

All Sorts of Other Affairs

Through founding the Philodramatic Society and leading it through several winters of continuing performances, I was back in a direct, intimate contact with the theater, so the old lust for the stage revived in me. "The lion has tasted blood and lusts for more," says the adage, and so the idea, the desire to establish a stable German theater in St. Louis grew in me more and more, leaving me no peace until I brought it to pass. I had to surrender the leadership of the Philodramatic Society to others after years of intense involvement.

St. Louis grew ever more, becoming important both in population and in business. Gradually it became a great city. The sixty-eight thousand residents I had found on my arrival had already grown to two hundred thousand. Germans constituted a good third of the general population, while Anglo-Americans not only failed to grow in the same proportion, but in fact showed a decline. This phenomenon, which is visible all over the United States, has become palpable in the course of a few decades, and it will be a frightening fact in a century's time. There will be a decline of the Anglo-American population and a rise of the German American and Irish American populations. The twofold cause of this decline is the continual new arrivals from Germany and Ireland via immigration, and the fact that every immigrating family brings ten more from the old homeland in following years through their reports. In contrast to this there is the solidly rooted Anglo-American system of only-two-children, which sets ever narrower limits to the expansion of the Anglo-American population. This narrow-hearted and egoistic reluctance of Anglo-Americans to have more than two children permits women to resort to terrifying means to make this plan a reality.[1] The system is maintained with the greatest rigor and offers only a few exceptions, while Germans and Irishmen are happy with a rich blessing of children, particularly in the countryside, where they increase the work force and are seen as an increase to the family's prosperity.

For this reason, the adopted population of America rises while the Anglo-American portion stands still or declines. It does not require any great gift of prophecy to predict that in a hundred years the Anglo-Americans will no longer be lords of the land, but rather a mere minority within it, while the immigrants and their descendents will, through the most marvelous cross-breeding and race-mixing, be a new race, the genuine American people

---

1. This is a tantalizing reference to the covert use of birth control and abortion by American women in the mid-nineteenth century.

of peoples. One can be just as sure that the Irish, if they continue to be slaves to drink, bigotry and priests, will not take the dominant position in the new race structure, and that the hard-working, active and persistent German element will win and assert a dominant, influential position.

But I have wandered into a consideration of the future when I was supposed to be talking about the past. St. Louis had grown to be a great city, as I said. The number of its German inhabitants had more than tripled, and with this growth the number of subscribers and the influence and prestige of my paper had grown. All of the paper's aspects grew along with the rise of population. The format grew ever larger; advertisements flowed in more massively; the printing shop was supplied with double-cylinder presses; folding machines and all the other modern equipment were added. When I took over there had been a single hand-press in the shop and the paper itself had been printed by another company. With this expansion of business my own burdens increased, since I never surrendered either the political or the technical leadership of the newspaper to anyone else. At the same time, as if I did not have enough to do in journalism, I was always ready to enter other enterprises, taking new labors onto my shoulders and new activities onto my head.

This need for activity, this tireless lust for enterprise, is in the American air itself, or perhaps better in American conditions.[2] Social life in America is so colorless, so monotonous. Excepting always the still life of family, of course, there is so little to excite the spirit and provide elevating or enlightening moments. This could hardly be otherwise in a country with a history only a century old. American tavern life is demoralizing, and it is avoided by every better person. Theatrical and musical enjoyments are sporadic phenomena, and at that time great America did not even have a single stable theater, neither English nor German, only wandering companies that came to one town after another for a few months at a time. Musical "stars" were imported from Europe to do hectic tours of a few months, organized by some enterprising speculator. But they rushed throughout America, often performing in three towns on the same day, with a matinee here, a midday show there, and an evening concert at yet another place, returning home rich in dollars but poor in artistic successes. This lack of higher enjoyments of an intellectual sort—so richly offered in Europe and accessible even to those of slender means—this emptiness and thinness of American social life, makes business the actual purpose and goal of existence. People live their whole day for business, and even during the few

---

2. The following observations are strikingly similar to those of Alexis de Tocqueville, who entitled a chapter in his famous *Democracy in America*, "Why the Americans are so restless in the midst of their Prosperity," vol. 2. Phillips Bradley, ed. (New York: Random House, 1945), 144-47.

hours they spend at home with their families they think only of business. Even during the night hours they dream only of business. This peace and these dreams will often be interrupted by telegram messengers, who might bring a business telegram in the middle of the night. And when one's own business is mediocre, he looks for other, new business or participates in the speculation of others. Loading new concerns and cares on his back, as is the case with most American businessmen, he has "too many irons in the fire."[3]

That was my situation as well. American social life had no appeal for me, and I avoided inns and public places on principle. So when journalism permitted me free hours, I threw myself into various activities, loading ever new labor and care upon myself. I did not do this out of a desire for profit, but only to satisfy my drive for action, my need for occupation. Most Americans are not moved to their restless occupation with business out of a mere desire for profit; for Americans, money and its winning is more a means than a end. The American looks upon money as a tool, the proper instrument or powerful machine by which he can do something. The heaping up of money is rarely an American's sole purpose in life. This is the reason American businesspeople so seldom withdraw from business activity. Only with difficulty do they place themselves at ease in comfort, which is the highest goal of life in Europe.

So it was with me. With every new business I undertook, there arose the drive to do more. Then I would look for another side occupation. In short, during the years between 1857 and 1861, at the same time and alongside my enormous newspaper business and the job-printing shop connected with it, I had three large beerhalls leased to tavernkeepers as well as a brewery. I had erected a German hotel with my friend S. Jacobi,[4] the Germania Hotel at the corner of Market and Third. I was also one of the directors of the St. Louis Building and Savings Institution, and beyond that I had leased the St. Louis Opera House and created a stable German theater there, leading it as director and even as a performer. That was certainly a great deal for the powers of one individual. Now, in the repose of cozy Europe, I can barely imagine where I found the time and strength to fulfill all these tasks. For I was no mere figurehead or place-filler: in each case I took full part in all the activities which I undertook.

---

3. This is precisely the phrase which is used three times for Boernstein himself in anonymous credit reports of 1856, 1857, and 1859. See R. G. Dun & Co. Collection, Baker Library, Harvard University Graduate School of Business Administration, Missouri vol. 36, p. 286, report of 1 January 1856; Missouri vol. 37, p. 589, report dated 19 October 1857; same page, report of (illegible date) 1859.

4. Samuel Jacoby is listed as a commission merchant and maltster in the St. Louis directories for 1860 (p. 262), 1864 (p. 312), 1866 (p. 483), but is not listed in 1867. On the Germania Hotel, see Rowan/Primm, 61, *AW,* 29 November 1857.

Many readers will find it hard to understand how I came to erect beer halls and become a brewer, considering my own views about tavern life. But it all came about in the most natural manner in the world, more to the liking of others than to me. For example, I had leased the entire building in which the *Anzeiger* printing plant was placed, but I did not yet need the ground floor. It happened that I came to know a fine, energetic man of whom I became very fond, Friedrich Schäfer from Ludwigsburg in Württemberg. One of the earliest German citizens of St. Louis, he had once served in the Württemberg military, then served with honor as a captain in the war of the United States against Mexico. After peace, he tried several enterprises, but none of them had borne fruit; despite his efforts and persistence, he lacked the capital required. So it was one day that he was complaining to me that he would have to give up his position as a tavernkeeper in south St. Louis because competition was too great. He was of the opinion that if he could establish a beer hall on the ground floor of my printing plant, whither many people came in the course of a day, he would have a splendid business. He only lacked the capital to make this work.

I wanted to help the good man, and as impulsive as I always was, I offered to let him have the location. Promising also to decorate it, furnish it and erect an elegant beer hall, I promised to enter into a partnership with him. No sooner was it said than done. The beer hall was done up like the best, and a supply contract for lager beer was made with the renowned Eimer Brewery in Belleville. The undertaking found general support, which rose even further when musical entertainment in the Viennese style was introduced, something quite novel then. Instrumental performances alternated with German songs done by a songstress, Demoiselle Salvini, and occasionally a virtuoso passing through would appear. One of the most popular tavernkeepers of St. Louis came from his dark establishment into the limelight by appearing as Schustertoni, performing Austrian *Vierzeilige Gstanzeln* and *Schnadahüpferln* on the guitar to general enjoyment.

As I said, the beer hall steadily gained in popularity with the public. But soon I had to recall the poet's words, "It is the curse of an evil deed that it stands out; evil must bellow." As early as the end of July, in the first year of our operation, the Eimer Brewery in Belleville was unable to deliver the lager beer promised by contract.[5] Either they had brewed too little beer or had sold too much to others; suffice it to say that we had a beer hall but no beer. We could get some beer from other breweries for a few weeks, but then their

---

5. Lager beer was brewed in the winter and stored for drinking after aging to acquire natural carbonation, which required that it be prepared long in advance. This requirement for storage space led to the use of limestone caverns located under St. Louis properties, some of which may still be seen and explored.

supplies would begin running out as well, and then we would literally run dry. This was a fate that many other establishments incidentally suffered as well, since almost all breweries were running out of lager beer; the autumn had turned out extraordinarily hot, so that it was impossible to resort to underfermented new beer. For Germans this was a true calamity, and genuine despair reigned among true beer fanatics.

Depressed over a business that was lamed through no fault of my own, I began listening to those who told me a large beer hall could only be operated securely and successfully if it had its own brewery. Such an enterprise could put down the beer it needed in stone cellars while completely covering the costs of the brewery by selling the surplus to other taverns. That made sense to me, all the more so because St. Louis was then in the grips of an obsession about building breweries. Some of the older brewers, such as Messrs. Lempp, Uhrig, Winkelmeier and others had become rich men through making beer. St. Louis beer had a good reputation, and it was even being sold out of town. The old brewers could not meet the demand, which rose with the increasing population, and so many people began to enter this profitable business and establish new breweries. Clever practicing physicians, soap makers, professors, and others became brewers. And so I allowed Schäfer to talk me into taking a lease for several years on old Wenger's brewery in south St. Louis, with its splendid stone cellars.

I did not understand the first thing about brewing beer, but I could get good advice from friends who knew the technical details. I hired a foreman who was highly recommended, the brewery was named *Salvator-Brauerei.* Our Salvator beer became popular. Then once again it was demonstrated that an evil deed must continually create evil, for now that we had assured beer for our beer hall, we had more beer than we needed or could sell to others. The next step was to convince myself that I had to establish another beer hall in order to consume my own beer. Now I bought a large house on Franklin Avenue near Tenth from the lawyer, Samuel Knox,[6] formerly belonging to his aunt Vendeventer. The lot was planted with beautiful shade trees reaching to Tenth. Here I established a beautiful beer hall with a beer garden for summer, leasing it to another tavernkeeper who was required to sell only my Salvator beer. When I eventually leased the St. Louis Opera House, I found there a large cellar area of huge dimensions that I rebuilt into yet another beer hall. The result is that I, a principled opponent of tavern life, had three beer halls and a brewery around my neck as a result of a strange

---

6. Samuel Knox (1815-1905), born in Massachusetts, graduated from Williams College and Harvard Law School and established himself in St. Louis in 1838. He was elected to Congress against Frank Blair in 1862 only after long dispute and served 10 June 1864 to March 1865, but he was defeated for reelection. He returned to the practice of law, and he retired eventually to Massachusetts. *EHSL,* 2: 1191; *BDUSC,* 1324-5.

contradiction in business relations. I never earned much at it, since I understood nothing about the business and had too little time to give it serious attention. I also had several runs of bad luck, such as an unexpected rise in the price of malt and hops and the souring of one lot of lager beer. I recall my experience as a brewer with regret.

My friend Jacobi and I established the German Germania Hotel as pretty as one would wish, letting it to a capable innkeeper who worked wonders in his specialty. Yet despite the cleanliness and order that reigned there, despite the excellent service and the fine French and German cuisine the innkeeper served, the enterprise never really found a market. American travelers would never set foot in a German hotel under any circumstances, prosperous German travelers went to the usual American hotels, and the less prosperous classes preferred German boarding houses and lodging houses of the second and third class because they were cheap. In time, such an undertaking probably could have been made profitable. But both of us had too many other businesses and we could not pay as much attention to managing the hotel as it would have needed. After a period of time we sold the whole business to an American, who took over the Germania Hotel, re-Americanized it and made it profitable.

Naturally, with such a burden of business and so many distractions, I had long since had to surrender leadership of the Philodramatic Society. My dear, proven friend Ferdinand Klünder, who was also an important member of the Philodramatic Society, leased the Variétés Theater for a winter after I dissolved the organization upon my resignation. There he gathered most of the former members of the Philodramatic Society, hiring some additional professional actors. I permitted my wife, who was a favorite of the public, to participate through the winter without a salary. I supported the undertaking to the extent of my power in my newspaper, always keeping in view the goal of popular education. The result was that Klünder, who was both a gifted performer in his own right and a capable businessman, had great success with his winter season.

As soon as the following year, however, there was considerable change in the Variétés Theater. The theater, which had been the most beautiful in St. Louis, had been constructed by a stock company consisting of a number of prosperous citizens from the best families of the city, and they had kept the stock in their own hands. The founders had leased the theater to English-speaking directors, but they had also built a club room into the theater where they gathered, entertained one another, held whist parties, dined, supped, and in short formed a closed society. The theater was what did not prosper, because its string of English-speaking directors did poor business. The founders did not manage the whole as energetically, either, as would have been the case if a single businessman had been in charge. All payments from the club treasury were in dispute and lax management prevailed. The result was that the stock company not only paid no dividends, but failed to make the normal interest payments on capital invested; every year extra payments were necessary, and the deficit mounted ever higher. In the end, the founders grew tired of continual losses, and a general meeting of stockholders decided to sell the theater. The sale took place, and two enterprising citizens, Captain Eads[7] and Mr. Dickson, bought the theater for a price which meant the stockholders lost half their capital. Yet the buyers did not regard the cheap purchase of this large, beautiful building as an ordinary monetary transaction; rather, they had more noble, artistic goals in mind. They had the entire theater renovated from the bottom up, made the hall into a gathering place that was as elegant as it was comfortable, and gave the theater the new name of the St. Louis Opera House. They proceeded to look for an enterprising, capable person to lease it. Either they had determined from the books of earlier management that profits from German presentations had always been higher than English-language shows, or they had been referred to me by third parties. In any case, I was offered the lease on the Opera House. My old lust for the theater, never quite stilled, was again awakened in me. I could not resist temptation. After a brief negotiation, we were in agreement, and in the autumn of 1859, I became leaseholder and director of the beautiful St. Louis Opera House.

---

7. James Buchanan Eads (1820-1887), born in Indiana, came to St. Louis in 1833. He invented a diving bell to recover the cargoes of sunken steamers. During the Civil War he manufactured ironclad river steamers, and after the war he constructed the Eads Bridge (1867-74), dredged the Southwest Passage entry to the Mississippi south of New Orleans, and proposed a railroad passage across Nicaragua to compete with the Panama Canal of Ferdinand de Lesseps. See *EHSL*, 2: 623-5.

The St. Louis Opera House
(1859-1860)

W hen I signed the contract granting me the lease on the St. Louis Opera
House for ten years in the summer of 1859, I had no idea how daring
an assignment I had taken on, one with an importance and difficulty beyond
my comprehension. I wanted to establish a stable German theater in
St. Louis, which then had 70,000 Germans out of a population of 200,000.
This theater was to operate summer and winter, offering the few
professional German actors in America a secure existence; we would then be
preferred by them to any other engagement, with the sole exception of New
York. It was my plan to organize the German actors scattered across the
broad expanse of the United States into a single, large, theatrical association.
Whether this could be done, or was even possible, was of little concern to
me. My sanguine temperament, my need for action, and the old lust for the
theater that had never died all allowed me to overcome hesitation easily and
with good courage.

In order to understand the difficulties, it is necessary to consider the
precarious situation of the German theater in the United States in those days.
I have already mentioned something of this. Even in mammoth New York,
the German director Haman had to play comedies in tavern saloons,
warehouses, and desanctified churches at a time when New York was already
a city of a half-million, including more than 70,000 Germans. He did this
until he finally succeeded in the mid-fifties in building his own theater, the
Deutsche Stadttheater, with the support of wealthy Germans. This theater was
the sole permanent German stage in all of America for twenty years. Even
today—when the number of inhabitants in New York has risen to a million,
with a population of 500,000 in neighboring communities, when 170,000
Germans live in New York and 75,000 in the suburbs, when there are twenty
legitimate theaters in New York—there are only two German theaters in that
city, with a third to be built in the coming year.

In the other cities of the United States there was not yet even such a
thing as a stable German theater. Rather, there were occasional shows, partly
by traveling companies, partly by dramatic clubs of Turners, singing societies
and other associations. These groups performed comedies in saloons,
gymnastic halls, and occasionally in English-language theaters. That was the
situation of the dramatic arts in St. Louis, despite the fact that the German
population was large and rather prosperous. Before 1842 there had never
been a German theatrical performance in St. Louis, which then had more

than 30,000 inhabitants. It is only in the 1840s that immigration from Germany really began to be important, becoming a numerous and influential element in the entire West. German immigration before 1820 had vanished without a trace, with the older persons dying out and the younger totally Americanizing themselves, so that the grandchildren knew nothing of their German ancestry. Only in the course of the 1840s did a German community develop in the cities; previously they had been isolated and scattered, mostly as farmers in the country, had vanished into the mass of the population and were respected little or not at all.

The first theatrical presentation in German in St. Louis took place in 1842. An old German actor whom destiny had driven to America, Herr Riese from Berlin, arrived in St. Louis in a condition of great want. Several young Germans, traveling salesmen or clerks, came to know the poor man and decided to support him in his hour of need. The young men had no money themselves, but they had good will and concern with the down-on-his-luck Riese. They encouraged him to give some theatrical performances, promising to assist him as amateurs. The money needed would come from charging a worthy public. No sooner was it said than done. The young men went to a German tavernkeeper whose inn, bearing the shingle *"Zum Bremer Schlüssel"* ["At the Sign of the Bremen Key"] was located on Third Street between Pine and Olive. They rented a long salon on the second floor, which served as a banquet hall for weddings and other festive occasions.

An emergency stage was cobbled together out of carpenters' trestles and boards, and the whitewashed walls of the salon were decorated by a housepainter to look like a forest, as well as one could. For the scenes taking place in rooms, cheap carpets were used as scenery and glued to a wall, and the curtain of bedclothes were sewn together. A couple wooden chairs and a table made up the room furnishings. The first performance of Schiller's *Robbers* was presented with this set decoration. The tower in which Old Moor is imprisoned was done by the artistic housepainter with such cunning that it looked like a giant cake. No armchair could be found for Old Moor, so an old crate was taken and one side sawed out at sitting height. The boards obtained from this were reattached as feet, the whole was covered with a bedsheet, and the armchair of the old count was ready. Either because some fellow was making a joke, or perhaps due to accident, one end of the bedsheet was caught up in the rope for the curtain. The performance began as the four-man orchestra struck up the overture, the prompter gave the bell signal and the curtain rose. But the bedsheet went right up with the curtain, and the armchair on which Old Moor sat was thrown over backwards. Loud laughter greeted this tragi-comic beginning. The curtain had to be brought back down to stormy jeering, and only after everything had been put back in its place on the stage did the performance resume its course.

Because it was impossible to find an actress, the character Amalie was entirely dropped; a great deal was said of her, but no one ever got to see her. The robber extras, all young volunteers, were always more numerous than the actors. They had all brought their revolvers and hunting rifles, and there was so much shooting in the robbery scene in the third act that the entire hall was filled with gunsmoke. The result was an impenetrable fog, through which the tallow candle lights shimmered like red points. Riese did not want to perform the fifth act without an Amalie to stab to death. In the end the tavernkeeper's cook had to put on a white dress, loosen her hair and throw herself on Riese in the midst of the thick gunsmoke. In response Riese spoke the lines of his role and stabbed her. When she would not fall over right away, he slugged her with his fist. Due to the smoke, almost nothing in the final acts could be seen, and because the audience was coughing, little could be heard. At the conclusion, however, all participants were applauded stormily, and then the entire income from the production was drunk up in the bar downstairs.

The newspapers of the day have preserved for us the names of the men who made the first German theatrical performance in St. Louis possible. Riese played Karl Moor; John D. Hill, a well-known lumber merchant, played Franz; Heinrich Fischer was Old Moor; Hippo Krug, later one of the most popular tavernkeepers in the city, played the Swiss as well as Hermann; Georg Bressler of Belleville played Schusterle; and Block, of the later respected firm of Block & Evers, played Spiegelberg.

The performance was a sensation in the fullest sense of the word. Not only was it repeated in St. Louis, but its reputation reached neighboring Belleville, and Riese was invited to come over with his company to play *The Robbers* there as well. The piece was played in Belleville with the same cast, but because no orchestra could be gathered there, Hippo Krug had to haul evening clothes over his costume when he was finished playing the Swiss or Hermann and walk out into the audience, where a piano stood. There he would play the incidental music accompanied by Herr Ochs on the clarinet and Herr Dann on the violin.

After the performance, the income was once more drunk up in the bar, and when day dawned, none of the performers had a penny to get back to St. Louis. The brewer Gottfried Busch took pity on them and had his large beer wagon hitched, loaded up the entire company and hauled them back to St. Louis for nothing. This was the premature end of a German theater in St. Louis. Riese, who had become known and popular among Germans, traveled from one German tavern to another, consuming untold quantities of beer, until his previous protectors tired of the pointless effort and took up a collection to send him to Philadelphia at their own expense. There he became a guest performer with an Italian opera company that had suddenly lost its baritone. Riese, who also had a pretty singing voice, offered himself as a replacement, and he was engaged after a tryout. The company, which had always taken its baritones from Italy and would have had to close for months to await a replacement, was as happy with Riese's efforts as was the public. His German name was changed to Benedetti, and he performed for years as an Italian opera singer in New York, Philadelphia, Boston and other cities. Then he rapidly went downhill, lost his voice, grew old and sickly, and died in 1859 in the poorhouse on Blackwell's Island near New York.

That was the origin of German theater in St. Louis seventeen years before I took over the St. Louis Opera House. During those seventeen years there were many other attempts to establish a German theater. Christian Thielemann, a German actor, came with his wife Elise, and they twice gave a series of performances with the assistance of amateurs. Then came the old theater director F. H. Strasser, who had a small company with his wife, his two daughters and a stepson, and who also combined talents with amateurs. Afterward there was a long pause before real professional theatrical presentations were made, until in 1852 the *St. Louiser Sänger-Bund* [St. Louis Singing League] arranged a series of performances by amateurs, first in Washington Hall, then in the Variétés Theater in 1853. Then came the Philodramatic Society I established, which performed for four years and which I have already described. All during this time theater directors would appear with their traveling companies, first of all Bötzow, then Benrodt, followed by A. R. Wolf and finally Ferdinand Klünder (whose efforts I have already mentioned). After him was the director Bonner once more. All of them did business which was occasionally good, but mostly poor.

During the same period as the performances by A. R. Wolf, who had some good actors, the *Deutsche Institut zur Beförderung deutscher Kunst und Wissenschaft in Amerika* [German Institute for the Promotion of German Art and Science in America] was established in St. Louis. In order to honor this cultural event in a suitable way, I arranged a benefit of the classic sort, uniting the members of the old Philodramatic Society with Wolf's theater company to present single acts from Goethe's *Egmont*, Schiller's *Kabal und Liebe* [*Conspiracy and Love*] and Lessing's *Minna von Barnheim*. The presentation was preceded by a verse prologue composed by me, and the expanded orchestra performed the overtures for Weber's *Freischütz* [*The Sharpshooter*], Beethoven's *Egmont*, Mozart's *Zauberflöte* [*The Magic Flute*], Weber's *Oberon*, Kreutzer's *Nachtlager in Granada* [*Night Camp in Granada*], and at the end of the production Mayerbeer's "Coronation March" from *The Prophets* was performed. This performance was without doubt the best and most perfect seen on the St. Louis stage up to that time. Its reception was extremely enthusiastic, and the income, directed to the German Institute, was the greatest ever collected, either before or after.

During this long period the only European guest performers in St. Louis were the infamous Lola Montez,[1] already a ruin, and the colossal Vestvali, a female dramatic opera singer.

This sums up the prehistory of the German theater in St. Louis through the day when I took over the lease for the St. Louis Opera House.[2] It had always been my intention and warmest desire to establish a stable German theater in St. Louis, which I now regarded as my home. I did everything I could to make the undertaking as perfect as American theatrical conditions permitted, sparing neither effort nor money. A favorable fate bestowed on me the person of a young Austrian painter, Ferdinand Kurz. He was a very capable, I would even say ingenious decorative painter, and I had him do a number of splendid set designs. Unfortunately this gifted, talented painter died in the bloom of his youth. I ordered from Vienna and Leipzig an extensive library containing the older classic repertoire, as well as the newer and most recent dramatic productions. An Italian opera company that had dissolved had pawned their rich, splendid costumes in St. Louis to cover debts, then had left them unclaimed. I bought the lot, ending up in possession of a fine, complete costume collection such as even one of the smaller court theaters in Germany would not possess.

My plan that the expectation of a continual engagement would draw the German dramatic talent available in America to St. Louis proved true. All German actors in the United States not already engaged at the *Stadttheater* in New York soon joined my enterprise. Of this company I will only name Alexander Pfeiffer, the splendid heroic and romantic lead from the court theater in Karlsruhe; Karoline Lindemann, née Müller, a fine actress who had won great acclaim under the direction of Birch-Pfeifer in Zürich and then at the Court Theater in Darmstadt, and who played maternal roles for me; then there was the excellent Friedrich Schwan; the many-sided Julius Grossmann; the capable character actor F. Röpenak; the youthful romantic leads A. Föllger and Gustav Ostermann; a former member of the Philodramatic

---

1. Lola Montez (1824-1861), born in Ireland as Maria Dolores Porris Gilbert, was a classic nineteenth-century adventuress who commenced her travels as a "Spanish dancer" in 1840 in Paris. In 1847 she became involved with King Ludwig I of Bavaria, who ennobled her as the Countess of Landsfeldt. Her meddling in Bavarian politics led to her own expulsion and eventually precipitated Ludwig's abdication in early 1848. She came to America in 1851 on the same ship that brought Lajos Kossuth, and she toured the nation before departing for Australia. On her return to America she tried to shift to a more serious message, but this found no market. Her health collapsed, and she died in a sanitary asylum on Long Island. *ACAB*, 4: 368.

2. Most of this chapter is a selection from an anonymous article with contributions by Adalbert Löhr, "Zur Geschichte des 'Deutschen Theaters' in St. Louis," in F. Kreuter, Carl Börnstein, eds., *Bühnen-Alamanach des. St. Louis Opern Hauses (mit Beiträgen der Herren Otto Ruppius, Georg Hillgärtner, A. Löhr und Andere)* (St. Louis, 1 January 1861), 12-23.

Society, G. W. Stierlin, whom I had trained for overwrought and comic roles; the amiable Alwine Dremmel as youthful female lead; the fine actress Mrs. Otto; as well as Mrs. Minna Ostermann, Miss Ludovika Pfeiffer, Mrs. Schaab-Meaubert, and Emil Höchster and Julius Ascher, the latter one of the most beloved character actors in Berlin.

Beyond this ensemble, of which I have only named the leads, there was my wife, who had already been married thirty-two years at that time and was surrounded by grown children and by grandchildren, so that she was already a grandmother, and yet was still one of the most charming phenomena on the stage. She was gifted with eternal youth, and in her fine makeup, the life and fire of her acting, in the tone and gesture still a model for all younger actresses, and still very much the darling of the public. At first I was active only as producer and director and had no intention of acting myself but simply to lead the undertaking. I remained true to this resolution for a long time, until in January 1860, we engaged the fine actress Miss Antonie Grahn, formerly of the court theater in Darmstadt, then at the *Stadttheater* in New York, for a visit of eighteen performances. This celebrated *artiste*, who was received with the greatest applause, excited enthusiasm among the public for her accomplishments as Deborah, Mary Stuart, Gretchen in *Faust,* The Maid of Orleans, Ophelia, Philippine Welser, Lucretia Borgia, Juliet Capulet, Thusnelda, Adrienne Lecouvreur, and other roles. Her benefit performance was *Donna Diana.* Pfeiffer played Don Cesar, Grahn did Donna Diana, my wife was Floretta, and I was asked by Grahn to play Perin, which I finally did do. The other roles were also well filled, and the performance was a model production which excited genuine enthusiasm. This threw me back into comic plays, reawakening with new power my old lust to act, and I was pressed by the public not to deprive their performances of my acting talents. The result was that I once more took my place as a performer in the ranks of my cast, at first rarely, then with increasing frequency.

The opening of the St. Louis Opera House took place on 15 September 1859, and for that purpose I engaged the Italian opera company of Signora Parodi with Angelo Torriani as musical conductor, Z. Ronzoni as director, the *prime donne* Theresa Parodi and Karoline Alaimo, tenor Giovanni Sbriglia, baritone F. Gnone and basso N. Barili. While the Italian singers were giving twenty-eight performances to grand applause, including *Trovatore, Lucia, Norma, Traviata, Rigoletto, Lucretia Borgia, Polliuto, Don Pasquale, Il Barbière,* and Mozart's *Don Giovanni,* I had time to organize my German acting company, holding numerous rehearsals and training the minor roles.

As a result, after the Italian series we could open the German season with Goethe's *Egmont* with music by Beethoven. German performances now ran continuously until political events and the outbreak of the Civil War brought the entire enterprise to a sudden end. During this season of nineteen months the classic works of the German stage as well as novelties which had attracted attention in Germany were performed in the fullest possible productions, and older friends of the theater in St. Louis still fondly recall our successful productions of *Faust, Don Carlos, Wallenstein, Hamlet, Karlsschüler, Romeo and Juliet, William Tell, Götz von Berlichingen* and *Montrose*, as well as sumptuously produced versions of *Zauberschleier [The Magic Veil], Barometermacher [The Barometer Maker], Leiermann und sein Kind [Leiermann and his Child]* and others. German productions made way for the visiting French Opera of New Orleans, with Madame Dalmont-Messmacre as *prima donna*, Demoiselle d'Arcy as second lead, Mr. Philippe as tenor, and so on. Then the Colson company came, with its singers Pauline Colson and Miss Kellogg, the tenor Brignoli, the bass Susini and the baritone Ferri. In addition, there was the Siegrist-Zamfretta ballet and pantomime company, with a large *corps de ballet* and fine solo dancers, and lastly Anna Bishop and her concert society. In short, it was a diverse and enjoyable season. In the next section I will tell how this enterprise, begun so finely, was suddenly interrupted and brought to a stop due to no fault of mine.

"The People Arise—The Storm Breaks"
(1861)

I had not chosen the best of moments for my theatrical undertaking, and if I or any other person could have foreseen what the near future would bring us, I would certainly not have launched the Opera House and a thousand others would not have begun their other businesses. Rather, we all would have limited our activities to passive waiting. Yet that is the way it is with prophets: they never imagine that the prophecies of their inspired moments could become hard realities. As early as 1852, I clearly predicted a war between the North and the South over the slavery question in the clearest terms in my *Mysteries of St. Louis*, at a time when no one even considered the *possibility* of such a thing.[1] Now, however, in 1859, the coming civil war was already casting shadows, and the presidential election of 1860 would be fateful for the republic of the United States, yet no more than millions of others did I believe that the fearsome event of a war between the citizens of the North and the South was immediately imminent. Despite the fact that tensions over slavery and its results rose ever higher from year to year, now reaching the point where it became hatred and embitterment, and despite the fact that signs were clearly visible that the South intended to loose the bands of the Union, aided by the treasonous President James Buchanan and his cabinet, particularly the Secretary of War, Jefferson Davis,[2] making preparations in all the slave states for separation. Despite the tearing apart of the American league of states and the division of the American people into two hostile halves, with dreadful consequences for the whole as well as for individuals, no one in the North or in the border slave states wanted to believe in the event's realization, not even in the possibility of such a catastrophe. Everyone pursued his ordinary business, entered commercial and industrial enterprises and speculations without concern, as if the deepest peace reigned in the country and the existence of the Union was assured for all time. Even I, who stood so near the stage of political events and could peek behind the scenes, still believed in summer 1859, that there would be peace, even as the dull thunder of an approaching storm sounded from the

---

1. Boernstein, *Mysteries*, 160, which pictures slavery being used as the pretext for a civil war fomented by the Catholic Church.

2. Jefferson Davis, future president of the Confederate States of America, was secretary of war under Franklin Pierce, 1853-57, not under Buchanan. Otherwise, Davis served continuously as U.S. Senator from Mississippi from 1847 to January 1861. *DAB*, 5: 123-31.

South, and I signed the lease of the St. Louis Opera House for ten years, taking on a heavy burden and responsibility. The lease was for ten years, and it was ten years in a time when no one could know what each new year would bring in terms of the unexpected or even the undesired.

Yet, as I just said, no one thought about such dark possibilities, and restless American business life continued along its regular course, driving everything and driven by everything. As a result, I was totally preoccupied by my newspaper business as well as my theatrical enterprises. The fact that I was able to manage at once two such large enterprises, both a newspaper and a theater, besides many other businesses on the side, was made possible by the fact that my friend Bernays had responded some years before to my friendly invitation, which became a pressing plea, to give up his residence in Highland and come to St. Louis as coeditor of my paper. In him I not only had one of the most gifted, hard-working German American publicists, but also a true friend and companion at my side on whom I could rely. Together with Bernays and me there was Georg Hillgärtner as permanent collaborator on the *Anzeiger,* and the technical portion of the paper, the printing plant, was under my eldest son. The result was that it was possible to do perfect justice to all the demands placed upon me by my double efforts. But 1860 was a hot time, a trying, event-filled year in this my life, which had already been eventful enough.

The winter season reaching from September 1859, to Easter, 1860, had been excellent. The dramatic company was fully staffed, the entire enterprise solidly based, and it seemed that the difficult task I had set myself, which was to found a stable German theater in St. Louis, had every expectation of success. Yet "there is no permanent alliance to be made with the powers of fate, and evil moves swiftly," as our great poet says. With the beginning of 1860 preparations began for electing a new president, which on this occasion would decide the destiny of the largest republic on earth, and with that the near future of the whole of mankind. The crass contrast between the enemies of Negro slavery and the friends or defenders of this repellent institution had risen to the greatest intensity over the course of recent years. There could be no talk of any understanding, and the time for cowardly compromise was forever past. What was needed was a powerful collision, and through this a final decision. With few exceptions, German Americans in the northern free states as well as in the border slave states of Missouri and Kentucky and others were decided opponents of slavery, and they were also principled enemies of what was called "states' rights," which was the sovereignty of each state toward the Union. Germans had learned the bitter lesson of *Kleinstaaterei* ["small-statism"] in Germany and had no desire to transform the splendid, dignified union of the United States into a mass of independent, petty state sovereignties.

Although Missouri was a slave state, all of Missouri's Germans were decided opponents to slavery, and they were so out of principle and conviction, for they directly suffered little from the evil of slavery. In Missouri, which then had a population of 1,200,000 persons, there were only something over 100,000 slaves, almost all of them in the countryside. In the city of St. Louis itself there were only 113 slaves as house servants for the wealthiest families, vanishing almost without a trace in a population of 200,000. Despite this, all political and legal institutions were predicated on the maintenance and promotion of the "peculiar institution." In the Missouri Code of Laws, it was still forbidden on pain of heavy penalty to teach a slave to read or write, and the Fugitive Slave Law passed by the last Congress required every citizen to catch escaped slaves and return them to their proper owners. Where these laws did not suffice, brutal force was applied, and opponents of slavery such as the Methodist preacher Lovejoy, who had damned slavery from his pulpit as well as in his newspaper, were assaulted by mobs, their property destroyed, were expelled from the state, mishandled, murdered.

Even if the cursed institution of slavery was unable to expand in the city of St. Louis, still there were Negro pens in the middle of the city where Negro slaves of both sexes being transported to another county or another state were kept overnight on their passage through St. Louis. If any one of them was unable or unwilling to march in proper order, or if they offended the strict discipline of slavery, they would be chastised and whipped, so that one heard the howls of these unfortunate persons in all the nearby streets, where primarily Germans lived. Then several times a year, but particularly on New Years Day, in the middle of the city, on the east side of the Court House, there were court-ordered sales and slave auctions, and German Americans watched with horror as human beings such as themselves, only distinguished by their black or dark skin color, were displayed for sale in the open air like cattle. They saw also how these poor people were tested by those seeking to buy, touched and investigated with cynical coarseness, how they were knocked down to the highest bidder, so that the wife was separated from her husband, the mother from her children, and each of them taken to separate counties or another state, never to see one another again in their lifetimes. German Americans watched all of this with horror, and their disinclination to slavery grew into a grim hatred of this accursed institution and its friends and defenders.

Until this time, the Germans could not express their hostility to slavery at elections, for no one had dared to present a Republican, antislavery ticket in the state of Missouri. Germans could only vote for Benton Democracy, which was at least opposed to every further expansion of slavery in the new territories. Now, however, in 1860, Benton Democracy had so gained in size

TENTH WARD
REPUBLICAN TICKET
EXCEPT FOR COUNTY RECORDER.

FOR GOVERNOR
JAMES B. GARDENHIRE
FOR LIEUT. GOVERNOR
JAMES LINDSAY
FOR SECRETARY OF STATE
William B. Adams
FOR TREASURER
G. W. H. Landon
FOR AUDITOR
Judge Ezra Hunt
FOR ATTORNEY GENERAL
Arnold Krekel
FOR REGISTER
Thomas C. Fletcher
FOR SUPT. OF COMMON SCHOOLS
Dr Henry Boernstein
FOR BOARD OF PUBLIC WORKS
John M. Richardson, Frederick Munch, William M. McPherson

For Representative in the 36th Congress, to fill vacancy
FRANCIS P. BLAIR, JR.
FOR THIRTY SEVENTH CONGRESS,
FRANCIS P. BLAIR, JR.
FOR THE STATE SENATE
Dr. Walter B. Morris
FOR THE HOUSE OF REPRESENTATIVES

George Partridge,	John S. Cavender,
Felix Coste,	John D. Stephenson,
John Sexton,	James Peckman,
John Doyle,	Charles F. Meyer,
Dr. Rudolph Doehn,	Madison Miller,
R. M. Hanna,	George M. Moore.

FOR COUNTY SCHOOL COMMISSIONER
JOHN H. TICE
For Sheriff—**JOHN H. ANDREWS**
For Jailor—**JOHN C. BLAKEY**
For Marshal—**CHARLES BORG**
For Recorder—**CHARLES KEEMLE**
For Coroner—**DR. ALFRED ARNAUD**
For Justice of the Peace

For Constable
WM. BLACKMORE

The first statewide ticket of the Missouri Republican Party, 1860, including Boernstein as candidate for Superintendent of Education. Courtesy of Western Historical Manuscripts Collection, University of Missouri—St. Louis, Freie Gemeinde Papers.

and strength that it presented a Republican ticket and people could vote for it.[3] The elections for municipal offices as well as those for Congress and the county in August brought complete victory for the Republican ticket. The presidential election was to take place on 6 November 1860; the campaign began in May and grew in intensity and bitterness from day to day.

In this situation I had the doubly difficult task of tirelessly leading the campaign in my newspaper, as the preeminent German paper, in order to assure the victory of Republican principles, and at the same time I was also successfully guiding a major theatrical enterprise through all the problems of a hot summer, a difficult time for theater. Today, looking back calmly, I have no idea how I managed to fulfill my double mission. What I do know is that during the campaign I had already read all the incoming letters and newspapers every morning in order to start writing the lead article by eight. At ten I rushed to the theater for rehearsals, and I rehearsed until two or even later, then after a hastily eaten meal I was back in the editorial office to make the remaining orders for the morning paper and to take care of business correspondence. Then it was back to the theater at six to get ready for the performance, in which I usually had to play a large, trying role. When this was at an end, duty called me once more to the editorial office, where I remained and worked until the paper was almost ready and all the telegrams had arrived. It was usually between two and three in the morning before I returned to my apartment and was able to enjoy the peace of sleep.

In addition to these daily occupations were added extraordinary events, particularly election rallies at which I was an orator. Carl Schurz came to St. Louis for the first time in this period, and I had the honor of introducing him to his compatriots in a great German assembly in the Courthouse.[4] Then Schurz spoke himself, representing Republican principles in a masterful manner to the stormy and enthusiastic applause of a gathering numbering in the thousands. William H. Seward[5] also came to St. Louis and held an enthusiastic oration from the balcony of the Barnum Hotel, in

---

3. Rowan/Primm, 119-20, *AW,* 12 July 1860.

4. It was during this visit that Schurz made a major English-language address which was published as *Speech of Carl Schurz delivered at Verandah Hall, August 1, 1860* (St. Louis: Missouri Democrat, 1860), in which he said, "This is the first time that I have had the honor to address a meeting in a slave State, and even now I owe the privilege of expressing my opinions freely and without restraint to the circumstance that, although in a slave State, I stand on the soil of a free city, and under the generous protection of free men."

5. William Henry Seward (1801-1872) of New York, began his career as a member of the Anti-Masonic Party, was Whig governor of New York, 1838-42, and U.S. Senator as a Whig and Republican, 1848-61. He was Lincoln's and Johnson's secretary of state, 1861-69. *DAB,* 16: 615-21.

which he praised the love of liberty of the German Americans in the most honorable manner by declaring that Missouri must be Germanized to win the state for freedom.

This commitment by the Germans brought upon them the entire hatred of the slaveholders, and this was soon expressed in terms of threats. Even if the Republicans were able to get their Republican candidates elected to Congress as well as to offices in the city and county, they still could do little against the slaveholders who lived in the interior of the state. Those had the undisputed majority in state elections, so that the entire government of the state of Missouri was composed of proslavery people, and a majority of slaveholders was elected to the Legislature as well. The new governor of the state, Claiborne Fox Jackson, and the lieutenant-governor, Thomas C. Reynolds, were bitter representatives of slavery, and they entered office on 3 January 1861 with the solid intent of tearing Missouri from the Union and delivering it to the Southern secession.

If it was true that Reynolds was no Missourian, not even a born American but, as many asserted, a German-Bohemian from Prague with the original name of Thomas Reinhardt, then it is inconceivable how he could have committed himself to this elevation and defense of accursed slavery. I knew him well for a long time, and I have never determined the basis for this rumor. All I know is that Reynolds could speak German well and fluently, though with a sort of Anglo-Saxon accent. Further, it was clear that he had received a European education, was quite at home with German literature, and claimed by his own account to have studied in Heidelberg. Here in Austria people claim to be certain he was from Prague, and they have ascribed to him a Semitic ancestry. The truth will probably never be established, for in any case Reynolds must have emigrated early and through the years he erased every trace of his origin. But however that is, it is certain that Jackson and Reynolds brought ruin on the state of Missouri, and they unleashed the fury of civil war there. As I said, I was very intimate with Reynolds for a long time; since he was an educated man, I enjoyed being with him, but the opposition of our views on the slavery question gradually alienated us from one another, and since neither could convert the other to his view, our friendship gradually chilled. Finally we ceased seeing one another, and in the end we stood against one another as armed enemies.

As mentioned, the legislature, with a slaveholder majority, was entirely of a piece with the new state government. When it assembled, South Carolina had already seceded from the Union on 20 December 1860, after Lincoln's election, and had raised the palmetto flag of the state. With that began the fearful Civil War, which lasted four long, bloody years, demanded the sacrifice of hundreds of thousands of human lives, and turned the once rich and blooming South into a desert occupied by impoverished persons. The other Southern states followed suit in the course of January and February 1861, and everything was done to separate the border slave states from the Union, particularly Missouri and Kentucky. Governor Jackson and his alter ego, Reynolds, and the state legislature worked tirelessly in this direction, and despite all protests by a pro-Union minority, a number of oppressive laws were passed preparing the way for secession. Thus a law was passed which decreed the death penalty for anyone who stole a horse or took a Negro slave from his master. Further, a militia law was passed which granted the governor unrestricted disposal of the persons, lives and property of all citizens. To pay for this militia, which was to join the Southern secessionist army, the funds of the public schools, madhouses and houses for the blind were seized, and through this mean act of violence ten thousand schoolchildren in St. Louis alone were thrown out of their institutions of learning into the streets.

Above all else, however, the Germans of St. Louis were to be punished for their love of liberty and their opposition to slavery, and the greatest city in the state was to be hobbled, unmanned, and hindered in every free expression of opinion. For this purpose the state legislature passed a law readily sanctioned by the governor which narrowed and painfully reduced the official power of the mayor and the city administration of St. Louis. The police, which had hitherto been administered by the city, was taken away from it and bestowed on the so-called Metropolitan Police, whose four commissioners were all committed secessionists named by the governor.[6] These commissioners in turn named only those favorable to slavery and hostile to Germans as policemen. The result was that the entire population of the city of St. Louis with its 200,000 persons were declared minors and placed under guardianship. The primary principle of American administration, which is that of self government, was openly slapped in the face. On 25 March 1861 this shameful law was passed and signed by the governor, who immediately named the new commissioners, who entered their offices with the greatest haste as well as with the determination to control St. Louis in general and the Germans in particular.

The law for the sanctification of Sunday was certainly in the Law Code of Missouri, but until now it had been a dead letter with the exception of the one year when the Know-Nothings held the municipal administration. Now it was suddenly enforced to the letter and with great strictness. Until then taverns had always been open on Sunday, and beer gardens gave musical performances in the evening with the edifying title of "Sacred Concerts,"

---

6. This institution is still in existence today, and it remains the object of controversy.

where anything but sacred music was presented. The German theater gave its most important performances on Sunday, and on this day it made the most profits, for since German citizens lived either in the far north or far south of the city, it was almost impossible for them to get to the German theater (located in the center of the city) after the end of work or once their businesses closed on most days.

On 8 April the new police commissioners entered office and reorganized the personnel of the department using their own fanatic adherents, excluding all Germans. On the very next Sunday, 14 April, they staged their first coup. Squads of police were sent in all directions forcefully to close all taverns, particularly German taverns, and to drive their guests into the street. At the same time all evening concerts were abolished, so that a police captain came to me at 6 p.m., an hour before the performance, informing me that there could be no further performances on Sunday by order of the commissioners. I responded to him that such as order was illegal, since it should have been communicated to me in advance, at least during the day, but that at 6 p.m. it was too late to cancel the performance and make that cancellation adequately known to the public. The police captain shrugged his shoulders and said that the commissioners would soon compel obedience to their orders. I hence ordered the box office to open and prepared for the performance, but a quarter-hour later the new chief of police, McDonough (hitherto a creature and front man for the *Missouri Republican*),[7] arrived with forty policemen, who occupied the box office and all entrances to the theater, preventing the audience which was arriving from entering the theater. I led the chief of police into my theater office and read to him from the Law Code of Missouri that there was no mention in the Sunday Law about theatrical presentations or concerts, but only against the opening of taverns or the holding of horse races or cockfights, and that there was no municipal ban on theatrical presentations or concerts on Sunday. The act of the police commissioners was hence illegal and violent, and that I was protesting against it, reserving all my legal claims for compensation.

The police chief conceded to me that there was no law forbidding theatrical presentations on Sunday, but that under the new police law the commissioners had the right to make and carry out all police regulations which appeared necessary to them. He had received the order to close the theater, and he must carry that order out, by force if necessary. I told him

---

7. James McDonough, who was involved in trading cattle and lumber when not being a policeman, would serve three times as St. Louis Chief of Police: 1861-62, 1870-74, 1876-81, see MHS, Genealogical and Biographical Collection, letter of Samuel R. Phillips to MHS, 12 February 1924.

in a written protest that I would only give in to force, and that I reserved my legal rights. Then I spoke to my company in the wardrobe that they should get dressed, since the performance was not taking place. In the meantime, not only many customers blocked by the police from entering, but also thousands of passersby and curious stood around, and soon there was a mass which filled not only the place in front of the theater but all the nearby streets as well as the Courthouse Square, and the dominant mood was hostile and agitated. Everyone was bitter about this shameful act of violence; there were threats, heads grew ever hotter, and some spoke out for charging the police and forcing entrance to the theater. The crowd before the theater grew larger by the minute and the mood steadily more bitter. All that was needed was a spark to move this heated mass to action. The chief of police and his forty policemen stood nervously in a little group in front of the theater, crowded in by the mass on all sides. They had ordered the doors of the theater closed behind them, so their escape route had been cut off. The police chief could certainly have called for assistance, but by the time this arrived and worked its way through the mass of people, they would have been given up to the wrath of an enraged mob.

The police chief, McDonough beseeched me in his anxiety and distress to pacify my compatriots and get them to go home, swearing that he would present my protest to the commissioners, and everything could be regulated in a legal manner during the next few days. I only needed a few moments to consider, and I found it more intelligent to avoid a street riot. The party of the slaveholders was the only one militarily organized in expectation of coming events, and several companies of so-called "Minute Men" had formed with their own weapons, marching through town and performing weapons drills. The Germans still did not have any military organization; on the contrary, two of the existing German militia companies had been dissolved and disarmed by the governor on dubious pretexts, and the other German militia units, particularly artillery, had been sent to the far border of the state, supposedly to protect against supposed attacks by irregulars from Kansas. If there had been street riots in front of the theater and the agitated mood had risen to violent outbreaks, the police chief and his people would have been pounded to a pulp and any group coming to his aid would have suffered the same fate, but the commissioners then could have called for armed help. The American militias, particularly the "Minute Men," the grimmest of German-haters, would have been summoned up, and the Irish and American mobs would have joined in. An armed attack would have been made on the defenseless crowd, and there would have been a dreadful bloodbath. These considerations, as well as my concern about further dangerous results of such an event, caused me to intervene and comply with the request of the police chief.

I had a table brought out from the theater, and I climbed up on it to make myself generally visible and capable of being heard. My appearance was greeted with thundering hurrahs from all sides, and eventually there was sufficient quieting of the crowd for me to be heard. I then exhorted my compatriots to disperse and quietly go home, and above all to provoke no scandal, since this would have terrible results for the innocent and defenseless. What had happened today was an illegal and brutal act of force, but for that very reason it behooved good citizens such as the Germans were to oppose them only by legal means, not to give a pretext for further crimes through their own illegal acts. I myself had given way to the illegal order only under duress, under protest and with assertion of legal redress. The performance had been canceled and would not take place, the actors had already left, and the gaslights had been extinguished. Remaining in front of the theater had no purpose. "Now go home quietly, my friends," my speech concluded, "and show through your conduct that you are peaceful, orderly, free citizens. There will be full compensation to me and to you for the injury of our rights and liberties. I guarantee this to you by my word as a man, and you know that I have always done what I have promised. With that, my friends, I wish all of you 'Good Evening' after this hot day."

There was stormy applause, and cries of "Good Evening!" followed my speech; those who stood nearby passed my words to those further out, and at least their gist was made understandable to the crowd of people. Gradually there was a little movement in the stalled mass. One by one, then several at a time, then whole groups began to withdraw, and the knot of people dissolved from minute to minute, leaving empty space behind. I finally stepped down from my table, and the police chief and his police thanked me earnestly for my "saving deed." An hour later the square and environs of the theater were entirely empty of people, and the police reserves which arrived in a rush returned home laughing. I went to my office and wrote down the events of the day and evening, making them into the lead article.[8] Yet I had told my compatriots the truth after all. We were indeed totally compensated, since the force of events quickly made the governor's police commissioners and all the police into relics of the past. A few weeks after this fifteenth of April, we Germans were represented by four volunteer regiments, and we were the lords of St. Louis. The Metropolitan Police was nowhere, and a few weeks later Governor Jackson,

---

8. Rowan/Primm, 175-8, *AW,* 19 April 1861.

Lieutenant Governor Reynolds and his entire government, as well as the slaveholder majority of the legislature, were in wild flight to safety before our approaching German regiments. The theatrical performances in the St. Louis Opera House were at an end forever, but the bloody tragedy of the American Civil War was about to begin on the great stage of the world, and in this tragedy we Germans played a leading role.

"What Coward Can Still Lay His Hands in His Lap?"
(1861)

The miniature *coup d'état* which the governor had performed with the police commissioners demonstrated how there was an intent on the part of the Democratic holders of power to punish German citizens for their antislavery attitude and to bring them under the control of the ruling slaveholders through oppressions of all sorts. Through the commissioners' proclamation of the principle that they had the right to declare and carry out all police regulations they thought necessary, all civil liberties were subject to oppression, and the right of self-government was simply obliterated. According to the same law by which the police entered the Opera House and closed it, they could violently enter any printing plant of a paper they disliked, close it and thus suppress the freedom of the press. By the same principle they could forcefully occupy the site of a public gathering of the people which was not desired by them, hindering the citizens' right of assembly and the orators' right of free speech. By this means all the rights guaranteed by the federal constitution were placed in question, and a door was opened to every sort of chicanery. By this means it could have gone to the point where the police would have been able to forbid citizens from taking a stroll on Sundays, and one could even have needed police permission to cook or dine on Sunday. At the same time there was a clear demonstration that these chicaneries and measures were aimed exclusively at German citizens, for it was German theaters which were closed by the police and German taverns which were barred, while the American drinking salons in the Planter's House and other hotels, the International Salon and other places, were left undisturbed.[1]

By this act of force, the fate of my theatrical enterprise was sealed. It became clear to me that I could not continue it under these conditions. Since Lincoln's election the symptoms had multiplied that hard and tumultuous days were coming. The agitation of the populace rose by the hour, the political situation of the country became almost the only public concern, and even more so because St. Louis lay in a slave state and the German population knew in advance what their lot would be if Missouri joined the

---

1. Rowan/Primm, 178, *AW,* 19 April 1861.

secessionist South and separated from the Union. There awoke the most serious concerns for the near future, spirits became increasingly uneasy, and in an atmosphere so agitated and distressed there was little sense or desire to go to the theater or participate in the other pastimes of earlier, more peaceful times. As a result, theatrical attendance dropped in the course of the 1860-61 season as political events grew increasingly grim and threatening. As early as New Years I found myself compelled to close the Opera House for six weeks in order to take my entire company on tour to friendly Cincinnati in the free state of Ohio. Here in Cincinnati the mood of the German population was happier and better than in St. Louis. For my company's performances I rented Pike's lovely Opera House, and my old friend Friedrich Hassaurek gave me the fullest support of his influential *Volksblatt*. The educated, prosperous German population of Cincinnati positively supported the enterprise, and for our performances we had large, enthusiastic audiences, consisting not only of Germans but also of educated Americans.

It was during this time that the new president, Lincoln, passed through Cincinnati on his way from Illinois to Washington to take office. He was greeted with enthusiastic jubilation by the people in Cincinnati, but to reach Washington he would have to pass through Baltimore in the slave state of Maryland. There he was threatened with genuine danger from Democratic slaveholders, who had sworn not to allow him to enter office. The traitor President Buchanan still ruled, and he did not do the least thing to prevent the falling away of the South. The officers of the federal army, almost all southerners, had resigned, with few exceptions, and had entered the secession army then forming. The old traitor General Twiggs, military commandant in Texas, handed over the arsenal there with all its war materiel to the secessionists. Many officers of the federal navy did the same with the ships they commanded. Partly through deception and partly through force, the governments of the southern states came into possession of almost all arsenals and forts of the United States. In February 1861, a Constitution of the "Confederate States" was adopted in a convention of the seceded states, and Jefferson Davis was elected as president. As a result, in order to pass Maryland and Baltimore, Lincoln had to resort to disguise, and after reaching Washington he took up the presidential office on 4 March, an office tied with tremendous cares and responsibility.

After the conclusion of our extended engagement in Cincinnati, I made another side trip with my company to Louisville, giving a series of performances there and also finding a friendly reception. After returning to St. Louis and resuming performances in the Opera House, I informed the members of my company, whose contracts expired at Easter, 1861, that I could still not commit to extending these contracts after Easter because the situation of the country was too uncertain. I expected to continue to perform after Easter, but without any long-term commitment and reserving the right to close the theater on a week's notice if political conditions grew even worse. Whoever could find an engagement elsewhere could receive a release. No one made use of this concession because the situation in the theater was equally bad everywhere in the Union, and none of the few German directors was interested in adding to his burdens by making new engagements.

So we continued to perform until the fatal 14 April and the forceful closing of the theater by the police commissioners on that Sunday evening. By this act the existence of German theater in St. Louis was rendered impossible, for the entire enterprise depended on good Sunday incomes, because attendance during the week was relatively weak since too many Germans lived in the more distant parts of town far away from the theater in the center to be able to attend performances in large numbers on weeknights. As agreed, then, I announced closing a week in advance, gave a number of very well attended farewell performances, and closed the Opera House on 20 April, forever.

During these final days, the situation grew extremely threatening. On the same 14 April the Opera House was closed, Fort Sumter in Charleston harbor, bravely defended by Major Anderson and federal troops, fell after a bombardment of several days by the secessionists. Over its shattered ruins, in the place of the American flag, the secessionist flag was raised. The next day, 15 April, President Lincoln issued a proclamation to the people of the United States calling for a levy of seventy-five thousand volunteers for three months service as United States Volunteers. The state of Missouri was to supply four thousand men, but in response to the official order by War Secretary Cameron,[2] our governor, C. F. Jackson, responded with the following brutal words:

Executive Department
Jefferson City, Mo., April 17, 1861

Hon. Simon Cameron,
Secretary of War:

Sir: Your dispatch of the 15th instant, making a call on Missouri for four regiments for immediate service, has been received. There can be, I apprehend, no doubt but the men are intended to form a part of the President's army to make war upon the people of the seceded states.

---

2. Simon Cameron (1799-1889), a political boss in Pennsylvania, often U.S. Senator, was secretary of war under Lincoln, March 1861 to January 1862. He was criticized for his handling of federal contracts. *DAB*, 3: 437-9.

Your requisition, in my judgment, is illegal, unconstitutional, and revolutionary in its object, inhuman and diabolical, and cannot be complied with. Not one man will the State of Missouri furnish to carry on any such unholy crusade.

C. F. Jackson
Governor of Missouri[3]

At the same time the Militia General D. M. Frost,[4] commandant of the First Military District of Missouri, wrote to the governor calling for the erection of a fortified camp of the State Militia near St. Louis in order to hold the liberal city within limits. He also recommended calling the state legislature into session to take Missouri out of the Union and join it with the southern states. The organization of the pro-southern Minute Men became more extensive with every passing day, and into their ranks came that same anti-German and lawless element which had once taken part in armed assault and arson in the First Ward as well as in later Know-Nothing disturbances. They were supplied with weapons and ammunition from the State Arsenal in Jefferson City, and a state building, a tobacco storage warehouse, was cleared and provided for their drills. Every day the Minute Men marched through the entire city with fife and drum—this much memory of the Prussian manner of drill introduced by General Steuben in the army of Independence in 1776 was preserved—making dreadful threats against Germans and other citizens loyal to the Union. But the Germans were not idle either, and a call for the formation of an *unabhängige schwarzer Jägercorps* [Independent Black Rifle Corps] inviting the participation of all citizens loyal to the Union, excited great response and many members.[5] The "Black Rifles," which the *Missouri Republican* translated as "black guards," comparing them with the Prussian Death's-Head Hussars—terrified the Minute Men, and dark rumors spread that

---

3. *WROR*, series 3, vol. I, 82-3, above text taken from the original rather than by retranslating Boernstein's translation.

4. General David Marsh Frost (1823-1900) graduated West Point in 1844, served in the Mexican War, resigning his commission in 1853. He served in 1861 as a brigadier general of the Missouri Militia. After Camp Jackson, he led a Missouri brigade at Pea Ridge, being named a brigadier general in the CSA, but he was dropped from the active list in late 1863. See Mark Mayo Boatner III, ed., *The Civil War Dictionary* (New York, 1959), 318. He returned to St. Louis after the war, and his family eventually donated enough to have the name of Frost Campus bestowed on the establishment of Saint Louis University at Lindell and Grand and precipitating the displacement of the Camp Jackson memorial to Lyon Park in 1960. See Winter, 37.

5. *AW*, vol. 26, no. 131, 17 April 1861, p. 2, call for volunteers signed by Julius Wagner, "Hauptmann."

there were over a thousand of them, and that they would neither give nor accept pardon. They were said to be bound to a fearsome oath to exterminate all slaveholders and friends of slavery. The result was that the Black Rifles appeared more dreadful and terrifying to the guilt-ridden secessionists than they in fact were.

During these days Frank P. Blair returned to St. Louis from Washington, meeting at once with his party friends, and his home on Washington Avenue became the mustering place for all true friends of the Union. Every day there were consultations there, and the steps to be taken were carefully weighed. Blair was already aware of the answer of the governor of Missouri to the secretary of war, and he knew precisely what plans the governor and the slaveholder majority of the state legislature were hoarding. Above everything else, Blair urged German and pro-Union officers in the militia to tender their resignations so they would no longer depend on the governor. The Minute Men under Frost's command had already put aside the Union flag, and in its place they had raised the flag of the southern states. As a result [Friedrich] Schäfer wrote to the governor, "I cannot justify it in terms of my views of military loyalty and discipline to follow a flag other than the sole true flag of the United States." General Frost interpreted this action by Schäfer as treason against the state of Missouri, rejected his resignation and called a court martial, which then gave Major Schäfer a dishonorable discharge for conduct unbecoming an officer.[6] Yet the very next day all pro-Union officers of the militia tendered their resignations, demanding to be put before a court martial, so that the militia organization of the First Military District was virtually dissolved, since the militia of that district consisted mostly of Germans.

As far as Blair and the friends of the Union, the primary concern was to secure and protect the St. Louis arsenal, which lay in what was then the far south of the city, in which vast supplies of weapons and munitions were stored. Under the treasonous administration of Buchanan, everything was prepared to assist the southern states in their separation from the Union. Under various pretexts, Buchanan's War Secretary Floyd had completely emptied the arsenals in the northern free states and transferred cannon, weapons and munitions to southern arsenals.[7] These arsenals were then forcefully seized by the slave states and their troops armed from

---

6. Rowan/Primm, 184, *MB*, 21 April 1861; Rowan/Primm, 186, *MB*, 28 April 1861.

7. John Buchanan Floyd (1806-1863) was governor of Virginia, 1849-52, 1855-57, and secretary of war under Buchanan from 1857 to December 1860. He was accused at the time of transferring arms to the South. In the war, he rose to Confederate major general, and he died on campaign. *DAB*, 6: 482-3.

them. Only the arsenal in St. Louis was still in the hands of the federal government. If this arsenal had fallen into the hands of the secessionists, then the western free states of Illinois, Indiana, Iowa, Wisconsin and others would have remained entirely unarmed, and even with the best will they would not have been able to obtain the weapons needed. This would have exposed them to invasions by the rebellious army, which would quickly have won out and moved the theater of civil war to the free states. The Union could have been smashed without any capacity for defense, helpless. The first priority of all was thus to secure the vast war supplies in the St. Louis Arsenal for federal forces.

Already under Buchanan's administration, the commander of the United States Army, General Winfield Scott,[8] had turned his eye to this problem. Using his powers as commander without asking President Buchanan, he sent Captain Nathaniel Lyon with two hundred men of the Second Infantry Regiment from Kansas to St. Louis and made Lyon commander of the arsenal.[9] Until that time the arsenal had been guarded by about twenty soldiers, mostly semi-invalids. Captain Lyon, a graduate of the military academy at West Point in 1841, had acquitted himself with honor in several Indian wars and the war against Mexico, and he had been advanced to the rank of captain. He was a decisive, energetic man, loyal to the Union, in sense and conviction a "freethinker," as they define it in America. At the same time, as is the case with many men from New England, he was a confirmed Know-Nothing and nativist who harbored a particularly decided dislike of Germans. Yet, through the strange workings of fate, it was precisely the Germans alone who would stand by him loyally and courageously, making his success and fame. As conditions grew steadily more perilous, he conferred with Blair, and swift agreements were made for the protection of the arsenal.

In the meantime, terrified by the threat of danger, the new governor of Illinois, Francis A. Hoffmann,[10] a German, came to St. Louis in order

---

8. Winfield Scott (1786-1866), a general in the U.S. Army from 1814, was commanding general of the army, 1841-1861, and Whig candidate for president in 1852. *DAB*, 16: 505-11.

9. Nathaniel Lyon (1818-1861) was born in Connecticut, served in Florida and in the Mexican War, and gained a reputation as one of the few abolitionists in the army during his service in Kansas. See *ACAB*, 4: 67-9, and most recently Christopher Phillips, *Damned Yankee: The Life of General Nathaniel Lyon* (Columbia: University of Missouri Press, 1990), which agrees with Boernstein's low estimate of Lyon as a commander, but which blames Lyon's personal psychoses for the Civil War in Missouri, barely mentioning Frank Blair or the hypocritical nature of Jackson's "neutrality" proposal.

10. Francis A. Hoffmann (1822-1903), born in Herford, Westphalia, emigrated to America c. 1840, a Lutheran minister. He became a lawyer in 1851 and was the editor of the

to inform himself of the situation on the spot, and he participated in the discussions. The pro-Union state of Illinois with its large population, consisting heavily of Germans, only awaited the proclamation of President Lincoln to take up weapons for the defense of the Union, but where should they get their weapons if the St. Louis arsenal should fall into the hands of the secessionists? In our discussions with Blair it was stressed above all else that it would be necessary to organize militarily the pro-Union citizens, who constituted the majority of the population, and to do so independently of the governor and the discipline of the state militia. During the week from 14-21 April there were numerous discussions, including one in my editorial office which included besides myself, Schäfer, Sigel[11] and other sympathizers. It was resolved to call at once for the formation of independent military companies, and we adopted this resolution despite Sigel's objection that such a measure was illegal and premature. The very next morning, the German papers carried the appeal, the first by Major Schäfer, the second by my son August Siegmund.[12] The German Turner Society of St. Louis had already begun a military organization in total secrecy, forming itself in companies numbering about three hundred men. They received weapons from the pro-Union gunsmith Albright.[13] A furloughed officer of the U.S. Army, Larned, placed himself at the disposal of the Turners as drillmaster, and they drilled zealously under the command of Hugo Gollmer and Julius Müller, making every preparation for the conflict to come. At the same time consultations at Blair's place set up a Committee of Public Safety

Illinois Staats-Zeitung in Chicago. He was an early organizer of the Republican Party, and he was lieutenant governor of Illinois, 1860-64. He was noted as a writer on agricultural matters. *DAB*, 9: 118-19. The governor of Illinois in this period was Richard Yates.

11. Franz Sigel (1824-1902), born in Sinsheim, Baden, graduated from the military academy in Karlsruhe but resigned from the Baden army in 1847. He was a leading military commander in both Baden revolts, and he was minister of war in the Baden provisional government of 1849. He fled to England, coming to America in 1852. He was teaching mathematics in St. Louis when called to arms in 1861. He was politically popular but a disastrous field commander, rising to the rank of major general despite his ineptitude in battle. After the war he moved to New York City, where he worked in journalism and pursued local political causes; see Zucker, 343. There are monuments to him in New York and in Forest Park in St. Louis.

12. *AW*, vol. 26, no. 134, 20 April 1861, p. 2, advertisement for the "Bildung eines freiwilligen Regiments" was signed by Carl Börnstein, and a call to form a battalion of rifles (*Jäger*) was signed by Fr. Schäfer.

13. Thomas J. Albright was proprietor of T. J. Albright & Son gun makers, located at "40 n. Main" in *Directory* 1860, 21.

consisting of Messrs. O. D. Filley,[14] John How, S. T. Glover,[15] J. O. Broadhead[16] and J. J. Witzig,[17] which took over supreme leadership.

The calls in the newspapers for the formation of volunteer companies had an indescribable success. Youths, men, even old men, had themselves registered at once, and many young men left good jobs and their own businesses to fight for the defense of the Union. Within three days the first two companies, each 120 men strong, were completely formed. Then followed another call, and there was intense effort everywhere at forming volunteer companies. Before April reached its end, the organization of the Union Volunteers had been completed, numbering 4,200 men, that is, four American regiments at a thousand men each. But these enthusiastic Union fighters still did not have weapons, for the new federal administration in Washington still wallowed in indecisiveness and hesitation. Important voices were raised that one should not use force against the "erring brothers" in the South, but rather that friendly negotiations should settle the dispute peacefully. The result was that Captain Lyon still had not received the order from Washington to arm the volunteers and to allow them to occupy the arsenal. By this means the impatience of the ardent volunteers was raised to the highest degree, even to active dissatisfaction. Still, drill continued with staves, hunting rifles and other surrogate weapons, as the leaders of the pro-Union movement were pressed on all sides to take decisive steps.

In the meantime, the commander of the Military Department of Missouri, General Harney of the United States Army, had been observing

---

14. Oliver Dwight Filley (1806-1881), born in Connecticut, came to St. Louis in 1833 to work as a tinner, and he became wealthy as a manufacturer and seller of stoves and tinware with his brother Giles F. Filley. He was a director of the Bank of Missouri, a friend of Thomas Hart Benton, and an early supporter of Frank Blair. He served as mayor of St. Louis, 1858-9. *EHSL*, 2: 745.

15. Samuel T. Glover (1813-1884) from Kentucky, moved as a lawyer to Palmyra, Missouri, in 1837, coming to St. Louis in 1849. An early supporter of emancipation, he supported the candidacy of Edward Bates for the Republican nomination in 1860 and worked closely with Frank Blair. After the end of the Civil War, he opposed Radical efforts, particularly the test oath. *EHSL*, 2: 905-7.

16. James Overton Broadhead (1819-1898) was born in Virginia, studied briefly at the University of Virginia, and arrived in Missouri in 1837, becoming a lawyer in Bowling Green. He entered state politics as a Whig. He was a political ally of Frank Blair, moving to St. Louis in 1859. He was president of the American Bar Association in 1878 and was elected to Congress in 1882 as a Democrat. *DAB*, 3: 58-9.

17. John J. Witzig was a "master mechanic" on the Iron Mountain Rail Road in 1860, living at 228 S. Third (*Directory* 1860, 555); by the time of *Directory* 1864, 568, he was U.S. Supervising Inspector at the Customs House, and he was similarly listed in 1866 and 1867, but in *Directory* 1869 he is not to be found.

all of this in inactivity.[18] A man intimately befriended with slaveholders, Harney allowed the armed Minute Men to multiply to such a degree that they could conceive of an attack on the arsenal, and he allowed General Frost of the militia to establish a camp of secessionist troops right by the city, in Lindell's Grove, including not only the Minute Men but also strong contingents from the interior of the state, formed into an army corps. The camp was already flourishing the secessionist flag. On 20 April came the news that the second U.S. Arsenal in Missouri, in Liberty, had been seized by the state militia with all its supply of weapons.

Now the secessionists decided to overrun the St. Louis arsenal through a *coup de main*, and they made all necessary preparations. But those on the pro-Union side also made preparations to resist this effort. A company of Minute Men was already on the march toward the arsenal as an *avant-garde*, and the other companies only awaited the advent of darkness to follow it and make an attack on the arsenal. But in order for this *avant-garde* to reach the arsenal, it would have to pass through the First Ward, occupied exclusively by Germans, and on their appearance an ever larger crowd gathered, so that the troop was literally pressed together on all sides by the crowd and greeted with threats. The commander with his hundred men perceived the untenable nature of his situation, lost his head, and when his scouts informed him that the house opposite the arsenal, belonging to Dr. A. Hammer, was jammed with armed students of the Humboldt Institute and other men sworn to resist, and that they would fall on the rear of anyone attacking the arsenal, he called "Halt!" Then, after consultation with his officers, it was "Right about face!" And then they marched back to the headquarters of the Minute Men to the tune of the mockery of the people. The mayor of the city, D. Taylor,[19] came to the headquarters and beseeched the Minute Men to desist from their plans, though he himself had southern sympathies. He portrayed the strength of the German military organizations, the terrifying Black Rifles, the feared Turners, and so on, in such a dramatic fashion, predicting a fearsome bloodbath which would

---

18. William Selby Harney (1800-1889), a military officer from 1818, Harney distinguished himself in various Indian wars, serving as Winfield Scott's ranking cavalry officer in the Mexican War, though there were severe conflicts. He was brevetted brigadier general in 1847 for bravery at Cerro Gordo. He served in other Indian commands before being placed in command of the Western District, 1858-61. After his removal from command in St. Louis in 1861, he was given no further commands and retired in 1863. *DAB*, 8: 280-1; Winter, 39.

19. Daniel Gilchrist Taylor (1819-1878) born in Cincinnati, worked on steamboats on the Mississippi and Ohio, participated in explorations in the West, then settled after 1849 as a wholesaler, serving in the city council after 1852. He was a Democratic mayor, 1861-62, and later served as city treasurer. *EHSL*, 4: 2221-22.

necessarily result from the extraordinary bitterness of the Germans, so that first there was uncertainty, then genuine reluctance, and finally the plan was canceled, at least for this night.

With this episode the arsenal with its rich supplies of weapons was saved, for two days later such an attack had been rendered impossible. F. P. Blair, whose brother Montgomery Blair sat in Lincoln's cabinet as postmaster general, had been trying vainly in Washington to have Captain Lyon empowered to arm the volunteers and have them occupy the arsenal. As often and as pressingly as he repeated his telegrams to Washington, the order he demanded did not come back in response. It finally appears that the news of the taking of the Liberty Arsenal opened the eyes of the administration, and during the night of 21-22 April the telegram arrived from Washington bestowing on Captain Lyon the commission which had been sought. When it was announced on the morning of the 22nd, three Turner companies, which had camped the entire night in the Turner Hall because an attack on the hall had been planned by the secessionists, were led by Blair into the arsenal, where they were immediately armed and provided with uniforms.[20]

Since the War of Independence, American volunteer organizations had the practice that the companies elected their own officers, and that all the officers of a regiment together elected their colonel, lieutenant colonel and majors. Now my son had already informed me two days earlier that the company he had organized had unanimously elected me its captain. I had sought to decline this honor on the grounds of my age, but finally I had to give in to the general demand. When Blair informed me on the morning of the 22nd that the arsenal was open to us, I called my company together in an instant and marched with them about midday into the arsenal. We were unarmed, but our march through the city excited some admiration and some distress, in that we were greeted in American neighborhoods with mockery and threats, and in the German areas with cries of jubilation. So we arrived in the arsenal, I immediately reported to Captain Lyon, and he had the company mustered, sworn in, armed and assigned quarters by Artillery Lieutenant Schofield (now a general and commandant of the military academy at West Point) as muster officer.[21] Soon Friedrich Schäfer arrived

---

20. Rombauer, 195-200, sketches the organization of the original regiments formed in the arsenal. The Turner Companies became Companies A to C of the First Missouri Volunteers under Colonel Frank Blair.

21. John McAllister Schofield (1831-1906), born in New York, graduated West Point in 1853, served in artillery before teaching at West Point. In 1860 he took leave to teach physics as a professor at Washington University in St. Louis. At the start of the Civil War, he became a close aide to Nathaniel Lyon, later rising to major general under General Sherman. He was superintendent of West Point, 1876-81, finally commanding general of the army, 1888-95, retiring as lieutenant general. Schofield Barracks at Pearl

with his company, then others, and by evening there was a battalion of five companies in the arsenal. Then the companies organized by Sigel arrived, and on this night the arsenal was occupied by 1,000 well-armed volunteers and 200 regular infantry, secure against any possible *coup de main*. In the next few days, the First Volunteer Regiment was formed out of the Turner companies and what joined them under Blair's leadership, the Second Regiment out of the companies under me and Schäfer, from Sigel's companies the Third, and a few days later these were joined by the Fourth Regiment under Schüttner.[22] These four regiments consisted of 4,200 men, almost all German Americans, with at the most 100 Americans and no Irish at all, for their priests had warned the pious Irishmen not to declare themselves for either party but to remain strictly neutral. This was in order not to alienate either party, for it was as yet unknown who would be victorious. With this uprising of the Germans, not only was the St. Louis arsenal secured together with its great supplies, but the state of Missouri was also saved for the Union, the arming of the Western free states was assured, and a great step was taken for the preservation of the Union.

Harbor, Hawaii, is named after him. *DAB*, 16: 453-4; James L. McDonough, "'And All for Nothing': Early Experiences of John M. Schofield in Missouri," *MHR*, 64 (1969-70): 306-21.

22. Nikolaus Schüttner (sometimes spelled Schittner), colonel commanding the Fourth Regiment, Missouri Volunteers *(Schwarze Jäger)*, was a manufacturer of brick molds and leader of a street gang devoted to terrifying secessionists in south St. Louis. He was noted as a man of little education but great enthusiasm for the Union cause; see Kaufmann, 551. He is mentioned in *Directory* 1857, 193, as a carpenter living in the alley between Barry and Park Avenues; in *Directory* 1860, 450, he is still a carpenter, living on the east side of Buell between Arrow and Ohio. In *Directory* 1864, 477, and 1866, 719, he is superintendent of the city engineer's office; in *Directory* 1867, he is street commissioner, and in *Directory* 1869, 689, his widow Catherine Schittner is listed.

Under Arms

(1861)

President Lincoln had demanded 4,000 volunteers from the state of Missouri, and Governor C. F. Jackson had rejected this legitimate demand in a crude, offensive manner. Now despite this, in response to a call by a couple of private citizens, more than the number demanded were placed under arms; 4,200 volunteers were mustered, with few exceptions almost all from the German population of a single city, St. Louis. These were true volunteers in the noblest sense of the word, leaving their jobs, businesses and families. Out of enthusiasm for a good cause, they took on the soldier's life, courageously bearing all cares and wants, cheerfully ready to lay down their lives for the victory of liberty and the preservation of the great star-spangled republic. In those days an elevated, enthusiastic mood dominated in the German American population, which exhibited an unequaled readiness for sacrifice, virtually the last flicker of the idealism of the remarkable year of 1848 they had brought from Europe. It was not only youths who thought and acted so, but also mature men, whose hair had gone gray. Even old men took up weapons to the best of their strength, joining in the great struggle for the liberty of a hemisphere.

If Lincoln and his cabinet, instead of anxiously trembling and shaking, had called up 200,000 men instead of 75,000 in April 1861, and not for three months but for two years, the accursed War of Secession would have been finished within twelve months and the country would have been spared much misery. Such a force, as enthusiastic and self-sacrificing as was the case with the three-month people, could not have been resisted by the secessionists. The Union Army would have advanced, put down all opposition, and throttled the entire rebellion before it had reached such a dangerous height as to extend the war to nearly four years. But in Washington in the spring of 1861, no one grasped that this was not a mutiny, an uprising of a few districts or states. No one saw it was the beginning of a great political and social revolution that would end with the complete abolition of slavery. On the contrary, everyone hoped that with the 75,000 volunteers scraped together in haste a few victories could be won, then there would be negotiations and a compromise with the "misled brothers," a restoration of domestic peace. For that reason the "peculiar institution" of slavery was handled with kid gloves, and the commanders of the Union Army had to issue solemn proclamations in the slave states that they would respect property in slaves with great scrupulousness, protecting the masters and lords of Negro slaves in their property. Indeed, when one of these commanders, General Frémont, acted against instructions a few months later by declaring those [Missouri] slaves whose owners had turned against the Union to be free, his order was declared null and void from Washington, and he was severely criticized.

It was a fact that Lincoln's administration was then almost entirely in the hands of older political leaders who had come to tolerate the institution of slavery as a "necessary evil," even if they did not much like it. As a result the government acted weakly and indecisively at the outset. The first victories did not go to the Union Army, but to the more decisive secessionist force. This was a momentary misfortune for the great cause, but in the long run it was fortunate for the future of the United States. The defeat that the Unionists endured in the first battle at Bull Run, the threat to the seat of government itself at Washington, began to open the eyes of the administration and the Northern states. This convinced them that there would be no "stroll to Richmond," a brief campaign of ninety days, but a war of long duration. The time for cowardly compromise was forever past. The end would inevitably be the abolition of slavery in the entire Union and the obliteration of the previous political domination by the South. Only from Bull Run were the great goals fixed in the sight of Washington, as well as the leading Northern states, and energetic measures taken. When an energetic commander with far sight, cunning decisiveness and tough persistence finally appeared in the person of Ulysses S. Grant, the dreadful Civil War was finally ended with victory and profit to the Union after years of struggle.

It is by no means my intention to write the history of the War of Secession here, and so I return to my narrative and the last days of April 1861. Those were beautiful, elevating days that made up the week from 22 to 29 April. From all parts of the city newly formed, unbidden German volunteer companies, headed by elected officers, streamed into the arsenal. There Captain Lyon and his officers had their hands full mustering in the thousands of volunteers, arming and housing them. What a happy, cheerful mood reigned among these volunteers! At all points of the great park surrounding the United States Arsenal, there was ceaseless drilling, and when this labor was done at the end of day, all nooks and crannies sounded with German war songs and soldiers' choirs, Lützow's *"Wilde Jagd"* and the *"Schwertlieb."* In the meantime there was cooking at the hastily organized field kitchens, and in the manner of soldiers they were fed by units. They ate with the best appetite, either standing or sitting on the ground. Even those who had once been wont to dine at the *table d'hôte* at the Planter's House or other hotels pronounced the cuisine excellent. The general happiness, the humorous mood, the awareness of doing a good deed and the physical exertions served as seasoning to stimulate the appetite. In my entire life I cannot recall days so cheerful, exciting or invigorating as those first few days at the arsenal when we were forming our volunteer regiments.

And yet all of us were well aware of the difficult mission we had accepted. We well knew that we were in a slave state in which slaveholders constituted a majority, and that we would find no reinforcements or help in the interior of the state. We further knew that we four thousand men could be pressed down by one hundred thousand slaveholders simply by their numbers. But these considerations, which the more reflective among us kept in our hearts, did not distract our little volunteer army in the least. Everyone was cheerful and of good spirits, and concerns or fears did not trouble us for even an hour. We pulled together into a true brotherhood of arms, so that each had joy in the enthusiasm of the other. Even if there had been a force ten times our size, if forty thousand secessionists had marched up and demanded the surrender of the arsenal, we would have laughed them to scorn, rejecting their demands rudely and accepting the unequal combat. Later events demonstrated that those three-month volunteers were indeed fine, proven soldiers. Most of them remained in the Union Army even after their three months were up, so that they would become the true core, the veterans of the three-year volunteer regiments of the Union Army.

But we soon outgrew the rather spread-out quarters of the arsenal and its outbuildings, and we had to consider eventually moving the companies to other quarters. Schäfer and I already had eight companies of 120 men each, and Captain Lyon ordered us to go to the vacated Marine Hospital, a building belonging to the United States on a hill south of the arsenal. There we would complete the regiment and carry out its required organization. On the morning of the 24th I marched there with my company to take possession of the building, with the other companies to follow in the afternoon. I found a large, roomy building with bright, well-aired rooms, situated in a fenced park that could easily be held by our people. The administrator for the hospital, awakened from his repose, protested and did not want to admit us. This of course was to no avail. Despite his resistance, I occupied the building, and while he was protesting to General Harney the other companies marched in and made themselves comfortable. Either General Harney was not in or he did not consider the matter important enough, but it sufficed that the administrator's protests were pointless. We remained undisturbed at the Marine Hospital.[1] I was disinclined to house myself or my men in the sickrooms of a former hospital, so I chose instead a

---

1. On the United States Marine Hospital, see Winter, 43, 54. C. F. W. Walther, leader of the Missouri Synod Lutherans, a loyal Missourian and principled sympathizer with secession and tolerator of slavery for religious reasons, was upset by the presence of his old enemy Boernstein with an armed force at the Marine Hospital near Concordia Seminary on South Jefferson. See Concordia Historical Society, letter of Pastor C. F. W. Walther to

bombproof bunker in the park that had once served as a powder magazine for the arsenal, but which now was empty. I quartered my company in this long, arched powder magazine, with only two openings. The furnishing was simple, consisting of absolutely nothing, but I requisitioned straw and made two long rows of mass bedding on which everyone slept following the exertions of the day. The next morning the administrator at the arsenal sent us two long tables and benches, and we were thus fully equipped. The field kitchen was set up in open air in the park.

On the evening of the next day, this peaceful still-life had a sudden end. We had drilled the whole day, and there had been many things to look after to assure the housing of the company; in short, I was exhausted. My feet were worn, and I had just pulled on my house slippers when an aide from the arsenal arrived with a handwritten note:

> Captain Boernstein is hereby ordered to march at once to the Arsenal and to report there with his company. N. Lyon, Captain and commandant of the Arsenal.

My first thought was that an attack on the arsenal was imminent, and that the commandant needed reinforcements. I alarmed the company and had them arm while I informed Captain Schäfer, who as the eldest officer was commander in the Marine Hospital. I told him to be ready, as well, and to keep the other companies under arms through the night. In order to defend our rather isolated position against possible attack, Captain Lyon had provided us with two cannon and a section of artillerists. These quickly loaded their guns and cartridges, and the other companies were placed in battle positions to defend against attack. I marched double-time with Company A to the arsenal. On arriving at the gate, we found a company of regular infantry drawn up in front, and we had to halt. Captain Totten, their company commander, recognized us, and after the password and call were exchanged, the ranks of the regulars opened and we were allowed to pass

---

Jacob Matthias Buehler, St. Louis, 21 May 1861: "After our governor refused to send the President soldiers to fight the South, significant military forces have been gathered by the latter, mostly consisting of local Germans, under the command of Boernstein, Blair and others. The Arsenal and its immediate vicinity all the way to the Marine Hospital is crawling with United States soldiers. Since it appeared to us as if the field of battle was being established here under the College's window (Colonel Boernstein, encamped in the Marine Hospital, swore with his hand on a cannon to shoot to pieces the secessionist nest, as he likes to call our college), and since the Governor expects to pass a military bill through the legislature, we saw ourselves moved in our conscience to dissolve the institution until further notice and send home all pupils and students, partly so that no one would be put in peril of his life by remaining here, partly so that northerners would not be put in peril of being pressed into the army, even to draw a sword against the North."

through into the arsenal. Under the prevailing conditions, there was a strong watch; entry into the arsenal was as strictly controlled as a fortress under siege. We had marched in such haste that I had not even found time to put on my boots, so that I performed my first military expedition in my slippers. I only lacked my dressing gown to make it complete. Thank heavens I had quit wearing a dressing gown in those troubled times, and I was fortunate that it was a dark night and no one saw my slippers.

I found Captain Lyon behind the officers' building of the arsenal, on the riverbank, and I reported to him. He told me my company and I, together with one of Blair's companies under Captain Stone's command, had been ordered on an expedition that required absolute silence and unconditional obedience. I would receive my instructions at once.

I shall never forget the imposing impression of this night and its mysterious proceedings. At the riverbank lay a huge steamer, its fore and aft decks beset with cannon by which artillerists stood, ready to fire. The moon shone weakly through torn clouds, casting ghostly illumination on our two companies lined up on the bank, left and right of the steamer. In the middle stood Captain Lyon, with his officers and the administrator of the arsenal, overseeing the loading. Regular soldiers hauled long, heavy chests on their shoulders, loading them continually onto the steamer. This whole business, carried out in utter silence and without a light visible either on the steamer nor on the shore, lasted until midnight. At last the loading was complete, and Captain Lyon gave me his instructions. He had received the order from Washington to deliver to Illinois the weapons and munitions necessary to equip its militia. On board there were twenty-one thousand rifles, eight cannon, the necessary sidearms, carts and corresponding munitions. All of this was to be taken to Alton and delivered to Illinois state officials by the U.S. officer aboard. The greatest quiet and care had to be observed so that this delivery of arms would not be betrayed and either attacked or blocked by friends of secession. No light would be allowed to burn on board, and in view of the gunpowder there was to be no smoking. Above all else, the most complete silence had to be observed so that our passage would not be observed from the banks of the Mississippi. Captain Stone and I were responsible for precisely fulfilling his orders. Captain Lyon hoped to see us back at the arsenal within twenty-four hours once the mission had been completed.

After we parted from him our companies marched aboard and took their places on the lower deck of the steamer, which was crammed full of weapons. In keeping with Lyon's orders, the crates of rifles were piled up in such a way along the exterior of the boat so that they formed an almost impenetrable wall around the men placed in the middle. Musket balls could not have penetrated them, and even cannon shot would have encountered resistance. The steamer moved soundlessly to the middle of the stream before moving against the current toward Alton. The boiler was heated as little as possible in order not to reveal our position through rising smoke, and deep silence reigned on the mighty steamer on which there were almost three hundred men.

On parting, Captain Lyon had addressed us commandants and called our attention to the fact that many Minute Men were encamped in the northern part of the city with two cannon. If the expedition were betrayed despite all efforts, either a heavy bombardment from the cannon or even an attack by a rented, heavily manned steamer was possible. For those reasons, the deepest silence should be observed, but the men should be ready to fight at any moment.

It was a cool, pleasant April night on which we made our journey to Alton. But the deep silence, the quiet whispers with which we spoke, the uncanny apprehension of what was to come, the deep agitation of spirits, all came together to make this evening a torment that never seemed to end. The swollen river rolled its powerful waves past us, and we made only very slow progress. As the first gray of morning shone and night gave way to dawn, a light mist enveloped us. Finally the boilers were heated up, so that about eight o'clock we were within sight of Alton. The steamer turned toward the levee just as the sun finally broke through the mist and illuminated the friendly town with a bright light.

Now a large United States flag was unfurled from our boat, together with a signal flag. The instant these were seen from the shore there was lively movement. Signal cannon fired into the air and the bells of all the churches and firehouses began to peal. The entire population streamed from all sides to the harbor, where we were landing, as the signal shots were returned. The representative of the governor of Illinois came on board immediately, and we delivered our cargo to him. Strong bridging was placed to the shore. Hundreds of volunteer workers, almost the entire male population of Alton, crowded around to unload the steamer's valuable cargo *gratis.* The men of Illinois were all loyal to the Union and had already organized militia regiments for its defense, but they largely lacked the weapons for the primary outfitting. General jubilation reigned because we had at last brought the longed-for weapons, and we were greeted with the greatest friendliness from all sides. Our companies formed a large circle on the shore, and with hundreds of hands to help, the entire steamer was emptied in a few hours. The representative of the governor accepted the entire shipment and issued a receipt, and within a few hours these weapons were on the railways, sent in all directions into the interior of Illinois according to a distribution plan already worked out. Thus loyal Illinois was armed, and within a few days their regiments moved to their marshaling places. The brave volunteers of Illinois fought

The riverfront at Alton, Illinois, during the Civil War, where weapons from the St. Louis arsenal were taken under Boernstein's guard in 1861. Boernstein waited three days at Alton for further orders. Photograph courtesy of the Missouri Historical Society, Civil War Box 2, Prisons.

loyally and well through the long war, doing their part for the preservation and defense of the Union.[2]

For the time being there was no talk about returning us within twenty-four hours as Captain Lyon had promised. In the midst of the trouble and agitation then reigning in St. Louis, they appeared to have forgotten completely about us in Alton. First twenty-four hours passed, then forty-eight, then three days. Still we were lying in the harbor at Alton without knowing what we were to do. In fact, it seemed that no one cared about us. We were unable to leave the steamer, which was kept ready with heated boiler. The captain told us he was not allowed to return to St. Louis without a telegraphic order, as his orders read, but when the order came he would be gone within ten minutes. As a result, everyone had to remain on board or in the immediate vicinity. There was nothing to do but give in to the unavoidable and patiently wait until we were called back.

The three days passed in intense boredom. In order to use the time to some purpose, we drilled from morning to night on the riverbank, close to the steamer, to the great enjoyment of the residents of Alton. It was also possible for me to replace the boots left behind at the Marine Hospital with a new pair made by a German shoemaker nearby in exchange for money and good words. At last I was back on my best foot and free of my accursed slippers. But as the fourth day dawned and there was still no command to return, the whole business became just "too dumb," and I did what I should have done the first day, telegraphing Blair and asking for our recall.

As I awaited a reply, a letter came from Schäfer informing me that the regiment had been completely formed. I had been unanimously elected by all the officers of the regiment as colonel, with Schäfer as lieutenant colonel, and Osterhaus[3] and Laibold as majors of the Second Missouri Volunteer Regiment. These appointments had been confirmed by the proper authorities. As soon as possible I was to return to take over command of the regiment provisionally headed by himself.

2. Rowan/Primm, 197, *AW*, 9 May 1861, reports that the Missouri Legislature regarded the taking of weapons from Missouri to Illinois by force of federal arms as tantamount to a declaration of war against Missouri.

3. Peter Joseph Osterhaus (1823-1917), born in Koblenz in the Rhineland, served in the Prussian army before emigrating to America in 1849, arriving in St. Louis in 1851. As captain and then major in Boernstein's Second Missouri Volunteers, he fought at Wilson's Creek. In December 1861, he became colonel of the Twelfth Missouri Volunteers, fighting at Pea Ridge in March 1862. He became a brigadier general in June 1862. He had numerous field commands, distinguishing himself particularly at Missionary Ridge. He was made major general in June 1864. After the war he was U.S. Consul at Lyons, 1866-1877, later at Mannheim, 1898-1900. He retired in Germany and died in Duisburg. *DAB*, 14: 88-9.

A few hours after I received this letter, a telegram came from Blair informing me that a command for the steamer's return had already been issued, and soon afterward the steamer captain received his orders by telegraph. We rushed on board with jubilation and steamed quickly to our St. Louis, much more quickly now that we were traveling with the stream. We landed at the arsenal, where I reported to Captain Lyon on the expedition and I received his congratulations on the success of our effort and his apology for having forgotten us. Then I went up to the Marine Hospital, where we were joyously received by the entire officer corps and men of the regiment. The new colonel was greeted with hearty toasts. A cheerful dinner, quite frugal in view of our limited means but spiced with joy and friendship, closed this reception, which lasted late into the night. So I lay down for the first time as colonel of an American regiment, consoled by the awareness of having 1,200 brave German men as true brothers in arms under my command, whose prosperity or woe depended on me. I felt twenty years younger the next morning, ready for anything, and despite my fifty-six years, I bore the strains of my time of service healthy and strong.

Black Friday
(1861)

As American and Irish professional office-hunters rushed in droves to Washington to finagle a fat little office through beseeching, begging and shameless impertinence, or by claiming some special privilege, Germans stood under arms defending the Union. It is an honor to the German name that in the days of peril, there was not a single German among those jockeying for offices and distinctions in Washington. The self-sacrifice and enthusiasm with which the Germans rushed to the flag of the Union grew from day to day, so that in St. Louis a fifth volunteer regiment was in the process of being formed. Captain Lyon also called for the formation of four regiments of Homeguards, consisting of married men and older citizens who were to serve only in St. Louis and preserve the peace and security of the city when the volunteer regiments went into the field.

The Homeguards also consisted entirely of German citizens, so that three weeks after the order finally came from Washington authorizing the arming of volunteers, there was a well-armed small army corps of almost ten thousand Germans at the disposal of federal authorities. All concerns of family or business had been put aside. Everyone thought only of the greater whole, the defense and preservation of the Union. No sacrifice was considered too great when it was to save the great American star-spangled republic. I myself, for example, placed my numerous, complex businesses in the hands of friends or employees, only seeing my print shop and editorial office again three months later. In the same regiment with me were my three sons and my son-in-law, and with the exception of my eldest son, who was elected my successor as captain of Company A, they all carried muskets as privates in the ranks.[1]

Everything was also being done on the secessionist side as well to strengthen their ranks. Everywhere in the state they were arming, in keeping with the governor's command. By his order, every man capable of bearing arms had to enter a militia unit, a situation of raw compulsion, mistreatment, and force. There were brave Union people who, refusing to bear arms against the legitimate authorities or the Union, were attacked by

---

1. Rombauer, 363-79, gives the complete original muster roll of the Second Regiment Infantry, Missouri Volunteers, giving Henry Boernstein as colonel, Charles Boernstein as sergeant major, and August Boernstein as captain, Company A. Gustav Boernstein was First Lieutenant of Company D. Adolf Wilharditz could not be located in this listing.

fanatic bands and driven from their property, house and home, so that these poor people had to flee into the woods while their houses were plundered and set ablaze. The armed levy of the secessionists was supplied with weapons state authorities robbed in their sudden attack on the United States Arsenal at Liberty. The intention, as soon as sufficient strength had been reached, was to march on St. Louis, attack the town under the command of General D. M. Frost of the state militia, and together with the secessionists and Minute Men there, to subject the city to the will of the slaveholders. For this purpose General Frost raised a camp on a hill west of St. Louis which was named Camp Jackson, in honor of the governor, and over which the secessionist flag was already raised. In the first days of May, the steamer *J. C. Swon* brought an entire shipload of cannon, rifles, sidearms, supplies and munitions from the United States Arsenal in Liberty to St. Louis, where they were unloaded by night and taken immediately to the secessionist camp.[2]

In these same first days of May, all the staff officers and chief officers of the four volunteer regiments gathered to elect a brigadier general, in keeping with the American practice. The election fell unanimously to Captain N. Lyon, who accepted the vote with thanks, and the record of the election with the signatures of all officers was sent at once by Blair to Secretary of War Cameron, requesting a confirmation of election. This vote of confidence from the volunteer regiments considerably strengthened Lyon's position, for as general Lyon could do a great deal that was not possible for him as a mere captain of infantry. Blair and Lyon were decisively of the opinion that they should no longer beguile themselves with the wishy-washy policies dominating Washington. Both of them saw waiting any longer without action to be dangerous for the cause of the Union and the security of St. Louis, because this would only make it possible for the secessionists to complete their military organization. Above all else, Camp Jackson had to be closed, the secessionist force there dispersed, and stolen federal property recovered.

For this purpose, General Lyon staged a personal reconnaissance of the secessionist camp in Lindell's Grove in disguise. While he was doing this, he also called for the members of the Committee of Public Safety and the colonels of the volunteer regiments to hold a council of war. It was in the afternoon of Thursday, 9 May, that we gathered in Lyon's apartment in a small house next to the armory. Present at this remarkable gathering were

---

2. The *J. C. Swon*, which arrived from Memphis, carried heavy military ordnance from United States installations further south, but not from the Liberty Arsenal, which was upstream from St. Louis on the Missouri. See Rowan/Primm, 205-6, *WP*, 15 May 1861.

Lieutenant Colonel Chester Harding,[3] Lyon's adjutant general; Franklin A. Dick,[4] Blair's brother-in-law, who also had adjutant functions; then the members of the Committee of Public Safety: O. D. Filley, Broadhead, Glover and Witzig; as well as Cols. Blair, Boernstein, Sigel and Schüttner. Only General Lyon himself was missing.

Finally, as dusk descended, Lyon appeared in clothing completely covered with dirt and mud from his reconnaissance (having crept through a ditch into the encampment).[5] He began the meeting at once. He declared that, since seeing the camp with his own eyes, he was convinced that Camp Jackson posed a great peril for the city and the arsenal, and that it was necessary to act quickly and dissolve the camp. There was no time to lose in this. The United States military commander in Missouri, General Harney, would be returning in three days from Washington, and in view of his personal friendship with leaders of secession, one could not expect any support from him, only restrictions and difficulties. The deed must be done in the next few days, before the propitious moment passed.

All of those present approved Lyon's proposal. Only the lawyer Glover raised objections of a legal sort, counseling delay until there was an order from a United States court for the recovery of federal property. Such an order would be served in Camp Jackson by the U.S. Marshal, and

3. Chester Harding, Jr., son of the noted portrait artist Chester Harding, served the entire war in various capacities in Missouri, receiving the rank of brevet brigadier general in 1865. See Boatner, ed., *Civil War Dictionary*, 375; Winter, 146.

4. Franklin A. Dick was aide to General Lyon at the time of the Camp Jackson raid; see *WROR*, section I, vol. 3, 5, report of Nathaniel Lyon, 11 May 1861. He later served as provost marshal in St. Louis; see Walter B. Stevens, *History of St. Louis, The Fourth City, 1764-1909*, vol. I (Chicago; St. Louis: S. L. Clarke, 1909): 835. He was related to Frank Blair by having married the sister of Blair's wife, Apolline Alexander, so that they shared Mrs. Alexander as a mother-in-law. After the war, Dick moved to Philadelphia. The guilty conscience of even some important participants in Lyon's operation is reflected by the postscript of a letter by Dick: "When we took Camp Jackson, we were not *regularly* authorized, for we had no authority from the U.S. to do that rash act. Lyon and his staff were irregulars in that proceeding, but we assumed an organization analogous to a legal one." MHS, Civil War Papers, F. A. Dick, Storrington, Conn., to Benson J. Lossing in Poughkeepsie, N.Y., 7 August 1865.

5. There is the irresistible story that Lyon made an exploration of Camp Jackson dressed as a lady and drawn about in a carriage, which Rombauer, 224, rejects out of hand. For confirmation of the story by a participant, see MHS, Civil War Papers, Charles D. Drake, St. Louis, to Benson J. Lossing in Poughkeepsie, N.Y., 20 December 1864. Drake refers to Dick, "who was Genl. Lyon's Asst. Adj't. Genl. at the time of, and prior to, the capture of Camp Jackson. Remembering your request for information in regard to Lyon's reconaissance of Camp Jackson, in the guise of a lady, I asked Col. Dick about it, and found that he was perfectly familiar with the whole matter, having suggested to Lyon that form of disguise, and furnished him with the apparel from the wardrobe of his mother-in-law, Mrs. Alexander."

the volunteers would then operate as a *posse comitatus* to carry it out. Blair and Lyon knew all too well that the members of the United States court were secret friends of secession, however, and that difficulties and delays would be introduced. So the two decided to act on their own responsibility. General Lyon posed the question to the colonels whether they could rely on their people without hesitation, which was answered with a unanimous yes. He informed us that the moment of action had not yet been determined, but that we should all hold ourselves ready to act at any moment.

It was very late when we returned to our headquarters. Here, as well as in the city at large, there was much agitation. Rumors about the council of war had passed through the walls of the arsenal into the population. They had seen long columns of harnessed dray horses being led into the arsenal, and it was inferred that there would soon be a movement by the federal troops. There were also rumors that a corps of secessionist troops from the interior of the state was on the march to St. Louis, or that it had already been seen there, to join with the troops in Camp Jackson and overrun the city and the arsenal that very night. As a precaution I had the watch at the Marine Hospital doubled, and the men were not allowed to undress. Instead, they had to be ready to respond ready for action on the mustering field at the first alarm.

In the meantime, the night passed quietly. Scouts reported that it had been quiet at Camp Jackson, where there had been a large party of the officers with toasts to the Union's demise and the victory of secession. No order came from the arsenal, so the regiment went out to drill early in the morning, as was the practice.

Teaching these men to drill in the American fashion in the short period between 22 April and 10 May was no easy matter. To be sure, the majority of the officers and men had already served in the military in Europe for some length of time. But one would have served in the Austrian army, another in the Prussian, and others with the Bavarian, Württemberg, Hessian, or other forces. Each of these had learned different grasps, movements and commands. The remainder of the men had never served, had never had a gun in their hands before. It was no simple thing to unite all these elements into a well-disciplined, harmonious whole and initiate them in American procedure in a matter of days.

In order to overcome these problems quickly, I conceived the idea of forming a model company. All of the officers, sergeants, and corporals were gathered at five o'clock in the morning in rank and file, standing shoulder to shoulder with muskets on their shoulders. The captains of the companies served as noncommissioned officers, and the three staff officers took their places on the wings or in the rear of the company. We worked through

American drill according to Hartnett's manual[6] step by step for two hours. First the grasps, then the tactical movements, and so on. When the exercise was over, the members of the model company rushed to their own companies and trained their own people for two hours, teaching what they had just learned. The same procedure was repeated in the afternoon, so that it happened that the Second Regiment made great progress and was fully trained in a relatively short time. I am happy to recognize that, besides the enthusiasm and lively zeal of officers and men, my own experience from five years in the Austrian army made the process considerably easier.

We had just finished training the model company on the morning of 10 May when a messenger came rushing from the arsenal with a written order from General Lyon. The general, it said, desired to see the Second Regiment in the arsenal at ten o'clock in order to have it pass in review. Two companies should remain behind to protect the Marine Hospital. I suspected at once that the time had come for action, so I took appropriate measures. When dray horses arrived to bring the cannons back, I knew what was afoot, and after nine o'clock we were marching toward the arsenal. Here we found the entire arsenal crammed with troops in long lines under the trees. General Lyon rode down the rows of the regiments and gave each a brief, forceful address. He then told the colonels to have the troops load their weapons. The artillerists loaded their cannon and at noon the gates of the arsenal opened for the expedition to march out. General Lyon, with two companies of regular infantry; Major Backhof with six cannon; and the First Regiment (Col. Blair) marched down Laclede Avenue. The Second Regiment (Col. Boernstein) went down Pine Street. The Third Regiment (Col. Sigel) marched down Olive Street, and the Fourth Regiment (Col. Schüttner) followed the course of Market Street. All four regiments arrived at Camp Jackson at almost the same moment. The Fifth Volunteer Regiment and the First and Second Home Guards Regiments remained in the arsenal as a garrison, while the Third and Fourth Home Guards Regiments were placed as reserves between the city and Camp Jackson.[7]

---

6. Boernstein is probably thinking of William Joseph Hardee, *The Manual of Arms, Adapted to the Rifle Musket, Model 1855, with Maynard's Primer* . . . (New York, 1860); idem., *Rifle and Light Infantry Tactics, for the Exercise and Manoeuvres of Troops When Acting as Light Infantry or Riflemen. Prepared under the Direction of the War Department by Brevet Lieutenant Colonel W. J. Hardee* (Philadelphia, 1855) and many subsequent editions. A German-language edition was published in New York in 1861. Hardee (1815-1873) a Georgian, later had his manuals issued as rules of drill for the Confederate States Army, revised by John H. Richardson. See *NUC*, 230, 473-75. On drill manuals in general, see J. W. A. Whitehorne, "Inspector General Sylvester Churchill's Efforts to Produce a New Army Drill Manual," *Civil War History 32* (1986): 159-168.

7. Rowan/Primm, 206-212, *WP,* 15 May 1861, for a contemporary account of the Camp Jackson raid. See the long account in Winter, 40-53.

There was no movement in the secessionist camp, except for riders passing in and out to scout the advance of the federal troops and to report to General Frost. In contrast, thousands of the curious, aroused by the march of the troops, streamed out and followed us, as if it were a peaceful maneuver rather than a bloody war exercise that threatened onlookers as well. When Camp Jackson had been surrounded on all sides by federal troops and our guns set up in such a way as to cover the entire secessionist camp and pound it to a pulp, Lyon sent Major Farrar under a flag of truce to Camp Jackson. Farrar presented General Frost with Lyon's written demand to surrender the camp to federal troops within half an hour, or he and his people would experience the worst. There was an uproar and panic in the secessionist camp. During the previous night and the course of that day, in the face of threatening preparations, 500 out of the 2,000 men had deserted to safety. Now, as federal troops appeared, several hundred more followed suit, throwing away their secessionist cockades and other insignia, crawling over the fences of the camp and mingling with the onlookers. The half hour of grace had not yet passed when Frost's adjutant general appeared before General Lyon and told him General Frost agreed to surrender the camp under protest, asking only that public property in the camp be placed under guard and that the officers be allowed to keep their swords. One company of Sigel's regiment under Captain Blandowski's[8] command occupied the entry to Camp Jackson, and the entire garrison (or what was left), amounting to 1,110 men and 78 officers, had to leave the camp and enter the custody of federal troops as prisoners of war. In addition, there were 12 cannon, 7 mortars, 1,200 rifles, a great amount of sidearms, equipment and tents. There also was a significant number of cannon and rifles unpacked in their crates, just as they had been delivered and unloaded from the *Swon*. An enormous supply of munitions was also seized by the federal troops and brought to the arsenal the following day.

As the prisoners of war were departing the camp under military escort and the Third Regiment under Col. Sigel was occupying it, the secessionist

---

8. Constantin Blandowski (died 25 May 1861) had been trained as an officer in Dresden, Saxony, and had served with the French army in Algeria and participated first in the Polish revolution and later in Italy. He was a close friend of the St. Louis German American artist Carl Wimar, accompanying him on a journey to the Rocky Mountains in 1858. Wimar did a portrait of Blandowski and included his posthumous image in a pro-Union *grisaille* painting of 1861 together with Nathaniel Lyon and John Charles Frémont. He commanded Company F, Third Regiment, Missouri Volunteers (Sigel). Kaufmann, 483; Rombauer, 389; Lincoln Bruce Spiess, "Carl Wimar: The Missouri Historical Society Collection," *GH*, vol. 3, no. 3 (Winter 1982-3), 16-29. Less reliable than Spiess on some details is Rick Stewart, Joseph D. Ketner II, Angela L. Miller, *Carl Wimar, Chronicler of the Missouri River Frontier* (Fort Worth, Tex.: Amon Carter Museum, 1991), esp. 225, n. 84.

flag was hauled down on Lyon's order. In its place, the star-spangled banner of the Union was raised and hailed by federal troops with a threefold hurrah. That was too much for the friends and adherents of secession, who had rushed there from all sides and among whom escapees from the camp were mingled. As soon as surrender of the camp without resistance became a foregone conclusion, the federal troops were enclosed on all sides and insulted with curses and mockery. Of these they took no notice. But when the Union flag was raised and hailed with hurrahs, the scorn of the secessionists rose to blind rage. Raw curses became stones and tiles and clots of dirt heaped on the troops from close range, wounding several in the rank and file. Despite this, the troops maintained model calm, not permitting themselves to be distracted. Rather, they directed their full attention to watching the war prisoners, who had been divided into two groups and placed in the middle of the columns of the First and Second Regiments.

The columns were about to begin their march back to the arsenal when suddenly, out of a house that was in the process of being built, and from the trees and the prairie, the troops were fired upon with revolvers. Two men in my regiment fell and several were wounded. Captain Blandowski, who commanded the watch at the entrance to the camp, had his shin shattered by a ball. His leg had to be amputated, and he died several days after the operation.[9] This treacherous attack exhausted the patience of the troops, who lifted their weapons and fired on their attackers without command, responding to the natural drive for self-defense. It was the regular infantry and men of my own regiment who opened fire, and cowardly attackers hidden high in the trees fired back. When the cowards saw that things had grown serious, a panic seized the raging mob and it flew in all directions. On the ground lay sixteen dead and more than fifty wounded. The number of victims was probably even larger, for many were taken away by friends and acquaintances and their participation in the lawless riot kept as quiet as possible.

As a result of my efforts and those of other officers, we managed to get the fire to cease after several minutes. We got our columns under way about six o'clock in the afternoon, marching the prisoners along Olive Street toward the arsenal. We had to march slowly, and our advance was not without peril. Enormous crowds had gathered along our way, seeking, they said, to seize the prisoners from us at any cost. They threatened a street battle at any moment. The secessionists stationed themselves in masses along the sidewalks, revolvers in their hands, and threats against "Hessian

---

9. Rowan/Primm, 211, 246-8, *WP,* 29 May 1861, on his death and elaborate military funeral. See also Winter, 64-67.

Peter Joseph Osterhaus, major of rifles in Boernstein's regiment, as a brigadier general. Photograph by Hoelke and Benecke, c. 1863. Courtesy of the Missouri Historical Society.

mercenaries" in their mouths.[10] They placed their wives and children in front of themselves, so that the troops would not shoot. It gradually grew darker the farther we went, and we contemplated the most dreadful prospect of a street battle at night, when one would not be able to distinguish friend from foe. It was only the calm, firm attitude of the troops that overawed the mob. The prisoners were also calm and silent, and they did not allow themselves to be provoked. The return march went without disturbance. But I only breathed freely once I turned into Fourteenth Street and headed nearer the southern neighborhoods inhabited by Germans.

When we reached Carondelet Street, however, a new peril threatened us. An endless mass of people filled the broad street, mostly women and children, whose their men were marching in the rank and file. The news of the treacherous attack at Camp Jackson, in which volunteers had fallen victim as both dead and wounded, had already reached them, and this had produced great distress and bitterness. Each of the women believed and feared her husband or her son was among the fallen, and rumor had greatly exaggerated our losses. There was a terrible bitterness among the women, who shouted threats from all sides. They wanted to revenge themselves on the cause of all this misfortune and lynch the secessionist prisoners. The columns had to be drawn closer, and it was only after long, kindly persuasion and the assurance that each would receive justice that the upset was dampened enough for us to bring our prisoners uninjured to the arsenal. It was eight in the evening. My people had been under arms for eleven hours. I myself had not left the saddle for as long. Yet it was another two hours before we had our desired rest, because the prisoners first had to be taken down in a list and swear never again to bear arms against the Union. All of them took this oath except one captain, Emmet Macdonald, who preferred to remain in the arsenal as a prisoner of war. With few exceptions, however, those who had sworn did not allow themselves to be hindered in the least from fighting against the Union in the ranks of the secessionists in the coming months.

At ten o'clock at night, after all formalities had been completed, we were finally able to leave the arsenal and return to the Marine Hospital, where we were greeted with jubilation and an illumination of all windows. We were tired unto death, however, and virtually starved. We desired nothing so much as to eat, drink and then to have undisturbed rest, all of which were supplied to us in plenty.

---

10. German soldiers in America were inevitably called "Hessian mercenaries," recalling Germans hired by the British crown to serve in the American Revolutionary War. This term is also witnessed in the chapter, "Camp Jackson," in Francis Grierson's minor masterpiece, *The Valley of Shadows*, Harold P. Simonson, ed. (New Haven, Conn.: College and University Press, 1970), 189-92.

In the meantime, the situation in the city had become quite stormy and agitated. Improvised assemblies took place in front of the Planter's House, at the court house and at other points. Enraged speeches were held against the "damned Dutch," "cheap Hessian mercenaries" who dared to fire on native-born Americans. Aliens had been so bold as to seize the troops of the state of Missouri and take them to the arsenal. This was a national insult that must be revenged by the extermination of all Germans. The orations grew ever more violent, and agitation grew ever higher. Individual Germans were mistreated on the street and a few murdered in a cowardly fashion. Soon the raging mob went into motion, intending to take their revenge for the dissatisfactions of the day by destroying the print shops of the *Missouri Democrat* or the *Anzeiger des Westens.* Yet the state police, which had hitherto openly or covertly taken the side of the secessionists, now understood that the mantle of power had fallen on other shoulders. They accommodated themselves to the new situation. Chief of Police McDonough threw himself and his entire police force in the way of the advancing mob, declaring that it was his duty to keep peace and order and to defend persons and property, and that he would counter force with force. If his people were too weak, he declared, everything would still be fine, because the dreaded Black Rifles already occupied the printing shop of the *Democrat* and would institute a dreadful bloodbath if it were attacked. The tactic worked. In the place of rage there arose quiet reason, and gradually the mob dispersed. In the meantime, another mob of almost a thousand advanced on the printing shop of the *Anzeiger* with the same intent, but here had been placed two companies of the Fourth Regiment, blocking the street at both ends. When the first threats of the crowd led the commandant to call out to load weapons and fix their long bayonets, peace and reason quickly returned. A quarter-hour later the street was empty and dead.

Thus ended that fateful Friday, the tenth of May, which the *Missouri Republican* the next day baptized Black Friday.

The Tenth of May and Its Consequences
(1861)

It was only the next morning that the extensive consequences of boldly taking the secessionist Camp Jackson could be seen in St. Louis, in Missouri, in the entire Union, in the southern slave states and particularly at the seat of government in Washington. Despite the fact that South Carolina had left the government at the end of 1860 and that the other southern states followed during January and February, there had not yet been any violent conflicts between the North and the South. Both parts were arming and gathering their forces for future operations, but all larger encounters had thus far been avoided; each side still hoped to achieve its goal through negotiation. In this way, President Lincoln had been solemnly inaugurated in Washington, very near to Richmond, Virginia, seat of the rebel government. In the same way the Southerners had come into possession of the great arsenal at Harper's Ferry and the government naval yards at Norfolk, more through deceit than force. The only open act of war yet undertaken was the bombardment of Fort Sumter in Charleston harbor, where Major Anderson and defending federal troops had to capitulate after three days of bombardment due to their lack of food and munitions, surrendering on condition of evacuating the garrison; more stones and mortar fell than human lives.[1] After this catastrophe, a long armistice set in, not negotiated but casually observed by both sides, ending only by the taking of Camp Jackson and its bloody sequel.

A military operation resulting in the seizure of the secessionist camp, the conquest of extensive booty of war and with the preemptive suppression of rebellion in a slave state—an engagement with the result of 16 dead, 50 wounded and 1,200 prisoners—was an important and ominous event for those still inclined to wait and negotiate and for a time still beguiled by its illusions. As a result, it had considerable influence beyond the borders of Missouri.

The impression in Missouri itself was enormous. The bitter rage of slavery men, who had had their plans thwarted and their hopes destroyed, was dreadful. Their chief mouthpiece, the *Missouri Republican*, brought out the very next morning a rabidly foaming article. Half a dozen headlines in bold type read, "Black Friday," "German Mercenaries Murder American

---

1. Here and elsewhere, Boernstein describes the bombardment of Fort Sumter as taking three days. In truth, the long siege culminated in a bombardment lasting thirty-three hours and ending in capitulation.

Citizens," "Old Men, Women and Children Killed by Bold Soldiery," and other similar provocations. The article itself described the self-defense of the troops against unjustified assault as an assassination of state sovereignty. It was a bold attack on honor, life and persons of free citizens by a band of mercenaries deteriorated into common criminals. All was portrayed in the most hateful colors, and revenge was called for against the alien intruders.

This rabid article in the *Missouri Republican* and similar portrayals in other papers of the events of the previous day combined to revive and increase (if possible) the agitation of the previous evening. Everywhere crowds discussed developments in the bitterest manner. The mayor of St. Louis issued a proclamation commanding all taverns and inns to close and to cease selling alcohol. He also advised parents not to permit their children on the street and all residents not to leave their houses after dark. This proclamation was little observed, however, and people talked and drank themselves into more of a blind rage. Not suspecting this state of affairs, I granted several men of my regiment a brief leave on the morning of 11 May in order to take care of their businesses or to visit parents. Most of them did not return to the Marine Hospital until it grew dark, with clothing torn, faces beaten bloody and all the signs of having suffered mistreatment. Although they were unarmed and dressed in civilian clothes, they had been recognized as Germans and volunteers, and they were insulted and mistreated by half-drunken gangs. Two of them never returned, and they were never heard of again. It is probable that they were beaten to death and their corpses thrown in the river.

On the afternoon of that same Saturday, 11 May, a battalion of the Sixth Homeguard Regiment marched to the arsenal to be armed there. During their unarmed march to the arsenal, they were insulted by the mob. When they marched back with weapons and came to the center of the city, an enormous crowd formed at the corner of Fifth and Walnut Streets, receiving the troop with mockery and abuse. This assembly shouted the most insulting curses, finally pelting them with a hail of stones and bricks. The Homeguards marched peacefully along their way, opposing the offenses of the mob with quiet contempt. Then, where the column turned into Walnut Street, revolver fire opened on them from the portico of the Presbyterian church, and rifles fired from the upper floors of neighboring houses.

On this treacherous attack from behind, the commandant of the battalion, Lieutenant Colonel White, ordered the troop to halt. They turned about and opened a well-aimed salvo at the attackers. It has never been established how many victims fell, because the rowdies who attacked the troops and were killed or wounded were quickly taken away by their comrades, their mishap hushed up. Several men of the Homeguards were wounded, and two peaceful citizens who happened to be on the street at the time, belonging neither to the Homeguard nor the mob, fell victims of the cowardly attack. Citizen Rebstock had his right arm shattered by a shot, and citizen Niederreuter was shot dead as he emerged into the street from his apartment. The Germans heard the shooting from the Turner Hall. An alarm was sounded, and in a few moments the entire First Volunteer Regiment was armed and on its way to help the Homeguards. At the same moment, General Lyon sent patrols through the city, and the regimental commanders had the areas around their headquarters and stations patrolled by strong detachments. In short, armed force showed itself ready to strike at once and everywhere, so that the cowardly scum of the mob vanished in a cloud of dust and crept away when it saw things had turned serious.[2] Now regret and bad consciences took over, and people came to their senses.

In aristocratic neighborhoods, where the most committed adherents to secession lived, the silliest, most dreadful rumors were being spread. Germans had supposedly sworn to take revenge for the cowardly attacks and would rise in hordes the following day, a Sunday, marching against the center of the city. There they would punish the friends and adherents of slavery, plundering their houses and setting them afire. It was thought in particular that the Black Rifles had sworn neither to give nor accept quarter, not even sparing the child in its mother's womb. With these old wives' tales and the bite of their own bad consciences, the people became so agitated that they did not even want to wait until morning to flee St. Louis, doomed as it was to destruction by German revenge, for the safety of Illinois.

And so Sunday morning presented the spectacle of a general flight of the "upper ten," the rich, proud slaveholders, who had looked down on the Germans only twenty-four hours before with such contempt. Coaches from every livery stable, furniture wagons, drays, and every sort of vehicle was requisitioned. The best furniture, trunks and chests with clothing and linen, women and children, and anything that was not nailed down were loaded up. In an endless procession, a column of wagons extended down to the river, waiting to be taken by ferry to the hospitable shore of Illinois. This exodus lasted until late into the evening, and livery stables and carriage owners did a wonderful business, for they were paid thirty dollars and more for a wagon.

I need not remark that all of these dreadful rumors were mere phantoms of overheated imagination and empty humbug, and that the Germans had no thought of acting against citizens in the center of the city. They remained peacefully in their wards, determined only to defend themselves against intentional injustices. In this hour of anxiety and terror, however, anxious slaveholders sent masses of telegrams to Washington. Partly to General

---

2. Rowan/Primm, 213-17, *WP*, 15 May 1861.

Harney, whom they beseeched to return at once to St. Louis and establish order before all were murdered, partly to Edward Bates,[3] Lincoln's attorney general, whom they beseeched as a citizen of St. Louis to protect his home town from plunder and destruction at the hands of the Germans. In all of these telegrams and as many letters, the episode at Camp Jackson was portrayed in the coarsest colors as an unjustified act of force, despicable murder by bestial soldiery. Such was the first impression that Washington received of developments in St. Louis.

Yet this unreasoned agitation, the panicky fear and cowardly flight, had the positive result of breaking the back of the secessionist movement in St. Louis. From this moment on the city had no more distress or revolt. All who fled returned to St. Louis within a few days when the feared Germans remained utterly peaceful; they did so in a much more subdued mood, however, conducting themselves more modestly and carefully than when they had left a few days before.

General Harney arrived in all haste from Washington on 12 May, bearing himself like a great personage. As military commandant of the Missouri District, he wanted to dissolve the Homeguard regiments at once, believing they had no legal standing. He also wanted to remove the volunteer regiments from St. Louis and scatter them across the state in small detachments. At least those had been the pressing demands of the secessionists, and General Harney was inclined to fulfill them as completely as possible. But at the first meeting and discussion with General Lyon and Frank P. Blair in which Harney revealed his plans, Blair presented an order from Secretary of War Cameron legitimizing the creation of the Homeguard regiments. With this same order, the volunteer regiments were commanded to guard the arsenal and federal property in St. Louis for the time being. General Harney had to submit to the orders of his superior, so he restricted himself to issuing a proclamation in St. Louis to the population of Missouri in his own pacific and conciliatory style, calling for peace and order. Four companies of regular infantry with two cannon were stationed in the center of the city near the courthouse to help municipal authorities keep order and to avoid conflicts between the two sides. Because all railway stations and the outer areas of the city were occupied by the volunteer regiments and Homeguards, keeping strict control over comings and goings, military

---

3. Edward Bates (1793-1869), born in Virginia, arrived in Missouri in 1814, and was licensed to practice law in 1816. He was a Whig member of Congress, 1827-29, and settled in St. Louis in 1842. He declined the secretary of war post under Millard Fillmore in 1850 and was elected judge of the St. Louis Land Court as a Benton Democrat with strong German support, 1853-56. After serving as attorney general under Lincoln, 1861-64, Bates stridently opposed Radicals in Missouri in 1865 and after. *DAB*, 2: 48-9; *BDUSC*, 588.

advances from the interior of the state were hindered. Gradually, agitation died out from a lack of fuel. As a result, the repose of St. Louis was no longer disturbed and business resumed its normal course.

The impression that the taking of Camp Jackson had in the capital city, Jefferson City, was almost greater than in St. Louis itself.[4] The governor and his cabinet were there, and the state legislature was in session. With one blow the entire plan for secession, which these brave people had worked on for months, was ruined. Plans had been made for armed bands from all parts of the state to converge on a particular day in St. Louis; an expected fifteen thousand men uniting with the force in Camp Jackson to take and occupy St. Louis and seize the arsenal. A night session of the legislature was called at once, which the majority attended in a rage, armed with revolvers. The bitterest, most passionate speeches were made, the most insane motions presented. Lyon, Blair, the other regimental commanders and I were declared outlaws, free to be killed by anyone. The city of St. Louis was to be destroyed with fire and sword and the place sown with ashes and salt, and similar mad, silly stuff. Since the session grew ever more tumultuous, there were no formal resolutions. On the rumor that General Lyon was on the march toward Jefferson City with the Volunteers, they dissolved in wild disorder. Later, as military commander in Jefferson City, I read in the capitol the minutes of this and other secret sessions of the legislature with shock, and after reading them for my own entertainment, I sent them to the Committee of Public Safety in St. Louis.

With the natural exception of the South, the news of Lyon's energetic deed and the taking of Camp Jackson worked throughout the entire Union in an encouraging and reinforcing direction. The last hesitations vanished, and with them any inclination to negotiate; it was necessary to act instead, quickly and energetically, and this news solidified public opinion more and more.

What was less good was the impression the news made at the seat of the government in Washington. I have already remarked about the one-sided and hateful style in which the first reports reaching Washington were framed. They made a deep impression on President Lincoln, by nature a gentle, good-natured man who only hardened in the course of events. In addition, Attorney General Edward Bates, himself a Missourian married to a leading slaveholding family, stormed poor Lincoln without mercy to disavow Lyon and Blair, arguing that the greatest care would be needed in the border slave states such as Missouri and Kentucky to keep from pressing them into secession, in which case the Union would be irretrievably lost. Wealthy businessmen in St. Louis, who did their major business with the South, and

---

4. Rowan/Primm, 212-13, *WP,* 15 May 1861.

who felt themselves unwilling tributaries to the North for its industrial articles, almost all stood in their sympathies on the side of secession. They sent two of their most respected citizens, James E. Yeatman and Hamilton R. Gamble[5] as deputies to Washington to join hand in hand with Edward Bates against Blair and Lyon, with the goal of revoking their measures.

But Blair had his own support in Lincoln's cabinet in the form of his brother Montgomery Blair, who was postmaster general and had great influence over Lincoln. Further, Blair sent his brother-in-law Franklin A. Dick to Washington and provided him with C. L. Bernays, my coeditor, as a representative of the German element. Bernays had been with Lincoln in Springfield on the day of his election as president, remaining with him through the night as the telegraphic reports of the election flowed in. He has often described this night as the most interesting in his entire life,[6] and he only left Lincoln as morning dawned and his election was irreversible. Bernays thus came to Washington both as a friend and confidant of Lincoln, and he was warmly received. In a private conversation, Bernays described the situation in Missouri to the president, eloquently informing him of the hopes and concerns of the friends of the Union, the loyalty of the Germans to the federal government, and all of the other local factors. Bernays portrayed the taking of Camp Jackson and its absolute necessity in a non-partisan, objective manner, presenting him convincing documents. Lincoln appeared quite satisfied with this conversation and from then on seemed to evaluate the situation in Missouri correctly.

Governor Jackson's arming and military organization of the state proceeded apace, and pro-Union citizens continued to be persecuted and mistreated everywhere. When General Harney finally entered negotiations with General Price,[7] commander of the state militia, and signed a formal

---

5. James E. Yeatman (1818-1901), born in Tennessee, came to St. Louis in 1842, retiring from banking in 1860. He was noted as a Unionist, but opposed to radicalism. He organized the Western Sanitary Commission in September 1861, which made a major contribution to the humane treatment of wounded or invalid soldiers. See *EHSL*, 4: 2563-5; *DAB*, 20: 606-7; William E. Parrish, "The Western Sanitary Commission," *Civil War History* 36 (1990): 17-35. Hamilton R. Gamble (1798-1864) was born and raised in Virginia, settled in Missouri in 1818, served as a lawyer and a judge, and as a member of the Missouri Supreme Court he rejected Dred Scott's petition for freedom. He retired in 1859 and went to Pennsylvania, returning only due to the political crisis in 1861. He was a leader of the Constitutional Unionists, and he was made governor of Missouri in June 1861. He opposed the immediate abolition of slavery. He died in office. *DAB*, 7: 120-1.

6. Rowan/Primm, 129-31.

7. Rowan/Primm, 236, *AW,* 23 May 1861, with the text of the Price-Harney agreement. Sterling Price (1809-1867) was born in Virginia and came to Missouri in 1830. He was a member of Congress in 1844. Price served with distinction in the Mexican War,

agreement completely ignoring the interests of the Union, M[ontgomery]. Blair, F[ranklin]. Dick, and Bernays energetically pressed Lincoln to remove General Harney and replace him with Lyon. On 16 May, after long resistance, Lincoln placed his signature on Harney's removal, but he directed Blair to use the order only in the case of extreme necessity. Frank Blair kept the order in his desk until reliable reports arrived from all sides that the newly organized State Militia displayed the flag of secession everywhere, that Union people were being generally persecuted, and that the governor was negotiating with the Indians of the border territories to use the savage redskins as allies against Union troops.[8] When Harney did absolutely nothing despite Blair's admonitions, even rebuffing all Unionists who sought to organize for Volunteer or Homeguard service with the statement, "The government has too many troops already," Frank Blair could no longer hesitate. On 30 May he sent Major B. Farrar to General Harney with Special Order of the United States War Department of 16 May, No. 135, which read as follows:

> Brig. Gen. W. S. Harney is relieved of his command of the Department of the West, and is granted leave of absence until further orders.
>
> L. Thomas
> Adjutant General[9]

Thus General Harney vanished from the scene, never to return. In his place as commandant of Missouri stepped General Lyon, and from this point on energetic action was possible.

Among the documents on the taking of Camp Jackson is my affidavit on the events of 10 May, which I wrote out and confirmed under oath in

---

becoming a brigadier general. He served one term as Missouri governor, and was president of the Missouri State Convention, which decided against secession. Along with Ben McCullough, he defeated Lyon at Wilson's Creek on 10 August 1861 and lost at Pea Ridge in March 1862. In Fall, 1864, he led a major cavalry raid into Missouri, where he was defeated at Westport on 23 October 1864. He fled to Mexico at the end of the war, establishing a colony for former Confederates, but he returned to St. Louis after the collapse of Maximilan's régime. He died of cholera in St. Louis. See Christopher Phillips in *EC*, 3: 1251-2; Winter, 121-22.

8. Some Cherokee always had strong sympathies with the slaveholding South, and negotiations between Albert Pike and Chief John Ross in late summer, 1861, led to the formation of Cherokee units under Confederate leadership. One such unit served under Pike's command at Pea Ridge in March 1862. See *EC*, 1: 296-7. The alliance with Native Americans was exploited by pro-Union propaganda to portray the Confederacy as uncivilized.

9. *WROR*, section I, vol. 3, 374.

response to Blair's pressing request. I felt myself all the more bound to do so because Lincoln knew me personally and regarded me as worthy of esteem, so that he would believe my calmly objective report. Further, because the fire had begun from my regiment, I felt myself responsible for it to some degree. This document, which Bernays later told me Lincoln read repeatedly and examined in all its details, made a great impression on the president. It was supported in essence by the other documents, also affidavits. Thus the howls of the secessionist noisemakers lost their impact, and Lyon and Blair were confirmed in their positions to work even more effectively in the future.

The draft of this sworn report is still in my hands, and I insert it here as material for future historians. It reads:

The report of Colonel H. Boernstein, Commanding the II. Missouri Volunteer Regiment, United States Army.

In obedience to the general order, I took my command, consisting of eight companies of the Second Missouri Volunteers; three companies of regular infantry, commanded by Captain Totten and Lieutenant Sexton; my two rifle companies under Major Osterhaus; and two cannon. I took the position allotted me behind Camp Jackson on the west of the encampment.

After the surrender of the camp, I received the order through Adjutant F. A. Dick to march up along the northern side of the camp and form a column behind Colonel Blair's regiment. Half of the prisoners of war were enclosed in Colonel Blair's column, and the other half, more than six hundred officers and men, were to be escorted in the column of my regiment. The column was organized in this fashion: as *avant-garde* there was Major Osterhaus with two companies of rifles, then Captain Totten with three companies of regular infantry, and finally my regiment with the war prisoners allotted to us. Because of the enormous group of men involved, the columns could move only very slowly, finally coming to a halt on the high road. A number of individuals, many of them drunk, gathered in increasing numbers around the troops and covered them with the most common insults and curses, insulting both officers and men. The cries of "Hurrah for Jefferson Davis" alternated with such dark threats as, "Today is your day, but tomorrow will be our day!" or "We will hang you all, Boernstein and Blair first of all!" The soldiers remained quiet and serious in rank and file, and there was no response to these insults. The only response was that the regimental band occasionally played the National Anthem and "Yankee Doodle." The column could not move, for Colonel Blair's regiment also stood still as a result of some hindrance. During this time I saw that Richard J. Howard, the U.S. Collector of St. Louis, was surrounded by a group of intoxicated individuals and being pelted with insults. He was thus a witness, as an official of the United States, to the entire episode, and I would refer to his report.

Finally the column got into motion again and moved slowly forward, about a hundred paces. Then came another obstacle, and we stood still. My *avant-garde* and the first two companies of regulars had just passed a building under construction on the south side of the street. Suddenly, as we halted, shots came from the building, from the trees and from the camp fence, and bullets went whistling past our heads. A quick look around revealed that about fifteen or twenty men with revolvers were firing from the window of the house under construction, while others fired from the limbs of the trees and from behind the fence at the entrance to the camp. There followed some confusion due to this unexpected attack. Two men from my regiment fell dead, and Captain Weckerlin of Company B had a bullet pass through his hat, grazing his scalp. My men continued to maintain their calm and made their weapons ready. In this moment I heard firing from my left and, as I looked around, saw the last section of regulars formed in a front, firing on the attackers. At the same time a company of the Third Regiment, which stood at the entrance to the camp, fired on the mob for the same reason. The firing spread to the ranks of my own regiment, where the people fired due to the instinct of self-preservation and without command.

Lieutenant Colonel Schaefer and I jumped down at once from our horses and threw ourselves into the ranks of the first battalion, ordering the people to cease fire at once; in fact, we threatened to cut down anyone who fired. As a result, the firing ceased at last, but not without taking victims. I can declare here under oath, however, that all of those who fell with weapons in their hands and on whom the troops fired deserved their fate. One individual, who was shot down out of a high tree, had five six-shooters with him in his hiding place, of which he had already emptied three. The men had endured curses, challenges, threats and finally the throwing of stones and sticks without resorting to their weapons. However, when one of the rowdies was bold enough to step up to an officer in Major Laibold's battalion and place a revolver against his breast and threaten to shoot him down, when the shots began ringing out, my soldiers as well returned fire. In my regiment, besides two dead, I had three men wounded by shots and two by stones. One of the latter, hit on the temple by a rock, fell unconscious over the edge of the highway and was assaulted by the rowdies, who beat him bloody and tore the clothes from his body in tatters. I am certainly sorry that some innocent victims also fell, but a military expedition to take a camp is no place for onlookers, nor for women and children as spectators. Firing took place without the command of the officers; on the contrary, the officers did their best to halt the fire as soon as possible. I am convinced, incidentally, that if this serious conflict had not taken place by the camp, giving our opponents fair warning and leading them to second thoughts, we would have certainly been attacked by the raging mob along our return march. We would have been in a very dangerous situation. As it was, we still had to endure cursing and dreadful threats on our way via Olive Street, but there were no more serious attacks. I have to remark in addition that, when the shooting began, I called to the prisoners to lie flat on the ground in order not to be hit, which they did, and they remained uninjured except for two who broke ranks in the first confusion, drawing out hidden revolvers and firing on the troops. Both of them were gunned down. The conduct of the arrested officers was rather decent, but the Minute Men conducted themselves during our march through the upper portions of the city in a crude and offensive manner. When we later came to the southern portion of the city, they grew ever quieter and more modest, and in the First Ward, when they saw many Germans gathered, they grew anxious and quite still. So we finally brought them into the arsenal, where we delivered them healthy and well.

Bernays took along many similar sworn accounts of witnesses, concerned especially with particular details. All of them were signed and sworn by honorable, well-known men, and they had a decisive effect on President Lincoln. The time for hesitation and wavering was at an end for Missouri, and the friends of the Union could finally breathe freely.

The Campaign *into the* Interior
(1861)

The removal of General Harney had greatly clarified the situation, and the cause of the Union took a great step forward as a result. To be sure, General Lyon was not put in Harney's place as commander of the entire Western Department. Rather he was simply confirmed as brigadier general of volunteer regiments in Missouri, while military authority over Missouri and the other western states was placed under the control of General McClellan.[1] Still, General Lyon could operate essentially unhindered because his superior, General McClellan, was commanding Union troops in western Virginia and knew virtually nothing about Missouri. This permitted General Lyon to do whatever he wanted in the interior of the state. As soon as Harney laid down his command, Lyon introduced complete supervision of communications by river and railroad, as well as a thorough securing of the city. The troops at his disposal for this amounted to about ten thousand men and consisted almost entirely of German volunteer and Homeguard regiments. All the exterior portions of the city of St. Louis were occupied militarily. At train stations and landings, water and land vehicles were precisely checked for war contraband, receiving passes to continue only after being found in order. This was extremely trying service, involving great responsibility and many discomforts. For example, with my regiment I had to control a frontier of three miles, beginning at Hyde Park on the river and running to St. Charles Plank Road. There the Third Regiment under Colonel Sigel took a similar stretch of the western suburbs reaching to the Pacific Railway, and so it went all the way to the river in the south. The entire greater city was enclosed by an iron belt by land as well as by water, making possible the most precise control.

My headquarters were located at the old water works, where a tent camp was pitched. There a battalion camped, and four cannon were posted at the water works themselves, controlling the entire area. Beside this encampment, called Camp Lincoln, was joined another outpost of my regiment called Fort Scott, while Major Osterhaus' rifle battalion camped at the station of

---

1. George Brinton McClellan (1826-1885) graduated West Point in 1846, resigning his commission in 1857. In 1861 he suppressed secession in western Virginia and he was made commander of the Army of the Potomac on 26 July 1861. He was removed in November 1862 for inaction. He was Democratic nominee for president in 1864. *DAB,* II: 580-5.

the Northern Missouri Railroad. At night, many patrols and relays maintained ties between the various encampments, guarding against the infiltration of suspicious persons or the smuggling of weapons and munitions. Every steamboat had to be hailed in by a competent officer with sufficient troops, then made to land and thoroughly searched. The same occurred with every arriving or departing train. Besides this, many tips on secret caches of weapons or munitions, nocturnal drills of rebels and the like had to be resolved by surprise visits, and drill had to proceed to perfect the maneuverability of the troops.[2]

In the meantime, the removal of General Harney had terrified the governor and his cohorts in Jefferson City, and they now attempted to make an agreement with Lyon, and deceive him as they had always managed to do with Harney. The lawyer T. Gantt[3] and Judge W. A. Hall[4] arranged a meeting of Governor Jackson and his military commander Price with General Lyon, issuing the two chiefs of the secession a letter of safe conduct to guarantee a secure trip from Jefferson City to St. Louis and back. Pocketing this letter, Governor Jackson and General Price came on 10 June by a special train to St. Louis, and the conference with Lyon and Blair took place in the Planter's House. Governor Jackson particularly demanded that federal troops be removed from the state, offering in return to dissolve the state militia. The state of Missouri would declare itself neutral, and neither party would permit any forces crossing the borders of the state. Lyon and Blair rejected this proposal, insisting that the authority of the federal government be maintained, that the protection of the state and its citizens rest with the federal government alone. This remarkable discussion went on for four hours, but it obviously could not lead to a resolution, so they parted without any result.[5]

Governor Jackson and General Price rushed from the Planter's House to the railway station, sprang aboard the locomotive being kept under steam, and rushed off to Jefferson City, afraid of being arrested despite the letter of

---

2. Rowan/Primm, 229-31, *AW,* 23 May 1861.

3. Thomas Tasker Gantt (1814-1889) was born in Maryland, coming to St. Louis as a lawyer in 1839 and working as a partner to Montgomery Blair. Although an unconditional Unionist in 1861, he was an anti-Radical by the end of the Civil War. See *EHSL,* 2, 865-6.

4. William Augustus Hall (1815-1888), born in Maine, graduated from Yale, moved to Randolph County, Missouri, in 1840. He was judge of the state circuit court, 1847-61, a member of the State Constitutional Convention, 1861, and was elected as a Democrat to take the place of a member expelled. He was subsequently reelected, serving 1862-65. *BDUSC,* 1116. His pro-Union sympathies made him subject to severe personal threats, see MHS, Sweringen Papers, M. W. Mitchell, Huntsville, Missouri, to James T. Sweringen, letters of 28 March, 19 June, and 23 September 1861.

5. Rowan/Primm, 254-5, *AW,* 12 June 1861.

CLAIBORNE F. JACKSON,
GOVERNOR OF MISSOURI FROM JANUARY, 1861, TO DECEMBER, 1862.

Claiborne Fox Jackson (1806-62), as portrayed in the Confederate War Journal, *1893. Courtesy of the Missouri Historical Society.*

safe conduct. On the way back, Jackson ordered that the rail bridges over the Gasconade and Osage rivers be burned. This was done right away, breaking all direct rail connections. The next day, Governor Jackson sent dispatches to all the slaveholders, demanding that they arm themselves and join him with their forces. On 12 June there was a further proclamation calling fifty thousand men of the state militia under arms with the words "for the protection of our endangered homes and firesides, and for the defense of their most sacred rights and dearest liberties." This fatal proclamation, which was an open declaration of war against the Union government in Washington, closed with the following apostrophe to the people of Missouri:

> But it is equally my duty to advise you that your first allegiance is due to your own State, and that you are under no obligation whatever to obey the unconstitutional edicts of the military despotism which has enthroned itself at Washington, nor to submit to the infamous and degrading sway of its wicked minions in this State. No brave and true-hearted Missourian will obey one or submit to the other. Rise, then, and drive out ignominiously the invaders who have dared to desecrate the soil which your labors have made fruitful, and which is consecrated by your homes.[6]

With that the die was cast and war declared. The arming and organization of the so-called state militia was pursued with the greatest zeal. Each man between eighteen and fifty years of age had to enter the state militia. At the same time, the governor's messengers were sent to Arkansas, Louisiana, and Texas to ask these states to make an incursion into Missouri with their troops to support the rebellion against federal troops. General Lyon and Blair both saw that it was no longer enough to remain on the defensive, but that an energetic effort had to be made. Only attack could smother the evil at its origin. On 12 June Governor Jackson issued his decree. On the thirteenth, when it became known in St. Louis, Lyon and Blair had already taken all measures to open the battle in the interior of the state. As early as the fourteenth, Colonel Sigel was under way with the Third and Fifth Volunteer Regiments to Rolla to occupy the southwest spur of the Pacific Railway, while on the fifteenth General Lyon and his troops were proceeding on two steamers up the Missouri to Jefferson City.

At the first news in Jefferson City of the movement of federal troops, great distress and panicky terror seized everyone. Governor Jackson and General Price departed Jefferson City in haste, fleeing with about six hundred hastily assembled men of the state militia to Boonville, which had

6. Rombauer, 264-5, 12 June 1861.

been designated as the rendezvous for all state troops. The governor's cabinet and the legislature also disappeared in a cloud of dust, and along with them fled the most thoroughly compromised secessionists. On the evening of the fourteenth, I received the order to go at once the next morning with my regiment to the Pacific Railway in order to be taken to Hermann, which was as far as the route was still intact. In Hermann I would find the steamer *Louisiana* awaiting me, which would then take my regiment to Jefferson City. We departed on the morning of the fifteenth for Hermann and were greeted there with jubilation by the pro-Union German population. We began at once to load the regiment on the steamer *Louisiana.* Getting our troops on board and loading provisions, munitions and the like which we had brought with us took much time; we knew we could count on little in the interior of the state, so that we brought everything from St. Louis. In addition, the Missouri was swollen, so that we only made slow progress upstream.

When it grew dark, we were still about fifty miles from Jefferson City, so that we had to put in and await the break of day. For this purpose, we found a rather open portion of the riverbank, providing a broad view of the area, and we made ready to remain there for the night. The greatest care was called for, as we had been informed that fanatic slaveowners intended to set troop-bearing steamers afire at night, so measures had to be taken for security. The rifle battalion of Major Osterhaus landed and set out a wide picket line that began below the landing on the riverbank and ran in a semi-circle around the boat, ending back at the river above the landing. Within these pickets large campfires were lit, brightly illuminating the area and allowing any approach of suspicious persons to be seen. The same care was observed on the river side of the boat, where a watch was kept on board and the pickets had live ammunition. At the same time, patrols were sent out beyond the pickets to penetrate the area and frustrate any attempts to approach.

One of these patrols, led by my younger son, discovered by dawn's early light a man dressed in urban clothing, obviously not local, who sought to avoid the troops. He was clearly one of the refugees from Jefferson City. When hailed by the patrol, the man tried to flee as quickly as possible, but he was brought to reason when they lowered their weapons and cocked them, warning that he would be shot if he did not stop. His confused, contradictory answers raised the suspicion of the patrol leader even more, so that prisoner was brought to me on board. Here his evasive responses were to no avail, for the captain of the boat recognized him as the secretary of the state treasury.[7] As

---

7. Alfred William Morrison (died 1883), a Democrat of Howard County, was appointed State Treasurer on 6 November 1851, elected in 1852, 1856, and 1860, and his office was "vacated for failure to file an oath of loyalty." *Official Manual, State of Missouri 1991-1992* (Jefferson City, Mo., 1991), 53.

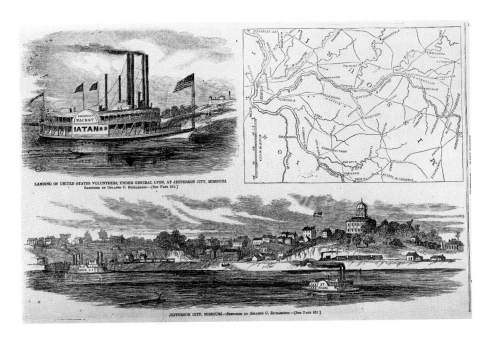

LANDING OF UNITED STATES VOLUNTEERS, UNDER GENERAL LYON, AT JEFFERSON CITY, MISSOURI.
SKETCHED BY ORLANDO C. RICHARDSON.—[SEE PAGE 431.]

JEFFERSON CITY, MISSOURI.—SKETCHED BY ORLANDO C. RICHARDSON.—[SEE PAGE 431.]

"Jefferson City, Missouri. Sketched by Orlando C. Richardson." Boernstein acted as military commandant here for several weeks in 1861. Wood engraving in Harper's Weekly, *vol. 5, July 6, 1861, p. 420. Courtesy of the Missouri Historical Society.*

soon as we established his identity, I had him searched. We discovered on him $100,000 of good notes of the Bank of Missouri, which he said were property of the state treasury entrusted to him. I took the secretary of the treasury and his money into custody, delivering them both to General Lyon the next afternoon when we arrived in Jefferson City. Lyon let the secretary of the treasury go, and he redeposited the money in the state treasury, which was placed under my supervision.

When we landed in Jefferson City on the afternoon of the sixteenth, we found the other steamers all under steam to take General Lyon and his expedition upriver to Boonville. The *Louisiana* also received the order to hold itself ready for departure. I rushed to the capitol to report to General Lyon, and I found him about to depart, issuing his last orders. The troops were already marching on board, and in the few minutes we had to speak, Lyon told me that he could afford to lose no time. He had to depart to pursue the governor and the state troops and to seize the camp of the secessionists near Boonville before this gathering could take on more threatening dimensions. He told me that I was to remain as military commandant in Jefferson City, but he could only leave me three companies of my regiment; he had to take all the other companies with him on his expedition. Still, I could eventually organize Homeguard companies, and in necessity Adjutant General Chester Harding would send me reinforcements from the arsenal. When I asked for instructions, he said that the most important thing was that I should keep his rear free. I was also to watch the river closely and inspect all steamships, and I was particularly to see to it that his munitions and provisions were sent to him punctually and securely from St. Louis to wherever he should be. In Jefferson City itself, the state government and the legislature had fled, and the state administration, consisting largely of secessionists, had also dissolved; I should therefore take executive authority provisionally into my own hands, caring particularly for peace, order and the security of persons and property.

I was to deal with these municipal affairs by choosing three or four reliable men as advisors, respectable old citizens and good Union men, and I should allow myself to be led by their experiences and views. As far as the affairs of state government went, Lyon empowered me to use those members of the state government who returned to their posts as soon as they had sworn an oath of loyalty to the United States. I was to keep them under my own control, see that they were capable of functioning and see that they would not be exploited to do anything against the Union or the legitimate government of the United States, or to help the secessionists. An hour passed during this discussion, significant in every manner, which was ended by the report that everyone was aboard and the steamers were ready for departure. Farewells were done in all haste. General Lyon promised to send me more detailed instructions, and Blair told me on his departure, "Don't worry about any instructions, act in keeping with the circumstances and your own best judgment!" Then they all rushed on board. Salutes thundered, cheers for the Union were stormed, the band played "Hail Columbia," and the steamers labored upstream until they vanished from our gaze.

I returned to the capitol in the state capital city, where I had placed my headquarters. First of all I ordered security arrangements for this exposed position. With three companies of 120 men each, I was supposed to oversee steamer traffic on the river; keep peace and order in the capital itself, hitherto the very center of secession; watch the region like a hawk; and not permit the slightest disorder. On top of that, I was to guard the entire Pacific Railway from St. Louis to Sedalia, including the bridges being rebuilt; make communications between the two banks of the river impossible; and above all else, as Blair had pressingly advised me, watch and dominate the two bordering counties of Boone and Howard, which were the blackest in the slavery question, sending frequent expeditions through them. All of this was to be done with 360 men, of whom three-quarters were combatants. I did not have a single cannon, not even a drummer boy, for Lyon had taken even these. If the secessionists had understood their craft a bit better, they could have taken my three companies and me some lovely summer night in the first days of our abandonment without anything to be done about it. There could have been no hope for reinforcements from St. Louis, because all disposable forces were in the field, partly with General Lyon and partly with Colonel Sigel. The federal government in Washington was allowing events in Missouri to run their course, showing the greatest indifference and carelessness.

Volunteer regiments were under arms everywhere in Illinois, Wisconsin, Iowa and Kansas, and an order from Washington would have brought all these eager troops to Missouri. Such numerical superiority alone would have been enough to drive the secessionist gangs out of Missouri, to expel the rebels from Arkansas, and bring the entire right bank of the Mississippi with its tributaries into the possession of the Union. But none of that happened. These troops were held inactive in their states for months, and they were then sent to places that needed them much less than sorely-pressed Missouri. The weak, indecisive administration of Cameron's War Department and the hesitation and palsy in government circles in Washington bore primary guilt for the first defeats of federal troops and the excessive length of this unfortunate war. It was only once Stanton took over the War Department and Lincoln grew harder and more autonomous that the situation improved.[8]

---

8. Edwin Stanton (1814-1869), a capable lawyer from Ohio who settled in Washington, D.C., to plead before the Supreme Court, was briefly attorney general under Buchanan, December 1860 to March 1861, then although a Democrat, secretary of war for Lincoln and Johnson, 1862-68; noted for his energy and overbearing manner. *DAB*, 17: 517-21.

The Capitol, Jefferson City, Missouri, in the 1850s. The building served as Boernstein's headquarters during his occupation of the town. Daguerreotype by Thomas M. Easterly, 1852. Missouri Historical Society. Easterly collection no. 127.

The result was that all of the pressing demands by General Lyon, all of the representations by Blair for sending reinforcements to Missouri, remained without success of any sort. Even when neighboring military commanders wanted to send assistance in response to pressing pleas, Washington would countermand orders and then usually send the troops to places less threatened than Missouri. Inactivity, *laisser-aller* and *laissez-faire,* appeared to be the leading principles of the entire military policy, and just as Lyon and Blair were left to themselves and their own limited strength, so Sigel was sent from Rolla toward Springfield and the Arkansas border with inadequate forces, and I was left behind in a difficult position, in the center of the state, with three companies whose men in even the best case were only recruits.

But all this reasoning helped not a bit and did not improve our situation. It was a matter of conforming to conditions and dealing according to my best judgment. I had my soldiers arm, and I explained to the officers and men as clearly as I could how we were almost alone, able to rely only on ourselves. We could figure only on our own alertness, strict performance of duty, decisiveness and valor. I remarked that we were in an isolated, perhaps hopeless position whose tenure was of the greatest importance for the whole; hence each individual must do his duty fully and precisely, just as all of us together must do our duty. I then established a temporary bivouac for the men in the three companies in the great hall of the house of representatives, and the officers were quartered in the hall of the senate. I myself took over the chamber of the secretary of state, and I never had time by day or night to enjoy the use of any other apartment.

First of all, the necessary pickets had to be set around the capitol and patrols organized to pass through town by the hour and care for peace and order. I invited the former governor Tom Price,[9] the German state senator Bruns,[10] and

---

9. Thomas L. Price (1809-1870), born in Virginia, came to Missouri in 1831 and settled in Jefferson City. As a Democrat of Cole County, he was lieutenant governor of Missouri, 1849-53, served as a general of state militia in 1847, and commissioned a brigadier general by Lincoln. *Official Manual, State of Missouri 1991-1992* (Jefferson City, Mo., 1991); Adolph Schroeder, Carla Schulz-Geisberg, eds., *Hold Dear, As Always Jette, a German Immigrant Life in Letters* (Columbia: University of Missouri Press, 1988), 179 n. 27.

10. Johann Bernhard (Dr. Bernhard) Bruns (1798-1864), married Henrietta (Jette) Geisberg (1813-1899) in 1832 and emigrated to America in 1835, establishing the community of Westphalia, Missouri; moved to Jefferson City in 1854. He lost two sons in the early combat of the Civil War. Bruns was commissioned a major in the Union Army and was serving as mayor of Jefferson City when he died. His wife Jette ran a virtual salon of radical German legislators in Jefferson City. Contrary to Boernstein's memory, Bruns was never a state senator. See Schroeder, Schulz-Geisberg, *Hold Dear,* 7-14.

a third citizen (whose name I have forgotten), to a meeting. There we drafted a proclamation to the population and published it the next morning.[11] After discussing and deciding this and other necessary things, I could finally go to rest with the elevating awareness of bearing the well being and woe of the whole on my shoulders as military governor of the state of Missouri. I could lay myself down and sleep the sleep of the just. But I got neither bed nor rest, for we were all too excited. The posts had to be visited again in the night, and the patrols had to be made ready. The officers leading the patrols were as yet unfamiliar with the town, and they were very nervous. After their return there were unsettling reports, whose truth had to be checked through other patrols. The result was that no one came to any peace. We passed the night in the senate chamber chattering and smoking cigars until it was day and the duties of service claimed us once again.

---

11. Rowan/Primm, 265-6, *AW,* 20 June 1861.

Military Government
(1861)

After the excitement of the first days and the enthusiasm with which we greeted advancing into the state's interior and opening the Missouri campaign, the next morning serious life began with all its cares and burdens. As early as the next day it became clear to me that I was in the presence of total chaos, a general collapse, and that everything needed to be done if the ordinary course of civil life were not to stop entirely. The governor and his secessionist brotherhood had fled in a cowardly manner, his cabinet and the legislature had vanished in a cloud of dust, and the legislature had even dissolved itself. Courts no longer sat to judge cases; public works were suspended; no taxes were being paid because, with the real question who was to be paid, the taxpayers chose the most prudent resolution and paid nothing. I faced this measureless confusion with no other commission than that given me orally by Lyon, who for his part was not entitled to make such a commission. In this situation there was no time for questions or consideration; rather, it was a matter of *à la guerre comme à la guerre.*[1] It was necessary to act without worrying greatly about later consequences. The fact that to act I had only three hundred soldiers and not one cent of money, and I relied on undependable ship traffic for my ties with St. Louis, since the railroads had not yet been rebuilt, and that I had to struggle with the hostility or at best the mistrust of the population—all were factors that made my mission difficult. In my heart, I envied my comrades who marched without cares into a fresh, joyful war. I had to lead the precarious existence of a military governor, heaped with responsibilities and activities, burdened with hundreds of cares and concerns, and possessing neither the legal authority nor the necessary resources. The fact that General Lyon never sent me the thorough written instructions he had promised was both natural and excusable in the tumult of war. I did write down his oral instructions immediately after our discussion, but I soon found that Blair's word of farewell, "Don't worry about any instructions, act in keeping with the circumstances and your own best judgment!" remained the only instructions I needed for practical action.

My first duty was to pacify the agitation and concern of the population, which had been surprised, terrified, even numbed by the sudden turn of

---

1. French, "To war as if to war."

events. Two days before, the secessionists had been masters of the government, the legislature, the state, and the town. The rebel flag had been displayed everywhere. Secessionists were in charge, making dire threats against the Union and its adherents. Hurrahs for Jefferson Davis sounded in the taverns, in the chambers of the Legislature and on the streets. Then overnight the witchery had vanished, fleeing in every direction. The star-spangled banner of the Union waved once more from the apex of the capitol, and federal troops held the state capital under occupation. In addition to the stress from this sudden change of scenery, there was also concern for the security of property. Slaveholders feared in all seriousness that the volunteer regiments, made up entirely of abolitionists, would forcefully take their slaves and free them. Most owners of Negro slaves, particularly slave breeders and slave traders, sought to bring their black wares into security as quickly as possible. A literal exodus began in which slaves were sent to southern counties or even to Southern states in masses of smaller and greater size, under the control of overseers. In response to the pressing desire of my civilian advisers, I stressed in my proclamation to the population that I would protect and preserve the property of residents. At the same time, I sent out search patrols that stopped all such columns of slaves and brought them back to town to their masters. This could be done in individual cases. But the evil, hostile attitude of the majority of the population, the distrust and concern, could not be lifted at once. In the course of the day—as I learned of the small proportion of pro-Union people; as I heard the most distressing reports about the upset mood, lying rumors and the dubious doings of some compromised persons; and when my own informers told me that the proclamation was almost everywhere torn down and destroyed to make room for rebellious placards—I decided to use a means of intimidation which the French call *la terreur blanche,* white or bloodless terror.[2]

---

2. A testimony to the almost flippant quality of Boernstein's arrest and detention policy from a hostile source is given in W. M. Leftwich, *Martyrdom in Missouri*, vol. I (St. Louis: S. W. Book and Publishing Co., 1870) 107-8: "Amongst the first arrests was that of the Rev. J. Ditzler.

"In 1860 and '61 Rev. J. Ditzler was stationed in Jefferson City, in charge of the M. E. Church, South. He was also chaplain to the lower House of the General Assembly.

"After Governor Jackson and General Price had evacuated the State capital and the United States forces under General Lyon had taken possession, Mr. Ditzler remained as a non-combatant, supposing that he would not be molested. In this he was mistaken. He was not allowed long to remain in his quiet study. . . . An 'orderly,' with a guard of seven men, called on him . . ., arrested and marched him through the city, and put him with others in an old meat (smoke) house. He was taunted and sneered at by his guard—the Dutch—though the cracks of the old log house. Mr. Ditzler talked back at them in

My opponents had no notion how small was the military force that stood at my disposal, because from the moment of seizure no one was allowed into the capitol. It was thus a matter of first importance to keep the population believing I had a large force, one with which I could hold the town within bounds. Almost all of my force was divided into small and large detachments that moved back and forth at all hours of day and night, not tolerating the slightest disturbance of the peace. At the same time I had five of the most compromised citizens arrested, including a tavern owner who had been the first to display the secessionist flag in Jefferson City, and I had them brought to the capitol and kept as prisoners in the cellars. These five, who had been denounced as chief conspirators of the rebels by Union people, had fled with the governor in the first terror, but they had returned, or perhaps had been sent back on particular missions, and they provided me with material to intimidate the others. When the news of the arrests spread through town, everything became suddenly very quiet, and a good number of dubious or ambiguous individuals grew anxious and fled the next night.

Naturally, I did not have the slightest right to hold these people, but there was at the time no court operating that could hear a plea of *habeas corpus,* so no one could get them away from me very easily. I kept them in the capitol, subjecting them to daily interrogations that told me many things which compromised others, and so I gained a good notion of how the threads of the movement ran. Once the people had been softened up by the isolation and continuous interrogations, declaring their penitence and regret, I provided them with the hope that they would be able to get away unpunished this time, but that they would have to demonstrate improvement through their future conduct. They promised everything you could think of, including swearing and signing a loyalty oath to the United States. When a delegation of the most respected ladies of the town appeared to me to beg mercy for the prisoners, the rumor having spread in town that all of those arrested were to be shot under martial law, I announced their release, on the condition of future good conduct. I later had no reason to complain about these people. On the contrary, they showed themselves in every circumstance to be the most loyal adherents to the Union.

Then I had to take measures to protect us from any attack by a rebel corps in the field. First of all I requisitioned the prisoners of the large penitentiary and had them build high earthworks around the elevated

---

German, Italian, Spanish, French, Greek, and Hebrew, quoting freely from Schiller, Goethe and other German authors of note, for his own relief and their amusement, until he was reported to Col. Boernstein, Post Commander, and by him unconditionally released, solely on literary grounds. No charges were preferred against him, nor could he ever find out why he was imprisoned."

"Rebel Prisoners in the Dungeon of the State House at Jefferson City." Boernstein's extra-legal arrests of "compromised persons" caused a stir in the town. Wood engraving from a drawing by James A. Guirl, Harper's Weekly, October 5, 1861, p. 633. Courtesy of the Missouri Historical Society.

capitol, under the supervision of my officers. This at least provided security against a *coup de main*, and it made any defense easier. In response to my repeated, pressing requests, the man handling military affairs in St. Louis, Adjutant General Chester Harding, sent two cannon and a section of artillerists. The guns were quickly mounted on the new fortifications. A house search on the basis of an informant produced two cannon barrels buried in a stall, and these were fixed on emergency carriages and set up in the capitol as well, to impress at least by their appearance. Using a seized ferry steamer, expeditions on the river soon put me in the position to seize flatboats, barges and the like forty miles above and below my location. What could be used was taken to Jefferson City, and what was less useful was destroyed on the spot and left sunk. In this way, all links between northern and southern Missouri were cut. An attack from the counties on the opposite shore was made more difficult, if not prevented, while I remained in possession of the ferry boats to undertake expeditions in all directions on the river.

At the same time, I began organizing Homeguard companies in Jefferson City and the immediately surrounding counties, mustering them, swearing them in, and drilling them under sergeants assigned to the task. The greatest hindrance in this remained getting weapons and equipment, which could be obtained from the St. Louis arsenal only after repeated pressure, and only in small quantities. It was once again pro-Union German farmers who provided the core of the Homeguard companies, supplying themselves with weapons at their own cost when those supplied by the government did not suffice. As a result a pro-federal military organization was created in almost all the bordering counties. Eventually organized as battalions and placed under a supreme leadership in Jefferson City cooperating with me, making the guarding of the rebuilt railway and river traffic, as well as pacification of the countryside, much easier. With the aid of this Homeguard, large expeditions were undertaken to more distant counties, consisting of a full company of my troops, which would then rendezvous with Homeguard companies and search for hidden, buried caches of cannon or powder left behind by the fleeing state militia. Each of these expeditions returned with a couple wagons full of confiscated contraband of war, and I soon had a full powder magazine in one of the rooms of the capitol, which I had closely watched in order to prevent disaster.

On return from one of these excursions, Captain Weckerlin of Company B brought me seven prisoners who were all Methodist preachers or other clerics, then the most rabid agitators for secession, and who had been accused in protocols by good Union people of severely compromising themselves, preaching everywhere against the Union and advocating rebellion. They had persecuted, pursued and mistreated adherents to the Union, and some of them were said to have participated in the nocturnal raid and murder of a company of Homeguards in Cole Camp.[3] I had these worthy servants of the Lord locked up in the cellars on bread and water, until I could send them to headquarters in St. Louis with the first available boat, which confinement at least neutralized them in their region for a while.

Soon, however, my son brought me the news that there was great agitation among the men. Their moods had been heated by reports from the returning company of the dreadful deeds of these fanatics, and a lynching was to be feared. I rushed at once with several officers to the rotunda of the capitol, where all the men were gathered, and there I found my worst fears confirmed. The highly agitated men had already suspended seven ropes from the gallery of the rotunda, and I arrived just as a speaker was being applauded for moving that the seven fellows be dragged out of the cellars and hanged. When I entered with my officers it fell instantly still, but the uncanny, shy eyes of the people told me that they had not given up their intentions. Calmly, without any comment, I ordered the captains to form up their companies and place them in front of the capitol, because an important report had arrived that would make necessary a new dispatch of troops. The command was instantly obeyed. In keeping with instructions, the captains marched their companies out of town, while half a company remained in the capitol under my son August. As soon as the other troops were out of sight, I had the prisoners fetched in order to move them as soon as possible and withdraw them from the revenge of my aroused men.

Fortunately, the steamer *January* had arrived a few hours before from St. Louis with a large guard force, on its way to take provisions and munitions to General Lyon in Boonville. I had my son gather the prisoners into the center of his half-company. After I told them how close they had come to receiving just punishment for their shameful deeds, they were paraded through the entire town, where everyone knew them, and wherever there was a Union flag they had to bare their heads and bow. Then they were brought on board the steamer and given to the commandant of the guards as prisoners, along with a sealed letter to the post commander in Boonville, Colonel J. C. Stevenson. In the evening, when the other companies returned from their forced march, I gave them a severe tongue lashing as they stood at attention. Briefly and pointedly detailing the despicable nature of their intentions and the shame that they could have brought on the regiment, I informed them that the prisoners had already been sent on for investigation and punishment. That settled this unpleasant episode in a peaceful manner. A few days later the returning steamer bore a response from Colonel Stevenson, saying that he had received the prisoners and that he had them

---

3. The massacre at Cole Camp on 19 June 1861 will be treated in greater detail later.

hard at work digging ditches in the fortifications of Boonville. I never did hear what eventually happened to them.

General Lyon reached Boonville on the eighteenth, there scattering the state militia lined up under the command of General Price. Their entire camp was taken with rich supplies, and the governor and the remnant of the rebel troops were driven in wild flight to the southwest of the state. Lyon now prepared to pursue the scattered enemy, to drive them even farther toward the Arkansas border and, through a combined attack with Sigel's expedition, out of the state. This success made my own position in Jefferson City less exposed, and so it was less painful for me that General Lyon took away another one of my companies. Another boat arrived going upstream with munitions and provisions for General Lyon, and I received the command to send a strong guard for the boat for the stretch from Jefferson City to Boonville. For this I assigned Company C under Captain Bendel, but once they arrived in Boonville, they were not permitted to return. Instead, they were ordered to accompany the other companies under Schäfer and Osterhaus, which were to join the corps under General Lyon and participate in the expedition into the interior. Instead of my returning company, I received a laconic note from the general saying that he needed the company himself and that I would have to make do until reinforcements arrived from St. Louis. The difficulties of my situation grew even worse, for I never did receive real reinforcements. The most that happened was that a few companies of Homeguards would arrive now and then on the railroad, march into the capitol for a night's sleep, and vanish on the railway in the silence of the next morning. It is only because I continued to forbid entry into the capitol that no one knew how weak my force was, and I used every possible means of deception, sending out patrols and expeditions as if I had a couple of thousand men at my disposal.

It was only after taking care of the most pressing business, ordering the most necessary measures, and particularly placing the telegraph office under the continual surveillance of one of my officers, that I could consider viewing and investigating the house of the governor, C. F. Jackson, which was a government building. The empty, locked-up structure was opened and entered in the presence of State Senator Bruns, two officers and newly-arrived reporters from the *New York Herald* and the *New York Tribune*.[4] The interior looked wasted and forlorn, although the entire complement of furniture and household and kitchen implements was present. Even the drapes remained hung at the windows, the carpets on the floors. There was

4. See the description of Albert D. Richardson of the *New York Tribune*, quoted by William E. Parrish, *A History of Missouri*, vol. 3: *1860 to 1875* (Columbia: University of Missouri Press, 1973), 24. See also Rowan/Primm, 266-8, *AW*, 27 June 1861.

still sheet music on the piano. Everything pointed to a rushed, wild flight in which there was only time to pack and remove the most necessary. The floor in the absconded governor's office was covered with papers, which I had carefully collected and ordered. Consisting of letters, telegrams and other documents, they cast a bright light on developments of the last weeks, severely compromising many persons in St. Louis. I sent this paper booty there at once.

Thus the month of June went to its end, and the celebration of the national holiday of the Declaration of Independence on 4 July approached. This I was determined to celebrate in as splendid and imposing a fashion as my limited means allowed. In the course of the previous weeks I had gradually adjusted to my tenuous position; I was encountering less opposition than expected, and I had even begun to receive support for my measures among the pacified landowning population. I had also discovered that a decisively honorable end will always find a corresponding means. I had gained in insight and serenity, as well as experience. Tired of the bachelor life, I invited my wife to come to Jefferson City. Now I placed my headquarters in Governor Jackson's home, where it was somewhat better and more comfortable than in my bivouac in the capitol.

Honorably Discharged
(1861)

Following the battle at Boonville and General Lyon's scattering of the secessionist troops, it became significantly quieter in the interior of the state. This peace and security increased to such a degree that, on command from Washington, a couple of volunteer regiments from Iowa and Kansas finally marched into Missouri to support General Lyon's operations. In the area around the state capital it grew ever quieter and more peaceful in the month of July. It was only from northern Missouri, beyond the river, that we received reports of attempts to form new rebel bands and create a force which could attack and take Jefferson City. I was rather well informed of developments in the northern part of the state, for the agents of the railways and the telegraph officials were almost all good Union people, informing me quickly and conscientiously of all developments and episodes. As a result, I was always in a position to nip any threats in the bud through the rapid dispatch of an armed expedition. I did this time and again, to the considerable astonishment of secessionist ringleaders. They were both astounded and intimidated by the precise information of my headquarters as well as by the quick, energetic repression of every attempt at rebellion.

I also increased my forces somewhat during the time when two companies of my regiment, left behind in Jefferson Barracks,[1] joined me. As a result of President Lincoln's proclamation calling two hundred thousand volunteers to arms for three years of service, a start was made to organize these new forces as well. Two companies of this levy had already been formed from volunteers in the city and environs, as well as young people who came and had themselves enrolled, and these were sworn in at once and drilled. Even the new Homeguard had considerably improved, and it contributed not a little to keeping peace and order in the countryside. The result was that I could carry out my long-harbored intention of celebrating the Independence Day of the American Union on 4 July in peace and order and in a particularly demonstrative fashion, so as to overawe the portion of the population inclined to secession. At the same time, I also decided to use the occasion to

---

1. Jefferson Barracks was a military post established by the War Department in 1826 on part of the commons of the village of Carondelet. It was a marshaling place for expeditions and a depot for cavalry and artillery. During the Civil War its main function was as the site of a military hospital. *EHSL,* 2: 1120-22. It was closed as a military facility on 30 June 1946, see "Jefferson Barracks Closes," *BMHS* 2, no. 4 (July 1946): 54-55. It is now managed by the St. Louis County Parks System. See Winter, 4-7.

demonstrate to the residents of the state capital, as well as the population of the entire state, the security and solidity of the Union government by restoring the earlier civilian government of the state, allowing the officers to resume their official functions (under my own control, of course).

Toward the end of June, higher state officials and members of the cabinet of the absconded ex-governor, Jackson, had gradually returned to Jefferson City. They were tired of the deprivations and stresses of refugee life, and most of them lacked either money or means to subsistence. Finally, they feared that their long absence from their posts would become a pretext for declaring their positions vacant and replacing them with new men. The result was that these refugees returned one by one to their homes and families. When they saw that they would not be harassed, and that no one at all would persecute them for their pasts, a delegation of two from their number came to me to ask me whether they could resume their offices and duties after swearing a loyalty oath to the Union. As I have mentioned, I had already received instructions from General Lyon covering this case, empowering me to do so under certain conditions and with certain precautions. My committee of three advisors from the population supported getting the ordinary business of the state back into motion, as there was such torpor there and, if these anarchic conditions continued, there would be great disadvantage and peril. I now had a long conversation with each of the prodigal cabinet members of the absconded governor. I came to the conviction that all of them, with one exception, were rather guiltless, benign people who swam with the stream, more driven than driving. All of them had returned deeply regretting the past and well aware of the disadvantages that had come to the state. Of Jackson's cabinet, the only one missing was his minister of finance, the secretary of the treasury, who resigned his position in writing and went back to civilian life after being captured (as I described earlier), in possession of the entire state treasury. That was just as well with me, for I would never have trusted this man with the state treasury or finances.

I told all them that they had to swear the loyalty oath to the government of the United States before everyone, then confirm this in writing in a document in front of witnesses. They would then be able to enter their offices again and fulfill their duties, although under my control; I would have to be informed of all their more important acts. Drafts of the auditor could be issued as payment for public works and necessary expenditures in the ordinary course of business, but the state treasury remained closed and sealed, as it was when General Lyon gave it to me. Drafts would only be paid when a new governor was elected and a legitimate government installed. In the meantime, they were to inform the committee of three, always at my side assisting me, and this committee would report any doubtful matters to me together with its recommendations for accepting or rejecting the measures proposed. Once we understood and were in complete agreement over all points, as well as the limits of their functions in all departments of government, I designated the holiday of 4 July as the day the officials would perform the oath of loyalty and be reinstated in their offices.

On 4 July, whose beginning was hailed with a reveille by the regimental band and a salute of twenty-one cannon shots, I had my troops march out on parade. After the review the officers of the garrison, the committee of three and several prominent Union people gathered in the great hall of the capitol. Before this solemn assembly, the chief officials of the state took an oath of loyalty to the Union, which I read to them individually and which each repeated with upheld hand. I had already described their responsibilities and duties in an oration. Afterward, documents with the text of the same oath of loyalty were signed by each state official, by me, and by all present as witnesses.

With one exception, all of them signed and swore. Attorney General J. Proctor Knott,[2] a born Kentuckian who had only settled in Missouri in 1850, obstinately refused to render the oath, and instead he indulged in severe abuse against his colleagues who had sworn, and in his hot-blooded temperament he made statements that were treasonous and offensive to the Union. To prevent him from serving as a bad example for the others, I had him arrested on the spot and placed under guard. After swearing the oath, the others were reinstalled in their offices, and each received an inventory of his working quarters. From then on the business of government went forward regularly, if under certain restrictions. I retained only issuance of payment vouchers in my own hands, so that all payments for services rendered, works, etc., were issued only after review and approval by the committee of three, countersigned by me. They then passed to the state auditor, to hinder any abuse. In any case, payment was delayed until later.

The loyalty oath, which I had expanded somewhat on this occasion, read as follows:

2. James Proctor Knott (1830-1911) was appointed Missouri attorney general as a Democrat of Scotland County in September 1858, was elected to the office in August 1860, and his office was vacated by ordinance in 1861. *Official Manual, State of Missouri 1991-1992*, 58. Knott was born in Kentucky and moved to Missouri in 1850. In 1863 he opened a law practice in Lebanon, Kentucky, serving as a Democratic representative in Congress, 1867-71 and 1875-83. He was governor of Kentucky, 1883-87. *DAB*, 10: 470; Helen Bartter Crocker, "J. Proctor Knott's Education in Missouri Politics," *BMHS* 30 (1974-75): 101-116; *BDUSC*, 1323-4. Knott spoke of Boernstein as "old Boernstein" in his correspondence, and his wife Sallie was very apprehensive of his surveillance: "I never heard an officer announced or see a soldier coming but my heart is in my mouth, and 'Boernstein says come down' rings through my ears until he is gone." Carter, "J. Proctor Knott's Education," 112-113.

I, N. N., hereby solemnly swear that I shall be loyal and obedient to the United States of America, conduct myself in all ways as a good, loyal citizen, that I shall unconditionally obey the command of the President of the United States and the officers and officials named by him, that I shall support and defend the Constitution, the laws and government of the United States with all my strength, that I shall never bear arms against nor resist the government of the United States in the current civil war, and that I shall never provide any aid or assistance to treason and rebellion against the United States. So help me God.

Following this solemn ceremony, which made a deep impression on the assembly, the rest of the day was given over to enjoyment. I had encouraged the citizens of the capital to decorate and beflag their houses in observance of the national holiday. My wish was willingly fulfilled with very few exceptions, and its fulfillment contrasted crassly with the wild, tumultuous conditions in the same town, under the secessionist flag, hardly four weeks earlier. A patriotic brewer donated several barrels of his excellent lager beer, and I supplied a substantial lunch. In the open space before the capitol, afternoon passed under the fluttering star-spangled banner of the Union. A charming camp life, this military picnic; to the music of the regimental band there were gymnastics, fencing, races and other games, German songs were sung and beer and lunch consumed. At sundown the flag of the Union was brought down to a twenty-one-gun salute, and with the onset of night, a brilliant fireworks display closed the day's festivities. I had ordered several crates of fireworks and a number of sparklers from Orcutt in St. Louis. As it grew dark, the men of my regiment stationed themselves on the roof and the fortifications of the capitol in order to give the final volley, for which each had received thirty blanks made by the artillerists from the excess of powder we had collected as booty. The fireworks tableaux were set off, one after another, to the great enjoyment of my people and the entire population of Jefferson City, who gathered in great crowds around capitol hill. On the last tableau the words "Our Union Forever!" were spelled out in brilliant fire, showing far into the countryside, and the cannon fired a salute. A rich salvo of rockets rose into the air, sending down red, white, and blue stars from above. The exploding balls of light illuminating the dark summer night in three colors. The men of the regiment began an uninterrupted fire in response as the regimental band played the patriotic melodies of "Hail Columbia," "Star-Spangled Banner," "Red, White, Blue" and so on. Thundering hurrahs for the Union sounded through the nocturnal stillness.

It was a beautiful, successful celebration, filling my people and all friends of the Union with patriotic joy, and making a deep impression on the population of the town and environs.

Following the holiday, regular military life resumed. The rest of the month of July passed with expeditions into neighboring counties to hold free the left flank of General Lyon, who was now on the march against the rebels in the southwest of the state. An effort was also made to contact the general as often as possible through expeditions or scouts. Besides that, the watch over the river and the railway was strictly continued, and I still had to control the operation of the state government, there was no lack of work.

On 26 July the service period of the three-month volunteers enlisted service was at an end. I confess that I had looked forward to this moment with longing. I had not indulged this military intermezzo out of pride or a desire for adventure, but in order to set a good example as a party leader. My age no longer corresponded to the great demands that the cares, efforts and stresses of service placed on me, however, and my absence from St. Louis was also extremely damaging to my business interests. I had been happy to fulfill my duty, and now I could pass it to younger and more capable persons with a good conscience.

I had worked hard to prepare everything for imminent change and the reorganization of the regiment for three-year service. Besides the two entirely new companies, I had already enrolled more than half of the men for three years and sworn them in. My successor in command, Colonel Friedrich Schäfer, had little trouble completing the regiment and going into the field with tested men. The Second Missouri Volunteer Regiment proved to be one of the best regiments through all four years of the War of Secession, fighting in more than twenty battles and distinguishing itself through its valor and discipline. Colonel Schäfer fell a year and a half later on 31 December 1862, at the head of his own brigade in the battle of Murfreesborough [Stones River], Tennessee. He died on the field of honor a brave defender of the Union, and the valiant regiment brought many other blood sacrifices for the defense and preservation of the Union. More than a third of the officers and men fell in various battles or received severe wounds, and the veterans of the regiment still living can today look back on their military career with pride.

The twenty-sixth of July finally did come, and with it the end of our original period of service. Colonel Mulligan, who was later besieged by the rebels in Lexington and forced to capitulate, and Colonel Brown, with part of an Iowa regiment, entered Jefferson City. I surrendered to them the capitol with all its supplies, as well as the governor's home and all the other property under my protection. After a hearty farewell from the local Homeguards and the population of the town, whose leading citizens sought me out and thanked me for the friendly, mild treatment of the town under my command, I marched back to St. Louis with half of my regiment. Lieutenant Colonel Schäfer was ordered to the same destination with the half of the regiment then at Boonville. Only the two rifle companies of

Major Osterhaus were lacking, which were with General Lyon's corps and had been newly sworn in for the three-year service.

Late in the evening we arrived at the arsenal. There we found dreadful disorder. With General Lyon's departure for the field, the good military spirit had vanished from the headquarters of the arsenal, and an overwhelming and irritating lawyerdom had spread. Lyon's adjutant general, who as a lieutenant colonel was leader of the department during Lyon's absence, was a lawyer himself, and he surrounded himself increasingly with lawyer colleagues. All one saw in the arsenal was lawyers with neither clients nor trials, clothed with the most varied charges and all possible shoulder-straps. Rattling about the arsenal with their sabres and clothed in various uniforms, they disposed of everything with arrogance and ignorance, treating the true defenders of the Union, the brave officers and men, with coarseness and disdain. Lieutenant Colonel Schäfer had arrived some hours before me, but despite all his efforts, he could not get housing in any of the broad rooms of the arsenal, which the lawyers had occupied with their entourages. We were promised tents, but none arrived, and so the men of our regiment had to spend the night in the open under the trees of the arsenal park. Because the cooking rations had not been issued, they also had to observe a day of fasting against their will. All the while, my lords the lawyers took their ease in brightly lit chambers at richly set tables. Through upright advocacy and some proper rudeness, I was finally able to get the adjutant general to do something to house and feed my men the next morning. I transferred the command of the regiment to Lieutenant Colonel Schäfer and occupied myself for the next several days with putting the muster rolls in order for final payment, which gave me plenty to do.

Here in the arsenal I learned more about the fate of the rebel Attorney General Knott, whom I had sent to the arsenal as a prisoner under the guard of an officer. I had been authorized to do so by a letter from General Lyon, to whom I had reported the episode in the line of duty.

One crow does not peck another's eyes out, as the old saying goes, and as soon as my officer departed, Adjutant General Chester Harding freed the rebel. Although he continued to refuse to swear an oath of loyalty, he was invited to the officers' table, where he was celebrated by the other lawyers as the hero of the day. Yet Mr. Knott did appear to be rather put out by his experiences in Missouri, for he did not return to Jefferson City. Instead, he resettled in his old home state of Kentucky. There he was held in high honor by the Democratic Party as a hard-boiled copperhead and a martyr for the South, and he was sent to Congress several times as a representative.

After fulfilling all formalities, comparing mustering-out rolls with mustering-in rolls, and settling all accounts with the quartermaster's department and the suppliers, the United States paymasters appeared. The payment of officers and men took its regular course. We were still paid in gold coin, and it was certainly almost the last time this happened, for all following payments were made in paper money.

I bade a warm, hearty farewell to Schäfer, the officer corps and all of my dear brothers in arms. Returning to modest civilian life, I renounced all further martial glory. But I still return in my thoughts long and often with pleasure to those three months of military service. Frequently I return in my dreams to those stormy times, when I would come home in the evening to the governor's mansion and could finally enjoy an hour of peace. This was after the stresses of military service, the cares of civil administration and often a hundred audiences, for the whole world wanted advice and help from me, the supreme officer. Then we would sit in the back garden, my wife and I, enjoying the warm summer night, its stillness disturbed only by the stomps of patrols and the guards' calls of, "Who's there?" Opposite us, above the cupola of the capitol, the great comet of 1861 flamed in its fullest glory. So we sat, quietly happy, discussing plans and hopes, until another official report arrived, demanding immediate attention or even a visit to posts. Or one of the scouts would arrive, taking a message from General Lyon or an important tip from a friend of the Union out of the sole of his boot. Then peace was at an end. I had to gird on my sabre and mount my horse, often passing the whole night in official activities. Yet it was a beautiful time, fresh and moving, filled with life and action, the memory of which shall never desert me.

Moral Hangover
(1861)

On my return, I found St. Louis essentially changed in both material and moral terms. The large, usually lively city had a troubled, depressed appearance. The streets and public places were empty of people. Many young Americans, particularly the Minute Men and other opponents of the Union, had secretly gone south to serve in the rebel army, despite their parole after the Camp Jackson affair not to serve against the United States. Young Germans were under arms in the field. As a result, St. Louis looked literally desolated; all one saw were women and old men. Business was dead, trade was low, and credit, which plays a great role in American business life, had utterly vanished. On top of that, spirits were burdened by the heavy concerns about the shape of the near future and the fear that Missouri, as a slave state, would yield after all to the weight of events and join the rebellious South.

Concern grew even greater, morale sank even lower, and the attitude of the population became even more anxious at the news of the Union army's decisive defeat under General McDowell on 21 July at the battle of Bull Run. At first it was prettied up and hidden, but within a few days after our return it became known in its full terror. This news was shattering to Union people. Secessionists and slaveholders, on the other hand, went around in triumph and jubilation, portraying the triumphant rebel army pressing into the federal capital of Washington, foretelling the imminent collapse of the Union. The Union army had in fact been dispersed in disgraceful flight and had rushed back to Washington in wild disorder, leaving their entire artillery and about two thousand prisoners in the hands of the rebels. Only brave old Blenker[1] with the New York German Volunteer Regiments had held his place. Defending the ground foot by foot, he held back the advancing enemy and prevented them from completely annihilating the federal army. The first great collision between the pro-Union North and the rebel South had fallen to the disadvantage of the North, seeming to place its military power in serious question. If this defeat invoked general distress and deep sorrow in the free states, it was even more so in the border slave states. There the two

---

1. Ludwig Blenker (1812-1863) served as a policeman in Greece, then as a colonel in the Baden revolt of 1849, rising to command in the New York volunteers and to brigadier general early in the Civil War, when his staff harbored many European immigrants to serve in the Union forces. Zucker, 280.

parties stood opposed, even ready for battle, and the outbreak of civil war could be expected any hour.

The impressions I received investigating the state of my own enterprises and businesses were just as dark. It seemed as if I had lost almost all the fruits of years of labor, and that my entire existence was in question. I have already mentioned that good fortune favored my undertakings, and that my strenuous efforts were repaid with success. I was already most of the way to being a successful businessman. The commercial agencies, those detectives for the business world, rated me (as I learned from a confidential report), as "worth $100,000."[2] In the list of the one hundred largest taxpayers of the city, which was always published at New Year's, my own name was not in the last place. I owned my own newspaper enterprise and a printing plant, for which I had already refused an offer of $60,000.[3] I owned seven houses, of which I had built five myself, and I was also strongly interested in various other businesses, such as beer halls, a brewery, the theater, etc. To be sure, there were obligations on my real property, for I had bought most of the lots according to the local custom, making a small down payment and paying the rest off in five, seven or even ten years. On the other hand, I had completely paid for the buildings built on the lots, and I had paid off most of the debt remaining on the lots.

First came the financial crash of 1857, when, after an enormous financial and commercial boom, the collapse of a single bank, the Kentucky Trust Bank, caused other banks to stop their payments as well. This provoked a general panic, a storm by the population to banks and savings institutions to withdraw their deposits. This made a bad situation even worse. Distress spread with elemental force across the entire land, leaving ruin and destruction in its wake. This crisis, the first I had experienced in America, caused me some injury as well. I had begun without property, hence without capital, but I had enjoyed extensive personal credit. In such times of panic and general distrust, however, all credit ceases, and one has to rely on himself and survive the storm with his own resources. I managed to do this in 1857, but it cost me extreme exertions and great sacrifice. And because the credit previously supplied me by financial institutions ceased for me as it did for everyone else, I had to flee to professional money lenders to

---

2. R. G. Dun & Co. Collection, Baker Library, Harvard University Graduate School of Business Administration, gives several estimates of the worth of Boernstein's business, but none so high. See Missouri vol. 37, p. 589, report of 19 October 1857, "We do not consider him worth over $40,000 to $50,000 clear." When he leased his printing establishment to his sons August and Charles, it was estimated as worth $60,000, ibid., Missouri vol. 37, p. 588, report of 22 January 1861.

3. Ibid., Missouri vol. 37, p. 589, report of 19 October 1857, " . . . for both the house and the newspaper he was offered $40,000, much more than it is really worth . . . "

cover momentary shortages. This helped me out, but at a rate of interest far above the prevailing one. In that way I was fortunate enough to survive the financial crisis, although I was only exchanging an acute illness for a chronic complaint whose results imposed on me great sacrifice and burden.[4] Once the time of terror passed, the results of the financial crash vanished more swiftly than expected, business revived, and credit gradually resumed. I was on the best way to return to my ordained path, and my paper gained significantly in circulation and influence.

Then came the baleful events of 1861. The Civil War, breaking out like a storm from a clear sky, lamed trade, exchange, enterprises and credit. Once more all that had been attained stood in question. In addition, there was the fact that my pet undertaking, the foundation of a stable German theater in St. Louis, had demanded tremendous sacrifice. Whoever knows the hot summers of St. Louis—where evenings and nights are hotter than days due to the absorption of heat from the sun by houses and pavement during the day, only to be radiated when night commences—could understand what a financial sacrifice it was for me to keep my theater open through the summer of 1860. I kept my company together by paying them their engagement fee without reduction and fulfilling all my obligations to them. I had been willing to make these sacrifices in expectation and hope of a better future, but then ever more unfavorable circumstances emerged with the presidential election of 1860, until the coup of the state police commissioners forced me to close the theater. All my sacrifices were in vain.

The events of early 1861 made a deep moral impression on my nervous and extremely sensitive temperament. I saw the threatening collapse of the Union occurring before my eyes in ever-sharper form, placing everything in question. I lost faith in the future, in the possibility of improvement, even in myself. In my depressed, irritated mood, loaded down with heavy cares, I lost my joy for business for the first time. My energy was lamed, and I was overpowered by an invincible sense of disgust. It had been to tear myself out of this dark mood, to do what little I could to oppose this monumental storm, that I had acceded to the military intermezzo described in previous chapters. The result was that my absorption in action brought me some peace of mind and a return of my ability to act.

Before entering military service, I had put my house in order, considering as I was a longer engagement. I had transferred my newspaper and printing plant to my sons by means of sale, which according to the agreement set the purchase price as equal to the capital, and even the interest was only to be

---

4. Ibid., Missouri vol. 37, p. 589, report of 21 December 1857, "A number of his outside speculations have failed, and it is feared he will become involved. . . . Is a talented man, and capable of getting out of a bad place."

paid after my death to my widow.[5] I sought to shed or dissolve my other enterprises, for I no longer had any desire to engage in business. In addition, my creditors pressed for payment, which was natural and excusable in view of the general state of affairs and the uncertainty of the future. The bills of my paper supplier, in particular, had mounted high in the last months, and the man had to be satisfied, so we settled accounts by my giving him as payment four family houses that I had built on Tenth Street near Franklin Avenue. I lost my other houses in a less honorable manner. The lawyer Samuel Knox, from whom I had purchased a large house on Franklin Avenue that still had a few payments to go, would not grant me an extension. Instead, he demanded payment at once, compelling a forced auction, and buying the house back at the auction for the price of the remaining installments. Another man of honor, Van Sweringen,[6] from whom I had bought a building lot, on Franklin Avenue, on which I constructed a house, was still owed a few hundred dollars. While I was with my regiment in the field, he demanded what is called a "snap judgment," without my knowledge, forcing the house and lot to be auctioned and buying it for about a tenth of its value, since with the insecurity of the situation then, all landed property had fallen tremendously in value. Everyone wanted to sell, no one was buying, and so there were often no bidders at these forced auctions than the creditors themselves, who then naturally got the property for a song.

This was the situation I found on my return to St. Louis. Even the newspaper business was in difficulties. The number of subscribers had not declined, but there was no expectation that there would be any increase. At the same time, the main source of income of a large American newspaper, which is advertisements, became more dubious every day. All businesses stagnated, trade and exchange were down, so why should people advertise? Upon our return from Jefferson City, my sons and I did everything to revive our newspaper business, which was all we had left intact. After all arrangements had been made and the machinery placed in motion again with even greater energy, I decided to go to Washington. There I would discover the state of affairs personally, for they appeared rather black at the time, and only then would I make my plans for the near future.

Before I departed, news arrived of General Lyon's defeat and death in the battle of Wilson's Creek on 10 August, which caused great distress and

---

5. Ibid., Missouri vol. 37, p. 588, report of 22 January 1861, the lease to his sons took place over four months before the outbreak of hostilities.

6. James Tower Sweringen or Van Sweringen (1806-1872), born and raised in Pennsylvania, arrived in St. Louis in 1828, working as a dry goods wholesaler. He was a prominent local financier and businessman of obscure political affiliations. *EHSL*, 4: 2204-6.

deep mourning. This news depressed me even more. General Lyon was an open, honorable sort, gifted with considerable understanding of people and liberal in his views. His sole weak side was his nativist hatred of foreigners. His military knowledge was rather modest, and in his last period he also surrounded himself with a small circle of sycophants who stoked his personal vanity and led him from the straight and narrow way with their whispers. He had no idea of Moltke's[7] proven principle, "March separately, strike together." He dissipated his forces, which were not strong to begin with, by sending Sigel with a corps to the south while he himself lingered for a long time in Boonville, supposedly due to a lack of transport. When he finally did get under way, Sigel had already been defeated at Carthage and forced to retreat, enabling the rebel State Militia of Missouri to join the Confederate troops that McCullough brought from Texas and Arkansas. The result was that when Lyon finally arrived, they were able to oppose him with a numerical superiority.

General Lyon is also often overrated as a soldier. He was neither a strategist nor a tactician, and whatever he might have learned in the Military Academy at West Point had long since been sweated out of him in the monotony of distracting military service in Indian forts. I recall, for example, that when I began to drill with my entire regiment and found inadequate information in the few military handbooks available, I asked General Lyon how the American army handled the formation of squares to ward off cavalry attacks.

"Yes, my dear colonel," came his answer, "you came to the wrong man, for I cannot give you any information even with the best will. I have never had more than a hundred men in one place at one time over the last several years, and we never drill by whole regiments, as we are scattered about at company strength. Even when we had to deal with a cavalry attack in the Mexican War, the column simply closed together in a mass and defended themselves in that way in all directions."

I responded to him that a square was always superior to a mass formation, because with a mass the people forced into the middle could not participate in defense and could not shoot without endangering those in front, and there was not even room to load. In a square, on the other hand, the entire force could participate in defense, and the empty room in the middle of a square could be used to protect baggage, and as a refuge for non-combatants and wounded. He agreed with me, but he shrugged his shoulders and rendered the opinion that there should be something on the

---

7. Field Marshal Helmuth Graf von Moltke (1800-1891), longtime chief of the Prussian Supreme General Staff, see *Meyers Enzyklopädisches Lexikon* (Mannheim: Bibliographisches Institut, 1981), 16: 406; the principle is also attributable to Clausewitz.

matter in Scott's regulations,[8] but he didn't know. Such a lack of tactical knowledge in the American army is the natural result of the whole system, which scatters a weak armed force of about thirty thousand men across the entire vast country. These troops are stationed at outer borders or Indian forts, rarely gathering together a force as large as a regiment. In border wars, the most that occurs is skirmish firing, and tactical maneuvers are completely neglected. In the case at the time, I resolved the matter myself by recalling formations from the Austrian drill system for forming battalions into squares, and I trained my regiment to do that.

As much as General Lyon owed his success and fame, which he was fortunate enough not to outlive, to German volunteers alone, he could still never quite overcome his hatred for foreigners in general and Germans in particular. On every occasion he preferred his American officers to brave German leaders, while German volunteers always received from him nothing but contempt. The massacre at Cole Camp was another demonstration of his hatred of Germans. Friedrich Schnake, who was then with the army and was certainly an unimpeachable eyewitness, gives various telling proofs of this in his *Geschichte des Bürgerkrieges in Missouri [History of the Civil War in Missouri].*[9] Among other things, Schnake reports the following on the Cole Camp affair:

> At Cole Camp, Benton County, where five roads run together, about thirty miles from Boonville, the Benton County Homeguards had gathered in a strength of about 800 men. New reinforcements arrived every day from Cole Camp, Hawk Creek, Lake Creek, Fleet Creek and Richland Creek, where thousands of German families lived. The people were armed with hunting rifles, which they owned or had borrowed from acquaintances. (The regiment had been authorized by General Lyon on 13 June, and according to the adjutant general's reports it consisted of six companies with a general strength of 602 men.) Captain Carl Brühl had taken over a large barn as his quarters with Company F. On the night of 19 June defeated state troops, Kelly's Company and the Warsaw Greys, moved toward the camp in a strength of about 300 men. They bore with them the Union flag, in order to deceive the watch, who expected reinforcements from Warsaw.

---

8. Winfield Scott, *Infantry Tactics; or, Rules for the Exercise and Manoeuvres of the United States Infantry* (New York, 1835) was reissued many times, and a "new edition" of 1857, republished through 1864, consisted of three volumes, 1. *School of the Soldier and Company;* 2. *School of the Battalion, and Instructions for Light Infantry and Rifle;* and 3. *Evolution of the Line.*

9. Friedrich Schnake, "Der Ausbruch des Bürgerkrieges in Missouri," *Der Deutsche Pionier,* 11 (1879), 12 (1880). Reference supplied by Don Heinrich Tolzmann of the University of Cincinnati.

The gates of the barn were opened. Then the state troops began firing on General Kelly's orders, and Captain Brühl and 25 men were shot to death as they slept. Because Kelly's company was Governor Jackson's body-guard, and since the governor was in the vicinity, it seems possible that he had knowledge of this treacherous attack under false colors. The companies of the Benton County Homeguard under Captain Cook assembled on a hill behind the barn and opened heavy fire on the state troops. The state troops were forced to withdraw after a battle lasting half an hour and costing them 31 dead and many wounded. Besides those murdered in their sleep, the Union people had lost only four dead, including Lieutenant Wilhelm Kanstreuer of Company B, and several wounded. This attack enraged the German settlements in Benton, Boone and bordering counties, leading to a merciless pursuit of the "Bushwackers" there that continued until after the end of the war.

General Lyon was informed at once of the massacre, which took place about thirty English miles from his own position, but he took absolutely no measures to pursue the state troops. Instead he remained quietly with his men in Camp Cameron, near Boonville, until 3 July, as if nothing had happened. This peculiar carelessness, which aided his enemies and placed them in a position to perfect their organization, is to be explained in only one way. Although the troops under his command were almost exclusively German Americans, Lyon demonstrated on more than one occasion that he was a hard-bitten Know-Nothing. As such, he hated Germans. At Cole Camp only German Americans were butchered, for which reason Lyon did not concern himself. He probably did not even make an official report on it, since the massacre is remembered in none of the histories.

Thus far Friedrich Schnake.

In person, General Lyon was unshakable and brave. He was always up front where the bullets were thickest, dressed in his simple blue campaign uniform, with an old straw hat on his head. He was always where there was the greatest danger. He was a bold officer, but he was not up to the mission that the course of events forced on him. What he could do was fight, risk his life and show a good example to his troops. That was how he died, in the middle of an attack on the Southerners. Encouraging his troops in a loud voice and storming out at their head, he caught an enemy bullet in the breast. He slowly sank from his horse. His servant caught him and bedded him down on the ground as the troops pressed forward, raging to revenge their leader. The general whispered to his servant, "John, I'm going . . . up!" Then he sank back, dead. Honor to his memory! Despite his New England nativism, he was a brave man and a good soldier.

Nathaniel Lyon, brigadier general commanding in St. Louis, 1861. In Boernstein's estimation, Lyon was brave but overrated. Carte de visite photograph by John A. Scholten. Courtesy of the Missouri Historical Society. Civil War carte de visite album.

In St. Louis in the meantime, General John C. Frémont had arrived to be commandant of the Military District of Missouri, and he was installed at once in his office.[10] He also was no strategist, but he had the understanding and insight to supplement his limited knowledge in this field through others. He surrounded himself with a general staff of former officers of European armies, particularly Hungarians from the recent revolutionary war against Austria. He always received me with friendship, and he even offered me a position in his staff. I declined this with thanks, explaining my intention to go to Washington. On this occasion, however, I also once more saw his intelligent wife, Jessie, the daughter of old Benton.[11] General Frémont gave me a message to Secretary of War Cameron, and I departed St. Louis to travel to Washington. Departure from the city where I had passed the best years of my adulthood and with which I was so profoundly tied was very hard to me, but I felt that I needed a change if I was not to decline physically and morally. In the worst of moods, depressed by concerns for the future of the country, almost in despair, I departed the city where I had lived for twelve years. Behind me I left children, grandchildren and business. Accompanied by my wife and my youngest son Carl, I departed for Washington.

10. John Charles Frémont (1813-1890), born in Georgia, the illegitimate son of one Jean Charles Frémon, served briefly in the U.S. Navy, then the Army, making a name as an explorer and soldier; he was U.S. Senator from California, 1850-51 and Republican candidate for president in 1856. He was commander of the Department of the West, July to November 1861, of the Mountain Department in Virginia, February 1862 to June 1864, and briefly promoted as an anti-Lincoln radical candidate for president, 1864. He was an egregious business failure after the war, and served as governor of Arizona Territory, 1878-1881. See *DAB*, 7: 19-23; *BDUSC*, 1027-8.

11. Jessie Benton Frémont (1824-1902), second of five daughters of Thomas Hart Benton, married John Charles Frémont, 1841. On her Missouri experiences, see her *The Story of the Guard: A Chronicle of the War* (1863). *DAB*, 7: 18-19.

In *the* Federal Capital

I found Washington, in our joking manner called "the great chief-wigwam of our Union," in a state of great agitation. In the broad streets, which often consisted of unbuilt lots on both sides, whose monotony was broken occasionally by a colossal government building; in front of the hotels and in public places; in the Capitol and around the White House, the place was infested with uniforms of all sort. One saw nothing but officers and soldiers and occasionally couriers on horseback, bearing dispatches between the various camps and the capital. We were in the midst of the great transformation that followed the defeat of the Union army at Bull Run, an event highly tragic in its moral impact, but actually comic in effect. Hitherto careless and indifferent, the North had been awakened out of its apathy into consciousness. Finally recognizing the scale of its peril, it had begun to reach for heroic means to defend itself. It was certainly high time for this to happen. In the South, everything had been done to prepare for separation during the administration of President Buchanan, which was if not treasonous at least ambiguous. Even after the outbreak of the Civil War virtually nothing was done in the North, which surrendered itself to careless optimism. Up to 4 March 1861, Secretary of War Floyd[1] not only hindered every attempt at armament and defense in the North, but also emptied all arsenals there and sent their valuable contents south. The result was that the whole North was actually bereft of weapons. After Lincoln entered office, there were attempts to correct this bad situation as quickly as possible. The new war secretary, Cameron, bought all the old, discarded weapons he could find one way or another through middlemen in Europe, but for his dear money he got only poor or entirely useless wares. Millions were paid for these poor weapons, most of which ended up in the hands of suppliers and middlemen. Only then did the government turn to American private industry to produce good rifles according to an improved English model. It was the same with artillery, ships of the fleet, telegraph services, trains and medical care. Everywhere a high tuition had to be paid, and everywhere there were costly experiments until they finally found the right way.

At the outset of the conflict, the population of the North particularly lacked any understanding of the seriousness of the situation or the

---

1. John Buchanan Floyd (1806-1863) of Virginia, was governor, 1849-52, 1855-57, and secretary of war under Buchanan, 1857 to December 1860. He was accused at the time of transferring weapons to the South to help a prospective revolt. He became a CSA general and died in service. *DAB*, 6: 182-3.

importance of this war. They consoled themselves by perilously underestimating their opponent, his strength and his means. The old commander of the American army, General Winfield Scott, had drafted a plan in which three army corps were to penetrate the South at once and, ever advancing, enclose the rebellion deeper in its iron arms, finally throttling it. But for this purpose there were only 20,000 men in regular units, and 75,000 volunteers whom Lincoln had called to arms for three months, and the militia of the pro-Union states, which was 3 million soldiers on paper but really amounted to about 50,000 men. Scott's aggressive plan of operations could not be carried out with this "mob of armed people," neither adequately drilled nor disciplined. In the first encounter at Bull Run, militia regiments fled in disorder to save themselves from tree trunks painted to look like cannon, "masked batteries" as they were called then. As a result a great deal of time was wasted and much money paid out without success. Above everything else, the prestige of the government of the United States was dramatically damaged. In the South, meanwhile, armament was vigorously pursued and perfected with time, while self-confidence and expectation of victory grew by the day. Now at last, after the unfortunate, ludicrous course of the battle of Bull Run, the entire population of the North was convinced that the peril of the Union's being torn into two portions was genuine and serious. All forces would have to be used, the most extreme means applied, and the greatest decisiveness and energy called up to oppose the South successfully and hinder its separation.

Congress had been convened in Washington in extraordinary session. This Congress, consisting only of representatives of the North and border states, had a Republican majority in both houses. That majority now proceeded to pass decisive measures, committing itself in a solemn resolution, "to vote any amount of money or troops necessary to assure a swift, effective suppression of rebellion." Now 500,000 volunteers were called to arms and the regular army strengthened to 40,000, $10 million approved for manufacturing weapons, $43 million for fitting new warships, $228 million for the Army. In addition, they bestowed on the executive branch the power to declare blockade and state of siege. In a word, they finally got serious.

I came to Washington just as it was awakening from its earlier state of carelessness and lethargy. This aroused living and striving made a great impression on me. It appeared as if the North only needed the desire to gather itself for a mighty blow and smash the South. The fact that this did not occur was largely the fault of the North completely lacking field commanders and strategic leaders. The best officers had all entered the Southern army, and it was only in the course of the war's four years that good military leaders were trained for the North as well. My originally sanguinary hopes of great success for a Union army equipped with overwhelming resources eventually paled once I learned the state of affairs from close quarters.

Adventurers of all sort and from every land were to be found in Washington. Trying to find positions in the reorganizing Union army, they sought to impress others, some through their aristocratic titles, some by wearing medals whose pedigree no one could vouch for, some through bold self-assertion and extraordinary smoothness. I am sorry to say that some of them managed to find positions. I spent a great deal of time with the officers of Blenker's staff, and from them I learned the personal details and pasts of many imported war heroes, often not of the most respectable variety. Blenker's staff consisted mostly of good officers, and I spent a good deal of time with them, particularly Otto von Corvin,[2] whom I had already known in Paris; Prince Salm, accompanied by his amiable young wife;[3] Captain Brandenstein and other educated men and fine officers whose names have slipped out of my memory. Corvin, a spirited popular writer and inexhaustible teller of anecdotes, has so thoroughly and wonderfully described the adventurous life and activities in Washington and the dubious types who appeared then in his *Erinnerungen an 1861 [Memories of 1861]*[4] that I, who was much more briefly there, do not need to add anything.

I had come to Washington with the idea and intention of staying there, writing columns for my newspaper and making myself as useful to the federal government as I could. My first visit was with Edward Bates, my fellow Missourian, who held the portfolio of justice in Lincoln's cabinet. I was received in the most friendly fashion by the old man, whom I had always esteemed, and was immediately invited to tea with his family that evening.

---

2. Otto von Corvin-Wiersbitzki (1812-1886) was a leader in the Baden revolution in 1849, commanding fortress Rastatt for a time. During the Civil War he held the rank of colonel and acted as correspondent for the *London Times*. He was close to the Salm-Salms, and either co-wrote or edited the writings of the Princess. See Kaufmann, 490; Zucker, 285.

3. Prince Felix Salm-Salm (1828-1870) served in the Prussian and Austrian armies before going to America, where he joined General Blenker's staff. He was colonel commanding two successive New York regiments, and he led a brigade on Sherman's March to the Sea. After the war, he joined the entourage of Emperor Maximilian of Mexico, barely escaping execution, and he died serving as a major in the Prussian army in the Franco-Prussian War. His wife, Princess Agnes Winona (Joy) Salm-Salm, née Leclerq (1844-1912), who was from a French-Canadian military family and married the Prince in August 1862, lobbied for her husband in Albany and Washington, and accompanied her him on campaign in America and Mexico. Her memoirs, *Zehn Jahren aus meinem Leben,* were famous at the time. She headed a field hospital in the Franco-Prussian War. See Kaufmann, 546-7; *ADB*, 30: 253-4; *NUC*, 516: 415.

4. A compendium of Otto von Corvin's autobiographical writings was *Erinnerungen aus meinem Leben*, 3d ed., 4 vols. (Leipzig, 1880).

There I sat in intense personal conversation with Mr. Bates, telling him my views and hopes, asking him to aid with advice and deed. In response, Bates told me that he had heard that Count Gurowski, who had been employed in the Foreign Office for years because of his linguistic ability and political experience, was thinking of resigning and returning to Europe. For this reason, I should pay a visit on Secretary of State Seward and present my desires. I could probably manage to take Gurowski's place, in which case Bates and Montgomery Blair would give me the strongest support.

As a result, I went the next morning to the State Department and had myself announced to Seward. I was admitted at once. You can imagine my surprise when, after the first greetings, Seward directed to me the question, "Well, Colonel, are you already ready to go to your post?"

Entirely astonished, I responded to him, "To what post?"[5]

"Well," he retorted with a smile, "you must already know that the president named you United States Consul in Bremen on 8 August?"

"I have not heard a word about it," was my answer, and that was in fact true. The dispatch with my appointment had passed me on the way to St. Louis as I was coming to Washington. I only received it several days later, forwarded from my son in St. Louis, along with the legally required bond for $10,000 required by law, underwritten by two prominent St. Louis citizens. Seward's message was so unexpected and surprising that in the first moment I did not know what I should say in response. I had not been looking for a consulate and had not even thought of going to Europe. Seward, who perceived my hesitation and indecision, now added that he had suggested me himself because he wanted reliable people in all the harbor towns. Overseeing weapons dealing, the arrival and the equipping of privateers for the South, they could prevent as much of this from happening as possible. He had also asked Blair whether I would take the position, to which Blair had replied positively. The post in Bremen was a pleasant one, and I would have a friendly reception there. Despite the fact that the Bremen consul Schuhmacher in Baltimore had objected to my appointment, portraying me to the Bremen senate as a dangerous agitator. Seward had completely and permanently overcome these objections in a conversation with the *chargé d'affaires* of the Hanseatic Cities, Herr von Schleiden. He could guarantee me the best reception there.

---

5. Although Boernstein declares his surprise over the consular appointment, he was mentioned for other positions at the very start of the Lincoln Administration, probably with his acquiescence. One W. W. Greene of St. Louis wrote to Secretary of War Cameron in April 1861, on the position of Collector of Customs in St. Louis, "While I should have preferred Capt. Barton Able, yet it is a matter of congratulations that the infidel Mr. Boernstein has not been appointed. I regret, too, the appointment of Dr. Hammer as physician for the marine hospital, for he is also an avowed infidel." *WROR*, series I, vol. I, 671-2.

"Finally," he added, "The financial situation of the consulate in Bremen has been improved, and I have recommended to the Committee for Ways and Means raising the annual salary from $2,000 to $3,000."

When he pressed me for my definitive answer, I responded, "Yes." He directed me to go to the Consular Bureau to get my appointment and instructions and to review the dispatches of my predecessor, Isaak R. Diller of Illinois, who was still serving. On parting, he urged me to depart for my post as quickly as possible, and to send him political dispatches from time to time, as often as important events or political changes might take place in European politics. This was an assignment that varied from the usual consular responsibility, usually restricted to commercial dispatches.

The word of the secretary proved to be literally true. In Bremen, I found the friendliest and most forthcoming reception from the senate and the citizenry, and the elevation of my salary had also been approved by Congress before I arrived in Bremen. It was only with my successor that the salary was reduced back to $2,000 from $3,000.

In the Consular Bureau I found a friendly reception from the person then its head, Mr. Abbot (later named consul in Sheffield). I received from him the printed consular instructions, which unfortunately suited neither the dignity nor the pride of a great republic, and which permitted little competence to its representatives overseas. Every line of these instructions breathed the anxiety that consuls might come to disputes with foreign officials or governments; on every page appeasement and courteous agreement was preached. The consul was to settle all differences, and when they persisted, arrange compromises. On the other hand, strict fulfillment of duty was demanded in representing the administration and the republic. This certainly would have been more easily accomplished by strong action than by continual appeasement and perpetual dissimulation. The worst of it was that foreign governments know of these pusillanimous instructions and know how to obtain copies of them. At the least attempt at energetic action by a consul, he would have this or that paragraph cited, his demands would be coolly rejected and he would even have protests lodged against him in Washington. I naturally only learned of this debility in our consular representation later, during my service. But the Consular Bureau in Washington gave me a foretaste of what a consul overseas could expect as protection and support, not to mention maintenance of his dignity by the authorities immediately over him.

With the exception of Abbot, I found the Consular Bureau in those days to consist entirely of ill-educated, mediocre clerks, thoroughly unfamiliar with foreign languages or direct knowledge of foreign conditions. In my five years of service in Bremen, I had many opportunities to learn the utter incompetence, indifference and passivity of the scriveners in this office. An old consul, who had grown gray in the service of his country and had managed to keep his post for many years through the change of various presidents, later told me these heartening words:

> Dear friend, you know that Talleyrand told his young diplomats when they departed for their posts, 'Surtout, monsieur, point de zèle!'[6] In our Consular Bureau in Washington, this is the highest principle. A consul who sends many dispatches is intolerable and must be neutralized as quickly as possible. Believe me, the consul who does not send a single dispatch through the entire year, contributing at the most a commercial report for the *Public Documents,* is the most beloved and respected of men in the eyes of the Consular Bureau. This is because every consular dispatch has to be transcribed, presented to the secretary of state, and either answered or at least acknowledged. That all creates trouble and work for the clerks, which they do not love.

I often had occasion to prove the veracity of these words myself and through others. Perhaps it has improved since, but at that the most critical moment of our development as a state it was as I have portrayed it. In addition to this was the fact that our gentlemen clerks in the State Department and the Treasury could never get over the fact that, for reasons easy enough to understand, we consuls overseas were paid our salary in gold coin. Those employed in the country were paid with paper money, which often lay 40 to 50 percent below gold in exchange. This distinction was mentioned at every opportunity in official dispatches. A particular Underwood, the fifth auditor in the Treasury and a man with whom consuls had to communicate a great deal, particularly indulged in the most biting remarks on this in his correspondence. When this had no effect he took his refuge in all sorts of discrepancies and trifles, which usually delayed final accounting and thus payment vouchers, making necessary a lengthy exchange of dispatches. Hence I recall being compelled to write at least ten dispatches over a discrepancy of one-and-a-half cents. The responses of this auditor grew ever harsher and more biting, until in the end he broke off the correspondence and I complained through Blair to Seward, who swiftly brought an end to this bureaucratic nonsense through Treasury Secretary Chase.[7]

---

6. French, "Above all, sir, no zeal!"
7. Salmon Portland Chase (1808-1873), an ardent antislavery man, settled in Ohio and was U.S. Senator from 1849-61. He was Treasury secretary, 1861-64, and Chief Justice of the Supreme Court, 1864-73, all along ardently seeking the presidency. *DAB,* 4: 27-34.

In short, what I did not see then but soon came to see was that I had committed the dumbest stunt in my life by taking the consular post in Bremen. I should have taken to heart the old saying, "Remain in the country and feed yourself honestly." I should have returned to St. Louis and my journalistic enterprise, but then much would have turned out differently from what actually came to pass. To be sure, I probably would not have long tolerated American living and striving, distress and depression, enmities and struggles which are part and parcel of American journalism. I would probably long since have been lying in the cool earth of Bellefontaine Cemetery.[8] Instead, I am now enjoying a healthy, quiet old age. But in principle it does not matter whether a person lives to be sixty or eighty, all the more so if great age leads one more to vegetate than to live. I regard it as an extraordinarily fortunate fate that I am graced with being continuously active, even though I am approaching eighty.

After completing my business in the federal capital and taking leave of new and old friends, I left Washington. Not without heavy cares for the future of the country, I traveled to New York to catch one of the North-German Lloyd ships there. Until the departure of the steamer *Bremen*, I passed some pleasant and cheerful days in this great city, especially in the company of my old friend Hermann Raster, then editor of the *New York Abendzeitung*, with whom I had been in active correspondence for many years but whom I now had the first opportunity to meet in person. They were beautiful days, on which I look back with pleasure. Friend Raster, now editor-in-chief of the paper for which I am writing these memoirs, has always proved a loyal, reliable and magnanimous friend. May the thankful recognition of an old man and veteran of the press, as well as his own consciousness, repay him. I will always recall his true friendship with thanks until these old eyes close forever. My hearty greetings and wishes will accompany him on his life's journey.

---

8. Bellefontaine Cemetery was established in 1850 as one of the so-called rural cemeteries patterned particularly after Mount Auburn Cemetery in Cambridge, Massachusetts. See *EHSL*, 1: 337-8; Winter, 110.

In Bremen

(1861-1862)

Our crossing of the Atlantic Ocean on the Lloyd steamer *Bremen* was graced by the finest autumn weather, and the company was entirely pleasant. There were some thirty cabin passengers, and only a few persons in the 'tween decks. Among those in the cabins were the newly named United States consul for Vienna, Theodor Canisius of Illinois, and his family. We spent a great deal of time together, partly studying the printed consular instructions, partly informing one another through harmless chat of our new destinations and what we would find there. I could give my colleague a fairly clear picture of Vienna and its pleasures, but he knew as little as I did of Bremen, so that I had to rely on the report of a Bremen merchant family who had been visiting relatives in America and were now returning home. Otherwise, we occupied ourselves on the crossing principally with the affairs of our republic, and we impatiently awaited the moment when we landed in Southampton and would once more receive newspapers from home.

Finally we reached Southampton, where we made a stop of several hours to load and unload goods. The pilot brought us the *Times,* and in the harbor we had plenty of English and American newspapers. But our expectations were disappointed. During the twelve days we were on board without newspapers, nothing important had happened, and matters stood precisely where we had left them at our departure. Only the Mexican question cast a shadow, soon to take on so much importance for our republic. The European papers, particularly the official mouthpieces of England, France and Spain, were then debating vigorously and with irritation the resolution of the Mexican congress to establish the dictatorship of Juárez and to cease all payments, even interest payments to foreign creditors of the state. This was a painful measure to Spanish, English, and French capitalists, who turned to their governments for protection and support, and it gave Napoléon III his sought-for pretext to realize what he called his "greatest political idea." In conjunction with other European powers, he intended to intervene in Mexico, reestablish the monarchy there, and use it as his Archimedean point from which to accelerate the dissolution of the American Union. He would convert first the South and then later the North of the United States to monarchical systems of government, finally turning all the other republics on the American continents into empires and kingdoms. This plan rested, to be sure, on mad assumptions about the North's weakness and lack of viability, but it was if anything at least a grandiose concept. Only a few weeks after I took office in Bremen, the Napoléonic idea took palpable shape with the conclusion of the Convention of London of 31 October 1861. England, France, and Spain thereby joined for mutual intervention in Mexico, as they said, in order to protect their subjects there and to compel the Mexican government to fulfill its obligations. Even the United States was invited to join, but Lincoln was decisively against it, and the mood of the American people favored Mexico. Secretary Seward therefore rejected the dubious invitation in unambiguous terms, referring to the Monroe Doctrine.[1]

I landed in Bremen in the middle of September and took over the consulate from my predecessor Isaak R. Diller. I received confirmation within three days from the Bremen senate, and I had the friendliest reception from the Bremen government. The rich merchant class of Bremen was, however, less favorable to our Union, and I found among them a strong inclination toward the South and its efforts at secession. This was an entirely natural result of the fact that Bremen did almost all of its business and trade with the southern states, and their products, such as cotton, sugar, tobacco, and so on were the main staple of Bremen shipping and overseas trade. It required several years and constant effort to transform these sympathies into pro-Union attitudes, and it only succeeded completely with the taking of Richmond, Lee's capitulation, and the final collapse of the secession idea.

As a journalist, I had always closely followed the course of European politics, and from the time of my residence in Paris I knew most of the persons and motivating forces that influenced it. Beyond that, I had the good fortune in Bremen to gather worthwhile hints and information from foreign diplomats as well as from senators. The result was that I was in a position to fill my political dispatches to Mr. Seward with useful reports, in which I pursued the Mexican situation as it unfolded. I could also supply our foreign office with excerpts from the many English, French, and Spanish newspapers I found in the splendid Bremen Museum.[2]

Bremen then was still an independent republic with its own oligarchic government, pursuing above all a policy of self-interest. It certainly did

---

1. On the "Grand Design," see Nancy Nichols Barker, *The French Experience in Mexico, 1821-1861: A History of Constant Misunderstanding* (Chapel Hill: University of North Carolina Press, 1979). After the suspension of payments by Mexico in 1861, a consortium of European powers intervened, but France was the sole power by 1862. In 1864 Archduke Maximilian of Austria was established as Emperor of Mexico. Napoléon III withdrew support in March 1867, due to threats by the United States. Maximilian's effort to sustain his government by himself failed, and he was executed.

2. Washington, D.C., National Archives Microfilm Publications, T184: "Despatches from United States Consuls in Bremen, Germany, 1794-1906," 21 rolls, rolls 11-14, 11 January 1860, to 31 December 1869, encompass the period of the Boernstein consulate.

belong to the German League, but everyone knows how weak this league was and to what small degree it united the various German states into a whole. The statesmen of Bremen who led the government were well informed about political developments and plans of the various powers through their *chargés d'affaires* and consuls. They also received valuable reports from their own merchant class, who had branches and business ties in all parts of the world and who, in their own interest, had to be sure to be well and precisely informed. At the head of the Bremen government in those days stood a man of thorough education and clear vision, Arnold Duckwitz,[3] who had been the minister of trade under Reich Administrator Archduke Johann in 1848 and 1849. Foreign affairs were led by Senator Henri Smidt, son of the old, respected Burghermaster Smidt, who often complained jestingly of the misfortune of being the "son of a famous father." I was well received by both of these capable men, and I have both of them to thank for their helpfulness and assistance of me in my official duties. I harbor the best memories of both of them.

The impression that Bremen itself made on me was less positive, with its narrow, crooked streets, the medieval gables poking out all over, and the small town feeling it gave me. I had become used to America's free, wide spaces, its expansiveness and progress, in short the "go-ahead" nature of Americans. My son Carl, who had come to America as a child and had grown up in an American setting, asked me in astonishment if all towns in Europe look like this. In contrast, the suburb, with its broad streets and cheerful villa-style houses usually occupied by a single family and with charming gardens in front, reminded us of America. This was even more the case with the "New Town" laid out with American regularity on the opposite side of the river. I envied Bremen for the lovely, park-like area around its walls, pierced with running waters and enlivened with swans and other swimming birds, and I would have loved to transfer the entire wall to St. Louis. We made our first visit to the world-famous Bremen Rathskeller, of which we had heard so much during our crossing and which was already an old friend to me through Hauff's *Phantasien*.[4] This old gothic town hall from the fifteenth century—with its antique halls and chambers above ground, its rather lascivious exterior carvings and its

Here and elsewhere, Boernstein uses the term "foreign office" (*Auswärtiges Amt*) to describe the professional diplomatic service of the United States, as distinguished from the political ministry, which we would call the Department of State. Such a distinct Foreign Office has an institutional existence in Great Britain as well as in Prussia, the German Empire, and the present-day German Federal Republic.

3. Arnold Duckwitz (1802-1881), *ADB*, 48: 133-140.

4. Wilhelm Hauff (1802-1827) was author of *Phantasien im Bremer Rathskeller* [Fantasies in the Bremen Town Hall Cellars], see *NUC*, vol. 234, p. 559.

vast underground Rathskeller—offered perennial interest throughout the years of my residence.

It was in the great salon of the town hall, with its guild chamber, in what once had been the loge reserved for patrician ladies during processions of the citizenry, among old ship models and similar junk preserved there, that I spied the statue of the most significant man Bremen had in modern times, the old burghermaster, Johann Smidt. The gifted sculptor Steinhäuser,[5] also a son of Bremen who always concerned himself with decorating his home town, had carved old Smidt life-size with great fidelity from Carrara marble, presenting it to the city as a gift. Instead of placing the statue in a public place as a tribute to an accomplished man, they placed it out of petty considerations in this curio collection of the council chamber. There it was certainly prominent, but it by no means had the place it deserved.

Burghermaster Johann Smidt,[6] who did so much for Bremen, came from the middle of the last century. He was born in 1773, when his native city still lived in a divided dependence, under Sweden and Hanover, due to the former bishopric of Bremen. In the restricted circumstances of those days, when Germany still was lamed by the impact of the Thirty Years War, Burghermaster Johann Smidt was never quite able, despite his thorough education, to free himself of the petty-bourgeois narrowness of a limited political and social horizon. The result is that his impact on his immediate fellow citizens, the corporation of Bremen burghers, was more narrowing than intellectually expansive. After completing his studies, he became a professor in Bremen, then a member of the council and a senator after 1800. During the War of Liberation, he was the diplomatic representative of Bremen in negotiations with the powers, and as such he came into close contact with the most important statesmen of that moving time. In 1821, in recognition of his great services, he was elected burghermaster, and he held this first office of his city for thirty-six years until his death on 7 May 1857.

His greatest service to Bremen beyond dispute was his transformation of the town, which had become a city of the interior, into a harbor and a trading city once more. He did this by obtaining a strip of land on the mouth of the Weser from the government of Hanover after long negotiations in 1828. Hanover was not then so hostile to Bremen as it would later become. On this new territory was founded the harbor of Bremerhaven. Prior to this Bremen was reachable only by flatboats of the smaller dimension, for the Weser filled increasingly with sand, and seagoing ships

---

5. Karl Steinhäuser (1813-1878), born in Dresden, though he spent his later career in Karlsruhe. *ADB*, 35: 716-17.

6. *ADB*, 34: 488-494.

had to be loaded in Vegesak or the harbors of Oldenburg. This occasioned great expense, so that Bremen's trade steadily declined. The establishment of Bremerhaven gave Bremen new life. This new, spacious harbor was soon surrounded by a Bremen colony which has now become a blooming, bustling town. Docks and warehouses were erected there, and all of the important houses established associated agencies. Steamer traffic grew in the next few years with the establishment of the great institution of North-German Lloyd, and steam tugs and transport steamers coursed the Weser up and down. This former stretch of sand dunes that Smidt bought for 100,000 Taler became the flourishing harbor town of Bremen, handling its entire traffic. The city of Bremen had the further advantage from this arrangement of being entirely spared the inconveniences of a seagoing town—the streaming together of sailors of all nations, and the rather mean housing and entertainment which comes with it. Bremen was able to do this while receiving the advantages of a seagoing harbor town. Since that time, not only has the Bremen merchant fleet grown, but its entire overseas business, and it has become the preferred trading port, particularly for emigration to America. Old Smidt had the good fortune to be able to see his creation flourish and grow, and when he closed his eyes at the age of eighty-four, Bremerhaven was at the height of its development.

I arrived in Bremen four years after the death of this man of honor, and I found the old Hanseatic city in a gradual process of unfolding. It was just beginning to become a modern city, which Hamburg had been for a long time but which Bremen had not become. This was because old Smidt had committed his entire prestige and influence to preserving the patriarchal, petty-bourgeois style of life of former German Imperial cities. At the start of this century, anyone who set foot in Bremen was immediately transported to that medieval time when compulsion to join guilds and associations kept the little people under control; when views and prejudices, values and customs ruled could not harmonize with the spirit of the century of the Enlightenment. Seizure by the French had wiped away much of Bremen's puritanical and petty-bourgeois nature, but after Napoléon's fall they did everything possible to resurrect the old conditions in their original form. They were successful in many things, for Bremen's isolated position on the extreme northwest of Germany, still without railway links in those days, gave the population few ties to other towns or countries.

A further painful rip in old conditions occurred by the stormy year of 1848, when the high council of patricians, consisting of 4 burghermasters and 24 senators, hitherto the sole government, was joined by popular representation, consisting of 150 members of the citizenry. But this political renewal had little impact on the social and intimate life of the population of Bremen. The rising reaction which prevailed in Germany in the 1850s directed all efforts to preserving old conditions as long as possible, and, where they had already vanished, to reestablish them. This was easier in Bremen than elsewhere, simply because of its rather special position and the moderating influence that custom and local patriotism, both strong aspects of Bremen people, impressed on the population. In Bremen what was traditional and customary had been regarded for centuries as the law of life, to be followed blindly; because things had been so before, they were supposed to be so today; because the grandfathers and fathers had done something, the sons and grandsons were to do the same. Any variation from what was traditional and customary was regarded as a crime and often even punished as such, partly through the courts, and partly through public opinion, shunning, and ostracism.

On the other hand, this local patriotism of Bremeners, who see everything customary and traditional as worth valuing and preserving, can also be seen as honorable. I do not believe there is any group of Germans so committed to local patriotism, to dependence on the soil where they were born, to love of the homeland. To them, Bremen is the city of cities, the most beautiful on earth. Wherever they might establish themselves and make a fine business—for they combine hard work, action, speculation and the honorable spirit of mercantilism to a high degree. Whether it is in the United States or furthest India, Ceylon, South Africa or West Africa, they maintain their Bremen values, customs and ways of life. They take a Bremen newspaper and read the advertisements and family notices with great interest, even if the paper has taken a month to arrive. They continue to make their favorite Bremen foods, particularly "brown coal with pimples," and on great holidays they bake their Bremen *Fladen*, order their wines from the Bremen Rathskeller at high cost, and when they are among themselves, *"snaken sie plattdütsch,"*[7] not excepting even the highest dignitary of the state. The highest honor in the course of their lives pales alongside the awareness of being a *"tugeborn Bremer Borjer."*[8]

Wherever there are more than half a dozen gathered abroad, particularly in lands beyond the seas, they buy a little land, build their houses with pretty gardens in the Bremen style, name their complex "New Bremen" and live there in the manner of their old homeland, for themselves and among themselves. In the United States alone, there are twelve Bremens and New Bremens. On the city boundaries of St. Louis itself, the wealthy Bremen families—Meier, Angelrodt, Eggers, Schütze, Barth, Wolf, Hoppe and others—built such a New Bremen, long since incorporated into the city and

7. Low German, "They speak Low German."
8. Low German, "Bremen Burgher by birth."

become an urban ward.[9] Other New Bremens are to be found in Illinois, Indiana, Kentucky, Ohio, Maine, New York and so on. In short, the local patriotism of Bremeners is nothing affected or manufactured, but rather a natural feeling of the heart, an expression of their attachment to their old homeland that is transformed into deeds. Bremeners, particularly those of the old school, are valued and respected both at home and abroad for their honesty and scrupulousness, as well as for their knowledge, their mercantile spirit and their sure-footed capacity for speculation.

The local patriotism of Bremeners sometimes leads them into comic episodes and excesses. Once I knew a Bremener in America who had a great kettle of "brown coal with pimples" made up for him and sent over one winter, which he devoured with great pleasure. In order to keep the air out, it was covered with a thick layer of grease and the kettle was enclosed in an airtight, soldered tin container. How the dish tasted when warmed up I have no idea, but it certainly was an expensive dish. In the same way, even the most educated Bremeners participated in the utterly medieval Free Market, the sole Saturnalia of this earnest old Hanseatic city. Making use of enjoyments of the coarsest sort that they usually would have avoided with indifference, they happily visited the cabarets and spectacles typical of a village fair, slinging down indigestible greasy pastries and honey cakes of all sorts as if they were being paid to do so. In short, all Bremeners, including the most decent, worthy and educated, went through the motions of a dissolute, mad, and bacchanalian life. Offering no real enjoyment, the ten-day Free Market closed with a universal hangover. No one really enjoyed it, but they did it anyway for the sole reason that it had always been so, because their fathers and grandfathers and their ancestors had participated in the Free Market in precisely the same way.

A population so possessed with tradition, custom and local dependence, also located in the extreme northwest corner of Germany and cut off from direct contact with other Germans, could still preserve these old patriarchal conditions for a while, particularly when encouraged by those below to comply, while striving to set a good example oneself. That was the goal and purpose of the patrician families, who saw their privileges threatened by the penetration of novelties. The universally esteemed Burghermaster Smidt worked in this direction, seeking by word, deed and example to conserve the old conditions of an Imperial city as long and as well as possible, in which he had considerable success.

---

9. Bremen, or New Bremen, was a development laid out by Emil Mallinckrodt, E. C. Angelrodt, and other partners north of St. Louis in 1844. It was still an independent municipality in the early 1850s, but it was soon annexed to the city of St. Louis. Today the area is usually described as the Hyde Park neighborhood.

As I said, Burghermaster Smidt had been dead for four years when I came to Bremen, and the impact of his more than half-a-century of official activity were still visible and tangible. But there was some subdued effort to accommodate a bit to new times and to advance as other towns had. This transformation was especially stimulated by the railway running from Hanover to Bremen, in those days Bremen's only rail link. In Hanover the Bremeners were not likely to receive much stimulation, for with the exception of a small new suburb, that court town still looked like a large medieval market center. But once on the railroad, the Bremeners went further, to Cologne or Berlin, to the Rhine and the Main, to Stuttgart and Munich, to Vienna and Trieste. They brought home with them many new ideas and accomplishments. All of that fermented, and I had many opportunities to observe the development and emergence of the old chrysalis of Bremen. When I left seven years later, it was already profoundly different from the Bremen of old Burghermaster Smidt. With Bremen's entry into the German Reich, this development took on an even faster tempo. Once Bremen abandons its status as a free port, which must happen sooner or later, and is incorporated into the *Zollverein* [Customs Union], only then shall it finally achieve its full development. Along with Hamburg it will become the most important seaport of the German Reich.[10] Whether its citizens will fare better then, or whether they will long for the patriarchal conditions of old Bremen, is a question that no one can answer. Only the future will tell.

10. The *Deutscher Zollverein* was a customs union combined with the creation of parallel fiscal systems in German states under Prussian leadership, and it is regarded as the preparatory phase of German unification. In keeping with the charter of the German League in 1815, the *Zollverein* was begun in 1828, encompassing almost all of Germany outside of Austrian control by 1854. Hamburg and Bremen, however, remained outside the union for many years because of their orientation to overseas trade, and they did not join the *Zollverein* until 1888, long after the unification of Germany under Prussian leadership in 1871. See *Der Grosse Brockhaus*, 18th ed. (Wiesbaden, 1978), 3: 140-1.

Patriarchal Still-Life
(1862)

Old Bremen, which was just awakening from the long stasis that had lasted until Burghermaster Smidt's death, was finally beginning to move forward. But with its narrow, small-scaled, Imperial-City conditions, it offered a striking contrast to me. I who had become used to American conditions; accustoming me to free movement, to unhindered expansion; above all else to individual independence, self-government, and self-administration. In truth, despite the storms of 1848 and the new constitution of 1854, the old patrician aristocracy still ruled this state of four and a half square German miles and seventy thousand residents. This aristocracy was drawn from about three dozen patrician families, from whose members the eighteen ruling senators were elected. They in turn elected two burghermasters from their own number. The citizenry, represented in the business of government by 150 deputies, could also speak as much as it wished, even bringing complaints and protests. But basically only the burghermasters and the senate decided matters. Respect for custom and tradition continued here, as well, to keep the citizenry within bounds, and sometimes to soothe irritated spirits as well. In short, the patriarchal situation still prevailed, one which Burghermaster Smidt had managed to extend half a century into modern times. In exchange, the Bremen burghers had the inestimable privilege of being free of any military. There was no obligation to serve in the military, neither a general one such as exists in Germany today, nor one restricted to particular classes of the population, as exists in other countries. Instead, each person born in Bremen was permanently free of military obligation. The Bremen government fulfilled its obligations to the German League in this regard by keeping under arms a battalion of Hanseatic infantry, whose seven hundred men were raised by free recruitment, as with the armies of America and England. The Hanseatic Battalion, then commanded by Lieutenant Colonel Niebour, had good officers, was well drilled, and later served well in the campaign of 1866.

The taxation system was just as archaic as the military obligation. For the direct tax, called the *Schoss*, each burgher decided himself what he was to contribute. On a certain day the burghers were invited to appear at the town hall for the *Schoss*. In the council chamber sat a taxation commission consisting of burghermasters, senators and accountants. Before them sat a great iron money chest which was closed but which had a large opening in the lid. Through this slot contributions could be thrown. The burghers always appeared on this occasion in full numbers, for they saw the *Schoss* as a matter of honor. When their name was called, each stepped up to the money chest, one after another, and placed his contribution without the amount being observed. Thus each one set his own taxes, paying in keeping with his own sense of equity and the amount of business he had done that year. No one asked him how much he paid, and no one asked for more or for an explanation. The word of a burgher and taxpayer was regarded as inviolable, and the state never had to complain. Almost every time, when the chest was opened and the contents counted, there was a surplus over the original amount called for in the tax assessment. In Bremen there were no tax collectors, nor were there seizures or forced auctions for back taxes. The burghers' self-assessment, through which they contributed to state expenses, was one of the most honorable sides of the Bremen state.

On the other hand, many of the remaining traditions of the old Imperial city were less uplifting. Everywhere there was the old pigtail style, in various guises, and everywhere it stalled the forward movement of the state and the free movement and progress of the population. Is it to be believed, for example, that until 1866 there were still three separate post offices, and one had to think which of these three should be used to send letters or called at to check if any had arrived. First of all there was the Princely Thurn und Taxis Reich Post Office, which preserved its ancient privilege to handle postal traffic with southern Germany and the smaller sovereign states. Then there was the Royal Prussian Post Office, which carried letters and newspapers for the Prussian state, England, and Russia. Finally there was the Hanoverian Post Office, which handled postal traffic for the Kingdom of Hanover. Three post offices, three sets of officials, three groups of letter carriers, and three different sets of postal rates. The same sort of confusion reigned in Bremen's postal service as had a hundred years before in most other places, but it had become an abnormality in our modern times.

There was as good as no direct connection with the sister-city of Hamburg, though it was a mere twelve German miles away. Every evening an old postal coach with six passenger seats, laden with baggage, would leave Bremen. Traveling on an extremely primitive military road, it crossed peat-bogs, stony wastelands and empty meadows, pausing here and there at an inn out of ancient times where there was nothing to order but cheese and *Schnaps*. It rolled and rocked through the entire night, only reaching Hamburg the next forenoon. It was such an uncomfortable, even painful, trip that whoever did it once would certainly not repeat it. If one wished to take the railway from Bremen to Hamburg, however, he had to make a great detour, going fourteen German miles to Hanover and from there twenty German miles to Harburg, then take a ship on the Elbe and finally reach Hamburg. As a result, to go a distance of twelve German miles, it was necessary to travel by railway thirty-four miles, and then spend some additional hours on a riverboat, which meant a considerable loss of money and time.

The city itself, with the exception of the largely modern suburb, had principally narrow streets snaking about in all directions. There were only a few straight, wide streets running from the railway station to the Weser River on which two wagons could pass one another easily, and this situation was a major hindrance to the loading and unloading of goods. There was little construction going on, and the narrow streets were lined with gabled houses two or three centuries old.

In these houses, the entry hall took up much of the space, and from this, area narrow wooden steps and landings passed to some very low rooms that resembled puppet theaters for children rather than decent homes for people. Each house had a parlor to receive visitors, called the *Bestestube,* which was roomier and better furnished than the rest, but which was never used by the residents, who entered it only in order to clean it thoroughly when a visit was expected. Otherwise, people lived and moved in the entryway and slept in the little doll rooms upstairs.

On the other hand, it is to the credit of Bremeners that in their narrow streets and in their houses, the most extraordinary cleanliness reigned, reminding one of Dutch conditions. Everything was clean and neat, and every Saturday everything was "made clean from the ground up." Houses being showered and scrubbed, windows washed, even façades and sidewalk in front were flooded with water and scrubbed with brushes on long poles. Whoever had anything to do on the street on Saturday could count himself lucky if he came out of it dry, without being soaked by a flood of water from above.

There were only a few guesthouses or coffee houses, and these had little business, for it was not regarded as proper to spend time there. One never saw anyone from the better classes at an inn, and visiting such establishments was frowned on for members of the female sex. In the place of the pleasures of the inn, however, there was the Rathskeller, which enjoyed particular privileges and rights in this regard thanks to the Bremeners' local patriotism. Families and women could visit the Rathskeller, of which Bremeners were very proud, without injury to their reputation. If they wished to they could even drink until the sun came up. What was improper for other places was proper there. As a result, the Rathskeller was the focus of public and social life, always heavily attended, and even the best persons had trouble finding a seat in that vast place at the time of the Free Market.

This old, peculiar drinking establishment had its special practices and restrictions. Only wine from the Rhine or the Moselle was served, for example, although of the best sorts. Rhine wines two hundred or three hundred years old, from the "Rose" or the "Twelve Apostles," as the great barrels were named in which these ancient Rüdesheim wines were stored, had once not been for sale but were only issued a few bottles at a time as gifts of esteem by the senate to foreigners, or occasionally as a result of a special prescription from a physician, to strengthen a person seriously ill. Foreigners of distinction, the *chargés d'affaires* or ambassador of a foreign power passing through, might be invited by the senate as a special honor to view the Rathskeller and sample the wine, as well as to dine grandly.

I participated in several such "samplings," and I can assure you from my own experience that these wines centuries old have the taste of repellent medicine, but that they also had extraordinary power to make one intoxicated. The best of these wines was a Rüdesheimer of 1624 kept in the barrel "Judas Iscariot," but it did not taste pleasant. Further, the ordinary guest only received cold foods and oysters, and at ten o'clock the Rathskeller was closed and no further guests admitted. Those who came before ten, however, could remain there and drink until morning, which tried-and-true "wine-biters" (as we said in Vienna) did with panache.

It was one of the patriarchal peculiarities of Bremen that the wine bar in the Rathskeller was an institution of state under the control of the government. Every autumn, at the time of the grape harvest, a senator and several experts were sent with the cellar master to the wine districts on the Rhine and the Moselle, entrusted with the official mission of sampling the pressing and the young wine everywhere in the good areas, buying at once only the best. Once a choice had been made, the seal of the city council of Bremen was placed on the barrel. When the wine was ripe, it was sent under guard to Bremen and given to the cellar master there for handling and improvement. The cellar master and his assistants were all sworn officials of the state. It was only in 1832 that a resolution of the senate permitted these ancient wines, which represented a capital of incomparable worth, to be sold by the bottle to private persons. Until then these wines, which had the aura of high old age, were the object of high esteem, and people ascribed to them astonishing value and healing powers. But when anyone could drink some, even if for a high price, there were few takers after the first samples, for the taste, as I said, was not conducive to enjoyment.

The Rathskeller was then, as it had been for three hundred years, one of the most interesting sights in the old Hanseatic city. It was the gathering place for all foreigners and residents, and in its fine rooms, dedicated to Bacchus, there was open cheer that never exceeded the limits of decency. Here friendships for life were sealed with *Schmollis*, here much mercantile business was reviewed and concluded, here acquaintances were made and marriages arranged. Distinguished foreigners were invited to the table of honor for "sampling the wine," which took place in a special hall which was otherwise closed. There the burghermasters and senate had once held its secret sessions and discussions. The most secret and significant state negotiations were held in a special cellar hollow, with an appearance like a chapel, in which there was only the great cask with the *Rosenwein*, with a large painted rose on the ceiling before it. The saying of entrusting someone with a secret *sub rosa* is supposed to have originated there. There I have passed many pleasant evenings with natives and foreign visitors, particularly my fellow Americans, and I look back with pleasure on the cheerful, respectable society that prevailed there.

In those days, the realms of fashion and elegance were not represented in Bremen. Sellers of fashionable articles were few, and the articles they sold had not a trace of Parisian elegance. They concentrated more on the useful than on the beautiful. As a result, the attire of women one saw on the street was very simple and modest, as Smidt would have loved to see it. Even the richest ladies wore simple dresses of black, brown or gray, buttoned closed at the neck. I still recall what an enormous furor was made when one freshly arrived beautiful young American woman appeared on the wall promenade with deep décolleté, a red shawl and a hat with an ostrich plume. Everyone marveled at her and the street youth pointed with their fingers at the extraordinary sight, following her and making mocking remarks. This was discussed in all the families, as if it were an extraordinary event, and it was spoken of by women as a matter of great offense. The result was that Bremen families to which the young lady had been recommended found themselves compelled to speak with her in a friendly manner and advise her to dress more modestly out of concern that they might themselves be compromised.

Now all of that has much changed, and the whole of Bremen life has taken on a more modern shape. The result is that Bremen can compete in many aspects with lively Hamburg. Much is being built, the old gable houses increasingly vanish and glittering stores for fashionable wares are much in evidence, finding a good market, with Bremen ladies who now participate in the fashions of Paris and Berlin. The population has increased considerably, already exceeding one hundred thousand. Even Jews and Jewish businesses are numerous in Bremen nowadays, while earlier a Jew could not even linger in the town, even overnight. In my days there were no more eighty Jews in all of Bremen. I left Bremen in 1868 and have not seen it since, so that I cannot judge from my own experience but only report what is written from there. What I saw then was a relatively general distribution of prosperity in the population, with no concerns about food or pressing poverty, and while I was there I never saw a beggar. Whether that is still the case, now that Bremen has taken a more modern direction, I do not know. The peace and charm of friendly old Bremen did me a great deal of good after my irritating, stimulating career as an American journalist and politician. The old Hanseatic city pleased me beyond measure, and I would not have minded closing my days there in peace and respectability. It was only that fate had condemned me to a restless life and would not permit it. My agitated life would not yet come to rest for a long time.

After a month in a hotel, I finally found an appealing rental home next to a mill before the Doven Gate. Such were not then very frequent in Bremen. In the midst of the splendid Wall Park was a small, two-story house and its lovely garden fulfilled all my modest wishes. I rented it, and here I led a peaceful still-life. I established the consulate in a large, new building on Oberen Strasse, in the center of the city. Having reserved the right with the Department of State to name my own deputy consul and consular agent for Bremerhaven, I appointed my son Carl as deputy consul. Despite his youth, he had already proved himself a capable, reliable businessman as my theatrical secretary in the St. Louis Opera House and later as regimental adjutant. He went on to prove himself as my representative through five whole years. As my agent in Bremerhaven, I named the merchant F. W. Specht, a capable, experienced businessman on whom I could rely for any matter. In those days the position in Bremerhaven was not provided with a set salary; instead, the agent relied on fees, half of which he gave to me and half of which he kept. My own income was $3,000 in salary, $300 for my quarters and about $800 from Bremerhaven.

Confirmation of my appointments arrived from Washington by return post, and I worked my way into my office, whose duties I soon understood intimately. My primary obligation, beyond the usual consular business and the political reports for Secretary of State Seward, was to keep a close watch on Bremerhaven, and the smaller nearby harbors, always remaining informed of shipments of weapons, munitions and other contraband of war for the rebel states and hindering them whenever possible. I remained in constant contact by letter with the extraordinarily watchful and ever well-informed United States consul in London, Mr. Morse; with his agents in other English harbors; and with Captain Winslow, the commander of the United States frigate *Kearsarge*, cruising the North Sea (this same Winslow ran the privateer *Alabama*, under Captain Semmes, aground off Cherbourg).[1] I telegraphed them on all suspicious matters. In return, they notified me and

---

1. John Ancrum Winslow (1811-1873), a career naval officer, was a captain when he received command of the *U.S.S. Kearsarge*, patrolling from the Azores to the English Channel for Southern privateers. He did battle near Cherbourg with the *C. S. S. Alabama* and captured it on 19 June 1864. *DAB*, 20: 397-8. Legal disputes over damage claims between the United States and Great Britain, where the *Alabama* had been built and supplied, led to chronic diplomatic wrangling between the United States and Great Britain, even leading some American politicians to demand the cession of Canada as a price of settlement. The *Alabama* claims case was settled by arbitration on 14 September 1872 in keeping with the Treaty of Washington, 1871, resulting in the payment by the British government of $15.5 million in gold. See James Truslow Adams, ed., *Dictionary of American History*, vol. I, 40-41.

Carl Boernstein, son of Henry Boernstein. Carte de visite photograph by Jean Baptiste Feilner, Vienna and Bremen, c. 1863. Courtesy of the Missouri Historical Society.

sent me their discoveries, so that it was often possible for me to make myself useful to our country and government in this way.

In order to come into direct contact with my colleague in Hamburg for this purpose, I visited the city of my birth as soon as I could. It was moving to see Hamburg again, the precious town to which all the memories of my childhood were tied. Fifty years had passed since I had left Hamburg with my parents, in the period of French rule. Yet on my first outing in the district where we had last lived, I knew where I was at once, needing no guide. So sharp and lasting are the impressions of childhood. Without asking, I found the house on the small towpath that was our home, the home of my uncle on the Venusberg, the Goose-Market, the theater, the *Jungfernsteig*, the school I had attended. Everything was just as I had seen it fifty years before. Only in the new districts, built after the great fire, could I not find my way. It was in vain that I sought the house where I was born, opposite the old town hall, for it had been destroyed by flames along with the town hall. In Hamburg I met Bernays and his family; Bernays had been transferred as consul from Zürich to Elsinore. We passed splendid days, finding a friendly reception with the accomplished Dr. Wolfsohn and his amiable family. I also discovered a sister of my mother, Aunt Fischer, who was still a strong old woman, as well as her son, the playmate of my childhood, now the wine merchant Eduard Fischer; another aunt, Kuffner; and finally my dear old friend from Linz, the Imperial Opera singer Adolf Schunk, who had long since left the theater and was leading a quiet, carefree life as an administrator of the *Johanneum*. Those were fine days I passed in Hamburg then, of which I cannot think without pleasure. Unfortunately I have never again seen my dear home town, as much as I would have liked to, but I hold it ever in cheerful memory.

Back *in* America Once More
(1862)

The winter of 1861-62 passed in a quiet repose, a genuine relief after twelve years of hectic, irritating labor in St. Louis. But this still-life was darkened by the general news from America, which spoke of the increasingly stronger organization of the secession states, their successes in the field, and the hesitation, unsteadiness, and inadequate development of military power by our Union government. I received bleak news from St. Louis about the political parties there, and about the direction of my own paper, which led me to expect the worst. As I mentioned before, John C. Frémont had been named commander of the Western Military District (Illinois, Kentucky, Missouri, Kansas) on 9 July 1861, assuming his command before I left St. Louis. This was a new lease on life for the so-called Radicals, those people who still nourished themselves on the illusions of 1848 and to whom the moderate American pace of public affairs was too ponderous and boring. They rallied around Frémont, pressing him to take radical measures, and his staff, consisting largely of Hungarian revolutionary officers, did its own bit. Frémont thus entered St. Louis not merely as military commandant, but as a sort of dictator, called to save his threatened fatherland through forceful measures. All of Missouri was declared in a state of siege, although he had no power to make this effective, and on 31 August he issued that premature proclamation declaring the slaves of all adherents to secession within his district to be free. In addition, he was moved by his quartermaster general, McKinstry, to all manner of unauthorized steps, even some contrary to regulations, so that an investigation was launched against Frémont and McKinstry in response to many complaints reaching Washington. The investigation was personally led by War Secretary Cameron and his adjutant general. The result was a report in the *Congressional Documents* series, a 1,000-page volume whose documents and testimony severely compromised McKinstry and portrayed Frémont as lacking independence and decisiveness, hence weak and unreliable.

Further, things went very poorly in the Western theater of the war once Frémont took over command. The brave General Lyon did his best to beg reinforcements, but Frémont sent him none, for his general staff had developed grandiose plans for decisive campaigns to create a base of operations in Cairo, a small town in the Mississippi on a swampy corner at the mouth of the Ohio. This base would serve, as these would-be Moltkes declared, to protect the entire northwest of the Union against attacks by the

Carl Wimar's gray-tone painting of the "radical trinity" of Franz Sigel, John Charles Frémont, and Constantine Blandowski, an early martyr to the Union cause in Missouri who died of a wound received in the Camp Jackson affair. Photograph by John A. Scholten. Courtesy of the Missouri Historical Society.

rebels. At the very moment this was happening, the Southern generals Price, McCullough, Pillow, and Thompson had already occupied all of southern Missouri and were preparing to march against St. Louis and conquer it, while poor Lyon, thrown back on his own weak forces and left in the lurch by Frémont, was defeated at Wilson's Creek and fell. In the meantime, a rebel corps of 20,000 men under Price made an advance against northern Missouri, overran Lexington, and forced Colonel Mulligan to surrender with a 2,000-man Union troop.

After these indubitable fruits of Frémont's military administration, the federal government in Washington opened its eyes to Frémont's utter incapacity. His emancipation proclamation was declared null and void by President Lincoln, and a disciplinary procedure was launched against him and McKinstry. As a result of this investigation, Frémont was finally deprived of his command on 2 November, and it was transferred to General Halleck.

Despite all of this, Frémont's adherents, the Radicals, continued to support him. Particularly those Germans who were still under the spell of 1848 rallied to Frémont, who knew how to flatter them and who had made himself popular. On his return to St. Louis, he was received by the Germans as a conquering *triumphator*. A sword of honor was presented to him and resolutions were passed against the acts of the federal government. Frémont's removal was damned in the harshest terms. With this occurred the worst thing that could happen in a land torn by civil war, a split within the Republican or Union Party, dividing into the "Emancipationists," who called themselves "Unconditional Union Men," demanding immediate and uncompensated abolition of slavery, led by the political demagogue B. Gratz Brown. The "Conservative Union Men," continued to cleave to Frank P. Blair, still supporting the gradual elimination of slavery in stages. If this split among Union people was perilous, it had the even worse result of dissolving German American unity in the process. Germans fell into two factions, fighting one another. My painstaking work of twelve years to form Germans into a single, compact, strong force that determined the course of events in all political questions, was destroyed with one blow. My enemies used this propitious opportunity to place themselves under the Frémont banner and attack the *Anzeiger* and me. Frémont was celebrated as a great hero and patriotic martyr, while Blair, up to that time the Germans' truest friend and tried leader, lost his popularity and was attacked, even made an enemy.

The Frémont movement, in hindsight only a straw fire that soon flickered out, took on ever-greater dimensions and drew in wider circles. Even the *Anzeiger* and its editor, Georg Hillgärtner, a Forty-Eighter and radical who was weak and easily misled, joined with the Frémont movement and turned against Blair, to my deep distress. The sad result of this split among Missouri Germans became visible much later. The strong

German American phalanx was broken, and the slaveholders, nativists and enemies of adoptive citizens triumphed, turning even more decisively against the Germans.

If Missouri today, twenty years later, has not progressed like other free states; if it still stands under the rule of proslavery Democrats to whom liberty, progress and cultural development are all equally hateful; if immigration does not flow to this state, so well located and richly supplied with resources; and if the population has not risen, as is the case in Illinois, for example, then the basis for this is to be sought solely in that split of the Germans in 1861-62. This division lamed the true vanguard of progress, the Missouri Germans, giving new strength to their reactionary opponents.

As a result of this split, there formed a Frémont party and a Blair party, which fought each other intensely and destroyed each other. To be sure, the Frémont fever was gone the next year as quickly as it came. But the split left a division in the Germans, once so solid and united, and its sad results have not been mended to this day. Frémont was placed once more at the head of an army corps in West Virginia, where he showed once again "his utter want of capacity," as Montgomery Blair often said in his letters to me. He left the army and allowed himself to be put up by the radicals as a presidential candidate against Lincoln in 1864, but he soon voluntarily withdrew when he saw the hopelessness of his candidacy.[1] Frémont the politician became Frémont the financier. Eventually he became president of the Southwest Pacific Railroad Company and of the Costa Rica Railroad Company, which was to bind the Atlantic and the Pacific Oceans with rails, as Lesseps is now trying to do with a canal. Due to non-fulfillment of the conditions of his charter, he lost his privilege. Then came the rather offensive stories about the Mariposa claim, which ended with a degrading condemnation of Frémont by French courts. The once-so-celebrated Frémont vanished in darkness and oblivion. In recognition of his earlier genuine service as pathfinder and creator of gold-rich California, has found decent provision as the governor of one of our western territories. In St. Louis, where he was once worshipped as a demigod, no one thinks of him or of his time of illusion anymore, but the results are far from being erased.

In those days it was a common cry among the German population that Blair attacked Frémont out of jealousy over his rise, and that Frémont had been brought down by the lowest of means. It was even said that the real enmity lay between the two wives—Blair's wife, who was a very well-

---

1. See on this candidacy generally, Jörg Nagler, *Frémont contra Lincoln. Die deutsch-amerikanische Opposition in der Republikanischen Partei während des amerikanischen Bürgerkriegs* (Frankfurt a. M.: Peter Lang, 1984); an English edition is in preparation with Northern Illinois University Press.

Georg Hillgärtner, Boernstein's editor at the Anzeiger des Westens, *1861–62. Photograph courtesy of the State Historical Society of Missouri.*

educated and energetic political figure in her own right, and Mrs. Frémont, Benton's favorite daughter Jessie—and that the husbands paid heavily for the evil results of this hostility between two women. I believe all of this is merely gossip popular in political circles in those days. I was a frequent, intimate guest in the Blair home, and never did I hear the least hint of such a hostility. On the contrary, I can assert that Frémont owed his original naming as commander of the Western Military District to the zealous, tireless efforts of both Blairs, and that it was only when he proved himself unsuited for this difficult post, even injurious to the Union, that the Blairs declared themselves opposed to him and sought his recall. In all the letters from both Blairs to me, which I still possess, there recurs the refrain of "Frémont's utter want of capacity." But the masses were not to be enlightened on this matter. Frémont's adherents composed a whole series of popular legends and myths that surrounded his head with a halo, while Blair was denigrated as a vile intriguer and enemy of Germans.

One may imagine how painfully these conditions touched me in Bremen, and with what sad feelings I pursued these new events. Once more everything I had created over years of intense struggle stood in question. In the course of the winter of 1861-62, I repeatedly wrote to my son and to Hillgärtner, analyzing the dreadful results of the German split and beseeching them to take a different position. But they both responded that they dared not act differently. Public opinion was too agitated for Frémont and against Blair, and any attempt to speak on behalf of Blair would bring the ruin of the *Anzeiger.*

In early 1862, conditions grew worse rather than better. State and congressional elections were scheduled for that November, and the split among Union people deepened. The radicals and Frémont supporters were opposing Blair, who had so successfully represented Missouri in Congress until then, with a Congressional candidate of their own in the person of the insignificant lawyer Samuel Knox. Certain ambitious politicians, such as Gratz Brown, Henry T. Blow[2] and others, who had hitherto played only a subordinate role, were trying to rise to the top. Meanwhile the *Missouri Republican* and proslavery and nativist opponents to the Union promoted this split among Unionists, fishing in troubled water in hopes of a victory for their slavery sympathies. Then in early May, to my great surprise, I received a

---

2. Henry Taylor Blow (1817-1875), born in Virginia, graduated from Saint Louis University. President of the Iron Mountain Railroad and a pioneer in lead mining, he was a major promoter of Dred Scott's suit for freedom. (See Walter Ehrlich, *They Have No Rights: Dred Scott's Struggle for Freedom* (Westport, Conn.: Greenwood Press, 1979). Blow was U.S. Minister to Venezuela, 1861-62, "Charcoal" (Unconditional Unionist) candidate for Congress in 1862, reelected in 1864, and left Congress in 1867. He was then U.S. Minister to Brazil, 1869-71. He was the father of the noted educator Susan Blow (1843-1916). *DAB*, 2: 391-2; *BDUSC*, 636.

long letter from Henry T. Blow informing me that he had returned from his ambassadorial position in South America in March, and as a precise and non-partisan observer of the political situation in Missouri he had come to the conclusion

> that if the future of the city of St. Louis and of the state of Missouri is to be a good one, it would only be achieved if the selfless and patriotic men of the party would set aside their small differences of opinion and sacrifice for the common good, joining together solidly and harmoniously.

The letter then continued:

Our party is divided and torn, and we must admit that a portion of our people has surrendered to an extreme radicalism bordering on madness, injuring both our good reputation and the constitutional rights of others, placing everything in question. Almost all of our friends approve of Lincoln's careful and measured policy, but another portion, primarily the German population, is giving the President only lukewarm support and inclines to the most extreme abolitionism. We must settle our differences and join together again, offering the federal government the strongest support and showing the world that the Republican Party is a strictly constitutional and pro-Union party, that it respects all rights and has earned the trust of the people. In this situation, and because we do not have a single newspaper in St. Louis supporting the government, I turn to you, trusting in the good will and friendship that you have always shown me, hoping that there be no suspicion of wrong motivation in what I am doing. I have always been a friend of our German fellow citizens. Now I come to the object of this letter. I know of no man in our West who has so great an influence on the German population as you have. Further, I believe that, should you come here, you will join us and provide powerful support for Lincoln's policy in Missouri. Under these assumptions, I went to Washington and found that those in the leading circles have placed the same trust in you. Hence I arranged for you a leave of four months, and I hope that you will use it to come to us and strongly to support President Lincoln and the policy of the federal government. Our situation has improved; the rebellion approaches its end, and thanks and hope are the feelings which fill us. With the best greetings to Dr. Bernays,

Yours sincerely,
Henry T. Blow.

Two days later the dispatch arrived in Bremen from the State Department, granting me four months leave without my ever having asked for it. I perceived myself to be obligated to obey this call instantaneously, so I ordered my affairs in a hurry. Giving the consulate to my son Carl as acting consul, I had paid my respects to Burghermaster Duckwitz and Senator Smidt, asking them to make my son's difficult task easier through their friendly cooperation. I then took ship with my wife for New York. We were already there in the last days of June, going without delay to St. Louis.

I have only related this episode in detail because, both then and later, it was said that Blair called on my assistance and also had Bernays return to help his election, while in truth it was Henry T. Blow who called me back to St. Louis, and later Bernays as well. I arrived in St. Louis in the first days of July, finding the situation profoundly deteriorated. The split among the Unionists and among the Germans was as sharp and ominous as I portrayed it at the start of this chapter, so I need add nothing now.

The election campaign had already begun in a lively fashion. St. Louis then had two representatives in Congress, one for the northern part and one for the southern. For the former, Unionists supported their old leader Blair, while the Frémont supporters had elevated Samuel Knox. In the southern part of the city, Henry T. Blow was the candidate, without a serious opponent. The Germans were all for Blow, while the battle for and against Blair was fought with great bitterness.

My first business was therefore to give the *Anzeiger* a different direction. After I had discussed everything with my son and we were in agreement over everything, I openly told Hillgärtner that the *Anzeiger* could no longer continue in its previous anti-Blair direction. My old friendship for Blair, his services for Germans and his advancement of liberty over the years obligated me in ways I neither wished to deny nor could deny. Further, the split of the Unionists, particularly within the German population, had to be ended at any price, because both divisions would bring great harm.

Hillgärtner, who had been fully informed that I was coming back and hence foresaw the coming change, had already taken precautions and made an agreement with the Frémont people. My earlier enemies, in particular, had promised him support in advance. He rejected my statement from the high horse of principles and loyalty to convictions. Declaring in a rather brutal manner that he would not alter the previous position of the *Anzeiger*, he insisted on leaving the editor's position at once. I had no alternative but to grant him the release he had so suddenly and rudely demanded, and I took over the editorship myself. With money from my enemies, Hillgärtner founded a new newspaper, the *Neue Zeit*, in which he fired away at me to his heart's content, heaping me with mockery and libel. But he could not keep it going, and he soon had to give the paper into other hands.[3]

I now applied in Washington through Blow for an extended leave for Bernays. Having had enough of his consulate already, he returned at once. I placed the editorship in his hands, and we united with all our force for the Union, for President Lincoln, and for the election of Blair and Blow to Congress. The telling French saying, *"Les absents ont toujours tort"*[4] soon proved itself on me, however. I had been three months in the field and nine months in Europe, and twelve months away from my theater of operations had significantly reduced my once-great popularity. Despite all the efforts I made, I was no longer able to draw the Germans into a compact whole.[5] The split had persisted too long, and the bitterness between the two factions had already sharpened into mutual hatred. Those who are absent are always wrong, and I had been gone too long. Popularity is a highly perishable commodity, won through continuous, tireless effort, but quickly lost through absence or inactivity. Other men and other newspapers had won influence in my absence, and I hit against a stubborn opposition, where I had to fight for every inch of terrain.

I did have the satisfaction of seeing Blair and Blow elected, but I left St. Louis after the election completely disappointed, with only the smallest hope for the future. Blair's election was badly damaged by the excessive zeal of some of his friends, and it was disputed by Knox in the Congress. According to the investigation, there were irregularities in some of the more distant northern precincts committed by some of Blair's overzealous friends, particularly a Mr. Elleard, without Blair's knowledge. Blair's election was annulled by Congress, and this humiliation injured the sensitive man to his

---

3. *Die Neue Zeit* was published from 1862 to 1864, during which time its editorship merged with the *Westliche Post* in 1863. Emil Preetorius, who was the dominant figure in St. Louis German journalism for decades with the *Westliche Post* began his career with *Die Neue Zeit.* See Arndt/Olson, I: 265-66.

4. French, "Those who are absent are always wrong."

5. Daniel Hertle, *Die Deutschen in Nordamerika* (Chicago, 1865), 110-111: "After some skirmishing in the press, Blair's high council decided to take the Germans by storm in a great popular rally to be held at Rudi's Garten on 28 July 1862. When Blair appeared on the platform, he was interrupted by 'Hurrahs' for Frémont. In his irritation, he repeated the unwise phrase, 'I have made him and I killed him.' Then the storm really broke. Blair's agents, scattered through the crowd, sought to silence Frémont's friends by force. In vain. It came to deeds, and the speeches lost all impact. In vain was raised the gentle voice of the Consul of Bremen, who had come all the long way from Europe to handle the embittered masses. He had to hear unpleasant calls as well. Their assault on the fortress of German will went badly awry, and the bitterness against Blair became all the more intense as a result of the mistreatment which individual Germans suffered, and his fate was sealed from that evening forward."

foundation. The rude treatment he had received, particularly from the Germans, turned his earlier friendship into hatred. He alienated himself from the Union Party and returned in the end to the Democratic camp. I never approved of the way he did this, but the mistreatment and persecution he received from the Germans, from whom he deserved only thanks, at least excuses it.

I left St. Louis in a dark mood. Traveling with the English steamer *Edinburgh* to Liverpool, I passed eight days viewing London, then spent fourteen pleasant days with my wife's sister, the Marquise de Bréme, in Paris before returning to Bremen. There I found the consulate in the best order and was able to resume my duties, breathing a sigh of relief to be back in quiet Bremen. I would have done better not to have returned then but to have remained in St. Louis, turning all my attentions to my newspaper. I would have recovered my popularity and influence with time, and then I could have assured a secure future for myself and my dependents. But that was not to be.

The Fall *of the Anzeiger*
(1863)

The concerns, unease and fears for the future with which I left St. Louis to return to my post would prove only too justified. It later became clear to me what an error I had committed when I interrupted my political and journalistic career, endangering my hard-won independence and material existence. Misled by the phantom of a consulate overseas, I had been moved to accept the position in Bremen. At least I can view the step objectively now, and I can only advise my journalist colleagues and other countrymen who have already established a place in life for themselves not to follow my example, giving up their previous activity and placing their existence in doubt. They will lose popularity, influence and leverage, and they will see their business go to ruin. For they will receive no more compensation than that, for a few years, they will have the pleasure of living in some town as United States consul, a position that will provide them with much labor and distress. They will enjoy no real respect and no true authority, since overseas they see the American *chargés d'affaires* and consuls not as permanent diplomatic officials who have a solid position and are real representatives of their government, but they are held for what they actually are, which is party hacks and election agitators thrown a consular tidbit after the victory. Their ephemeral existence will be ended at most in four years when the elemental flood of the next presidential election sweeps everything away, and they will be replaced by new grandees made of the same material. That is, if a change is not made even earlier through the unceasing boring and pressing of hungry office hunters and the representative patronage system.

I had rather little trouble with this system, for I was a consul in a trading city where there was no court, no courtly etiquette, no bureaucracy, and also no prideful aristocracy. I officially dealt only with merchants, at the most with an elected burghermaster, and the entire coloration of life was bourgeois and the form that of a republic. Yet in my near vicinity I had the example of our consul in Hanover, who had his position and status painfully narrowed by the royal Hanoverian court circles. Our consuls have had similar experiences in small and large court towns. During the eight years I passed in Germany, I spent a great deal of time with our consuls, and everywhere I heard the same complaints. American consuls enjoyed relatively good status in seagoing towns, but in interior cities, particularly where the courts reside, they were not regarded as of full weight or as officials of the United States government. They were neither respected nor viewed as part of the diplomatic hierarchy. They were simply temporary party hacks who might play consul today or tomorrow, but who would return to their counters or desks in a few years, earning their daily bread as journalists or plowing their acres on their farms and watching their cattle. Hence in the eyes of European diplomats and bureaucrats they were only volunteers, replacements and straw men, not representatives of the great American republic.

This problem is most visible in Germany when the posts are filled with German Americans. There the English and French consuls and the representatives of Russia, Austria, and Italy receive greater respect, for they are permanent state officials. Conversely, the position of our consuls in France, England, and Italy is always more tolerable. In addition, there is the inadequate pay of most consular positions, despite the fact that the United States consul has to keep a household (if a modest one), represent his country, and as one of the men of position be approached first in subscriptions and collections for charity or social purposes.

Traveling Americans of reduced means who have lost their travel money for some reason make similar claims on the purse of the consul. When they are thus in difficulty, they consider it the least the consul can do to send him back home. To support poor Americans overseas, the United States consuls have no funds at all, and if they turn to Washington for compensation in especially needy cases, they will receive none. Only American sailors who have somehow been left behind somewhere overseas can be returned at government cost, and this in the cheapest possible way. In this regard I have paid a considerable tuition, and I have had to pay the costs for supporting poor Americans entirely out of my own pocket.

The situation is even worse for those United States consuls who happen to be at the site of a so-called American colony. There they are exploited as business agents, brokers, arrangers of housing or servants and representatives to the police or taxation authorities for the "upper tens" who live for a while in Germany, Italy, Switzerland and so forth to save money or other reasons. These people often misuse the consuls' friendliness and willingness to please fellow citizens. Brentano in Dresden,[1] Klauprecht in Stuttgart, and our consuls in Rome, Florence, and Naples could tell many such stories. If the wishes, or rather the preemptory demands of these "American colonists" are not immediately and unconditionally fulfilled by the consul, bitter letters of complaint and denunciation go to Washington, either directly to the State

---

1. Lorenz Brentano (1813-1891), a lawyer from Mannheim, participated as a moderate leftist in the 1848 revolutions, being named president of the provisional republic in 1849 and emigrating to America in 1850. After almost a decade as a farmer in Kalamazoo, Michigan, he went to Chicago and became editor of the *Illinois Staatszeitung*. He was a leader of German politics in Chicago, U.S. Consul in Dresden, 1872-76, and a Republican representative in Congress, 1877-79. Zucker, 281-2; *BDUSC*, 666.

Department or to influential members of congress. The consul will be portrayed in the most bilious colors as incapable, unpatriotic, incompatible with his compatriots, even as forgetful of his duties, and the end result of these railings will be his recall. I was spared this misery in Bremen, where no one would live for the pleasure of it. The Americans who live there are merchants and manufacturers who understand European conditions and make no unseemly demands of the consul. What I know about it rests on the stories told by my colleagues of those days. But the complaints of distressed emigrants, mutinies on American trading vessels, and other episodes give the consul more than enough to do, and it is often not the most pleasant work.

It once happened that a dreadful mutiny broke out on an American packet ship that had just arrived in Bremerhaven. The mutineers had ejected the captain and steersman from the ship by brute force, and they did not want to allow them back on board. The captain came to me for help and protection, and I went with him to Bremerhaven and onto the ship. Convincing talk and efforts to arbitrate all accomplished nothing with these furious people. My next visit, which I made with the harbormaster and two Bremen land dragoons, had no more success, so force had to be used. For this purpose I had to requisition Hanoverian military help from nearby Geerstemünde, and after much running about and writing, it was permitted. Only when I appeared on board for the third time with a military escort was it possible to bind the mutineers as prisoners and bring them ashore, after a stormy confrontation that degenerated into a brawl. They remained in prison for several weeks while the consulate bore the costs of their imprisonment, food, and so on until another American ship was found whose captain was willing to take the prisoners on board and deliver them in New York. Meanwhile, the captain of the mutiny ship had to raise a new crew to take his ship back to the United States. Only when he returned there was the investigation begun, and I had to send over sworn testimony, affidavits, official reports and the like to be used as exhibits in the trial. In short, it was one of the least uplifting episodes in my service.

All this should be enough to show that the position of an American consul overseas is not the most comfortable. I can only repeat my warning, declaring it a result of my own experiences, that any independent man in a respectable situation and an assured existence should stay far away from the offer of a consulate. Only when we have a standing consular corps like other countries, when the representatives of the great republic are financially better situated, when they can also do something for their compatriots seeking help and especially when our consular instructions (whose continual theory of appeasement and agreement I have already dealt with) are revised into something worthy of a great republic—only then will it get better and an

American consulate be a position of trust and honor. Until then, it will be advisable in every way to avoid this dubious honor.

A hard blow which struck me in 1863 was the sudden and utterly unnecessary closure of my newspaper, the *Anzeiger des Westens.* When I left St. Louis in November 1862 for the second and last time, the newspaper had lost few of its subscribers, despite the bitter struggle the Frémont people led against it. It was the income from advertisements, rather, that had painfully dropped, for almost all business was suffering due to the war. Now, during the winter, times grew steadily worse. The number of subscribers also fell, while the price of paper, printing materials and wages went up along with all things due to the devaluation of paper currency. Newspapers temporarily reduced their formats, though that did not suffice over the long run, and I was deeply involved in correspondence with my son and Bernays to come to agreement with our party friends over how to assure the survival of the paper. We already gathered considerable support when my son, who was leading the business, distressed over the thanklessness of the Germans, for whom the *Anzeiger* had done so much over the years, and embittered over the continuing attacks of the Frémont party, suddenly made a *coup de tête* without asking me. He abruptly ceased publishing the paper. This not only robbed me of my last support, but also endangered my current situation.

Over the course of time, I have come to the conviction that my son had another motive that moved him to this unexpected and rash act. During his three months of military service my son, young and lively in character, had come to have a taste for the military life. He would read every day what successes his earlier comrades had won in battle or other distinctions, seeing they had risen to staff officers and regimental commanders. This impelled him to return to the military career. On top of that, there were the continual struggle with financial cares, the hateful attacks of opponents, the gradual loss of the paper's earlier popularity. In short, without even Bernays knowing about it, my son had a notice posted at the top of the paper of 13 February 1863: "The *Anzeiger* will cease to appear beginning tomorrow." He released the typesetters and the rest of the personnel, delivering the material of the newspaper and the printing plant to my old good friend Sam Jacoby as trustee. He then went east, where he was at once taken on as a major commanding a newly formed Negro battalion. He distinguished himself at its head in all the operations of the following years on the Peninsula, and he was one of the first to enter Richmond. It was only after the end of the war that he departed the army, a lieutenant colonel.

The news of the newspaper's sudden end hit me without warning in Bremen, and it hurt me profoundly. No great newspaper was ever ended so suddenly, so unnecessarily or so disgracefully. The paper had existed almost thirty years and had taken the leading position in the entire West. If my son had taken the proper steps with the leaders of the party before making his rash decision, Blair and his friends would have raised the financial means at once to assure its survival, which was their most dependable mouthpiece.[2] Bernays could have taken over operations and my son could have satisfied his military desires. If he had informed me earlier of his decision, I would even have thrown down my consular position in an instant and rushed to St. Louis to lead the paper myself. But he did neither of these things. I had no inkling of his hasty decision, and the news hit me like a lightning bolt from a clear sky. I only learned it from the issue of 13 February, which was followed by letters from my son, Bernays, and my St. Louis friends on the next steamer. From all of these I learned that the cessation of the *Anzeiger* had been unnecessary, that the settlement of financial problems had already been assured by Bernays' efforts and the decision of the party. It was a true *coup de tête*, the rash, passionate decision of a hot-blooded young man who regrets it deeply today.

What was to be done? All complaint, all reasoning about how it could have been avoided was of no use. When I think back on whether I could have rushed back and revived the *Anzeiger*, I also have to tell myself that it would have been an extremely difficult, almost impossible mission. Three weeks had already passed in which the *Anzeiger* had not appeared when I received the news in Bremen. Five weeks or more would have been required to order my affairs in Bremen, send in my resignation, receive confirmation and to return to St. Louis. A further fourteen days would have been needed to prepare for the reappearance of the paper. In short, it would have taken a full quarter of a year, and in the meantime my subscribers and advertising businessmen would have gone to other papers. It would have been necessary to start over, to win a new public, starting from the beginning. In addition, the news from over the sea grew ever darker. Business stagnated even more, and the population's mood grew ever more depressed and discouraged. This was actually the worst period of the long Civil War. I knew all of the enormous hindrances and problems that would oppose my efforts, and in

---

2. R. G. Dun & Co. Collection, Harvard University Graduate School of Business Administration, Missouri vol. 37, p. 612, report of 11 July 1862, describes the paper's situation: "Have the largest German circulation of any paper in the city, but like other publishers feel the pressure of the times and short patronage. But personal friends and party interests will keep them up. Called good for current expenses." Ibid., report of 27 August 1862 records further debts, but holds the firm still "Good for wants." Ibid., report of 9 February 1863, "Doing a good business. Has some means and out to [illegible] money. Good for wants." Same date, "The 'Anzeiger des Westens' for some reason has been discontinued." Ibid., reports of 1 August 1863 and 18 February 1864, on chances for resumption and on liquidation.

the meantime I had become fifty-eight years old and feared that my strength and energy would not suffice to for me to start over and revive the closed paper. I was then physically a bit sickly, as well as psychologically depressed, and so after a hard internal struggle I decided to suspend my efforts and give in to fate.

I sent full powers to my friend Sam Jacoby, who proved himself a true and tireless friend in this crisis and in following years. I transferred to him a deed of trust securing the property of the *Anzeiger* until my sons had paid the balance of their contract (which never happened). Jacoby then got in touch with the leaders of our party. But the aspect of things had changed in the meantime. The same people who a few months ago were eager to promise support for the paper and bring it through its hardest times were very cool and hesitant to make sacrifices, now that I was no longer the feared journalist and influential leader. *"Les absents ont toujours tort"* proved itself once more. I was regarded by these people, who were considering only their own interests, as a "squeezed-out lemon," a "fallen great," etc. I was handled accordingly. After long negotiations, Messrs. John How, O. D. Filley and whoever the other leaders were—for whom the *Anzeiger* had done innumerable services and who had been made great by the paper—now declared that they would buy the material holdings of the paper and printing plant, the type, buildings, steam press and machines, for cheap. They would do nothing more, and so for the entire property they offered about a fifth of the value, $12,000. When Jacoby sent me this message, I sent my approval. Jacoby returned to complete the exchange, and these noble patrons and party friends told him that times had worsened during the six weeks my consent had required, and they could offer no more than $8,000 in paper money. Paper money then stood at a 40 percent discount from gold, so that the gentlemen offered a mere $5,000. Unfortunately, there was no alternative. I could not keep the materials, which would mean paying expensive rent for the building, and they would eventually be ruined or stolen. With a heavy heart I approved the sale, and my magnanimous former party friends walked off with the entire property of the *Anzeiger des Westens* for a joke of a price.

They even allowed it to appear again, but with the difference that what had once been a progressive, liberal paper was now an organ of the Democratic Party and fanatical proslavery men.[3] I must confess that this turn of events hurt me more than all the losses I had suffered, even my hopes for a secured old age for me and a sure future for my family. But bygones are

---

3. The paper appeared briefly as *Neue Anzeiger des Westens* in 1863, soon reverting to its original title. It continued as an independent paper to 1898, when it became the evening edition of the *Westliche Post* as the *Abend-Anzeiger*, 1898-1912. See Arndt/Olson, I: 250-1.

bygones, and the old proverb about spilt milk has its application here. With time, grass has grown over this memory, I have recovered from my hard blow and forgotten it as is the case with so much else. Friend Jacoby applied most of the sales amount, as agreed, to cover arrears and obligations. He showed himself once more as a true friend through his friendly settlement of these painful problems. So long as I live, this service will earn my deepest thanks, and I recognize it before the whole world. Such true and selfless friends are seldom found in life.

A New Friend

After the hard blows that struck me with the loss of the *Anzeiger*, the last hard-won property I still had, I figured that nothing worse could happen to me. And yet I forgot my own misfortune in the course of the next two years through my lively concern about the dreadful events in my adopted homeland and in my worry about the future of the fatherland. We Americans in Europe experienced a dark, hard time, awaiting the arrival of each steamer with tension and impatience. The news they brought was usually not good for the Union. We had to watch as Englishmen and some French expressed pleasure at the misfortune and decline of the American republic. How the reactionary parties of all countries rejoiced and triumphed. The agents of the South were extraordinarily active, spending the large amounts of money available to them to influence the opinion of European peoples increasingly in favor of the secession. Eventually the North lost all popular sympathy. On the side of the Union government, nothing whatsoever was done in this regard to influence public opinion for the Union cause. At the most, our ambassador and a few U.S. consuls in England made a weak attempt to respond to universal lies and errors, correcting the libels and hateful attacks against the North. But in the rest of Europe virtually nothing was done. Only a few consuls (mostly German Americans) sought on their own behalf to write newspaper articles and brochures as well as spread oral propaganda to influence public opinion. It is thus no wonder that through the first three years of the war people were almost never in favor of Americans or the cause of the Union. The considerable social and political revolution which took place, the massive struggle to extirpate the curse of Negro slavery, found little sympathy.

After my arrival in Bremen, it took little time to discover the source of this indifference on the part of Europe. I had observed to my regret how incomplete, imprecise, and negative were the prevailing views of conditions in our republic, even among the more educated classes of Europe. It was necessary to act against these false perceptions, to combat the unjust condemnation of our form of state and life, to correct these errors and replace them with more sound perceptions. Particularly in the monumental crisis in which America now found itself, it seemed doubly necessary to turn public opinion of civilized people in our direction, winning friends and sympathy everywhere. I wrote an extensive memorandum on this subject at the time and suggested what it would cost to set up literary bureaus in the larger cities of Europe, which would be supplied with reliable news reports from the foreign office in Washington and thus be well informed on the actual course of events. Such bureaus would then be in a position to influence public opinion in Europe in the direction of the Union in a correct and enlightened way, winning the sympathy of both governments and peoples for our good cause. I demonstrated how these institutions would be of great importance, showing that they existed already in more or less all states. In France there is even a special division of the ministry called *direction de l'esprit public*,[1] which has shown itself very effective. I sent this memorandum to Postmaster General Montgomery Blair, along with a long letter to my friend and patron, explaining my idea and my proposal for erecting these institutions. Blair answered me that he had immediately sent the memorandum to Secretary of State Seward, and recommended it to President Lincoln, since it completely agreed with Blair's own ideas. Seward had spoken highly of the project and gave him hope that it would be done, and the President's opinion was as positive. But the war and domestic problems, gaining in intensity from month to month, soon claimed all available interest and action of government circles. Nothing came from Washington. Influencing public opinion remained as ever a matter of *propria diligentia*[2] and good will of individual representatives of the United States. My memoir either slumbered away in the archives of the Foreign Office or was placed straightaway in a wastepaper basket. I mention this effort here only because I still believe in the usefulness of such an institution, and because nothing has been done in this regard during the almost twenty years that have passed.

European journals continue to judge the institutions and ways of life of the great, powerful, star-spangled republic in a most one-sided and restrictive manner. The small shadow sides are exaggerated and individual incidents expanded into unjustified conclusions about general conditions. Our failings are magnified and exaggerated to monstrous dimensions, and our advantages and good qualities passed over in silence. Those desiring to emigrate are terrified with horrifying fairy tales, and in conversation even with educated men I have been surprised and discouraged by erroneous and distorted views on American conditions. It is only in the most recent time, only now, when our last census shows a population over 50 million, and we are behind only China and Russia as the most populous country on the globe; only now, when our prosperity and productivity astonish Europe; only now they are beginning to grasp the present great importance of the United States and its imminent future, dominating the world. Yet the old restricted, erroneous perception of America still dominates, a last echo of the distortion of our national life that has continued for one hundred years. Because public

---

1. French, "direction of the public spirit."
2. Latin, "individual attention."

opinion has become an important factor in modern state life, our government should devote more attention to it and seek to lead it along the proper path, even if only out of truth and justice.

When I came to Bremen in 1861, as I already reported, I found a reception that was personally friendly, together with a cool, thoroughly negative view about our Union, which was viewed as lost. That was also the feeling in the rest of Germany, in France, Italy, Austria, even in our sister-republic of Switzerland. In England the opinion of the majority of the people was singularly, decisively hostile, and we had only a few friends. Even Gladstone, who now wishes to free all oppressed peoples, and his friends the Liberals, were on the side of slaveowners and Negro-barons. With the entire might of the British government they granted them protection and help. It was only at the start of 1865—when the decisiveness and persistence of the North finally won great successes, when Grant advanced in victory on the Peninsula and Sherman commenced and carried out his bold march through the South—that the repressed mood of Americans abroad would lift again. Their hope and confidence revived. When ever more positive news flowed in and the last barriers of secession were thrown down, Union troops entered Richmond, Lee and Johnston capitulated, and the last blood-drenched, wretched undertaking of secession collapsed into nothing, then we again raised our heads proudly. We could once again present ourselves to the Europeans with elevated feelings, with justified national pride, and public opinion there finally came over to our side.

I still recall with enthusiasm that happiest of days, when the report of victory arrived in Bremen. As it happened, I was one of the first who could announce it, because the newspapers would only come out the next morning. I had the telegram posted at the entrance to the consulate, and I had the entire large consulate decorated with hundreds of flags and with bunting. Across the street ropes were hung with the flags of all friendly countries flapping lustily in the wind, as was the custom in harbor towns on great occasions. Almost the entire population streamed in to read news of peace, news which soon spread across the town. All of the Americans, the senators, the representatives of the burghers and the chief merchants came to the consulate to extend their congratulations. Old ship captains and gray-haired boatmen and seamen who had been often and long in America, came by just to shake my hand and state their pleasure in their folksy Low German. In short, it was a day of jubilation, joy, and enthusiasm which I always look back on and that I shall never forget. Only the unfortunate owners of worthless Confederate paper money or ruined blockade-running speculators shuffled by sadly with hanging head.

What a dramatic, terrible contrast it was then, when the shattering news arrived of Lincoln's murder a few weeks later. The large flag in front of the consulate was lowered to half staff, and black bunting of mourning wrapped around it, announcing the distressing news. There was general mourning, and distress reigned in the entire population. The same men who had shortly before congratulated me on the victory now came to express their profound regrets, painfully seized with sadness and compassion. These, too, were days full of powerful impressions that I shall not forget.

In these writings I cannot mention all the many greater and lesser events or episodes in my service. They were sometimes serious, often unpleasant but sometimes pleasant, even funny or stimulating. Both aspects are demonstrated in the efforts of present and former officers of the various armies of Europe to enter the United States Army, naturally at a higher rank. I was literally overwhelmed with such offers in the first years, and often I could not fight off the applicants. Overseas representatives of the United States had no commission in this regard; on the contrary, most of the recommendations of foreign military sent in by U.S. ministers or consuls received a courteous but decisive rejection in Washington. In those days it was the same with officers' positions as with our agricultural and industrial production, because we could cover any demand completely from within our own country. The United States had a large number of German, Italian, Hungarian, Polish, French and other officers of the revolutions and revolts of the previous decades, as well as large numbers of mustered-out military of all nations, so that the officer billets of volunteer regiments could be filled completely. There was no need to spend large sums of money to bring these gentlemen and their unlimited pretensions from Europe. In addition, a considerable portion of these foreign officers, so impressive with their European titles and medals, proved in the course of the war to be incapable or simply unsuitable. This is partly because the American national character and the peculiarities of volunteer service were alien to them, but partly because they proved to be adventurers if not worse. A strict directive from Washington was issued to all representatives of the United States abroad at the start of 1862 not to send any officers, in fact to give no hope whatsoever for any position. Whoever wished to offer his services to the United States could come over at his own expense, like any other immigrant, and offer himself for a position. The government was not about to recruit *condottieri* or *Landsknechte*[3] from Europe. However, I personally had these applications for positions in the U.S. Army to thank for the acquaintance of a man with whom I have been bound by twenty years of intimate friendship, and who has had an influence on the further course of my life.

Bremen then had a good theater under the leadership of the directors Behr and Ritter. I was an avid visitor of their presentations, for my interest

---

3. These are archaic Italian and German terms for mercenaries.

in the stage has always remained the same, and I was happy to learn the newer dramatic productions after my long deprivation in America. In fact, my involvement in the theater rose so high that in the long winters in Bremen I once again wrote four plays, of which two, *Eine stumme Frau* [*A mute Woman*] and *Ein Mädchen vom Ballet* [*A Girl from the Ballet*] have made the rounds of most German stages. Because our consular instructions strictly forbad representatives of the United States from publishing literary works without requesting and receiving permission from the Foreign Office in Washington, I named myself as author H. Germamer (an abbreviation of "German American"), and these pieces are still performed today under this pseudonym.

One morning a young man of handsome appearance and winning nature presented himself in my consular office, whom I at once recognized from having him on stage as the treasured baritone of the Bremer Theater. Carl Bukovics, who had come to offer his services as an officer of the United States. Carl Bukovics von Kis Alacska, the son of a valorous Austrian soldier, was educated in the Imperial Officers' School in Wiener Neustadt. He then entered the army, and at the end of the 1850s he was assigned as first lieutenant and first adjutant with Prince von Mensdorf-Dietrichstein, commanding general in Bohemia. Through his service and military ability, he won the full favor of the Prince, soon becoming indispensable and being seen as a member of the family and the princely house. During the evening entertainments that normally took place in the salon of Prince Mensdorf, Bukovics received great recognition and won many friends in the prince's social circles through his singing of the *Lieder* of Schubert and Mendelssohn. With his truly beautiful voice and his soulful presentation, he soon participated in all of the aristocratic amateur circles. When Emperor Franz Joseph came to Prague and appeared at an evening gathering in Prince Mensdorf's home, Bukovics won the applause and recognition of the monarch through his masterful presentation of several *Lieder.* This reception, rapidly spread by all young officers interested in music, raised the young officer's reputation even higher than before.

At that precise moment there was a great need for good first tenors, and even the Vienna Court Opera did not have a really good heroic tenor. So on the motion of the Emperor, the directors of the Court Opera House asked Bukovics if he would give up his officer's position to be trained as first tenor at the expense of the Emperor, with a permanent position in the Court Opera after the end of training. The young officer accepted this enticing proposal and left his position as an officer. He went to Vienna, where he received a solid contract that would pay a decent salary during his training, followed by a brilliant engagement at the Opera House. In Vienna he was put into the hands of the court conductor, Heinrich Proch, for training.

Conductor Proch went to work zealously to fulfill the mission the Emperor had imposed on him; he practiced and worked tirelessly with Bukovics, but he overlooked the fact that the vocal range of his charge was actually a high baritone and not a tenor. As a result, Bukovics was artificially driven through the ceaseless practice of scales and the singing of sol-fa's into a higher range. He appeared at the Court Opera House as Max in the *Freischütz* with great success. He also pleased the public through his excellent delivery and expressive dramatic expression. But soon the sad results of the senseless elevation of a deeper organ into a higher tone began to show. After early success in heroic tenor parts, his voice would be exhausted and hoarse. Finally his teacher, as well as the theater director and the public realized that an error had been made, and that a lovely baritone had been artificially elevated into an inadequate tenor range.

Bukovics became what he should have been all along, which was a baritone. He left Vienna, where this specialty was fully staffed, and began to perform baritone parts at the theaters of Berlin, Hamburg, Riga, Königsberg and finally Bremen, where I met him. He told me of his artistic career up until then, and he spoke also of his fear that excessive strain and elevation of his tone had damaged his voice permanently. Fearing that he would not long be able to sing first-baritone parts, he was inclined to take up his earlier military career again, desiring to go to America and serve in the U.S. Army for the Union cause. I could naturally not encourage him; in fact, I had to advise against his plan from innermost conviction. But I promised him that I would send his application to Washington and support it as best I could. The young man made a very good impression on me. His winning ways, his education and his *savoir-faire* as a man of the world won me for himself, and I invited him to visit more often. He came to our house and soon bonded with my son Carl in intimate friendship, and he was treated as a close friend by the entire household. This is a relationship which has remained to the present day with the same intimacy and heartfeltness.

Through his friend Bukovics, my son Carl was introduced to the family of a respectable Bremen burgher, the photographer Eberhart Feilner, and he was received with friendship in the house and by the family. Bukovics later married one daughter of the house, Katharina, while my son Carl asked for the hand of the younger daughter Agnes a year later. With the approval of the parents, they also married. As a result the two friends also became brothers-in-law, and I became a sort of relative to the Feilner family and the Bukovics family. I was called uncle by all of them, a dignity I still hold, and I am not a little proud of my nephew Jean Baptiste Feilner, who is now one of the premier and artistically outstanding photographers in Germany. His work has been shown in England, France, Italy, Germany, Austria, Holland, even in Australia, receiving first prizes.

Unfortunately, Bukovics soon lost his voice completely, as he feared. He had to give up his engagement in Bremen, as well as his career on the stage as a whole, for he did not then trust his talent as an actor and thought his vocation was solely as a singer. He left the stage then and, in order to support himself and his wife decently, took the position of a traveling sales representative for a Bordeaux wine merchant covering Russia, Poland, Austria and the German North. He had all the necessary talents for this position, especially the charm as a man of the world, that won him access to all, even the highest circles. In this manner he held his position for several years, to the great satisfaction of his house.

During a winter visit to Russia and the strain and deprivation which that with it, however, he damaged his health. As soon as he returned to Germany from his journey through all of Russia, he fell very sick in Berlin. After several months in bed he was declared incurable by the physicians. Because his lower extremities were lamed and general weakness periodically appeared, he was sent by physicians to a milder climate and warm baths. His long illness cost him much money, and all of the family's resources were exhausted. In his necessity he had to give up his position, which he could no longer perform, and there was no obvious prospect that would earn him anything. So he determined to return to his homeland and seek a situation in the sulfur baths in Baden near Vienna, where his mother lived. How I found him there, and how our lives were bound together from then on will be told later. Here I only want to say, in order to justify this long and seemingly unnecessary excursus, that the ruined singer, my dear friend and "nephew" Carl von Bukovics, is now one of the most important of actors, playing humorous fathers and comic characters, not only in Vienna but all over the German stage. He was able to decline a very advantageous engagement offered him two years ago at the Imperial Court Theater by Director Dingelstedt, and now (1881) he is the darling of the public as an actor and Heinrich Laube's successor as director of the Vienna *Stadttheater.* He has led this stage with great ability, artistic and material success since I July 1880. We are still good friends and comrades today, as we have been for twenty years.

The End of Splendor
(1866)

"No matter how fine the sun shines, it must eventually go down" says Raimund's *Jugend.* Another poet says, "Even the loveliest days must have an end." And so the splendor of an American consul overseas, so widely longed for, is all the more mortal. He is never secure any day of his life, either of his position or his office. If he has great luck, he can remain at his post for a full four years, until a new presidential election and the general division of party booty washes him away, back into the great mass of the insignificant and unremarked we call "the people." Even these four years are not secure to him. A boundless stream of office-hunters and the patronage system of the senators and representatives bore and press in Washington without cease until all their protégés (that is, all those who have served to elect the member of Congress in question), have been paid off at state expense and found positions somewhere as consuls, harbor collectors, postmasters and the like. Any sort of oversight in the performance of an office, no matter how small, even a simple complaint, will suffice to bring down the office holder in question and bring a protégé into his place. It is certainly not in keeping with the power and dignity of the United States that the government changes all of its officials every four years, releasing tried and experienced workers and replacing them with inexperienced novices. All of this is because insatiable party leaders demand it, and if it were refused there would be a strike by party wire-pullers. They have invented a term for this nonsense, which is found in no other country in the world, and call it "rotation in office." But among themselves the gentlemen speak quite openly of the "division of the spoils."

So it is that the powerful United States of America has no true diplomatic corps. It is continually represented abroad by inexperienced novices, and that there is no higher school for diplomacy, such as have produced the most significant statesmen and diplomats in Europe. Our entire diplomatic representation overseas is a pitiful improvisation. Both ambassadors and consuls come to their posts as novices, without any experience or office routine. First they must orient themselves with great trouble, and then they are misled and misused by sly intriguers or sharper colleagues. When they have finally learned something through the experiences of their first years, finding their way at last and understanding something, their time has run out and they are recalled to make way for another novice. The British consul in Bremen in my time had been at his post for thirty years. The French consul had also been active for many years, despite all the revolts and changes in France, while the American consul changed every four years, and often sooner. I have already mentioned how this precarious and unsure position of our representatives overseas damages their status and influence, as well as how they are never taken seriously by foreign governments or their mouthpieces.

My conviction is that the United States would do much better simply to give up the whole system of diplomatic representation as currently practiced, which would save a great deal of money. One clerk of the foreign office could take care of the business with each government and each mercantile city that is currently handled by ambassadors and consuls in a pompous and hence expensive manner. The clerk in question, for instance in Paris, could deliver the dispatches of our State Department coming from Washington, receive the responses of the French government and send these to Washington. In ordinary times, that is about all our ambassadors overseas do anyway. Other clerks in mercantile towns could confirm the customs manifests and perform other minor consular services. This would save a great deal of money, and our representation overseas would certainly be no worse, in many points probably better. It would be a unity, with unified leadership from the seat of government. Now it has neither goal nor sense, and it is regarded both at home and abroad as simply a welfare agency for party hacks, election agents, stump speakers, and protégés of nepotism.

If this great turnover of officials only took place when one of the two large political parties is defeated and withdraws to make way for the other, when the "ins" become the "outs" and vice versa, it would have a certain justification. But people have unfortunately become used to this so-called rotation in office, and the demands of office-hunters are so profound that even when a party is confirmed in its possession of governmental power, they descend like hungry predators in Washington. There, supported by their protectors in Congress, they demand with loud howling a general massacre of all previous employees to make way for themselves. Even when the same party remains in office, when the same president is elected for the second time, this repellent drama is repeated. We experienced it when Lincoln and Grant were reelected; even if both of them manfully resisted the tumultuous pressure, they still had to succumb in many cases and release a number of their employees for no reason, sacrificing them as victims to rotation in office.

That was the situation for me when President Lincoln was elected the second time in November 1864. A friendly party in Washington informed me that a representative in Congress from St. Louis had been expending every effort with Lincoln, as well as with Seward, to have me recalled and replaced by one of his own protégés. As it later turned out, this congressman was my dear friend and patron Henry T. Blow, who had written me so many tender letters, had caused me to return from Europe on his own initiative to support his election to Congress, whom I had often done good services, and who had always assured me of his warmest thanks and respect. I was not the least astounded by this. I knew the self-seeking style and nature of the average American politician, who sees all persons as tools for his own elevation, and, when these have been used, throws them away like squeezed-out lemons. Since the closure of the *Anzeiger*, I was no longer the feared journalist, the influential popular leader. How was he supposed to show thanks for earlier obligations? One of my friends in St. Louis wrote to me privately in a ruthless, straightforward manner about the affair. Dropping his Attic preciosity of style, he wrote the following on 15 March 1865:

> Early this morning I had breakfast at Captain Eads', and there I met your friend H. T. Blow, that congressed, whisky-belching political turd. I gave him rather a hard time, speaking to him as if you were one of his friends whom he was dumping, as he did Frank Blair. We exchanged many biting words, which did not come to shouting because we were in someone else's house. Blow asserted that he never did anything against you with the President. It was certainly true that he had supported a few protégés, whom he did not name, in case the post in Bremen should fall vacant, but he had gone no further. The truth is that he could get nothing out of Lincoln against you, and now he is acting as if he was only operating *for* others, not *against* you. He is a .... (etc. etc.).

In the meantime I had written to Seward asking him to tell me the truth without restraint about whether a change was being considered, so that I could make plans for my future. As an answer there came a letter from Assistant Secretary of State Frederick Seward[1] assuring me that I could rest assured that the president was not considering any change of the consular post in Bremen. I was mollified by that, for I knew Lincoln's straight, reliable character, and he would not recall me without cause or motivation. With at least four years thus ahead of me, I took a favorable opportunity and purchased a small one-family house in the Remberti-Strasse, large enough for us to live in and offering the added pleasure of a pretty little garden. In the still half-patriarchal conditions of Bremen, one could very easily become a homeowner: by making a relatively low cash payment and taking over the obligation resting on the land, capitalized at only 4 percent. Because one

---

1. Frederick William Seward (1830-1915), son of William Henry Seward, graduated from Union College in 1849 and dedicated himself to being his father's secretary. He served as assistant secretary of state, 1861-69, and he would return to the post 1877-79. He edited his father's memoirs. *DAB*, 16: 612-13.

could get 6 percent on his own money, in American bonds for example, a homeowner paid no more and usually less than one had to pay as a renter in someone else's house, and then one was not dependent on another. I bought the house for 8,200 Bremen Taler, of which I paid 2,000 cash and the remnant with a payment of 4 percent in interest for an indefinite time.

Yet on the same day the sale was complete, when the cash payment had been made and the notary had delivered the keys of the house, there came the telegraphic notice of Lincoln's murder, and everything was up in the air again. I had been sure of Lincoln, but how would it be with his successor, former Vice President Andrew Johnson? I could not undo what had been done, and I quietly had to await what was to come.

A year passed in this way without my being bothered. I began to think that I was in peace and security, when I suddenly and unexpectedly received notice of my own recall. I learned this on a significant historical day, 16 June 1866. On that day when the foundation was laid for the unity of Germany and the German War began.[2] The German Federal Assembly in Frankfurt had made the decision on 14 June, and on 15 June Prussian ambassadors in Dresden, Hanover, Nassau and Kassel presented identical notes in which the respective governments were offered neutrality, with assurances of their territorial integrity and sovereignty. If there were no positive answer by midnight, then war was declared. On the 15 June, I received an invitation from Burghermaster Mohr to an official dinner the following day in honor of the newly named Italian ambassador to Hanover and the Hanseatic cities. One can imagine the agitation of the guests at the dinner. The Italian ambassador apologized at the outset that he was only able to remain a brief period of time, for he had to take the night train to Hanover to present his credentials to the king and, in view of the tense situation, he could not lose any time. He departed the table before dessert, but he still got to Hanover too late, for on 15 June, despite the fact that a deputation from the magistracy and the citizenry pressingly asked the king to compromise with Prussia, the Prussian ultimatum had been rejected. On the same day, General Manteuffel crossed the Elbe, occupied Harburg and advanced on Hanover. King George V left Hanover by 16 June, gathering his troops around him in retreat at Göttingen. The Italian ambassador was unable to find the king, and on the same day, 17 June, a Prussian division under General Göben entered Hanover. General Vogel von Falkenstein took over the government, and the Italian ambassador had to return home, never having been accredited.

---

2. The "War of Brothers" of 1866 pitted Prussia against Austria and her allies, leading to the annexation of the Kingdom of Hanover, an ally of Austria. Under Prussian leadership, a North German League was formed, a major stepping-stone to the foundation of the German *Reich* under Prince Bismarck's leadership in 1871.

As we were at dessert after the Italian ambassador's departure, there was a pause in the lively discussion. Senator Smidt, who sat next to me, suddenly asked whether I had already received notice of my recall and the appointment of General Dodge. Most unpleasantly surprised, I responded truly that I had not heard a thing about it, and he told me that he had the news from Consul General Rösing that my recall had taken place on 2 June and he could guarantee the precision of Rösing's reports. That is another of the lovely aspects of our diplomatic service, that the overseas representatives of the United States usually have to learn from others what affects them most. I left the dinner painfully hurt by the sudden blow and deeply depressed. The next day the mail brought a letter from Bernays of 2 June confirming the news. Bernays wrote:

> I just received news of your recall and General Dodge's naming to Bremen. My own problems have suddenly become light, since I am thinking of yours. What shall you do? Write me at once. Wherever I can advise and help, you would not call upon me in vain. Find some way we may live together somewhere. Business here is dreadful, and the most natural thing for everyone to do is to look on and start nothing, etc., etc.

A week later, the official dispatch of the State Department finally arrived which announced my termination. My successor came to Bremen only at the end of August, and I transferred the consulate to him in the first days of September, when the war was already at an end. Peace had been made at Prague, the alliance with the south German states had been completed, and the North German League had been established. Lincoln was dead, his successor had no obligation to me, and the pressure of office-hunters was too strong for the weak Johnson to resist. The war of secession had long since ended, the armies had been reduced to their small peacetime size, and the mass of ex-generals, ex-colonels and so forth besieged the president and Seward, stormily demanding compensation for their services and support for their near futures. A worthy friend in New York, who now lives in Europe, wrote me then about this pressure:

> You have absolutely no idea of the pressure of mustered-out high officers and all possible sorts of *milites gloriosi*[3] in Washington. At the end of June I was there for a day and a half, and at almost every step I stumbled over a general or colonel who wanted to be sent overseas as a consul. Osterhaus hoped for the consulate in London or Liverpool, but got only Lyon.

---

3. Latin, "Bragging Soldiers," a play on the title of a comic play by Plautus, *Miles gloriosus.*

Otherwise the German officers have been pushed down into very subordinate positions, although in the eyes of the Administration they have received plenty, for they also count Hungarians as Germans. In this way Asboth was sent to Buenos Aires as resident minister, Stahel to Japan as consul general, and several other Hungarians to Bucharest, Tarento, Palermo, etc. Many another will have to give way to this pressure. In the best case you would only have been able to resist the pressure for a few more months, and without an energetic and influential voice in the cabinet, every officeholder is doomed.

That was not the case with me. Montgomery Blair had long since parted company with Johnson over his dubious domestic policy, and old Bates was just that, an old man who "would let five be an even number." Hence I was doomed, and I surrendered to my destiny.

What was I to do? That was the question which I directed to myself, as Bernays had done earlier. My preference would have been to return to the United States and resume my journalistic career, but in the meantime I had become sixty-one years old. I felt that I could no longer claim the energy and strength one needed for this profession in America. It also repelled me to think that I would have to start over from nothing in this career. I decisively rejected the advice that I go to Washington and seek another office with the support of my earlier patrons. Bernays' suggestion that I should come to America, buying into a small, growing town in the West, and waiting for times to get better and offer a proper occupation, did not appeal to me either. I could linger just as well in Bremen and await better prospects. For the time being I decided for the latter plan.

At precisely this point, my friend Hassaurek wrote me from Cincinnati and asked me to recommend a correspondent in North Germany, for German conditions and events were currently exciting great interest. Naturally I recommended myself to him as a correspondent, which he accepted. And so I became a journalist once more and a correspondent for the Cincinnati *Volksblatt*. Our relationship was a heartfelt friendship borne by mutual respect. The connection lasted eight years, and it was broken not by Hassaurek, but by his partner at the time, Hof, because the poor business conditions in America then required a reduction of expenditures.

The result was that I remained in Europe, postponing my return to America year by year, until finally nothing more came of it nor ever shall come of it. During this time, I have received numerous inquiries and invitations to take over the editing of German American newspapers, including two very advantageous offers, but I declined them with thanks. America is the proper soil for young people. There they can move their elbows and be unhindered; they can satisfy their need for action to the full.

But America is no country for old people. Old men cannot even take their leisure there in a comfortable, pleasant manner to live their life to the end. This is because repose is alien to America. Rentiers, pensioned officers and officials, in short the sort of people who are retired either do not exist there, or they are an infinitesimally small number. Everyone works as long as he can, and he only lives as long as he works. In my days in St. Louis, heads with silver-gray or white hair were a great rarity, found almost exclusively among old Black house-slaves. Everyone worked and acted as long as he could, and when he could not go any further, he laid himself down and died. Wanting to retire in America, that country of tireless activity and continual labor, would be nonsense. Even if one were determined to remain a passive observer, still one would not be able to carry it off. He would soon be pulled into the morass of business life, political struggle and storm, but without having the fresh strength required.

In contrast, Europe is the continent for those seeking repose, the land for old men who live more in the past than in the present. In addition, German events at the time were extremely stimulating, and they claimed my lively interest. As a result, I remained in Europe and have never regretted my decision. To be sure, my retirement is no absolute inactivity, merely an abstention from the struggles of the day. I remain active and involved with intellectual work—if not according to American standards (which demand extreme exertion), at least according to a milder European measure, which has the motto, *"Est modus in rebus, sunt certi denique fines."*[4]

---

4. Latin, "There is a measure in things, and there are also definite limits."

Summary *of the* Final Chapters

Through Italy *to* Vienna (1866-1869)

After handing over the consulate to his successor, Boernstein managed a booking agency in Bremen with his son Carl. He also worked as the American correspondent for American newspapers, and he caught up on lost time in his pursuit of drama and literature. An injury led him to seek a warmer climate and visit baths, so he took a tour with a granddaughter through Italy, resulting in the publication of a book on his travels. While traveling, he encountered several St. Louisans, not all of them happy to meet him. He then settled in Baden near Vienna, intending to make his residence there permanent.

Theater-Director Once Again (1869-1871)

Boredom in Baden soon drove Boernstein to Vienna to manage a booking agency, and he was persuaded there to lease the Theater in der Josephstadt with Bukovics as his partner. The result was a great success, although at the price of great exertions, particularly by adapting dialect plays to the local Viennese language.

The End *of* Theater Direction (1871)

As a result of a fit of depression, Boernstein finally gave up the lease over the theater. Eventually his friend Bukovics took over the directorship of the Stadttheater, in which Boernstein would take a subordinate role.

A Hard Loss (1872-1878)

Boernstein's Bremen "nephew" came to Vienna and established a photography salon, and Carl Boernstein undertook to help him. When Carl died of smallpox, Boernstein took his place in the management of the photography business until other arrangements could be made. This coincided with an international financial panic and depression.

Final Chapter *and* Conclusion

While in Baden, Boernstein had begun writing his memoirs. He left them unfinished at roughly the point where he left for America until urged by Hermann Raster to complete and publish them. In 1879 Boernstein saw Prince Otto von Bismarck on his visit to Vienna, hence completing the trinity of the three greatest persons of the nineteenth century he had seen with his own eyes (the others being Napoléon I and Goethe).

Conclusion

So I live on in continual intellectual activity, quiet to the end. I am free of the primary plague of old age, which is boredom, and I hope it shall remain so until the conclusion. I consider death's arrival to do his duty while I am still fully armed and in the midst of strenuous activity to be the finest of fates.

With this I would like to conclude these sketches of an old man. All that remains is to make excuse that I, a nobody, should have regaled you with such a thorough account of my life, perhaps too thorough. This talkativeness is one of the weaknesses of old age, and I ask your indulgence. At the same time, I would like to thank the readers for the friendliness with which they have accompanied me in my reminiscences and excused so many asides. May you continue to preserve of me a friendly memory. This is my only wish.

Abbreviations of Frequently Cited Works

ACAB	James Grant Wilson and John Fiske, eds., *Appleton's Cyclopaedia of American Biography* (New York: Appleton and Company, 1898).
ADB	*Allgemeine deutsche Biographie*, Historische Commission bei der königlichen Akademie der Wissenschaften (München), 56 vols. (Leipzig: Duncker & Humblot, 1875-1912).
Arndt/Olson	Karl J. R. Arndt and May E. Olson, eds., *Die deutschsprachige Presse der Amerikas*, vol. 1, *Geschichte und Bibliographie 1732-1968: Vereinigte Staaten von Amerika*, 3d ed. (Munich: Verlag Dokumentation, 1976).
AW	*Anzeiger des Westens*
BDUSC	*Biographical Dictionary of the United States Congress, 1774-1989* (Washington, D.C.: United States Government Printing Office, 1989).
BMHS	*Bulletin of the Missouri Historical Society*
Boernstein, *Memoiren*	Heinrich Börnstein, *Fünfundsiebzig Jahre in der Alten und Neuen Welt. Memoiren eines Unbedeutenden*, [reprint of the 1st edition, 1881], introduction by Patricia Herminghouse (Frankfurt; New York; Bern: Peter Lang, 1983).
Boernstein, *Mysteries*	Henry Boernstein, *The Mysteries of St. Louis*, Friedrich Münch, tr., Steven Rowan and Elizabeth Sims, eds. (Chicago: Charles H. Kerr Publishing House, 1990).
Cazden, *Social History*	Robert E. Cazden, *A Social History of the German Book Trade in America to the Civil War* (Columbia, S.C.: Camden House, 1984).
DAB	Allan Johnson et al., eds.,*Dictionary of American Biography*, 22 vols. (New York: Charles Scribner's Sons, 1928-1958).
Directory 1854-5	*St. Louis Directory for 1854-55* (St. Louis: Chambers and Knapp, 1854).
Directory 1857	*Kennedy's St. Louis Directory for 1857* (St. Louis, 1856).
Directory 1860	*Kennedy's St. Louis Directory, 1860* (St. Louis, 1859).
Directory 1864	*Edwards's St. Louis Directory . . . 1864* (St. Louis, 1863).
Directory 1866	*Edwards's St. Louis Directory . . . 1866* (St. Louis, 1865).
Directory 1867	*Edwards's St. Louis Directory . . . 1867* (St. Louis, 1867).
Directory 1869	*Edwards's St. Louis Directory . . . 1869* (St. Louis, 1868).
Directory 1871	*Edwards's Annual Directory to the inhabitants . . . in the City of St. Louis for 1871* (St. Louis : Southern Publishing Co., c. 1870).
EC	*Encyclopedia of the Confederacy*, Richard N. Current, ed. (New York, 1993).
Edwards's	Richard Edwards and M. Hopewell, *Edwards's Great West* (St. Louis, 1860).
EHSL	William Hyde and Howard L. Conard, eds., *Encyclopedia of the History of St. Louis*, 4 vols. (New York; Louisville; St. Louis: Southern History Co., 1899).
GH	*Gateway Heritage*
Kaufmann	Wilhelm Kaufmann, *Die Deutschen im amerikanischen Bürgerkriege (Sezessionskrieg, 1861-1865)* (Munich; Berlin: Oldenbourg, 1911).

Körner, *Element*   Gustav Phillip Körner, *Das deutsche Element in den Vereinigten Staaten von Nordamerika 1818-1848* (Cincinnati, 1880), reprinted with an introduction by Patricia Herminghouse (New York: Peter Lang, 1986).

MB   *Mississippi Blätter*

MEGA 2   *Karl Marx Friedrich Engels Gesamtausgabe*, 2d ed., Institut für Marxismus-Leninismus beim Zentralkommittee der Kommunistischen Partei der Sowjetunion und...Institut für Marxismus-Leninismus beim Zentralkommittee der Sozialistischen Einheitspartei Deutschlands, eds., 3rd division, *Briefwechsel* (Berlin: Dietz, 1975 ff.).

MEW   *Karl Marx Friedrich Engels Werke*, Institut für Marxismus-Leninismus beim Zentralkommittee der Sozialistischen Einheitspartei Deutschlands, eds. (Berlin: Dietz, 1982 ff.).

MHR   *Missouri Historical Review*

MHS   Missouri Historical Society

MR   *Missouri Republican*

NUC   *The National Union Catalog of Pre-1956 Imprints*, 754 vols. (Chicago: Mansell, 1968-81).

Rombauer   Robert Rombauer, *The Union Cause in St. Louis in 1861. An Historical Sketch* (St. Louis, 1909).

Rowan/Primm   Steven Rowan, with James Neal Primm, *Germans for a Free Missouri: Translations from the St. Louis Radical Press, 1857-1862* (Columbia: University of Missouri Press, 1983).

WHM   Western Historical Manuscripts Collection

Winter   William C. Winter, *The Civil War in St. Louis: A Guided Tour* (St. Louis: Missouri Historical Society Press, 1994).

WP   *Westliche Post*

WROR   Robert N. Scott et al., eds., *The War of the Rebellion: Official Records of the Union and Confederate Armies*, 3 sections (Washington, D.C.: Government Printing Office, 1880-1901; repr., Harrisburg, Pa.: National Historical Society, 1971).

Zucker   A. E. Zucker, ed., *The Forty-Eighters* (New York, 1950).

Index